U.S. History

Volume 3: 1900 to Present

By OpenStax College
at Rice University

Arranged by Traci Hodgson
Chemeketa Community College

A Chemeketa Press Reprint

U.S. History, Volume 3: 1900 to Present

ISBN: 978-1-943536-09-2

The contents of this book are reprinted directly from U.S. History by OpenStax College. © May 15, 2015 by OpenStax College. Textbook content produced by OpenStax College is licensed under a Creative Commons Attribution 4.0 license.

Chemeketa Press
Managing Editor: Steve Richardson

Production Editor: Brian Mosher

Production Designer: Kristen MacDonald

Cover Layout: Cierra Maher

Printed in the United States of America.

Volume 3: 1900 to Present

CHAPTER 1

Leading the Way: The Progressive Movement, 1890-1920

Figure 1.1 The western states were the first to allow women the right to vote, a freedom that grew out of the less deeply entrenched gendered spheres in the region. This illustration, from 1915, shows a suffragist holding a torch over the western states and inviting the beckoning women from the rest of the country to join her.

Chapter Outline

1.1 The Origins of the Progressive Spirit in America
1.2 Progressivism at the Grassroots Level
1.3 New Voices for Women and African Americans
1.4 Progressivism in the White House

Introduction

Women's suffrage was one of many causes that emerged in the Progressive Era, as Americans confronted the numerous challenges of the late nineteenth century. Starting in the late 1800s, women increasingly were working outside the home—a task almost always done for money, not empowerment—as well as pursuing higher education, both at universities that were beginning to allow women to enroll and at female-only schools. Often, it was educated middle-class women with more time and resources that took up causes such as child labor and family health. As more women led new organizations or institutions, such as the settlement houses, they grew to have a greater voice on issues of social change. By the turn of the century, a strong movement had formed to advocate for a woman's right to vote. For three decades, suffragist groups pushed for legislation to give women the right to vote in every state. As the illustration above shows (Figure 1.1), the western states were the first to grant women the right to vote; it would not be until 1920 that the nation would extend that right to all women.

1.1 The Origins of the Progressive Spirit in America

By the end of this section, you will be able to:
- Describe the role that muckrakers played in catalyzing the Progressive Era
- Explain the main features of Progressivism

The Progressive Era was a time of wide-ranging causes and varied movements, where activists and reformers from diverse backgrounds and with very different agendas pursued their goals of a better America. These reformers were reacting to the challenges that faced the country at the end of the nineteenth century: rapid urban sprawl, immigration, corruption, industrial working conditions, the growth of large corporations, women's rights, and surging anti-black violence and white supremacy in the South. Investigative journalists of the day uncovered social inequality and encouraged Americans to take action. The campaigns of the Progressives were often grassroots in their origin. While different causes shared some underlying elements, each movement largely focused on its own goals, be it the right of women to vote, the removal of alcohol from communities, or the desire for a more democratic voting process.

THE MUCKRAKERS

A group of journalists and writers collectively known as **muckrakers** provided an important spark that ignited the Progressive movement. Unlike the "yellow journalists" who were interested only in sensationalized articles designed to sell newspapers, muckrakers exposed problems in American society and urged the public to identify solutions. Whether those problems were associated with corrupt machine politics, poor working conditions in factories, or the questionable living conditions of the working class (among others), muckrakers shined a light on the problem and provoked outraged responses from Americans. President Theodore Roosevelt knew many of these investigative journalists well and considered himself a Progressive. Yet, unhappy with the way they forced agendas into national politics, he was the one who first gave them the disparaging nickname "muckrakers," invoking an ill-spirited character obsessed with filth from *The Pilgrim's Progress*, a 1678 Christian allegory written by John Bunyan.

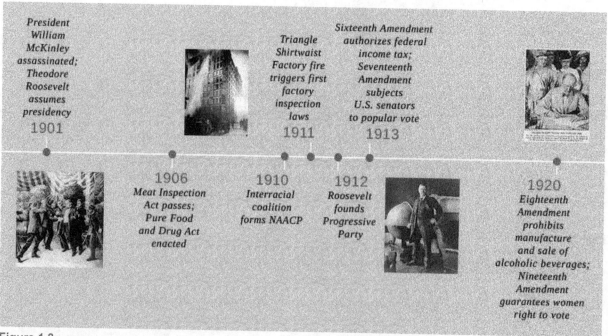

Figure 1.2

Beginning in the second half of the nineteenth century, these Progressive journalists sought to expose critical social problems and exhort the public to take action. In his book, *How the Other Half Lives* (1890), journalist and photographer Jacob Riis used photojournalism to capture the dismal and dangerous living conditions in working-class tenements in New York City (**Figure 1.3**). Ida Tarbell, perhaps the most well-known female muckraker, wrote a series of articles on the dangers of John D. Rockefeller's powerful monopoly, Standard Oil. Her articles followed Henry Demarest Lloyd's book, *Wealth Against Commonwealth*, published in 1894, which examined the excesses of Standard Oil. Other writers, like Lincoln Steffens, explored corruption in city politics, or, like Ray Standard Baker, researched unsafe working conditions and low pay in the coal mines.

Figure 1.3 Jacob Riis's images of New York City slums in the late nineteenth century, such as this 1890 photograph of children sleeping in Mulberry Street, exposed Americans all over the country to the living conditions of the urban poor.

The work of the muckrakers not only revealed serious problems in American society, but also agitated, often successfully, for change. Their articles, in magazines such as *McClure's*, as well as books garnered attention for issues such as child labor, anti-trust, big business break-ups, and health and safety. Progressive activists took up these causes and lobbied for legislation to address some of the ills troubling industrial America.

Click and Explore

openstax

To learn more about one of the most influential muckrakers of the late nineteenth century, peruse the photographs, writings, and more at the Ida M. Tarbell archives (http://openstaxcollege.org/l/tarbell) that are housed at Tarbell's alma mater, Allegheny College, where she matriculated in 1876 as the only woman in her class.

THE FEATURES OF PROGRESSIVISM

Muckrakers drew public attention to some of the most glaring inequities and scandals that grew out of the social ills of the Gilded Age and the hands-off approach of the federal government since the end of Reconstruction. These writers by and large addressed a white, middle-class and elite, native-born audience, even though Progressive movements and organizations involved a diverse range of Americans.

What united these Progressives beyond their different backgrounds and causes was a set of uniting principles, however. Most strove for a perfection of democracy, which required the expansion of suffrage to worthy citizens and the restriction of political participation for those considered "unfit" on account of health, education, or race. Progressives also agreed that democracy had to be balanced with an emphasis on efficiency, a reliance on science and technology, and deference to the expertise of professionals. They repudiated party politics but looked to government to regulate the modern market economy. And they saw themselves as the agents of social justice and reform, as well as the stewards and guides of workers and the urban poor. Often, reformers' convictions and faith in their own expertise led them to dismiss the voices of the very people they sought to help.

The expressions of these Progressive principles developed at the grassroots level. It was not until Theodore Roosevelt unexpectedly became president in 1901 that the federal government would engage in Progressive reforms. Before then, **Progressivism** was work done by the people, for the people. What knit Progressives together was the feeling that the country was moving at a dangerous pace in a dangerous direction and required the efforts of everyday Americans to help put it back on track.

1.2 Progressivism at the Grassroots Level

By the end of this section, you will be able to:
* Identify specific examples of grassroots Progressivism relating to the spread of democracy, efficiency in government, and social justice
* Describe the more radical movements associated with the Progressive Era

A wide variety of causes fell under the Progressive label. For example, Wisconsin's Robert M. ("Fighting Bob") La Follette, one of the most Progressive politicians of his day, fought hard to curb the power of special interests in politics and reform the democratic process at state and local levels. Others sought out safer working conditions for factory workers. Different groups prioritized banning the sale of alcohol, which, they believed, was the root of much of the trouble for the working poor. No matter what the cause, Progressive campaigns often started with issues brought to the public's attention by muckraking journalists.

EXPANDING DEMOCRACY

One of the key ideals that Progressives considered vital to the growth and health of the country was the concept of a perfected democracy. They felt, quite simply, that Americans needed to exert more control over their government. This shift, they believed, would ultimately lead to a system of government that was better able to address the needs of its citizens. Grassroots Progressives pushed forward their agenda of direct democracy through the passage of three state-level reforms.

The first law involved the creation of the **direct primary**. Prior to this time, the only people who had a hand in selecting candidates for elections were delegates at conventions. Direct primaries allowed party members to vote directly for a candidate, with the nomination going to the one with the most votes. This was the beginning of the current system of holding a primary election before a general election. South Carolina adopted this system for statewide elections in 1896; in 1901, Florida became the first state to use the direct primary in nominations for the presidency. It is the method currently used in three-quarters of U.S. states.

Another series of reforms pushed forward by Progressives that sought to sidestep the power of special interests in state legislatures and restore the democratic political process were three election innovations—the **initiative**, **referendum**, and **recall**. The first permitted voters to enact legislation by petitioning to place an idea, or initiative, on the ballot. In 1898, South Dakota became the first state to allow initiatives to appear on a ballot. By 1920, twenty states had adopted the procedure. The second innovation allowed voters to counteract legislation by holding a referendum—that is, putting an existing law on the ballot for voters to either affirm or reject. Currently twenty-four states allow some form of initiative and referendum. The third element of this direct democracy agenda was the recall. The recall permitted citizens to remove a public official from office through a process of petition and vote, similar to the initiative and referendum. While this measure was not as widely adopted as the others, Oregon, in 1910, became the first state to allow recalls. By 1920, twelve states had adopted this tool. It has only been used successfully a handful of times on the statewide level, for example, to remove the governor of North Dakota in 1921, and, more recently, the governor of California in 2003.

Progressives also pushed for democratic reform that affected the federal government. In an effort to achieve a fairer representation of state constituencies in the U.S. Congress, they lobbied for approval of the Seventeenth Amendment to the U.S. Constitution, which mandated the direct election of U.S. senators. The Seventeenth Amendment replaced the previous system of having state legislatures choose senators. William Jennings Bryan, the 1896 Democratic presidential candidate who received significant support from the Populist Party, was among the leading Progressives who championed this cause.

EXPERTISE AND EFFICIENCY

In addition to making government more directly accountable to the voters, Progressives also fought to rid politics of inefficiency, waste, and corruption. Progressives in large cities were particularly frustrated with the corruption and favoritism of machine politics, which wasted enormous sums of taxpayer money and ultimately stalled the progress of cities for the sake of entrenched politicians, like the notorious Democratic Party Boss William Tweed in New York's Tammany Hall. Progressives sought to change this corrupt system and had success in places like Galveston, Texas, where, in 1901, they pushed the city to adopt a commission system. A hurricane the previous year (**Figure 1.4**) had led to the collapse of the old city government, which had proved incapable of leading the city through the natural disaster. The storm claimed over eight thousand lives—the highest death toll from a natural disaster in the history of the country—and afterwards, the community had no faith that the existing government could rebuild. The commission system involved the election of a number of commissioners, each responsible for one specific operation of the city, with titles like water commissioner, fire commissioner, police commissioner, and so on. With no single political "boss" in charge, the prevalence of graft and corruption greatly decreased. The commissioner system is widely used in modern cities throughout the United States.

Figure 1.4 The 1900 hurricane in Galveston, Texas, claimed more lives than any other natural disaster in American history. In its wake, fearing that the existing corrupt and inefficient government was not up to the job of rebuilding, the remaining residents of the town adopted the commission system of local government.

Another model of municipal government reform took shape in Staunton, Virginia, in 1908, where the citizens switched to the city manager form of government. Designed to avoid the corruption inherent in political machines, the city manager system separated the daily operations of the city from both the electoral process and political parties. In this system, citizens elected city councilors who would pass laws and handle all legislative issues. However, their first job was to hire a city manager to deal with the daily management operation of the city. This person, unlike the politicians, was an engineer or businessman who understood the practical elements of city operations and oversaw city workers. Currently, over thirty-seven hundred cities have adopted the city manager system, including some of the largest cities in the country, such as Austin, Dallas, and Phoenix.

At the state level, perhaps the greatest advocate of Progressive government was Robert La Follette (**Figure 1.5**). During his time as governor, from 1901 through 1906, La Follette introduced the **Wisconsin Idea**, wherein he hired experts to research and advise him in drafting legislation to improve conditions in his state. "Fighting Bob" supported numerous Progressive ideas while governor: He signed into law the first workman's compensation system, approved a minimum wage law, developed a progressive tax law, adopted the direct election of U.S. senators before the subsequent constitutional amendment made it mandatory, and advocated for women's suffrage. La Follette subsequently served as a popular U.S. senator from Wisconsin from 1906 through 1925, and ran for president on the Progressive Party ticket in 1924.

Figure 1.5 An energetic speaker and tireless Progressive, Governor Robert "Fighting Bob" La Follette turned the state of Wisconsin into a flagship for democratic reform.

Click and Explore

Read how Robert La Follette's legacy (http://openstaxcollege.org/l/follette) still inspires progressives in Wisconsin.

Many Progressive reformers were also committed to the principle of efficiency in business as well as in government. The growth of large corporations at the time fostered the emergence of a class of professional managers. Fredrick Winslow Taylor, arguably the first American management consultant, laid out his argument of increased industrial efficiency through improvements in human productivity in his book *The Principles of Scientific Management* (1911). Through time-motion studies and the principles of standardization, Taylor sought to place workers in the most efficient positions of the industrial process. Management, he argued, should determine the work routine, leaving workers to simply execute the task at hand. The image below (**Figure 1.6**) shows a machinist in a factory where Taylor had consulted; he is alone and focused solely on his job. Progressive in its emphasis on efficiency, the use of science, and the reliance on experts, **Taylorism**, as scientific management became known, was not widely popular among workers who resented managerial authority and the loss of autonomy over their work. Many workers went on strikes in response, although some favored Taylor's methods, since their pay was directly linked to the productivity increases that his methods achieved and since increased efficiency allowed companies to charge consumers lower prices.

Figure 1.6 This machinist works alone in a factory that adopted Taylorism, the scientific time management principle that sought to bring ultimate efficiency to factories. Many workers found the focus on repetitive tasks to be dehumanizing and unpleasant.

SOCIAL JUSTICE

The Progressives' work towards social justice took many forms. In some cases, it was focused on those who suffered due to pervasive inequality, such as African Americans, other ethnic groups, and women. In others, the goal was to help those who were in desperate need due to circumstance, such as poor immigrants from southern and eastern Europe who often suffered severe discrimination, the working poor, and those with ill health. Women were in the vanguard of social justice reform. Jane Addams, Lillian Wald, and Ellen Gates Starr, for example, led the settlement house movement of the 1880s (discussed in a previous chapter). Their work to provide social services, education, and health care to working-class women and their children was among the earliest Progressive grassroots efforts in the country.

Building on the successes of the settlement houses, social justice reformers took on other, related challenges. The National Child Labor Committee (NCLC), formed in 1904, urged the passage of labor legislation to ban child labor in the industrial sector. In 1900, U.S. census records indicated that one out of every six children between the ages of five and ten were working, a 50-percent increase over the previous decade. If the sheer numbers alone were not enough to spur action, the fact that managers paid child workers noticeably less for their labor gave additional fuel to the NCLC's efforts to radically curtail child labor. The committee employed photographer Lewis Hine to engage in a decade-long pictorial campaign to educate Americans on the plight of children working in factories (**Figure 1.7**).

(a)   (b)

Figure 1.7 As part of the National Child Labor Committee's campaign to raise awareness about the plight of child laborers, Lewis Hine photographed dozens of children in factories around the country, including Addie Card (a), a twelve-year-old spinner working in a mill in Vermont in 1910, and these young boys working at Bibb Mill No. 1 in Macon, Georgia in 1909 (b). Working ten- to twelve-hour shifts, children often worked large machines where they could reach into gaps and remove lint and other debris, a practice that caused plenty of injuries. (credit a/b: modification of work by Library of Congress)

Although low-wage industries fiercely opposed any federal restriction on child labor, the NCLC did succeed in 1912, urging President William Howard Taft to sign into law the creation of the U.S. Children's Bureau. As a branch of the Department of Labor, the bureau worked closely with the NCLC to bring greater awareness to the issue of child labor. In 1916, the pressure from the NCLC and the general public resulted in the passage of the Keating-Owen Act, which prohibited the interstate trade of any goods produced with child labor. Although the U.S. Supreme Court later declared the law unconstitutional, Keating-Owen reflected a significant shift in the public perception of child labor. Finally, in 1938, the passage of the Fair Labor Standards Act signaled the victory of supporters of Keating-Owen. This new law outlawed the interstate trade of any products produced by children under the age of sixteen.

Florence Kelley, a Progressive supporter of the NCLC, championed other social justice causes as well. As the first general secretary of the National Consumers League, which was founded in 1899 by Jane Addams and others, Kelley led one of the original battles to try and secure safety in factory working conditions. She particularly opposed sweatshop labor and urged the passage of an eight-hour-workday law in order to specifically protect women in the workplace. Kelley's efforts were initially met with strong resistance from factory owners who exploited women's labor and were unwilling to give up the long hours and low wages they paid in order to offer the cheapest possible product to consumers. But in 1911, a tragedy turned the tide of public opinion in favor of Kelley's cause. On March 25 of that year, a fire broke out at the Triangle Shirtwaist Company on the eighth floor of the Asch building in New York City, resulting in the deaths of 146 garment workers, most of them young, immigrant women (**Figure 1.8**). Management had previously blockaded doors and fire escapes in an effort to control workers and keep out union organizers; in the blaze, many died due to the crush of bodies trying to evacuate the building. Others died when they fell off the flimsy fire escape or jumped to their deaths to escape the flames. This tragedy provided the National Consumers League with the moral argument to convince politicians of the need to pass workplace safety laws and codes.

Figure 1.8 On March 25, 1911, a fire broke out at the Triangle Shirtwaist Factory in New York City. Despite the efforts of firefighters, 146 workers died in the fire, mostly because the owners had trapped them on the sweatshop floors.

MY STORY

❂ *William Shepherd on the Triangle Shirtwaist Factory Fire*

The tragedy of the Triangle Shirtwaist Factory fire was a painful wake-up call to a country that was largely ignoring issues of poor working conditions and worker health and safety. While this fire was far from the only instance of worker death, the sheer number of people killed—almost one hundred fifty—and the fact they were all young women, made a strong impression. Furthering the power of this tragedy was the first-hand account shared by William Shepherd, a United Press reporter who was on the scene, giving his eyewitness account over a telephone. His account appeared, just two days later, in the *Milwaukee Journal*, and word of the tragedy spread from there. Public outrage over their deaths was enough to give the National Consumers League the power it needed to push politicians to get involved.

> I saw every feature of the tragedy visible from outside the building. I learned a new sound—a more horrible sound than description can picture. It was the thud of a speeding, living body on a stone sidewalk.
>
> Thud-dead, thud-dead, thud-dead, thud-dead. Sixty-two thud-deads. I call them that, because the sound and the thought of death came to me each time, at the same instant. There was plenty of chance to watch them as they came down. The height was eighty feet.
>
> The first ten thud-deads shocked me. I looked up—saw that there were scores of girls at the windows. The flames from the floor below were beating in their faces. Somehow I knew that they, too, must come down. . . .
>
> A policeman later went about with tags, which he fastened with wires to the wrists of the dead girls, numbering each with a lead pencil, and I saw him fasten tag no. 54 to the wrist of a girl who wore an engagement ring. A fireman who came downstairs from the building told me that there were at least fifty bodies in the big room on the seventh floor. Another fireman told me that more girls had jumped down an air shaft in the rear of the building. I went back there, into the narrow court, and saw a heap of dead girls. . . .
>
> The floods of water from the firemen's hose that ran into the gutter were actually stained red with blood. I looked upon the heap of dead bodies and I remembered these girls were the shirtwaist makers. I remembered their great strike of last year in which these same girls had demanded more sanitary conditions and more safety precautions in the shops. These dead bodies were the answer.

What do you think about William Shepherd's description? What effect do you think it had on newspaper readers in the Midwest?

Another cause that garnered support from a key group of Progressives was the prohibition of liquor. This crusade, which gained followers through the Women's Christian Temperance Union (WCTU) and the Anti-Saloon League, directly linked Progressivism with morality and Christian reform initiatives, and saw in alcohol both a moral vice and a practical concern, as workingmen spent their wages on liquor and saloons, often turning violent towards each other or their families at home. The WCTU and Anti-Saloon League moved the efforts to eliminate the sale of alcohol from a bar-to-bar public opinion campaign to one of city-to-city and state-by-state votes (**Figure 1.9**). Through local option votes and subsequent statewide initiatives and referendums, the Anti-Saloon League succeeded in urging 40 percent of the nation's counties to "go dry" by 1906, and a full dozen states to do the same by 1909. Their political pressure culminated in the passage of the Eighteenth Amendment to the U.S. Constitution, ratified in 1919, which prohibited the manufacture, sale, and transportation of alcoholic beverages nationwide.

Figure 1.9 This John R. Chapin illustration shows the women of the temperance movement holding an open-air prayer meeting outside an Ohio saloon. (credit: Library of Congress)

RADICAL PROGRESSIVES

The Progressive Era also witnessed a wave of radicalism, with leaders who believed that America was beyond reform and that only a complete revolution of sorts would bring about the necessary changes. The radicals had early roots in the labor and political movements of the mid-nineteenth century but soon grew to feel that the more moderate Progressive ideals were inadequate. Conversely, one reason mainstream why Progressives felt the need to succeed on issues of social inequity was because radicals offered remedies that middle-class Americans considered far more dangerous. The two most prominent radical movements to emerge at the beginning of the century were the Socialist Party of America (SPA), founded in 1901, and the Industrial Workers of the World (IWW), founded in 1905, whose emphasis on worker empowerment deviated from the more paternalistic approach of Progressive reformers.

Labor leader Eugene Debs, disenchanted with the failures of the labor movement, was a founding member and prominent leader of the SPA (**Figure 1.10**). Advocating for change via the ballot box, the SPA sought to elect Socialists to positions at the local, state, and federal levels in order to initiate change from within. Between 1901 and 1918, the SPA enjoyed tremendous success, electing over seventy Socialist mayors, over thirty state legislators, and two U.S. congressmen, Victor Berger from Wisconsin and Meyer London from New York. Debs himself ran for president as the SPA candidate in five elections between 1900 and 1920, twice earning nearly one million votes.

Figure 1.10 This image of Eugene Debs speaking to a crowd in Canton, Ohio, in 1918, illustrates the passion and intensity that made him such a compelling figure to the more radical Progressives.

As had been true for the Populist and Progressive movements, the radical movement suffered numerous fissures. Although Debs established a tenuous relationship with Samuel Gompers and the American Federation of Labor, some within the Socialist Party favored a more radical political stance than Debs's craft union structure. As a result, William "Big Bill" Haywood formed the more radical IWW, or **Wobblies**, in 1905. Although he remained an active member of the Socialist Party until 1919, Haywood appreciated the outcry of the more radical arm of the party that desired an industrial union approach to labor organization. The IWW advocated for direct action and, in particular, the general strike, as the most effective revolutionary method to overthrow the capitalist system. By 1912, the Wobblies had played a significant role in a number of major strikes, including the Paterson Silk Strike, the Lawrence Textile Strike, and the Mesabi Range Iron Strike. The government viewed the Wobblies as a significant threat, and in a response far greater than their actions warranted, targeted them with arrests, tar-and-featherings, shootings, and lynchings.

Both the Socialist Party and the IWW reflected elements of the Progressive desire for democracy and social justice. The difference was simply that for this small but vocal minority in the United States, the corruption of government at all levels meant that the desire for a better life required a different approach. What they sought mirrored the work of all grassroots Progressives, differing only in degree and strategy.

1.3 New Voices for Women and African Americans

By the end of this section, you will be able to:
- Understand the origins and growth of the women's rights movement
- Identify the different strands of the early African American civil rights movement

The Progressive drive for a more perfect democracy and social justice also fostered the growth of two new movements that attacked the oldest and most long-standing betrayals of the American promise of equal opportunity and citizenship—the disfranchisement of women and civil rights for African Americans. African Americans across the nation identified an agenda for civil rights and economic opportunity during the Progressive Era, but they disagreed strongly on how to meet these goals in the face of universal discrimination and disfranchisement, segregation, and racial violence in the South. And beginning in the late nineteenth century, the women's movement cultivated a cadre of new leaders, national organizations, and competing rationales for women's rights—especially the right to vote.

LEADERS EMERGE IN THE WOMEN'S MOVEMENT

Women like Jane Addams and Florence Kelley were instrumental in the early Progressive settlement house movement, and female leaders dominated organizations such as the WCTU and the Anti-Saloon League. From these earlier efforts came new leaders who, in their turn, focused their efforts on the key goal of the Progressive Era as it pertained to women: the right to vote.

Women had first formulated their demand for the right to vote in the Declaration of Sentiments at a convention in Seneca Falls, New York, in 1848, and saw their first opportunity of securing suffrage during Reconstruction when legislators—driven by racial animosity—sought to enfranchise women to counter the votes of black men following the ratification of the Fifteenth Amendment. By 1900, the western frontier states of Colorado, Idaho, Utah, and Wyoming had already responded to women's movements with the right to vote in state and local elections, regardless of gender. They conceded to the suffragists' demands, partly in order to attract more women to these male-dominated regions. But women's lives in the West also rarely fit with the nineteenth-century ideology of "separate spheres" that had legitimized the exclusion of women from the rough-and-tumble party competitions of public politics. In 1890, the National American Women's Suffrage Association (NAWSA) organized several hundred state and local chapters to urge the passage of a federal amendment to guarantee a woman's right to vote. Its leaders, Elizabeth Cady Stanton and Susan B. Anthony, were veterans of the women's suffrage movement and had formulated the first demand for the right to vote at Seneca Falls in 1848 (**Figure 1.11**). Under the subsequent leadership of Carrie Chapman Catt, beginning in 1900, the group decided to make suffrage its first priority. Soon, its membership began to grow. Using modern marketing efforts like celebrity endorsements to attract a younger audience, the NAWSA became a significant political pressure group for the passage of an amendment to the U.S. Constitution.

Figure 1.11 Women suffragists in Ohio sought to educate and convince men that they should support a woman's rights to vote. As the feature below on the backlash against suffragists illustrates, it was a far from simple task.

For some in the NAWSA, however, the pace of change was too slow. Frustrated with the lack of response by state and national legislators, Alice Paul, who joined the organization in 1912, sought to expand the scope of the organization as well as to adopt more direct protest tactics to draw greater media attention. When others in the group were unwilling to move in her direction, Paul split from the NAWSA to create the Congressional Union for Woman Suffrage, later renamed the National Woman's Party, in 1913. Known as the **Silent Sentinels** (**Figure 1.12**), Paul and her group picketed outside the White House for nearly two years, starting in 1917. In the latter stages of their protests, many women, including Paul, were arrested and thrown in jail, where they staged a hunger strike as self-proclaimed political prisoners. Prison guards ultimately force-fed Paul to keep her alive. At a time—during World War I—when women volunteered as army nurses, worked in vital defense industries, and supported Wilson's campaign to "make the world safe for democracy," the scandalous mistreatment of Paul embarrassed President Woodrow Wilson. Enlightened to the injustice toward all American women, he changed his position in support of a woman's constitutional right to vote.

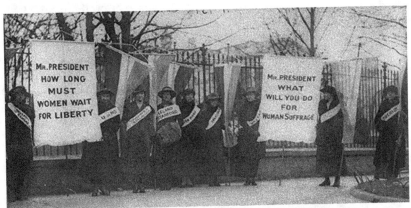

Figure 1.12 Alice Paul and her Silent Sentinels picketed outside the White House for almost two years, and, when arrested, went on hunger strike until they were force-fed in order to save their lives.

While Catt and Paul used different strategies, their combined efforts brought enough pressure to bear for Congress to pass the Nineteenth Amendment, which prohibited voter discrimination on the basis of sex, during a special session in the summer of 1919. Subsequently, the required thirty-six states approved its adoption, with Tennessee doing so in August of 1920, in time for that year's presidential election.

DEFINING "AMERICAN"

⊕ *The Anti-Suffragist Movement*

The early suffragists may have believed that the right to vote was a universal one, but they faced waves of discrimination and ridicule from both men and women. The image below (Figure 1.13) shows one of the organizations pushing back against the suffragist movement, but much of the anti-suffrage campaign was carried out through ridiculing postcards and signs that showed suffragists as sexually wanton, grasping, irresponsible, or impossibly ugly. Men in anti-suffragist posters were depicted as henpecked, crouching to clean the floor, while their suffragist wives marched out the door to campaign for the vote. They also showed cartoons of women gambling, drinking, and smoking cigars, that is, taking on men's vices, once they gained voting rights.

Figure 1.13 The anti-suffrage group used ridicule and embarrassment to try and sway the public away from supporting a woman's right to vote.

Other anti-suffragists believed that women could better influence the country from outside the realm of party politics, through their clubs, petitions, and churches. Many women also opposed women's suffrage because they thought the dirty world of politics was a morass to which ladies should not be exposed. The National Association Opposed to Woman Suffrage formed in 1911; around the country, state representatives used the organization's speakers, funds, and literature to promote the anti-suffragist cause. As the link below illustrates, the suffragists endured much prejudice and backlash in their push for equal rights.

Click and Explore

Browse this collection of anti-suffragist cartoons (http://openstaxcollege.org/l/postcard) to see examples of the stereotypes and fear-mongering that the anti-suffragist campaign promoted.

LEADERS EMERGE IN THE EARLY CIVIL RIGHTS MOVEMENT

Racial mob violence against African Americans permeated much of the "New South"—and, to a lesser extent, the West, where Mexican Americans and other immigrant groups also suffered severe discrimination and violence—by the late nineteenth century. The Ku Klux Klan and a system of Jim Crow laws governed much of the South (discussed in a previous chapter). White middle-class reformers were appalled at the violence of race relations in the nation but typically shared the belief in racial characteristics and the superiority of Anglo-Saxon whites over African Americans, Asians, "ethnic" Europeans, Indians, and Latin American populations. Southern reformers considered segregation a Progressive solution to racial violence; across the nation, educated middle-class Americans enthusiastically followed the work of eugenicists who identified virtually all human behavior as inheritable traits and issued awards at county fairs to families and individuals for their "racial fitness." It was against this tide that African American leaders developed their own voice in the Progressive Era, working along diverse paths to improve the lives and conditions of African Americans throughout the country.

Born into slavery in Virginia in 1856, Booker T. Washington became an influential African American leader at the outset of the Progressive Era. In 1881, he became the first principal for the Tuskegee Normal and Industrial Institute in Alabama, a position he held until he died in 1915. Tuskegee was an all-black "normal school"—an old term for a teachers' college—teaching African Americans a curriculum geared towards practical skills such as cooking, farming, and housekeeping. Graduates would often then travel through the South, teaching new farming and industrial techniques to rural communities. Washington extolled the school's graduates to focus on the black community's self-improvement and prove that they were productive members of society even in freedom—something white Americans throughout the nation had always doubted.

In a speech delivered at the Cotton States and International Exposition in Atlanta in 1895, which was meant to promote the economy of a "New South," Washington proposed what came to be known as the **Atlanta Compromise** (**Figure 1.14**). Speaking to a racially mixed audience, Washington called upon African Americans to work diligently for their own uplift and prosperity rather than preoccupy themselves with political and civil rights. Their success and hard work, he implied, would eventually convince southern whites to grant these rights. Not surprisingly, most whites liked Washington's model of race relations, since it placed the burden of change on blacks and required nothing of them. Wealthy industrialists such as Andrew Carnegie and John D. Rockefeller provided funding for many of Washington's self-help programs, as did Sears, Roebuck & Co. co-founder Julius Rosenwald, and Washington was the first African American invited to the White House by President Roosevelt in 1901. At the same time, his message also appealed to many in the black community, and some attribute this widespread popularity to his consistent message that social and economic growth, even within a segregated society, would do more for African Americans than an all-out agitation for equal rights on all fronts.

Figure 1.14 In Booker T. Washington's speech at the Cotton States and International Exposition in Atlanta, he urged his audience to "cast down your bucket where you are" and make friends with the people around them.

Visit George Mason University's History Matters website for the text and audio of Booker T. Washington's famous Atlanta Compromise (http://openstaxcollege.org/l/booker) speech.

Yet, many African Americans disagreed with Washington's approach. Much in the same manner that Alice Paul felt the pace of the struggle for women's rights was moving too slowly under the NAWSA, some within the African American community felt that immediate agitation for the rights guaranteed under the Thirteenth, Fourteenth, and Fifteenth Amendments, established during the immediate aftermath of the Civil War, was necessary. In 1905, a group of prominent civil rights leaders, led by W. E. B. Du Bois, met in a small hotel on the Canadian side of Niagara Falls—where segregation laws did not bar them from hotel accommodations—to discuss what immediate steps were needed for equal rights (**Figure 1.15**). Du Bois, a professor at the all-black Atlanta University and the first African American with a doctorate from Harvard, emerged as the prominent spokesperson for what would later be dubbed the **Niagara Movement**. By 1905, he had grown wary of Booker T. Washington's calls for African Americans to accommodate white racism and focus solely on self-improvement. Du Bois, and others alongside him, wished to carve a more direct path towards equality that drew on the political leadership and litigation skills of the black, educated elite, which he termed the "talented tenth."

Figure 1.15 This photo of the Niagara Movement shows W. E. B. Du Bois seated in the second row, center, in the white hat. The proud and self-confident postures of this group stood in marked contrast to the humility that Booker T. Washington urged of blacks.

At the meeting, Du Bois led the others in drafting the "Declaration of Principles," which called for immediate political, economic, and social equality for African Americans. These rights included universal suffrage, compulsory education, and the elimination of the convict lease system in which tens of thousands of blacks had endured slavery-like conditions in southern road construction, mines, prisons, and penal farms since the end of Reconstruction. Within a year, Niagara chapters had sprung up in twenty-one states across the country. By 1908, internal fights over the role of women in the fight for African American equal rights lessened the interest in the Niagara Movement. But the movement laid the groundwork for the creation of the National Association for the Advancement of Colored People (**NAACP**), founded in 1909. Du Bois served as the influential director of publications for the NAACP from its inception until 1933. As the editor of the journal *The Crisis*, Du Bois had a platform to express his views on a variety of issues facing African Americans in the later Progressive Era, as well as during World War I and its aftermath.

In both Washington and Du Bois, African Americans found leaders to push forward the fight for their place in the new century, each with a very different strategy. Both men cultivated ground for a new generation of African American spokespeople and leaders who would then pave the road to the modern civil rights movement after World War II.

1.4 Progressivism in the White House

By the end of this section, you will be able to:
- Explain the key features of Theodore Roosevelt's "Square Deal"
- Explain the key features of William Howard Taft's Progressive agenda
- Identify the main pieces of legislation that Woodrow Wilson's "New Freedom" agenda comprised

Progressive groups made tremendous strides on issues involving democracy, efficiency, and social justice. But they found that their grassroots approach was ill-equipped to push back against the most powerful beneficiaries of growing inequality, economic concentration, and corruption—big business. In their fight against the trusts, Progressives needed the leadership of the federal government, and they found it in Theodore Roosevelt in 1901, through an accident of history.

In 1900, a sound economic recovery, a unifying victory in the Spanish-American War, and the annexation of the Philippines had helped President William McKinley secure his reelection with the first solid popular majority since 1872. His new vice president was former New York Governor and Assistant Secretary of the Navy, Theodore Roosevelt. But when an assassin shot and killed President McKinley in 1901 (**Figure 1.16**) at the Pan-American Exposition in Buffalo, New York, Theodore Roosevelt unexpectedly became the youngest president in the nation's history. More importantly, it ushered in a new era of progressive national politics and changed the role of the presidency for the twentieth century.

(a)   (b)

Figure 1.16 President William McKinley's assassination (a) at the hands of an anarchist made Theodore Roosevelt (b) the country's youngest president.

BUSTING THE TRUSTS

Roosevelt's early career showed him to be a dynamic leader with a Progressive agenda. Many Republican Party leaders disliked Roosevelt's Progressive ideas and popular appeal and hoped to end his career with a nomination to the vice presidency—long considered a dead end in politics. When an assassin's bullet toppled this scheme, Mark Hanna, a prominent Republican senator and party leader, lamented, "Now look! That damned cowboy is now president!"

As the new president, however, Roosevelt moved cautiously with his agenda while he finished out McKinley's term. Roosevelt kept much of McKinley's cabinet intact, and his initial message to Congress gave only one overriding Progressive goal for his presidency: to eliminate business trusts. In the three years prior to Roosevelt's presidency, the nation had witnessed a wave of mergers and the creation of mega-corporations. To counter this trend, Roosevelt created the Department of Commerce and Labor in 1903, which included the Bureau of Corporations, whose job it was to investigate trusts. He also asked the Department of Justice to resume prosecutions under the Sherman Antitrust Act of 1890. Intended to empower federal prosecutors to ban monopolies as conspiracies against interstate trade, the law had run afoul of a conservative Supreme Court.

In 1902, Roosevelt launched his administration's first antitrust suit against the Northern Securities Trust Company, which included powerful businessmen, like John D. Rockefeller and J. P. Morgan, and controlled many of the large midwestern railroads. The suit wound through the judicial system, all the way to the U.S. Supreme Court. In 1904, the highest court in the land ultimately affirmed the ruling to break up the trust in a narrow five-to-four vote. For Roosevelt, that was enough of a mandate;

he immediately moved against other corporations as well, including the American Tobacco Company and—most significantly—Rockefeller's Standard Oil Company.

Although Roosevelt enjoyed the nickname "the Trustbuster," he did not consider all trusts dangerous to the public welfare. The "good trusts," Roosevelt reasoned, used their power in the marketplace and economies of scale to deliver goods and services to customers more cheaply. For example, he allowed Morgan's U.S. Steel Corporation to continue its operations and let it take over smaller steel companies. At the same time, Roosevelt used the presidency as a "bully pulpit" to publicly denounce "bad trusts"—those corporations that exploited their market positions for short-term gains—before he ordered prosecutions by the Justice Department. In total, Roosevelt initiated over two dozen successful anti-trust suits, more than any president before him.

Roosevelt also showed in other contexts that he dared to face the power of corporations. When an anthracite coal strike gripped the nation for much of the year in 1902, Roosevelt directly intervened in the dispute and invited both sides to the White House to negotiate a deal that included minor wage increases and a slight improvement in working hours. For Roosevelt, his intervention in the matter symbolized his belief that the federal government should adopt a more proactive role and serve as a steward of all Americans (**Figure 1.17**). This stood in contrast to his predecessors, who had time and again bolstered industrialists in their fight against workers' rights with the deployment of federal troops.

THE WASHINGTON SCHOOLMASTER
From the *Chronicle* (Chicago)

Figure 1.17 This cartoon shows President Roosevelt disciplining coal barons like J. P. Morgan, threatening to beat them with a stick labeled "Federal Authority." It illustrates Roosevelt's new approach to business.

THE SQUARE DEAL

Roosevelt won his second term in 1904 with an overwhelming 57 percent of the popular vote. After the election, he moved quickly to enact his own brand of Progressivism, which he called a **Square Deal** for the American people. Early in his second term, Roosevelt read muckraker Upton Sinclair's 1905 novel and exposé on the meatpacking industry, *The Jungle*. Although Roosevelt initially questioned the book due to Sinclair's professed Socialist leanings, a subsequent presidential commission investigated the industry and corroborated the deplorable conditions under which Chicago's meatpackers processed meats for American consumers. Alarmed by the results and under pressure from an outraged public disgusted with the revelations, Roosevelt moved quickly to protect public health. He urged the passage of two laws to do so. The first, the Meat Inspection Act of 1906, established a system of government inspection for meat products, including grading the meat based on its quality. This standard was also used for imported meats. The second was the Pure Food and Drug Act of 1906, which required labels on all food and drug products that clearly stated the materials in the product. The law also prohibited any "adulterated" products, a measure aimed at some specific, unhealthy food preservatives. For Sinclair, this outcome was a disappointment nonetheless, since he had sought to draw attention to the plight of workers in the slaughterhouses, not the poor quality of the meat products. "I aimed at the public's heart, and by accident I hit it in the stomach," he concluded with frustration.

Another key element of Roosevelt's Progressivism was the protection of public land (**Figure 1.18**). Roosevelt was a longtime outdoorsman, with an interest that went back to his childhood and college days, as well as his time cattle ranching in the West, and he chose to appoint his good friend Gifford Pinchot as the country's first chief of the newly created U.S. Forestry Service. Under Pinchot's supervision, the department carved out several nature habitats on federal land in order to preserve the nation's environmental beauty and protect it from development or commercial use. Apart from national parks like Oregon's Crater Lake or Colorado's Mesa Verde, and monuments designed for preservation, Roosevelt conserved public land for regulated use for future generations. To this day, the 150 national forests created under Roosevelt's stewardship carry the slogan "land of many uses." In all, Roosevelt established eighteen national monuments, fifty-one federal bird preserves, five national parks, and over one hundred fifty national forests, which amounted to about 230 million acres of public land.

Figure 1.18 Theodore Roosevelt's interest in the protection of public lands was encouraged by conservationists such as John Muir, founder of the Sierra Club, with whom he toured Yosemite National Park in California, ca. 1906.

In his second term in office, Roosevelt signed legislation on Progressive issues such as factory inspections, child labor, and business regulation. He urged the passage of the Elkins Act of 1903 and the Hepburn Act of 1906, both of which strengthened the position of the Interstate Commerce Commission to regulate railroad prices. These laws also extended the Commission's authority to regulate interstate transportation on bridges, ferries, and even oil pipelines.

As the 1908 election approached, Roosevelt was at the height of popularity among the American public, if not among the big businesses and conservative leaders of his own Republican Party. Nonetheless, he promised on the night of his reelection in 1904 that he would not seek a third term. Roosevelt stepped aside as the election approached, but he did hand-pick a successor—Secretary of War and former Governor General of the Philippines William Howard Taft of Ohio—a personal friend who, he assured the American public, would continue the path of the "Square Deal" (**Figure 1.19**). With such a ringing endorsement, Taft easily won the 1908 presidential election, defeating three-time Democratic presidential nominee William Jennings Bryan, whose ideas on taxes and corporate regulations reminded voters of the more far-reaching Populist platforms of Bryan's past candidacies.

(a)   (b)

Figure 1.19 This photograph (a) of Theodore Roosevelt (left) and his hand-picked successor William Howard Taft (right) just before Taft's inauguration in 1909, was echoed in a Puck magazine cartoon (b) where "cowboy" Roosevelt hands off his "Policies" baby to "nurse-maid" Taft. Taft was seen, initially at least, as being a president who would continue Roosevelt's same policies.

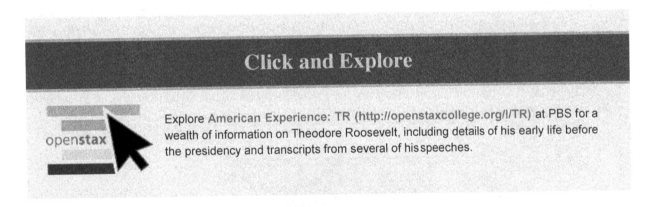

Click and Explore

Explore American Experience: TR (http://openstaxcollege.org/l/TR) at PBS for a wealth of information on Theodore Roosevelt, including details of his early life before the presidency and transcripts from several of his speeches.

THE TAFT PRESIDENCY

Although six feet tall and nearly 340 pounds, as Roosevelt's successor, Taft had big shoes to fill. The public expected much from Roosevelt's hand-picked replacement, as did Roosevelt himself, who kept a watchful eye over Taft's presidency.

The new president's background suggested he would be a strong administrator. He had previously served as the governor of the Philippines following the Spanish-American War, had a distinguished judicial career, and served as Roosevelt's Secretary of War from 1904 to 1908. Republican leaders, however, were anxious to reestablish tighter control over the party after Roosevelt's departure, and they left Taft little room to maneuver. He stayed the course of his predecessor by signing the Mann-Elkins Act of 1910, which extended the authority of the Interstate Commerce Commission over telephones and telegraphs. Additionally, during his tenure, Congress proposed constitutional amendments to authorize a federal income tax and mandate the direct election of U.S. senators. But even though Taft initiated twice as many antitrust suits against big business as Roosevelt, he lacked the political negotiating skills and focus on the public good of his predecessor, who felt betrayed when Taft took J.P. Morgan's U.S. Steel Corporation to court over an acquisition that Roosevelt had promised Morgan would not result in a prosecution.

Political infighting within his own party exposed the limitations of Taft's presidential authority, especially on the issue of protective tariffs. When House Republicans passed a measure to significantly reduce tariffs on several imported goods, Taft endorsed the Senate version, later known as the Payne-Aldrich Act of 1909, which raised tariff rates on over eight hundred products in the original bill. Taft also angered Progressives in his own party when he created the U.S. Chamber of Commerce in 1912, viewed by many as an attempt to offset the growing influence of the labor union movement at the time. The rift between Taft and his party's Progressives widened when the president supported conservative party candidates for the 1910 House and Senate elections.

Taft's biggest political blunder came in the area of land conservation. In 1909, Taft's Secretary of the Interior, Richard Ballinger, approved the sale of millions of acres of federal land to a company for which he had previously worked over Gifford Pinchot's objections. Pinchot publicly criticized the secretary for violating the principle of conservation and for his conflict of interest—a charge that in the public debate also reflected on the president. Taft fired Pinchot, a move that widened the gap between him and the former president. Upon his return from Africa, Roosevelt appeared primed to attack. He referred to the sitting president as a "fathead" and a "puzzlewit," and announced his intention to "throw my hat in the ring for the 1912 presidential election."

THE 1912 PRESIDENTIAL ELECTION

Although not as flamboyant or outwardly progressive as Roosevelt, Taft's organizational skills and generally solid performance as p resident aligned with the party leadership's concerns over another Roosevelt presidency and secured for him the Republican Party's nomination. Angry over this snub, in 1912, Roosevelt and the other Progressive Republicans bolted the Republican Party and formed the **Progressive Party**. His popularity had him hoping to win the presidential race as a third-party candidate. When he survived an assassination attempt in Milwaukee, Wisconsin, in October 1912—the assassin's bullet hit his eyeglass case and only injured him superficially—he turned the near-death experience into a political opportunity. Insisting upon delivering the speech before seeking medical attention, he told the crowd, "It takes more than a bullet to kill a bull moose!" The moniker stuck, and Roosevelt's Progressive Party would be known as the Bull Moose Party for the remainder of the campaign (**Figure 1.20**).

Figure 1.20 Theodore Roosevelt, now running as the Progressive Party, or Bull Moose Party, candidate, created an unprecedented moment in the country's history, where a former president was running against both an incumbent president and a future president.

The Democrats realized that a split Republican Party gave them a good chance of regaining the White House for the first time since 1896. They found their candidate in the Progressive governor of New

Jersey, Woodrow Wilson. A former history professor and president at Princeton University, Wilson had an academic demeanor that appealed to many Progressive reformers. Many Democrats also viewed Wilson as a Washington outsider who had made far fewer political enemies than Roosevelt and Taft.

Taft never truly campaigned for the post, did not deliver a single speech, and did not seem like a serious contender. In their campaigns, Roosevelt and Wilson formulated competing Progressive platforms. Wilson described his more moderate approach as one of **New Freedom**, which stood for a smaller federal government to protect public interests from the evils associated with big businesses and banks. Roosevelt campaigned on the promise of **New Nationalism**, a charge that he said required a vigorous and powerful federal government to protect public interests. He sought to capitalize on the stewardship approach that he had made famous during his previous administration.

Wilson won the 1912 election with over six million votes, with four million votes going to Roosevelt and three and one-half million for Taft. The internal split among Republicans not only cost them the White House but control of the Senate as well—and Democrats had already won a House majority in 1910. Wilson won the presidency with just 42 percent of the popular vote, which meant that he would have to sway a large number of voters should he have any aspirations for a second term.

DEFINING "AMERICAN"

✪ *The Unprecedented Election of 1912*

In his 2002 article on the 1912 election, historian Sidney M. Milkis writes,

> The Progressive Party's "compromise" with public opinion in the United States points to its legacy for American politics and government. Arguably, the failure of the 1912 experiment and the Progressive Party's demise underscore the incoherence of the Progressive movement. Nevertheless, it was neither the Democrats, nor the Republicans, nor the Socialists who set the tone of the 1912 campaign. It was the Progressives. Beyond the 1912 election, their program of political and social reform has been an enduring feature of American political discourse and electoral struggle. The Progressive Party forged a path of reform that left both social democracy and conservatism—Taft's constitutional sobriety—behind. Similarly, T.R.'s celebrity, and the popularity of the Progressive doctrine of the people's right to rule, tended to subordinate the more populist to the more plebiscitary schemes in the platform, such as the initiative, the referendum, and the direct primary, which exalted not the "grass roots" but mass opinion. Indeed, in the wake of the excitement aroused by the Progressive Party, Wilson, whose New Freedom campaign was far more sympathetic to the decentralized state of courts and parties than T.R.'s, felt compelled, as president, to govern as a New Nationalist Progressive.

It is interesting to think of how this most unusual election—one with three major candidates that pitted a former president against an incumbent and a major party contender—related to the larger Progressive movement. The cartoon below is only one of many cartoons of that era that sought to point out the differences between the candidates (**Figure 1.21**). While Roosevelt and the Progressive Party ultimately lost the election, they required the dialogue of the campaign to remain on the goals of Progressivism, particularly around more direct democracy and business regulation. The American public responded with fervor to Roosevelt's campaign, partly because of his immense popularity, but partly also because he espoused a kind of direct democracy that gave people a voice in federal politics. Although Wilson and his New Freedom platform won the election, his presidency undertook a more activist role than his campaign suggested. The American public had made clear that, no matter who sat in the White House, they were seeking a more progressive America.

Figure 1.21 This cartoon, from the 1912 election, parodies how the voters might perceive the three major candidates. As can be seen, Taft was never a serious contender.

WILSON'S NEW FREEDOM

When Wilson took office in March 1913, he immediately met with Congress to outline his New Freedom agenda for how progressive interests could be best preserved. His plan was simple: regulate the banks and big businesses, and lower tariff rates to increase international trade, increasing competition in the interest of consumers. Wilson took the unusual step of calling a special session of Congress in April 1913 to tackle the tariff question, which resulted in the Revenue Act of 1913, also known as the Underwood Tariff Act. This legislation lowered tariff rates across the board by approximately 15 percent and completely eliminated tariffs on several imports, including steel, iron ore, woolen products, and farm tools. To offset the potential loss of federal revenue, this new law reinstituted the federal income tax, which followed the ratification of the Sixteenth Amendment. This first income tax required married couples who earned $4000 or more, and single people who earned $3000 or more, to pay a 1-percent, graduated income tax, with the tax rate getting progressively higher for those who earned more.

Late in 1913, Wilson signed the Federal Reserve Act to regulate the banking industry and establish a federal banking system (**Figure 1.22**). Designed to remove power over interest rates from the hands of private bankers, the new system created twelve privately owned regional reserve banks regulated by a presidentially appointed Federal Reserve Board. The Board, known informally as the Fed, regulated the interest rate at which reserve banks loaned or distributed money to other banks around the country. Thus, when economic times were challenging, such as during a recession, the Fed could lower this "discount rate" and encourage more borrowing, which put more currency in circulation for people to spend or invest. Conversely, the Fed could curb inflationary trends with interest hikes that discouraged borrowing. This system is still the basis for the country's modern banking model.

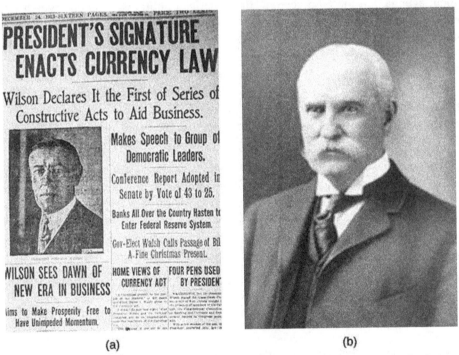

(a)   (b)

Figure 1.22 With the creation of the Federal Reserve Board, President Wilson set the stage for the modern banking system (a). This restructuring of the American financial system, which included the authorization of a federal income tax, was supported in large part by an influential Republican senator from Rhode Island, Nelson Aldrich (b), co-author of the Payne-Aldrich Act of 1909.

In early 1914, Wilson completed his New Freedom agenda with the passage of the Clayton Antitrust Act. This law expanded the power of the original Sherman Antitrust Act in order to allow the investigation and dismantling of more monopolies. The new act also took on the "interlocking directorates"—competing companies that still operated together in a form of oligopoly or conspiracy to restrain trade. His New Freedom agenda complete, Wilson turned his attention to foreign affairs, as war was quickly encompassing Europe.

THE FINAL VESTIGES OF PROGRESSIVISM

As the 1916 election approached, Wilson's focus on foreign affairs, as well as the natural effect of his small government agenda, left the 60 percent of the American public who had not voted for him the first time disinclined to change their minds and keep him in office. Realizing this, Wilson began a flurry of new Progressive reforms that impressed the voting public and ultimately proved to be the last wave of the Progressive Era. Some of the important measures that Wilson undertook to pass included the Federal Farm Act, which provided oversight of low-interest loans to millions of farmers in need of debt relief; the Keating-Owen Child Labor Act, which, although later deemed unconstitutional by the U.S. Supreme Court, prohibited the interstate distribution of products by child workers under the age of fourteen; and the Adamson Act, which put in place the first federally mandated eight-hour workday for railroad workers.

Wilson also gained significant support from Jewish voters with his 1916 appointment of the first Jewish U.S. Supreme Court justice, Louis D. Brandeis. Popular among social justice Progressives, Brandeis went on to become one of the most renowned justices on the court for his defense of freedom of speech and right to privacy issues. Finally, Wilson gained the support of many working-class voters with his defense of labor and union rights during a violent coal strike in Ludlow, Colorado, as well as his actions to forestall a potential railroad strike with the passage of the aforementioned Adamson Act.

Wilson's actions in 1916 proved enough, but barely. In a close presidential election, he secured a second term by defeating former New York governor Charles Evans Hughes by a scant twenty-three electoral votes, and less than 600,000 popular votes. Influential states like Minnesota and New Hampshire were decided by less than four hundred votes.

Despite the fact that he ran for reelection with the slogan, "He Kept Us Out of the War," Wilson could not avoid the reach of World War I much longer. For Wilson and the American public, the Progressive Era was rapidly winding down. Although a few Progressive achievements were still to come in the areas of women's suffrage and prohibition, the country would soon be gripped by the war that Wilson had tried to avoid during his first term in office. When he took the oath for his second term, on March 4, 1917, Wilson was barely five weeks away from leading the United States in declaring war on Germany, a move that would put an end to the Progressive Era.

CHAPTER 2

Americans and the Great War, 1914-1919

Figure 2.1 *Return of the Useless* (1918), by George Bellows, is an example of a kind of artistic imagery used to galvanize reluctant Americans into joining World War I. The scene shows German soldiers unloading and mistreating imprisoned civilians after their return home to Belgium from German forced-labor camps.

Chapter Outline

2.1 American Isolationism and the European Origins of War

2.2 The United States Prepares for War

2.3 A New Home Front

2.4 From War to Peace

2.5 Demobilization and Its Difficult Aftermath

Introduction

On the eve of World War I, the U.S. government under President Woodrow Wilson opposed any entanglement in international military conflicts. But as the war engulfed Europe and the belligerents' total war strategies targeted commerce and travel across the Atlantic, it became clear that the United States would not be able to maintain its position of neutrality. Still, the American public was of mixed opinion; many resisted the idea of American intervention and American lives lost, no matter how bad the circumstances.

In 1918, artist George Bellows created a series of paintings intended to strengthen public support for the war effort. His paintings depicted German war atrocities in explicit and expertly captured detail, from children run through with bayonets to torturers happily resting while their victims suffered. The image above, entitled *Return of the Useless* (**Figure 2.1**), shows Germans unloading sick or disabled labor camp prisoners from a boxcar. These paintings, while not regarded as Bellows' most important artistic work, were typical for anti-German propaganda at the time. The U.S. government sponsored much of this propaganda out of concern that many American immigrants sympathized with the Central powers and would not support the U.S. war effort.

2.1 American Isolationism and the European Origins of War

By the end of this section, you will be able to:
- Explain Woodrow Wilson's foreign policy and the difficulties of maintaining American neutrality at the outset of World War I
- Identify the key factors that led to the U.S. declaration of war on Germany in April 1917

Unlike his immediate predecessors, President Woodrow Wilson had planned to shrink the role of the United States in foreign affairs. He believed that the nation needed to intervene in international events only when there was a moral imperative to do so. But as Europe's political situation grew dire, it became increasingly difficult for Wilson to insist that the conflict growing overseas was not America's responsibility. Germany's war tactics struck most observers as morally reprehensible, while also putting American free trade with the Entente at risk. Despite campaign promises and diplomatic efforts, Wilson could only postpone American involvement in the war.

WOODROW WILSON'S NEW FREEDOM

When Woodrow Wilson took over the White House in March 1913, he promised a less expansionist approach to American foreign policy than Theodore Roosevelt and William Howard Taft had pursued. Wilson did share the commonly held view that American values were superior to those of the rest of the world, that democracy was the best system to promote peace and stability, and that the United States should continue to actively pursue economic markets abroad. But he proposed an idealistic foreign policy based on morality, rather than American self-interest, and felt that American interference in another nation's affairs should occur only when the circumstances rose to the level of a moral imperative.

Wilson appointed former presidential candidate William Jennings Bryan, a noted anti-imperialist and proponent of world peace, as his Secretary of State. Bryan undertook his new assignment with great vigor, encouraging nations around the world to sign "cooling off treaties," under which they agreed to resolve international disputes through talks, not war, and to submit any grievances to an international commission. Bryan also negotiated friendly relations with Colombia, including a $25 million apology for

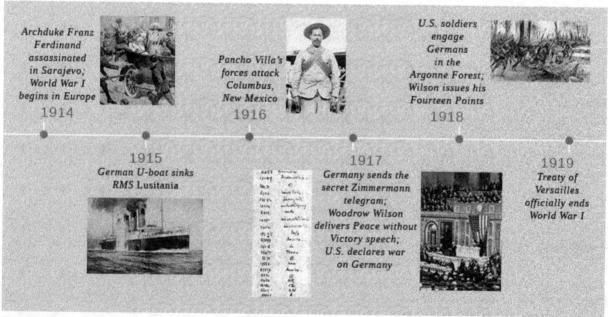

Figure 2.2

Roosevelt's actions during the Panamanian Revolution, and worked to establish effective self-government in the Philippines in preparation for the eventual American withdrawal. Even with Bryan's support, however, Wilson found that it was much harder than he anticipated to keep the United States out of world affairs (**Figure 2.3**). In reality, the United States was interventionist in areas where its interests—direct or indirect—were threatened.

THE BRONCHO-BUSTER.

Figure 2.3 While Wilson strove to be less of an interventionist, he found that to be more difficult in practice than in theory. Here, a political cartoon depicts him as a rather hapless cowboy, unclear on how to harness a foreign challenge, in this case, Mexico.

Wilson's greatest break from his predecessors occurred in Asia, where he abandoned Taft's "dollar diplomacy," a foreign policy that essentially used the power of U.S. economic dominance as a threat to gain favorable terms. Instead, Wilson revived diplomatic efforts to keep Japanese interference there at a minimum. But as World War I, also known as the Great War, began to unfold, and European nations largely abandoned their imperialistic interests in order to marshal their forces for self-defense, Japan demanded that China succumb to a Japanese protectorate over their entire nation. In 1917, William Jennings Bryan's successor as Secretary of State, Robert Lansing, signed the Lansing-Ishii Agreement, which recognized Japanese control over the Manchurian region of China in exchange for Japan's promise not to exploit the war to gain a greater foothold in the rest of the country.

Furthering his goal of reducing overseas interventions, Wilson had promised not to rely on the Roosevelt Corollary, Theodore Roosevelt's explicit policy that the United States could involve itself in Latin American politics whenever it felt that the countries in the Western Hemisphere needed policing. Once president, however, Wilson again found that it was more difficult to avoid American interventionism in practice than in rhetoric. Indeed, Wilson intervened more in Western Hemisphere affairs than either Taft or Roosevelt. In 1915, when a revolution in Haiti resulted in the murder of the Haitian president and threatened the safety of New York banking interests in the country, Wilson sent over three hundred U.S. Marines to establish order. Subsequently, the United States assumed control over the island's foreign policy as well as its financial administration. One year later, in 1916, Wilson again sent marines to Hispaniola, this time to the Dominican Republic, to ensure prompt payment of a debt that nation owed. In 1917, Wilson sent troops to Cuba to protect American-owned sugar plantations from attacks by Cuban rebels; this time, the troops remained for four years.

Wilson's most noted foreign policy foray prior to World War I focused on Mexico, where rebel general Victoriano Huerta had seized control from a previous rebel government just weeks before Wilson's inauguration. Wilson refused to recognize Huerta's government, instead choosing to make an example of Mexico by demanding that they hold democratic elections and establish laws based on the moral principles he espoused. Officially, Wilson supported Venustiano Carranza, who opposed Huerta's military control of the country. When American intelligence learned of a German ship allegedly preparing to deliver weapons to Huerta's forces, Wilson ordered the U.S. Navy to land forces at Veracruz to stop the shipment.

On April 22, 1914, a fight erupted between the U.S. Navy and Mexican troops, resulting in nearly 150 deaths, nineteen of them American. Although Carranza's faction managed to overthrow Huerta in the summer of 1914, most Mexicans—including Carranza—had come to resent American intervention in their affairs. Carranza refused to work with Wilson and the U.S. government, and instead threatened to defend Mexico's mineral rights against all American oil companies established there. Wilson then turned to support rebel forces who opposed Carranza, most notably Pancho Villa (**Figure 2.4**). However, Villa lacked the strength in number or weapons to overtake Carranza; in 1915, Wilson reluctantly authorized official U.S. recognition of Carranza's government.

Figure 2.4 Pancho Villa, a Mexican rebel who Wilson supported, then ultimately turned from, attempted an attack on the United States in retaliation. Wilson's actions in Mexico were emblematic of how difficult it was to truly set the United States on a course of moral leadership.

As a postscript, an irate Pancho Villa turned against Wilson, and on March 9, 1916, led a fifteen-hundred-man force across the border into New Mexico, where they attacked and burned the town of Columbus. Over one hundred people died in the attack, seventeen of them American. Wilson responded by sending General John Pershing into Mexico to capture Villa and return him to the United States for trial. With over eleven thousand troops at his disposal, Pershing marched three hundred miles into Mexico before an angry Carranza ordered U.S. troops to withdraw from the nation. Although reelected in 1916, Wilson reluctantly ordered the withdrawal of U.S. troops from Mexico in 1917, avoiding war with Mexico and enabling preparations for American intervention in Europe. Again, as in China, Wilson's attempt to impose a moral foreign policy had failed in light of economic and political realities.

WAR ERUPTS IN EUROPE

When a Serbian nationalist murdered the Archduke Franz Ferdinand of the Austro-Hungarian Empire on June 29, 1914, the underlying forces that led to World War I had already long been in motion and seemed, at first, to have little to do with the United States. At the time, the events that pushed Europe from ongoing tensions into war seemed very far away from U.S. interests. For nearly a century, nations had negotiated a series of mutual defense alliance treaties to secure themselves against their imperialistic rivals. Among the largest European powers, the Triple Entente included an alliance of France, Great Britain, and Russia. Opposite them, the Central powers, also known as the Triple Alliance, included Germany, Austria-Hungary, the Ottoman Empire, and initially Italy. A series of "side treaties" likewise entangled the larger European powers to protect several smaller ones should war break out.

At the same time that European nations committed each other to defense pacts, they jockeyed for power over empires overseas and invested heavily in large, modern militaries. Dreams of empire and military supremacy fueled an era of nationalism that was particularly pronounced in the newer nations of Germany and Italy, but also provoked separatist movements among Europeans. The Irish rose up in rebellion against British rule, for example. And in Bosnia's capital of Sarajevo, Gavrilo Princip and his accomplices assassinated the Austro-Hungarian archduke in their fight for a pan-Slavic nation. Thus, when Serbia failed to accede to Austro-Hungarian demands in the wake of the archduke's murder, Austria-Hungary declared war on Serbia with the confidence that it had the backing of Germany. This action, in turn, brought Russia into the conflict, due to a treaty in which they had agreed to defend Serbia. Germany followed suit by declaring war on Russia, fearing that Russia and France would seize this opportunity to move on Germany if it did not take the offensive. The eventual German invasion of Belgium drew Great Britain into the war, followed by the attack of the Ottoman Empire on Russia. By the end of August 1914, it seemed as if Europe had dragged the entire world into war.

The Great War was unlike any war that came before it. Whereas in previous European conflicts, troops typically faced each other on open battlefields, World War I saw new military technologies that turned war into a conflict of prolonged trench warfare. Both sides used new artillery, tanks, airplanes, machine guns, barbed wire, and, eventually, poison gas: weapons that strengthened defenses and turned each military offense into barbarous sacrifices of thousands of lives with minimal territorial advances in return. By the end of the war, the total military death toll was ten million, as well as another million civilian deaths attributed to military action, and another six million civilian deaths caused by famine, disease, or other related factors.

One terrifying new piece of technological warfare was the German *unterseeboot*—an "undersea boat" or U-boat. By early 1915, in an effort to break the British naval blockade of Germany and turn the tide of the war, the Germans dispatched a fleet of these submarines around Great Britain to attack both merchant and military ships. The U-boats acted in direct violation of international law, attacking without warning from beneath the water instead of surfacing and permitting the surrender of civilians or crew. By 1918, German U-boats had sunk nearly five thousand vessels. Of greatest historical note was the attack on the British passenger ship, RMS *Lusitania*, on its way from New York to Liverpool on May 7, 1915. The German Embassy in the United States had announced that this ship would be subject to attack for its cargo of ammunition: an allegation that later proved accurate. Nonetheless, almost 1,200 civilians died in the attack, including 128 Americans. The attack horrified the world, galvanizing support in England and beyond for the war (**Figure 2.5**). This attack, more than any other event, would test President Wilson's desire to stay out of what had been a largely European conflict.

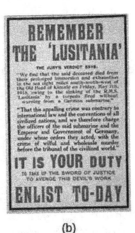

(a)   (b)

Figure 2.5 The torpedoing and sinking of the *Lusitania*, depicted in the English drawing above (a), resulted in the death over twelve hundred civilians and was an international incident that shifted American sentiment as to their potential role in the war, as illustrated in a British recruiting poster (b).

THE CHALLENGE OF NEUTRALITY

Despite the loss of American lives on the *Lusitania*, President Wilson stuck to his path of **neutrality** in Europe's escalating war: in part out of moral principle, in part as a matter of practical necessity, and in part for political reasons. Few Americans wished to participate in the devastating battles that ravaged Europe, and Wilson did not want to risk losing his reelection by ordering an unpopular military intervention. Wilson's "neutrality" did not mean isolation from all warring factions, but rather open markets for the United States and continued commercial ties with all belligerents. For Wilson, the conflict did not reach the threshold of a moral imperative for U.S. involvement; it was largely a European affair involving numerous countries with whom the United States wished to maintain working relations. In his message to Congress in 1914, the president noted that "Every man who really loves America will act and speak in the true spirit of neutrality, which is the spirit of impartiality and fairness and friendliness to all concerned."

Wilson understood that he was already looking at a difficult reelection bid. He had only won the 1912 election with 42 percent of the popular vote, and likely would not have been elected at all had Roosevelt not come back as a third-party candidate to run against his former protégée Taft. Wilson felt pressure from all different political constituents to take a position on the war, yet he knew that elections were seldom won with a campaign promise of "If elected, I will send your sons to war!" Facing pressure from some businessmen and other government officials who felt that the protection of America's best interests required a stronger position in defense of the Allied forces, Wilson agreed to a "preparedness campaign" in the year prior to the election. This campaign included the passage of the National Defense Act of 1916, which more than doubled the size of the army to nearly 225,000, and the Naval Appropriations Act of 1916, which called for the expansion of the U.S. fleet, including battleships, destroyers, submarines, and other ships.

As the 1916 election approached, the Republican Party hoped to capitalize on the fact that Wilson was making promises that he would not be able to keep. They nominated Charles Evans Hughes, a former governor of New York and sitting U.S. Supreme Court justice at the time of his nomination. Hughes focused his campaign on what he considered Wilson's foreign policy failures, but even as he did so, he himself tried to walk a fine line between neutrality and belligerence, depending on his audience. In contrast, Wilson and the Democrats capitalized on neutrality and campaigned under the slogan "Wilson—he kept us out of war." The election itself remained too close to call on election night. Only when a tight race in California was decided two days later could Wilson claim victory in his reelection bid, again with less than 50 percent of the popular vote. Despite his victory based upon a policy of neutrality, Wilson would find true neutrality a difficult challenge. Several different factors pushed Wilson, however reluctantly, toward the inevitability of American involvement.

A key factor driving U.S. engagement was economics. Great Britain was the country's most important trading partner, and the Allies as a whole relied heavily on American imports from the earliest days of the war forward. Specifically, the value of all exports to the Allies quadrupled from $750 million to $3 billion in the first two years of the war. At the same time, the British naval blockade meant that exports to Germany all but ended, dropping from $350 million to $30 million. Likewise, numerous private banks in the United States made extensive loans—in excess of $500 million—to England. J. P. Morgan's banking interests were among the largest lenders, due to his family's connection to the country.

Another key factor in the decision to go to war were the deep ethnic divisions between native-born Americans and more recent immigrants. For those of Anglo-Saxon descent, the nation's historic and ongoing relationship with Great Britain was paramount, but many Irish-Americans resented British rule over their place of birth and opposed support for the world's most expansive empire. Millions of Jewish immigrants had fled anti-Semitic pogroms in Tsarist Russia and would have supported any nation fighting that authoritarian state. German Americans saw their nation of origin as a victim of British and Russian aggression and a French desire to settle old scores, whereas emigrants from Austria-Hungary and the Ottoman Empire were mixed in their sympathies for the old monarchies or ethnic communities that these empires suppressed. For interventionists, this lack of support for Great Britain and its allies among recent immigrants only strengthened their conviction.

Germany's use of submarine warfare also played a role in challenging U.S. neutrality. After the sinking of the *Lusitania*, and the subsequent August 30 sinking of another British liner, the *Arabic*, Germany had promised to restrict their use of submarine warfare. Specifically, they promised to surface and visually identify any ship before they fired, as well as permit civilians to evacuate targeted ships. Instead, in February 1917, Germany intensified their use of submarines in an effort to end the war quickly before Great Britain's naval blockade starved them out of food and supplies.

The German high command wanted to continue unrestricted warfare on all Atlantic traffic, including unarmed American freighters, in order to cripple the British economy and secure a quick and decisive victory. Their goal: to bring an end to the war before the United States could intervene and tip the balance in this grueling war of attrition. In February 1917, a German U-boat sank the American merchant ship, the *Laconia*, killing two passengers, and, in late March, quickly sunk four more American ships. These attacks increased pressure on Wilson from all sides, as government officials, the general public, and both Democrats and Republicans urged him to declare war.

The final element that led to American involvement in World War I was the so-called **Zimmermann telegram**. British intelligence intercepted and decoded a top-secret telegram from German foreign minister Arthur Zimmermann to the German ambassador to Mexico, instructing the latter to invite Mexico to join the war effort on the German side, should the United States declare war on Germany. It further went on to encourage Mexico to invade the United States if such a declaration came to pass, as Mexico's invasion would create a diversion and permit Germany a clear path to victory. In exchange, Zimmermann offered to return to Mexico land that was previously lost to the United States in the Mexican-American War, including Arizona, New Mexico, and Texas (**Figure 2.6**).

Figure 2.6 "The Temptation," which appeared in the *Dallas Morning News* on March 2, 1917, shows Germany as the Devil, tempting Mexico to join their war effort against the United States in exchange for the return of land formerly belonging to Mexico. The prospect of such a move made it all but impossible for Wilson to avoid war. (credit: Library of Congress)

The likelihood that Mexico, weakened and torn by its own revolution and civil war, could wage war against the United States and recover territory lost in the Mexican-American war with Germany's help was remote at best. But combined with Germany's unrestricted use of submarine warfare and the sinking of American ships, the Zimmermann telegram made a powerful argument for a declaration of war. The outbreak of the Russian Revolution in February and abdication of Tsar Nicholas II in March raised the prospect of democracy in the Eurasian empire and removed an important moral objection to entering the war on the side of the Allies. On April 2, 1917, Wilson asked Congress to declare war on Germany. Congress debated for four days, and several senators and congressmen expressed their concerns that the war was being fought over U.S. economic interests more than strategic need or democratic ideals. When Congress voted on April 6, fifty-six voted against the resolution, including the first woman ever elected to Congress, Representative Jeannette Rankin. This was the largest "no" vote against a war resolution in American history.

DEFINING "AMERICAN"

⊛ *Wilson's Peace without Victory Speech*

Wilson's last-ditch effort to avoid bringing the United States into World War I is captured in a speech he gave before the U.S. Senate on January 22, 1917. This speech, known as the "Peace without Victory" speech, extolled the country to be patient, as the countries involved in the war were nearing a peace. Wilson stated:

> It must be a peace without victory. It is not pleasant to say this. I beg that I may be permitted to put my own interpretation upon it and that it may be understood that no other interpretation was in my thought. I am seeking only to face realities and to face them without soft concealments. Victory would mean peace forced upon the loser, a victor's terms imposed upon the vanquished. It would be accepted in humiliation, under duress, at an intolerable sacrifice, and would leave a sting, a resentment, a bitter memory upon which terms of peace would rest, not permanently, but only as upon quicksand. Only a peace between equals can last, only a peace the very principle of which is equality and a common participation in a common benefit.

Not surprisingly, this speech was not well received by either side fighting the war. England resisted being put on the same moral ground as Germany, and France, whose country had been battered by years of warfare, had no desire to end the war without victory and its spoils. Still, the speech as a whole illustrates Wilson's idealistic, if failed, attempt to create a more benign and high-minded foreign policy role for the United States. Unfortunately, the Zimmermann telegram and the sinking of the American merchant ships proved too provocative for Wilson to remain neutral. Little more than two months after this speech, he asked Congress to declare war on Germany.

Click and Explore

Read the full transcript of the Peace without Victory speech (http://openstaxcollege.org/l/15WWilson) that clearly shows Wilson's desire to remain out of the war, even when it seemed inevitable.

2.2 The United States Prepares for War

By the end of this section, you will be able to:
- Identify the steps taken by the U.S. government to secure enough men, money, food, and supplies to prosecute World War I
- Explain how the U.S. government attempted to sway popular opinion in favor of the war effort

Wilson knew that the key to America's success in war lay largely in its preparation. With both the Allied and enemy forces entrenched in battles of attrition, and supplies running low on both sides, the United States needed, first and foremost, to secure enough men, money, food, and supplies to be successful. The country needed to first supply the basic requirements to fight a war, and then work to ensure military leadership, public support, and strategic planning.

THE INGREDIENTS OF WAR

The First World War was, in many ways, a war of attrition, and the United States needed a large army to help the Allies. In 1917, when the United States declared war on Germany, the U.S. Army ranked seventh in the world in terms of size, with an estimated 200,000 enlisted men. In contrast, at the outset of the war in 1914, the German force included 4.5 million men, and the country ultimately mobilized over eleven million soldiers over the course of the entire war.

To compose a fighting force, Congress passed the Selective Service Act in 1917, which initially required all men aged twenty-one through thirty to register for the draft (**Figure 2.7**). In 1918, the act was expanded to include all men between eighteen and forty-five. Through a campaign of patriotic appeals, as well as an administrative system that allowed men to register at their local draft boards rather than directly with the federal government, over ten million men registered for the draft on the very first day. By the war's end, twenty-two million men had registered for the U.S. Army draft. Five million of these men were actually drafted, another 1.5 million volunteered, and over 500,000 additional men signed up for the navy or marines. In all, two million men participated in combat operations overseas. Among the volunteers were also twenty thousand women, a quarter of whom went to France to serve as nurses or in clerical positions.

But the draft also provoked opposition, and almost 350,000 eligible Americans refused to register for military service. About 65,000 of these defied the conscription law as conscientious objectors, mostly on the grounds of their deeply held religious beliefs. Such opposition was not without risks, and whereas most objectors were never prosecuted, those who were found guilty at military hearings received stiff punishments: Courts handed down over two hundred prison sentences of twenty years or more, and seventeen death sentences.

Figure 2.7 While many young men were eager to join the war effort, there were a sizable number who did not want to join, either due to a moral objection or simply because they did not want to fight in a war that seemed far from American interests. (credit: Library of Congress)

With the size of the army growing, the U.S. government next needed to ensure that there were adequate supplies—in particular food and fuel—for both the soldiers and the home front. Concerns over shortages led to the passage of the Lever Food and Fuel Control Act, which empowered the president to control the production, distribution, and price of all food products during the war effort. Using this law, Wilson created both a Fuel Administration and a Food Administration. The Fuel Administration, run by Harry Garfield, created the concept of "fuel holidays," encouraging civilian Americans to do their part for the war effort by rationing fuel on certain days. Garfield also implemented "daylight saving time" for the first time in American history, shifting the clocks to allow more productive daylight hours. Herbert Hoover coordinated the Food Administration, and he too encouraged volunteer rationing by invoking patriotism. With the slogan "food will win the war," Hoover encouraged "Meatless Mondays," "Wheatless Wednesdays," and other similar reductions, with the hope of rationing food for military use (**Figure 2.8**).

Figure 2.8 With massive propaganda campaigns linking rationing and frugality to patriotism, the government sought to ensure adequate supplies to fight the war.

Wilson also created the War Industries Board, run by Bernard Baruch, to ensure adequate military supplies. The War Industries Board had the power to direct shipments of raw materials, as well as to control government contracts with private producers. Baruch used lucrative contracts with guaranteed profits to encourage several private firms to shift their production over to wartime materials. For those firms that refused to cooperate, Baruch's government control over raw materials provided him with the necessary leverage to convince them to join the war effort, willingly or not.

As a way to move all the personnel and supplies around the country efficiently, Congress created the U.S. Railroad Administration. Logistical problems had led trains bound for the East Coast to get stranded as far away as Chicago. To prevent these problems, Wilson appointed William McAdoo, the Secretary of the Treasury, to lead this agency, which had extraordinary war powers to control the entire railroad industry, including traffic, terminals, rates, and wages.

Almost all the practical steps were in place for the United States to fight a successful war. The only step remaining was to figure out how to pay for it. The war effort was costly—with an eventual price tag in excess of $32 billion by 1920—and the government needed to finance it. The Liberty Loan Act allowed the federal government to sell **liberty bonds** to the American public, extolling citizens to "do their part" to help the war effort and bring the troops home. The government ultimately raised $23 billion through liberty bonds. Additional monies came from the government's use of federal income tax revenue, which was made possible by the passage of the Sixteenth Amendment to the U.S. Constitution in 1913. With the financing, transportation, equipment, food, and men in place, the United States was ready to enter the war. The next piece the country needed was public support.

CONTROLLING DISSENT

Although all the physical pieces required to fight a war fell quickly into place, the question of national unity was another concern. The American public was strongly divided on the subject of entering the war. While many felt it was the only choice, others protested strongly, feeling it was not America's war to fight. Wilson needed to ensure that a nation of diverse immigrants, with ties to both sides of the conflict, thought of themselves as American first, and their home country's nationality second. To do this, he initiated a propaganda campaign, pushing the "America First" message, which sought to convince Americans that they should do everything in their power to ensure an American victory, even if that meant silencing their own criticisms.

AMERICANA

✪ *American First, American Above All*

At the outset of the war, one of the greatest challenges for Wilson was the lack of national unity. The country, after all, was made up of immigrants, some recently arrived and some well established, but all with ties to their home countries. These home countries included Germany and Russia, as well as Great Britain and France. In an effort to ensure that Americans eventually supported the war, the government pro-war propaganda campaign focused on driving home that message. The posters below, shown in both English and Yiddish, prompted immigrants to remember what they owed to America (**Figure 2.9**).

(a)   (b)

Figure 2.9 These posters clearly illustrate the pressure exerted on immigrants to quell any dissent they might feel about the United States at war.

Regardless of how patriotic immigrants might feel and act, however, an anti-German xenophobia overtook the country. German Americans were persecuted and their businesses shunned, whether or not they voiced any objection to the war. Some cities changed the names of the streets and buildings if they were German. Libraries withdrew German-language books from the shelves, and German Americans began to avoid speaking German for fear of reprisal. For some immigrants, the war was fought on two fronts: on the battlefields of France and again at home.

The Wilson administration created the Committee of Public Information under director George Creel, a former journalist, just days after the United States declared war on Germany. Creel employed artists, speakers, writers, and filmmakers to develop a propaganda machine. The goal was to encourage all Americans to make sacrifices during the war and, equally importantly, to hate all things German (**Figure 2.10**). Through efforts such as the establishment of "loyalty leagues" in ethnic immigrant communities, Creel largely succeeded in molding an anti-German sentiment around the country. The result? Some schools banned the teaching of the German language and some restaurants refused to serve frankfurters, sauerkraut, or hamburgers, instead serving "liberty dogs with liberty cabbage" and "liberty sandwiches."

Symphonies refused to perform music written by German composers. The hatred of Germans grew so widespread that, at one point, at a circus, audience members cheered when, in an act gone horribly wrong, a Russian bear mauled a German animal trainer (whose ethnicity was more a part of the act than reality).

Figure 2.10 Creel's propaganda campaign embodied a strongly anti-German message. The depiction of Germans as brutal apes, stepping on the nation's shores with their crude weapon of "Kultur" (culture), stood in marked contrast to the idealized rendition of the nation's virtue as a fair beauty whose clothes had been ripped off her.

In addition to its propaganda campaign, the U.S. government also tried to secure broad support for the war effort with repressive legislation. The Trading with the Enemy Act of 1917 prohibited individual trade with an enemy nation and banned the use of the postal service for disseminating any literature deemed treasonous by the postmaster general. That same year, the Espionage Act prohibited giving aid to the enemy by spying, or espionage, as well as any public comments that opposed the American war effort. Under this act, the government could impose fines and imprisonment of up to twenty years. The Sedition Act, passed in 1918, prohibited any criticism or disloyal language against the federal government and its policies, the U.S. Constitution, the military uniform, or the American flag. More than two thousand persons were charged with violating these laws, and many received prison sentences of up to twenty years. Immigrants faced deportation as punishment for their dissent. Not since the Alien and Sedition Acts of 1798 had the federal government so infringed on the freedom of speech of loyal American citizens.

Click and Explore

openstax   For a sense of the response and pushback that antiwar sentiments incited, read this newspaper article (http://openstaxcollege.org/l/15antiDraft) from 1917, discussing the dissemination of 100,000 antidraft flyers by the No Conscription League.

In the months and years after these laws came into being, over one thousand people were convicted for their violation, primarily under the Espionage and Sedition Acts. More importantly, many more war critics were frightened into silence. One notable prosecution was that of Socialist Party leader Eugene Debs, who received a ten-year prison sentence for encouraging draft resistance, which, under the Espionage Act, was considered "giving aid to the enemy." Prominent Socialist Victor Berger was also prosecuted under the Espionage Act and subsequently twice denied his seat in Congress, to which he had been properly elected by the citizens of Milwaukee, Wisconsin. One of the more outrageous prosecutions was that of a film producer who released a film about the American Revolution: Prosecutors found the film seditious, and a court convicted the producer to ten years in prison for portraying the British, who were now American allies, as the obedient soldiers of a monarchical empire.

State and local officials, as well as private citizens, aided the government's efforts to investigate, identify, and crush subversion. Over 180,000 communities created local "councils of defense," which encouraged members to report any antiwar comments to local authorities. This mandate encouraged spying on neighbors, teachers, local newspapers, and other individuals. In addition, a larger national organization—the American Protective League—received support from the Department of Justice to spy on prominent dissenters, as well as open their mail and physically assault draft evaders.

Understandably, opposition to such repression began mounting. In 1917, Roger Baldwin formed the National Civil Liberties Bureau—a forerunner to the American Civil Liberties Union, which was founded in 1920—to challenge the government's policies against wartime dissent and conscientious objection. In 1919, the case of *Schenck v. United States* went to the U.S. Supreme Court to challenge the constitutionality of the Espionage and Sedition Acts. The case concerned Charles Schenck, a leader in the Socialist Party of Philadelphia, who had distributed fifteen thousand leaflets, encouraging young men to avoid conscription. The court ruled that during a time of war, the federal government was justified in passing such laws to quiet dissenters. The decision was unanimous, and in the court's opinion, Justice Oliver Wendell Holmes wrote that such dissent presented a **"clear and present danger"** to the safety of the United States and the military, and was therefore justified. He further explained how the First Amendment right of free speech did not protect such dissent, in the same manner that a citizen could not be freely permitted to yell "fire!" in a crowded theater, due to the danger it presented. Congress ultimately repealed most of the Espionage and Sedition Acts in 1921, and several who were imprisoned for violation of those acts were then quickly released. But the Supreme Court's deference to the federal government's restrictions on civil liberties remained a volatile topic in future wars.

2.3 A New Home Front

By the end of this section, you will be able to:
- Explain how the status of organized labor changed during the First World War
- Describe how the lives of women and African Americans changed as a result of American participation in World War I
- Explain how America's participation in World War I allowed for the passage of prohibition and women's suffrage

The lives of all Americans, whether they went abroad to fight or stayed on the home front, changed dramatically during the war. Restrictive laws censored dissent at home, and the armed forces demanded unconditional loyalty from millions of volunteers and conscripted soldiers. For organized labor, women, and African Americans in particular, the war brought changes to the prewar status quo. Some white women worked outside of the home for the first time, whereas others, like African American men, found that they were eligible for jobs that had previously been reserved for white men. African American women, too, were able to seek employment beyond the domestic servant jobs that had been their primary opportunity. These new options and freedoms were not easily erased after the war ended.

NEW OPPORTUNITIES BORN FROM WAR

After decades of limited involvement in the challenges between management and organized labor, the need for peaceful and productive industrial relations prompted the federal government during wartime to invite organized labor to the negotiating table. Samuel Gompers, head of the American Federation of Labor (AFL), sought to capitalize on these circumstances to better organize workers and secure for them better wages and working conditions. His efforts also solidified his own base of power. The increase in production that the war required exposed severe labor shortages in many states, a condition that was further exacerbated by the draft, which pulled millions of young men from the active labor force.

Wilson only briefly investigated the longstanding animosity between labor and management before ordering the creation of the National Labor War Board in April 1918. Quick negotiations with Gompers and the AFL resulted in a promise: Organized labor would make a "no-strike pledge" for the duration of the war, in exchange for the U.S. government's protection of workers' rights to organize and bargain collectively. The federal government kept its promise and promoted the adoption of an eight-hour workday (which had first been adopted by government employees in 1868), a living wage for all workers, and union membership. As a result, union membership skyrocketed during the war, from 2.6 million members in 1916 to 4.1 million in 1919. In short, American workers received better working conditions and wages, as a result of the country's participation in the war. However, their economic gains were limited. While prosperity overall went up during the war, it was enjoyed more by business owners and corporations than by the workers themselves. Even though wages increased, inflation offset most of the gains. Prices in the United States increased an average of 15–20 percent annually between 1917 and 1920. Individual purchasing power actually declined during the war due to the substantially higher cost of living. Business profits, in contrast, increased by nearly a third during the war.

Women in Wartime

For women, the economic situation was complicated by the war, with the departure of wage-earning men and the higher cost of living pushing many toward less comfortable lives. At the same time, however, wartime presented new opportunities for women in the workplace. More than one million women entered the workforce for the first time as a result of the war, while more than eight million working women found higher paying jobs, often in industry. Many women also found employment in what were typically considered male occupations, such as on the railroads (**Figure 2.11**), where the number of women tripled, and on assembly lines. After the war ended and men returned home and searched for work, women were fired from their jobs, and expected to return home and care for their families. Furthermore, even when they were doing men's jobs, women were typically paid lower wages than male workers, and unions were ambivalent at best—and hostile at worst—to women workers. Even under these circumstances, wartime employment familiarized women with an alternative to a life in domesticity and dependency, making a life of employment, even a career, plausible for women. When, a generation later, World War II arrived, this trend would increase dramatically.

(a)

(b)

Figure 2.11 The war brought new opportunities to women, such as the training offered to those who joined the Land Army (a) or the opening up of traditionally male occupations. In 1918, Eva Abbott (b) was one of many new women workers on the Erie Railroad. However, once the war ended and veterans returned home, these opportunities largely disappeared. (credit b: modification of work by U.S. Department of Labor)

One notable group of women who exploited these new opportunities was the Women's Land Army of America. First during World War I, then again in World War II, these women stepped up to run farms and other agricultural enterprises, as men left for the armed forces (**Figure 2.11**). Known as Farmerettes, some twenty thousand women—mostly college educated and from larger urban areas—served in this capacity. Their reasons for joining were manifold. For some, it was a way to serve their country during a time of war. Others hoped to capitalize on the efforts to further the fight for women's suffrage.

Also of special note were the approximately thirty thousand American women who served in the military, as well as a variety of humanitarian organizations, such as the Red Cross and YMCA, during the war. In addition to serving as military nurses (without rank), American women also served as telephone operators in France. Of this latter group, 230 of them, known as "Hello Girls," were bilingual and stationed in combat areas. Over eighteen thousand American women served as Red Cross nurses, providing much of the medical support available to American troops in France. Close to three hundred nurses died during service. Many of those who returned home continued to work in hospitals and home healthcare, helping wounded veterans heal both emotionally and physically from the scars of war.

African Americans in the Crusade for Democracy

African Americans also found that the war brought upheaval and opportunity. Blacks composed 13 percent of the enlisted military, with 350,000 men serving. Colonel Charles Young of the Tenth Cavalry division served as the highest-ranking African American officer. Blacks served in segregated units and suffered from widespread racism in the military hierarchy, often serving in menial or support roles. Some troops saw combat, however, and were commended for serving with valor. The 369th Infantry, for example, known as the **Harlem Hellfighters**, served on the frontline of France for six months, longer than any other American unit. One hundred seventy-one men from that regiment received the Legion of Merit for meritorious service in combat. The regiment marched in a homecoming parade in New York City, was remembered in paintings (**Figure 2.12**), and was celebrated for bravery and leadership. The accolades given to them, however, in no way extended to the bulk of African Americans fighting in the war.

Figure 2.12 African American soldiers suffered under segregation and second-class treatment in the military. Still, the 369th Infantry earned recognition and reward for its valor in service both in France and the United States.

On the home front, African Americans, like American women, saw economic opportunities increase during the war. During the so-called Great Migration (discussed in a previous chapter), nearly 350,000 African Americans had fled the post-Civil War South for opportunities in northern urban areas. From 1910–1920, they moved north and found work in the steel, mining, shipbuilding, and automotive industries, among others. African American women also sought better employment opportunities beyond their traditional roles as domestic servants. By 1920, over 100,000 women had found work in diverse manufacturing industries, up from 70,000 in 1910. Despite such opportunities, racism continued to be a major force in both the North and South. Worried about the large influx of black Americans into their cities, several municipalities passed residential codes designed to prohibit African Americans from settling in certain neighborhoods. Race riots also increased in frequency: In 1917 alone, there were race riots in twenty-five cities, including East Saint Louis, where thirty-nine blacks were killed. In the South, white business and plantation owners feared that their cheap workforce was fleeing the region, and used violence to intimidate blacks into staying. According to NAACP statistics, recorded incidences of lynching increased from thirty-eight in 1917 to eighty-three in 1919. These numbers did not start to decrease until 1923, when the number of annual lynchings dropped below thirty-five for the first time since the Civil War.

Click and Explore

Explore photographs and a written overview of the African American experience (http://openstaxcollege.org/l/15Africana) both at home and on the front line during World War I.

THE LAST VESTIGES OF PROGRESSIVISM

Across the United States, the war intersected with the last lingering efforts of the Progressives who sought to use the war as motivation for their final push for change. It was in large part due to the war's influence that Progressives were able to lobby for the passage of the Eighteenth and Nineteenth Amendments to the U.S. Constitution. The Eighteenth Amendment, prohibiting alcohol, and the Nineteenth Amendment, giving women the right to vote, received their final impetus due to the war effort.

Prohibition, as the anti-alcohol movement became known, had been a goal of many Progressives for decades. Organizations such as the Women's Christian Temperance Union and the Anti-Saloon League linked alcohol consumption with any number of societal problems, and they had worked tirelessly with municipalities and counties to limit or prohibit alcohol on a local scale. But with the war, prohibitionists saw an opportunity for federal action. One factor that helped their cause was the strong anti-German sentiment that gripped the country, which turned sympathy away from the largely German-descended immigrants who ran the breweries. Furthermore, the public cry to ration food and grain—the latter being a key ingredient in both beer and hard alcohol—made prohibition even more patriotic. Congress ratified the Eighteenth Amendment in January 1919, with provisions to take effect one year later. Specifically, the amendment prohibited the manufacture, sale, and transportation of intoxicating liquors. It did not prohibit the drinking of alcohol, as there was a widespread feeling that such language would be viewed as too intrusive on personal rights. However, by eliminating the manufacture, sale, and transport of such beverages, drinking was effectively outlawed. Shortly thereafter, Congress passed the Volstead Act, translating the Eighteenth Amendment into an enforceable ban on the consumption of alcoholic beverages, and regulating the scientific and industrial uses of alcohol. The act also specifically excluded from prohibition the use of alcohol for religious rituals (**Figure 2.13**).

Figure 2.13 Surrounded by prominent "dry workers," Governor James P. Goodrich of Indiana signs a statewide bill to prohibit alcohol.

Unfortunately for proponents of the amendment, the ban on alcohol did not take effect until one full year following the end of the war. Almost immediately following the war, the general public began to oppose—and clearly violate—the law, making it very difficult to enforce. Doctors and druggists, who could prescribe whisky for medicinal purposes, found themselves inundated with requests. In the 1920s, organized crime and gangsters like Al Capone would capitalize on the persistent demand for liquor, making fortunes in the illegal trade. A lack of enforcement, compounded by an overwhelming desire by the public to obtain alcohol at all costs, eventually resulted in the repeal of the law in 1933.

The First World War also provided the impetus for another longstanding goal of some reformers: universal suffrage. Supporters of equal rights for women pointed to Wilson's rallying cry of a war "to make the world safe for democracy," as hypocritical, saying he was sending American boys to die for such principles while simultaneously denying American women their democratic right to vote (**Figure 2.14**). Carrie Chapman Catt, president of the National American Women Suffrage Movement, capitalized on the growing patriotic fervor to point out that every woman who gained the vote could exercise that right in a show of loyalty to the nation, thus offsetting the dangers of draft-dodgers or naturalized Germans who already had the right to vote.

Alice Paul, of the National Women's Party, organized more radical tactics, bringing national attention to the issue of women's suffrage by organizing protests outside the White House and, later, hunger strikes among arrested protesters. By the end of the war, the abusive treatment of suffragist hunger-strikers in prison, women's important contribution to the war effort, and the arguments of his suffragist daughter Jessie Woodrow Wilson Sayre moved President Wilson to understand women's right to vote as an ethical mandate for a true democracy. He began urging congressmen and senators to adopt the legislation. The amendment finally passed in June 1919, and the states ratified it by August 1920. Specifically, the Nineteenth Amendment prohibited all efforts to deny the right to vote on the basis of sex. It took effect in time for American women to vote in the presidential election of 1920.

Figure 2.14 Suffragists picketed the White House in 1917, leveraging the war and America's stance on democracy to urge Woodrow Wilson to support an amendment giving women the right to vote.

2.4 From War to Peace

By the end of this section, you will be able to:

- Identify the role that the United States played at the end of World War I
- Describe Woodrow Wilson's vision for the postwar world
- Explain why the United States never formally approved the Treaty of Versailles nor joined the League of Nations

The American role in World War I was brief but decisive. While millions of soldiers went overseas, and many thousands paid with their lives, the country's involvement was limited to the very end of the war. In fact, the peace process, with the international conference and subsequent ratification process, took longer than the time U.S. soldiers were "in country" in France. For the Allies, American reinforcements came at a decisive moment in their defense of the western front, where a final offensive had exhausted German forces. For the United States, and for Wilson's vision of a peaceful future, the fighting was faster and more successful than what was to follow.

WINNING THE WAR

When the United States declared war on Germany in April 1917, the Allied forces were close to exhaustion. Great Britain and France had already indebted themselves heavily in the procurement of vital American military supplies. Now, facing near-certain defeat, a British delegation to Washington, DC, requested immediate troop reinforcements to boost Allied spirits and help crush German fighting morale, which was already weakened by short supplies on the frontlines and hunger on the home front. Wilson agreed and immediately sent 200,000 American troops in June 1917. These soldiers were placed in "quiet zones" while they trained and prepared for combat.

By March 1918, the Germans had won the war on the eastern front. The Russian Revolution of the previous year had not only toppled the hated regime of Tsar Nicholas II but also ushered in a civil war from which the Bolshevik faction of Communist revolutionaries under the leadership of Vladimir Lenin emerged victorious. Weakened by war and internal strife, and eager to build a new Soviet Union, Russian delegates agreed to a generous peace treaty with Germany. Thus emboldened, Germany quickly moved upon the Allied lines, causing both the French and British to ask Wilson to forestall extensive training to U.S. troops and instead commit them to the front immediately. Although wary of the move, Wilson complied, ordering the commander of the American Expeditionary Force, General John "Blackjack" Pershing, to offer U.S. troops as replacements for the Allied units in need of relief. By May 1918, Americans were fully engaged in the war **(Figure 2.15)**.

Figure 2.15 U.S. soldiers run past fallen Germans on their way to a bunker. In World War I, for the first time, photographs of the battles brought the war vividly to life for those at home.

In a series of battles along the front that took place from May 28 through August 6, 1918, including the battles of Cantigny, Chateau Thierry, Belleau Wood, and the Second Battle of the Marne, American forces alongside the British and French armies succeeded in repelling the German offensive. The Battle of Cantigny, on May 28, was the first American offensive in the war: In less than two hours that morning, American troops overran the German headquarters in the village, thus convincing the French commanders of their ability to fight against the German line advancing towards Paris. The subsequent battles of Chateau Thierry and Belleau Wood proved to be the bloodiest of the war for American troops. At the latter, faced with a German onslaught of mustard gas, artillery fire, and mortar fire, U.S. Marines attacked German units in the woods on six occasions—at times meeting them in hand-to-hand and bayonet combat—before finally repelling the advance. The U.S. forces suffered 10,000 casualties in the three-week battle, with almost 2,000 killed in total and 1,087 on a single day. Brutal as they were, they amounted to small losses compared to the casualties suffered by France and Great Britain. Still, these summer battles turned the tide of the war, with the Germans in full retreat by the end of July 1918 **(Figure 2.16)**.

Figure 2.16 This map shows the western front at the end of the war, as the Allied Forces decisively break the German line.

MY STORY

⊕ *Sgt. Charles Leon Boucher: Life and Death in the Trenches of France*

Wounded in his shoulder by enemy forces, George, a machine gunner posted on the right end of the American platoon, was taken prisoner at the Battle of Seicheprey in 1918. However, as darkness set in that evening, another American soldier, Charlie, heard a noise from a gully beside the trench in which he had hunkered down. "I figured it must be the enemy mop-up patrol," Charlie later said.

> I only had a couple of bullets left in the chamber of my forty-five. The noise stopped and a head popped into sight. When I was about to fire, I gave another look and a white and distorted face proved to be that of George, so I grabbed his shoulders and pulled him down into our trench beside me. He must have had about twenty bullet holes in him but not one of them was well placed enough to kill him. He made an effort to speak so I told him to keep quiet and conserve his energy. I had a few malted milk tablets left and, I forced them into his mouth. I also poured the last of the water I had left in my canteen into his mouth.

Following a harrowing night, they began to crawl along the road back to their platoon. As they crawled, George explained how he survived being captured. Charlie later told how George "was taken to an enemy First Aid Station where his wounds were dressed. Then the doctor motioned to have him taken to the rear of their lines. But, the Sergeant Major pushed him towards our side and 'No Mans Land,' pulled out his Luger Automatic and shot him down. Then, he began to crawl towards our lines little by little, being shot at consistently by the enemy snipers till, finally, he arrived in our position."

The story of Charlie and George, related later in life by Sgt. Charles Leon Boucher to his grandson, was one replayed many times over in various forms during the American Expeditionary Force's involvement in World War I. The industrial scale of death and destruction was as new to American soldiers as to their European counterparts, and the survivors brought home physical and psychological scars that influenced the United States long after the war was won (Figure 2.17).

Figure 2.17 This photograph of U.S. soldiers in a trench hardly begins to capture the brutal conditions of trench warfare, where disease, rats, mud, and hunger plagued the men.

By the end of September 1918, over one million U.S. soldiers staged a full offensive into the Argonne Forest. By November—after nearly forty days of intense fighting—the German lines were broken, and their military command reported to German Emperor Kaiser Wilhelm II of the desperate need to end the war and enter into peace negotiations. Facing civil unrest from the German people in Berlin, as well as the loss of support from his military high command, Kaiser Wilhelm abdicated his throne on November 9, 1918, and immediately fled by train to the Netherlands. Two days later, on November 11, 1918, Germany and the Allies declared an immediate armistice, thus bring the fighting to a stop and signaling the beginning of the peace process.

When the armistice was declared, a total of 117,000 American soldiers had been killed and 206,000 wounded. The Allies as a whole suffered over 5.7 million military deaths, primarily Russian, British, and French men. The Central powers suffered four million military deaths, with half of them German soldiers. The total cost of the war to the United States alone was in excess of $32 billion, with interest expenses and veterans' benefits eventually bringing the cost to well over $100 billion. Economically, emotionally, and geopolitically, the war had taken an enormous toll.

Click and Explore

This Smithsonian interactive exhibit (http://openstaxcollege.org/l/15PriceFree) offers a fascinating perspective on World War I.

THE BATTLE FOR PEACE

While Wilson had been loath to involve the United States in the war, he saw the country's eventual participation as justification for America's involvement in developing a moral foreign policy for the entire world. The "new world order" he wished to create from the outset of his presidency was now within his grasp. The United States emerged from the war as the predominant world power. Wilson sought to capitalize on that influence and impose his moral foreign policy on all the nations of the world.

The Paris Peace Conference

As early as January 1918—a full five months before U.S. military forces fired their first shot in the war, and eleven months before the actual armistice—Wilson announced his postwar peace plan before a joint session of Congress. Referring to what became known as the **Fourteen Points**, Wilson called for openness in all matters of diplomacy and trade, specifically, free trade, freedom of the seas, an end to secret treaties and negotiations, promotion of self-determination of all nations, and more. In addition, he called for the creation of a **League of Nations** to promote the new world order and preserve territorial integrity through open discussions in place of intimidation and war.

As the war concluded, Wilson announced, to the surprise of many, that he would attend the Paris Peace Conference himself, rather than ceding to the tradition of sending professional diplomats to represent the country (**Figure 2.18**). His decision influenced other nations to follow suit, and the Paris conference became the largest meeting of world leaders to date in history. For six months, beginning in December 1918, Wilson remained in Paris to personally conduct peace negotiations. Although the French public greeted Wilson with overwhelming enthusiasm, other delegates at the conference had deep misgivings about the American president's plans for a "peace without victory." Specifically, Great Britain, France, and Italy sought to obtain some measure of revenge against Germany for drawing them into the war, to secure themselves against possible future aggressions from that nation, and also to maintain or even strengthen their own colonial possessions. Great Britain and France in particular sought substantial monetary reparations, as well as territorial gains, at Germany's expense. Japan also desired concessions in Asia, whereas Italy sought new territory in Europe. Finally, the threat posed by a Bolshevik Russia under Vladimir Lenin, and more importantly, the danger of revolutions elsewhere, further spurred on these allies to use the treaty negotiations to expand their territories and secure their strategic interests, rather than strive towards world peace.

Figure 2.18 The Paris Peace Conference held the largest number of world leaders in one place to date. The photograph shows (from left to right) Prime Minister David Lloyd George of Great Britain; Vittorio Emanuele Orlando, prime minister of Italy; Georges Clemenceau, prime minister of France; and President Woodrow Wilson discussing the terms of the peace.

In the end, the Treaty of Versailles that officially concluded World War I resembled little of Wilson's original Fourteen Points. The Japanese, French, and British succeeded in carving up many of Germany's colonial holdings in Africa and Asia. The dissolution of the Ottoman Empire created new nations under the quasi-colonial rule of France and Great Britain, such as Iraq and Palestine. France gained much of the disputed territory along their border with Germany, as well as passage of a "war guilt clause" that demanded Germany take public responsibility for starting and prosecuting the war that led to so much death and destruction. Great Britain led the charge that resulted in Germany agreeing to pay reparations in excess of $33 billion to the Allies. As for Bolshevik Russia, Wilson had agreed to send American troops to their northern region to protect Allied supplies and holdings there, while also participating in an economic blockade designed to undermine Lenin's power. This move would ultimately have the opposite effect of galvanizing popular support for the Bolsheviks.

The sole piece of the original Fourteen Points that Wilson successfully fought to keep intact was the creation of a League of Nations. At a covenant agreed to at the conference, all member nations in the League would agree to defend all other member nations against military threats. Known as Article X, this agreement would basically render each nation equal in terms of power, as no member nation would be able to use its military might against a weaker member nation. Ironically, this article would prove to be the undoing of Wilson's dream of a new world order.

Ratification of the Treaty of Versailles

Although the other nations agreed to the final terms of the Treaty of Versailles, Wilson's greatest battle lay in the ratification debate that awaited him upon his return. As with all treaties, this one would require two-thirds approval by the U.S. Senate for final ratification, something Wilson knew would be difficult to achieve. Even before Wilson's return to Washington, Senator Henry Cabot Lodge, chairman of the Senate Foreign Relations Committee that oversaw ratification proceedings, issued a list of fourteen reservations he had regarding the treaty, most of which centered on the creation of a League of Nations. An isolationist in foreign policy issues, Cabot feared that Article X would require extensive American intervention, as more countries would seek her protection in all controversial affairs. But on the other side of the political spectrum, interventionists argued that Article X would impede the United States from using her rightfully attained military power to secure and protect America's international interests.

Wilson's greatest fight was with the Senate, where most Republicans opposed the treaty due to the clauses surrounding the creation of the League of Nations. Some Republicans, known as **Irreconcilables**, opposed the treaty on all grounds, whereas others, called **Reservationists**, would support the treaty if sufficient amendments were introduced that could eliminate Article X. In an effort to turn public support into a weapon against those in opposition, Wilson embarked on a cross-country railway speaking tour. He began travelling in September 1919, and the grueling pace, after the stress of the six months in Paris, proved too much. Wilson fainted following a public event on September 25, 1919, and immediately returned to Washington. There he suffered a debilitating stroke, leaving his second wife Edith Wilson in charge as de facto president for a period of about six months.

Frustrated that his dream of a new world order was slipping away—a frustration that was compounded by the fact that, now an invalid, he was unable to speak his own thoughts coherently—Wilson urged Democrats in the Senate to reject any effort to compromise on the treaty. As a result, Congress voted on, and defeated, the originally worded treaty in November. When the treaty was introduced with "reservations," or amendments, in March 1920, it again fell short of the necessary margin for ratification. As a result, the United States never became an official signatory of the Treaty of Versailles. Nor did the country join the League of Nations, which shattered the international authority and significance of the organization. Although Wilson received the Nobel Peace Prize in October 1919 for his efforts to create a model of world peace, he remained personally embarrassed and angry at his country's refusal to be a part of that model. As a result of its rejection of the treaty, the United States technically remained at war with Germany until July 21, 1921, when it formally came to a close with Congress's quiet passage of the Knox-Porter Resolution.

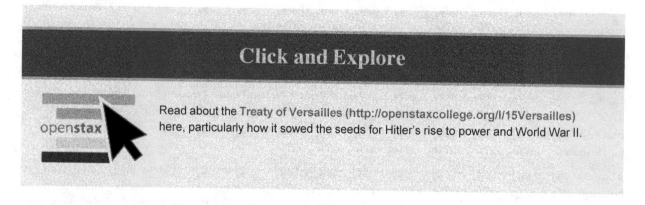

Click and Explore

openstax

Read about the Treaty of Versailles (http://openstaxcollege.org/l/15Versailles) here, particularly how it sowed the seeds for Hitler's rise to power and World War II.

2.5 Demobilization and Its Difficult Aftermath

By the end of this section, you will be able to:
- Identify the challenges that the United States faced following the conclusion of World War I
- Explain Warren G. Harding's landslide victory in the 1920 presidential election

As world leaders debated the terms of the peace, the American public faced its own challenges at the conclusion of the First World War. Several unrelated factors intersected to create a chaotic and difficult time, just as massive numbers of troops rapidly demobilized and came home. Racial tensions, a terrifying flu epidemic, anticommunist hysteria, and economic uncertainty all combined to leave many Americans wondering what, exactly, they had won in the war. Adding to these problems was the absence of President Wilson, who remained in Paris for six months, leaving the country leaderless. The result of these factors was that, rather than a celebratory transition from wartime to peace and prosperity, and ultimately the Jazz Age of the 1920s, 1919 was a tumultuous year that threatened to tear the country apart.

DISORDER AND FEAR IN AMERICA

After the war ended, U.S. troops were demobilized and rapidly sent home. One unanticipated and unwanted effect of their return was the emergence of a new strain of influenza that medical professionals had never before encountered. Within months of the war's end, over twenty million Americans fell ill from the flu (**Figure 2.19**). Eventually, 675,000 Americans died before the disease mysteriously ran its course in the spring of 1919. Worldwide, recent estimates suggest that 500 million people suffered from this flu strain, with as many as fifty million people dying. Throughout the United States, from the fall of 1918 to the spring of 1919, fear of the flu gripped the country. Americans avoided public gatherings, children wore surgical masks to school, and undertakers ran out of coffins and burial plots in cemeteries. Hysteria grew as well, and instead of welcoming soldiers home with a postwar celebration, people hunkered down and hoped to avoid contagion.

Figure 2.19 The flu pandemic that came home with the returning troops swept through the United States, as evidenced by this overcrowded flu ward at Camp Funstun, Kansas, adding another trauma onto the recovering postwar psyche.

Another element that greatly influenced the challenges of immediate postwar life was economic upheaval. As discussed above, wartime production had led to steady inflation; the rising cost of living meant that few Americans could comfortably afford to live off their wages. When the government's wartime control over the economy ended, businesses slowly recalibrated from the wartime production of guns and ships to the peacetime production of toasters and cars. Public demand quickly outpaced the slow production, leading to notable shortages of domestic goods. As a result, inflation skyrocketed in 1919. By the end of the year, the cost of living in the United States was nearly double what it had been in 1916. Workers, facing a shortage in wages to buy more expensive goods, and no longer bound by the no-strike pledge they made for the National War Labor Board, initiated a series of strikes for better hours and wages. In 1919 alone, more than four million workers participated in a total of nearly three thousand strikes: both records within all of American history.

In addition to labor clashes, race riots shattered the peace at the home front. The sporadic race riots that had begun during the Great Migration only grew in postwar America. White soldiers returned home to find black workers in their former jobs and neighborhoods, and were committed to restoring their position of white supremacy. Black soldiers returned home with a renewed sense of justice and strength, and were determined to assert their rights as men and as citizens. Meanwhile, southern lynchings continued to escalate, with white mobs burning African Americans at the stake. During the "**Red Summer**" of 1919, northern cities recorded twenty-five bloody race riots that killed over 250 people. Among these was the Chicago Race Riot of 1919, where a white mob stoned a young black boy to death because he swam too close to the "white beach" on Lake Michigan. Police at the scene did not arrest the perpetrator who threw the rock. This crime prompted a week-long riot that left twenty-three blacks and fifteen whites dead, as well as millions of dollars' worth of damage to the city (**Figure 2.20**). Riots in Tulsa, Oklahoma, in

1921, turned out even more deadly, with estimates of black fatalities ranging from fifty to three hundred. Americans thus entered the new decade with a profound sense of disillusionment over the prospects of peaceful race relations.

(a)   (b)

Figure 2.20 Riots broke out in Chicago in the wake of the stoning of a black boy. After two weeks, thirty-eight more people had died, some were stoned (a), and many had to abandon their vandalized homes (b).

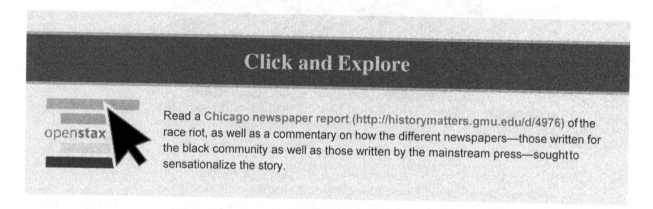

Click and Explore

Read a Chicago newspaper report (http://historymatters.gmu.edu/d/4976) of the race riot, as well as a commentary on how the different newspapers—those written for the black community as well as those written by the mainstream press—sought to sensationalize the story.

While illness, economic hardship, and racial tensions all came from within, another destabilizing factor arrived from overseas. As revolutionary rhetoric emanating from Bolshevik Russia intensified in 1918 and 1919, a **Red Scare** erupted in the United States over fear that Communist infiltrators sought to overthrow the American government as part of an international revolution (**Figure 2.21**). When investigators uncovered a collection of thirty-six letter bombs at a New York City post office, with recipients that included several federal, state, and local public officials, as well as industrial leaders such as John D. Rockefeller, fears grew significantly. And when eight additional bombs actually exploded simultaneously on June 2, 1919, including one that destroyed the entrance to U.S. attorney general A. Mitchell Palmer's house in Washington, the country was convinced that all radicals, no matter what ilk, were to blame. Socialists, Communists, members of the Industrial Workers of the World (Wobblies), and anarchists: They were all threats to be taken down.

Figure 2.21 Some Americans feared that labor strikes were the first step on a path that led ultimately to Bolshevik revolutions and chaos. This political cartoon depicts that fear.

Private citizens who considered themselves upstanding and loyal Americans, joined by discharged soldiers and sailors, raided radical meeting houses in many major cities, attacking any alleged radicals they found inside. By November 1919, Palmer's new assistant in charge of the Bureau of Investigation, J. Edgar Hoover, organized nationwide raids on radical headquarters in twelve cities around the country. Subsequent "Palmer raids" resulted in the arrests of four thousand alleged American radicals who were detained for weeks in overcrowded cells. Almost 250 of those arrested were subsequently deported on board a ship dubbed "the Soviet Ark" (**Figure 2.22**).

Figure 2.22 This cartoon advocates for a restrictive immigration policy, recommending the United States "close the gate" on undesirable (and presumably dangerous) immigrants.

A RETURN TO NORMALCY

By 1920, Americans had failed their great expectations to make the world safer and more democratic. The flu epidemic had demonstrated the limits of science and technology in making Americans less vulnerable. The Red Scare signified Americans' fear of revolutionary politics and the persistence of violent capital-labor conflicts. And race riots made it clear that the nation was no closer to peaceful race relations either. After a long era of Progressive initiatives and new government agencies, followed by a costly war that did not end in a better world, most of the public sought to focus on economic progress and success in their private lives instead. As the presidential election of 1920 unfolded, the extent of just how tired Americans were of an interventionist government—whether in terms of Progressive reform or international involvement—became exceedingly clear. Republicans, anxious to return to the White House after eight years of Wilson idealism, capitalized on this growing American sentiment to find the candidate who would promise a return to normalcy.

The Republicans found their man in Senator Warren G. Harding from Ohio. Although not the most energetic candidate for the White House, Harding offered what party handlers desired—a candidate around whom they could mold their policies of low taxes, immigration restriction, and noninterference in world affairs. He also provided Americans with what they desired: a candidate who could look and act presidential, and yet leave them alone to live their lives as they wished.

Click and Explore

Learn more about President Harding's campaign promise of a return to normalcy (http://openstaxcollege.org/l/15Readjustment) by listening to an audio recording or reading the text of his promise.

Democratic leaders realized they had little chance at victory. Wilson remained adamant that the election be a referendum over his League of Nations, yet after his stroke, he was in no physical condition to run for a third term. Political in-fighting among his cabinet, most notably between A. Mitchell Palmer and William McAdoo, threatened to split the party convention until a compromise candidate could be found in Ohio governor James Cox. Cox chose, for his vice presidential running mate, the young Assistant Secretary of the Navy, Franklin Delano Roosevelt.

At a time when Americans wanted prosperity and normalcy, rather than continued interference in their lives, Harding won in an overwhelming landslide, with 404 votes to 127 in the Electoral College, and 60 percent of the popular vote. With the war, the flu epidemic, the Red Scare, and other issues behind them, American looked forward to Harding's inauguration in 1921, and to an era of personal freedoms and hedonism that would come to be known as the Jazz Age.

CHAPTER 3

The Jazz Age: Redefining the Nation, 1919-1929

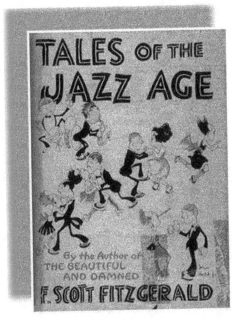

Figure 3.1 The illustrations for F. Scott Fitzgerald's *Tales of the Jazz Age*, drawn by John Held, Jr., epitomized the carefree flapper era of the 1920s.

Chapter Outline

3.1 Prosperity and the Production of Popular Entertainment
3.2 Transformation and Backlash
3.3 A New Generation
3.4 Republican Ascendancy: Politics in the 1920s

Introduction

Following the hardships of the immediate postwar era, the United States embarked upon one of the most prosperous decades in history. Mass production, especially of the automobile, increased mobility and fostered new industries. Unemployment plummeted as businesses grew to meet this increased demand. Cities continued to grow and, according to the 1920 census, a majority of the population lived in urban areas of twenty-five hundred or more residents.

Jazz music, movies, speakeasies, and new dances dominated the urban evening scene. Recent immigrants from southern and eastern Europe, many of them Catholic, now participated in the political system. This challenged rural Protestant fundamentalism, even as quota laws sought to limit new immigration patterns. The Ku Klux Klan rose to greater power, as they protested not only the changing role of African Americans but also the growing population of immigrant, Catholic, and Jewish Americans.

This mixture of social, political, economic, and cultural change and conflict gave the decade the nickname the "Roaring Twenties" or the "Jazz Age." The above illustration (**Figure 3.1**), which graced the cover of F. Scott Fitzgerald's *Tales of the Jazz Age*, embodies the popular view of the 1920s as a nonstop party, replete with dancing, music, flappers, and illegal drinking.

3.1 Prosperity and the Production of Popular Entertainment

By the end of this section, you will be able to:
- Discuss the role of movies in the evolution of American culture
- Explain the rise of sports as a dominant social force
- Analyze the ways in which the automobile, especially the Model T, transformed American life

In the 1920s, prosperity manifested itself in many forms, most notably in advancements in entertainment and technology that led to new patterns of leisure and consumption. Movies and sports became increasingly popular and buying on credit or "carrying" the debt allowed for the sale of more consumer goods and put automobiles within reach of average Americans. Advertising became a central institution in this new consumer economy, and commercial radio and magazines turned athletes and actors into national icons.

MOVIES

The increased prosperity of the 1920s gave many Americans more disposable income to spend on entertainment. As the popularity of "moving pictures" grew in the early part of the decade, "movie palaces," capable of seating thousands, sprang up in major cities. A ticket for a double feature and a live show cost twenty-five cents; for a quarter, Americans could escape from their problems and lose themselves in another era or world. People of all ages attended the movies with far more regularity than today, often going more than once per week. By the end of the decade, weekly movie attendance swelled to ninety million people.

The silent movies of the early 1920s gave rise to the first generation of movie stars. Rudolph Valentino, the lothario with the bedroom eyes, and Clara Bow, the "It Girl" with sex appeal, filled the imagination of millions of American moviegoers. However, no star captured the attention of the American viewing public more than Charlie Chaplin. This sad-eyed tramp with a moustache, baggy pants, and a cane was the top box office attraction of his time (**Figure 3.3**).

Figure 3.2

Figure 3.3 Charlie Chaplin's nickname "The Tramp" came from the recurring character he played in many of his silent films, such as 1921's *The Kid*, which starred Jackie Coogan in the title role.

In 1927, the world of the silent movie began to wane with the New York release of the first "talkie": *The Jazz Singer*. The plot of this film, which starred Al Jolson, told a distinctively American story of the 1920s. It follows the life of a Jewish man from his boyhood days of being groomed to be the cantor at the local synagogue to his life as a famous and "Americanized" jazz singer. Both the story and the new sound technology used to present it were popular with audiences around the country. It quickly became a huge hit for Warner Brothers, one of the "big five" motion picture studios in Hollywood along with Twentieth Century Fox, RKO Pictures, Paramount Pictures, and Metro-Goldwyn-Mayer.

Southern California in the 1920s, however, had only recently become the center of the American film industry. Film production was originally based in and around New York, where Thomas Edison first debuted the kinetoscope in 1893. But in the 1910s, as major filmmakers like D. W. Griffith looked to escape the cost of Edison's patents on camera equipment, this began to change. When Griffith filmed *In Old California* (1910), the first movie ever shot in **Hollywood**, California, the small town north of Los Angeles was little more than a village. As moviemakers flocked to southern California, not least because of its favorable climate and predictable sunshine, Hollywood swelled with moviemaking activity. By the 1920s, the once-sleepy village was home to a majorly profitable innovative industry in the United States.

AUTOMOBILES AND AIRPLANES: AMERICANS ON THE MOVE

Cinema was not the only major industry to make great technological strides in this decade. The 1920s opened up new possibilities of mobility for a large percentage of the U.S. population, as automobile manufacturers began to mass produce what had once been a luxury item, and daring aviators both demonstrated and drove advancements in aircraft technology. The most significant innovation of this era was Henry Ford's **Model T** Ford, which made car ownership available to the average American.

Ford did not invent the automobile—the Duryea brothers in Massachusetts as well as Gottlieb W. Daimler and Karl Friedrich Benz in Germany were early pioneers. By the early twentieth century, hundreds of car manufacturers existed. However, they all made products that were too expensive for most Americans. Ford's innovation lay in his focus on using mass production to manufacture automobiles; he revolutionized industrial work by perfecting the assembly line, which enabled him to lower the Model T's price from $850 in 1908 to $300 in 1924, making car ownership a real possibility for a large share of the population (**Figure 3.4**). As prices dropped, more and more people could afford to own a car. Soon, people could buy used Model Ts for as little as five dollars, allowing students and others with   low incomes to enjoy the freedom and mobility of car ownership. By 1929, there were over twenty-three million automobiles on American roads.

Figure 3.4 This advertisement for Ford's Model T ran in the New Orleans *Times Picayune* in 1911. Note that the prices have not yet dropped far from their initial high of $850.

The assembly line helped Ford reduce labor costs within the production process by moving the product from one team of workers to the next, each of them completing a step so simple they had to be, in Ford's words, "no smarter than an ox" (**Figure 3.5**). Ford's reliance on the **moving assembly line**, scientific management, and time-motion studies added to his emphasis on efficiency over craftsmanship.

Figure 3.5 In this image from a 1928 *Literary Digest* interview with Henry Ford, workers on an assembly line produce new models of Ford automobiles.

Ford's emphasis on cheap mass production brought both benefits and disadvantages to its workers. Ford would not allow his workers to unionize, and the boring, repetitive nature of the assembly line work generated a high turnover rate. However, he doubled workers' pay to five dollars a day and standardized the workday to eight hours (a reduction from the norm). Ford's assembly line also offered greater equality than most opportunities of the time, as he paid white and black workers equally. Seeking these wages, many African Americans from the South moved to Detroit and other large northern cities to work in factories.

Ford even bought a plot of land in the Amazonian jungle twice the size of Delaware to build a factory town he called Fordlandia. Workers there rejected his midwestern Puritanism even more than his factory discipline, and the project ended in an epic failure. In the United States, however, Ford shaped the nation's mode of industrialism—one that relied on paying decent wages so that workers could afford to be the consumers of their own products.

The automobile changed the face of America, both economically and socially. Industries like glass, steel, and rubber processing expanded to keep up with auto production. The oil industry in California, Oklahoma, and Texas expanded, as Americans' reliance on oil increased and the nation transitioned from a coal-based economy to one driven by petroleum. The need for public roadways required local and state governments to fund a dramatic expansion of infrastructure, which permitted motels and restaurants to spring up and offer new services to millions of newly mobile Americans with cash to spend. With this new infrastructure, new shopping and living patterns emerged, and streetcar suburbs gave way to automobile suburbs as private automobile traffic on public roads began to replace mass transit on trains and trolleys.

The 1920s not only witnessed a transformation in ground transportation but also major changes in air travel. By the mid-1920s, men—as well as some pioneering women like the African American stunt pilot Bessie Coleman (**Figure 3.6**)—had been flying for two decades. But there remained doubts about the suitability of airplanes for long-distance travel. Orville Wright, one of the pioneers of airplane technology in the United States, once famously declared, "No flying machine will ever fly from New York to Paris [because] no known motor can run at the requisite speed for four days without stopping." However, in 1927, this skepticism was finally put to rest when Charles Lindbergh became the first person to fly solo across the Atlantic Ocean, flying from New York to Paris in thirty-three hours (**Figure 3.6**).

(a)   (b)

Figure 3.6 Aviator Charles Lindbergh stands in front of the *Spirit of St Louis* (a), the plane in which he flew from New York to Paris, France, in 1927. Because American flight schools barred black students, stunt pilot Bessie Coleman (b), the daughter of Texas sharecroppers, taught herself French to earn her pilot's license overseas.

Lindbergh's flight made him an international hero: the best-known American in the world. On his return, Americans greeted him with a ticker-tape parade—a celebration in which shredded paper thrown from surrounding buildings creates a festive, flurry effect. His flight, which he completed in the monoplane *Spirit of St. Louis*, seemed like a triumph of individualism in modern mass society and exemplified Americans' ability to conquer the air with new technology. Following his success, the small airline industry began to blossom, fully coming into its own in the 1930s, as companies like Boeing and Ford developed airplanes designed specifically for passenger air transport. As technologies in engine and passenger compartment design improved, air travel became more popular. In 1934, the number of U.S. domestic air passengers was just over 450,000 annually. By the end of the decade, that number had increased to nearly two million.

Technological innovation influenced more than just transportation. As access to electricity became more common and the electric motor was made more efficient, inventors began to churn out new and more complex household appliances. Newly developed innovations like radios, phonographs, vacuum cleaners, washing machines, and refrigerators emerged on the market during this period. While expensive, new consumer-purchasing innovations like store credit and installment plans made them available to a larger segment of the population. Many of these devices promised to give women—who continued to have primary responsibility for housework—more opportunities to step out of the home and expand their horizons. Ironically, however, these labor-saving devices tended to increase the workload for women by raising the standards of domestic work. With the aid of these tools, women ended up cleaning more frequently, washing more often, and cooking more elaborate meals rather than gaining spare time.

Despite the fact that the promise of more leisure time went largely unfulfilled, the lure of technology as the gateway to a more relaxed lifestyle endured. This enduring dream was a testament to the influence of another growing industry: advertising. The mass consumption of cars, household appliances, ready-to-wear clothing, and processed foods depended heavily on the work of advertisers. Magazines like *Ladies' Home Journal* and *The Saturday Evening Post* became vehicles to connect advertisers with middle-class consumers. Colorful and occasionally provocative print advertisements decorated the pages of these publications and became a staple in American popular culture (**Figure 3.7**).

Figure 3.7 This advertisement for Palmolive soap, which appeared in *Ladies' Home Journal* in 1922, claimed that the soap's "moderate price is due to popularity, to the enormous demand which keeps Palmolive factories working day and night" and so "the old-time luxury of the few may now be enjoyed the world over."

The form of the advertisements, however, was not new. These colorful print ads were merely the modern incarnations of an advertising strategy that went back to the nineteenth century. The new medium for advertisers in the 1920s, the one that would reach out to consumers in radically new and innovative ways, was radio.

THE POWER OF RADIO AND THE WORLD OF SPORTS

After being introduced during World War I, radios became a common feature in American homes of the 1920s. Hundreds of radio stations popped up over the decade. These stations developed and broadcasted news, serial stories, and political speeches. Much like print media, advertising space was interspersed with entertainment. Yet, unlike magazines and newspapers, advertisers did not have to depend on the active participation of consumers: Advertisers could reach out to anyone within listening distance of the radio. On the other hand, their broader audience meant that they had to be more conservative and careful not to offend anyone.

Click and Explore

Listen to a recording of a broadcast (http://openstaxcollege.org/l/15Showboat) of the "WLS Showboat: "The Floating Palace of Wonder," a variety show from WLS Chicago, a radio station run by Sears Roebuck and Co. What does the clip tell you about the entertainment of the 1920s?

The power of radio further sped up the processes of nationalization and homogenization that were previously begun with the wide distribution of newspapers made possible by railroads and telegraphs. Far more effectively than these print media, however, radio created and pumped out American culture onto the airwaves and into the homes of families around the country. Syndicated radio programs like *Amos 'n' Andy*, which began in the late 1920s, entertained listeners around the country—in the case of the popular *Amos 'n' Andy*, it did so with racial stereotypes about African Americans familiar from minstrel shows of the previous century. No longer were small corners of the country separated by their access to information. With the radio, Americans from coast to coast could listen to exactly the same programming. This had the effect of smoothing out regional differences in dialect, language, music, and even consumer taste.

Radio also transformed how Americans enjoyed sports. The introduction of play-by-play descriptions of sporting events broadcast over the radio brought sports entertainment right into the homes of millions. Radio also helped to popularize sports figures and their accomplishments. Jim Thorpe, who grew up in the Sac and Fox Nation in Oklahoma, was known as one of the best athletes in the world: He medaled in the 1912 Olympic Games, played Major League Baseball, and was one of the founding members of the National Football League. Other sports superstars were soon household names. In 1926, Gertrude Ederle became the first woman to swim the English Channel. Helen Wills dominated women's tennis, winning Wimbledon eight times in the late 1920s (**Figure 3.8**), whereas "Big Bill" Tilden won the national singles title every year from 1920 to 1925. In football, Harold "Red" Grange played for the University of Illinois, averaging over ten yards per carry during his college career. The biggest star of all was the "Sultan of Swat," Babe Ruth, who became America's first baseball hero (**Figure 3.8**). He changed the game of baseball from a low-scoring one dominated by pitchers to one where his hitting became famous. By 1923, most pitchers intentionally walked him. In 1924, he hit sixty homeruns.

Figure 3.8 Babe Ruth (a) led the New York Yankees to four World Series championships. In this 1921 photograph, he stands outside of the New York Yankees dugout. Helen Wills (b) won a total of thirty-one Grand Slam titles in her career, including eight singles titles at Wimbledon from 1927 to 1938. (credit a: modification of work by Library of Congress)

3.2 Transformation and Backlash

By the end of this section, you will be able to:

- Define nativism and analyze the ways in which it affected the politics and society of the 1920s
- Describe the conflict between urban Americans and rural fundamentalists
- Explain the issues in question in the Scopes trial

While prosperous, middle-class Americans found much to celebrate about the new era of leisure and consumption, many Americans—often those in rural areas—disagreed on the meaning of a "good life" and how to achieve it. They reacted to the rapid social changes of modern urban society with a vigorous defense of religious values and a fearful rejection of cultural diversity and equality.

NATIVISM

Beginning at the end of the nineteenth century, immigration into the United States rocketed to never-before-seen heights. Many of these new immigrants were coming from eastern and southern Europe and, for many English-speaking, native-born Americans of northern European descent, the growing diversity of new languages, customs, and religions triggered anxiety and racial animosity. In reaction, some embraced **nativism**, prizing white Americans with older family trees over more recent immigrants, and rejecting outside influences in favor of their own local customs. Nativists also stoked a sense of fear over the perceived foreign threat, pointing to the anarchist assassinations of the Spanish prime minister in 1897, the Italian king in 1900, and even President William McKinley in 1901 as proof. Following the Bolshevik Revolution in Russia in November 1917, the sense of an inevitable foreign or communist threat only grew among those already predisposed to distrust immigrants.

The sense of fear and anxiety over the rising tide of immigration came to a head with the trial of Nicola Sacco and Bartolomeo Vanzetti (**Figure 3.9**). Sacco and Vanzetti were Italian immigrants who were accused of being part of a robbery and murder in Braintree, Massachusetts, in 1920. There was no direct evidence linking them to the crime, but (in addition to being immigrants) both men were anarchists who favored the destruction of the American market-based, capitalistic society through violence. At their trial, the district attorney emphasized Sacco and Vanzetti's radical views, and the jury found them guilty on July 14, 1921. Despite subsequent motions and appeals based on ballistics testing, recanted testimony, and an ex-convict's confession, both men were executed on August 23, 1927.

(a)   (b)

Figure 3.9 Bartolomeo Vanzetti and Nicola Sacco (a) sit in handcuffs at Dedham Superior Court in Massachusetts in 1923. After the verdict in 1921, protesters demonstrated (b) in London, England, hoping to save Sacco and Vanzetti from execution.

Opinions on the trial and judgment tended to divide along nativist-immigrant lines, with immigrants supporting the innocence of the condemned pair. The verdict sparked protests from Italian and other immigrant groups, as well as from noted intellectuals such as writer John Dos Passos, satirist Dorothy Parker, and famed physicist Albert Einstein. Muckraker Upton Sinclair based his indictment of the American justice system, the "documentary novel" *Boston*, on Sacco and Vanzetti's trial, which he considered a gross miscarriage of justice. As the execution neared, the radical labor union Industrial Workers of the World called for a three-day nationwide walkout, leading to the Great Colorado Coal Strike of 1927. Protests occurred worldwide from Tokyo to Buenos Aires to London (**Figure 3.9**).

One of the most articulate critics of the trial was then-Harvard Law School professor Felix Frankfurter, who would go on to be appointed to the U.S. Supreme Court by Franklin D. Roosevelt in 1939. In 1927, six years after the trial, he wrote in *The Atlantic*, "By systematic exploitation of the defendants' alien blood, their imperfect knowledge of English, their unpopular social views, and their opposition to the war, the District Attorney invoked against them a riot of political passion and patriotic sentiment; and the trial judge connived at—one had almost written, cooperated in—the process."

To "preserve the ideal of American homogeneity," the Emergency Immigration Act of 1921 introduced numerical limits on European immigration for the first time in U.S. history. These limits were based on a quota system that restricted annual immigration from any given country to 3 percent of the residents from that same country as counted in the 1910 census. The National Origins Act of 1924 went even further, lowering the level to 2 percent of the 1890 census, significantly reducing the share of eligible southern and eastern Europeans, since they had only begun to arrive in the United States in large numbers in the 1890s. Although New York congressmen Fiorello LaGuardia and Emanuel Celler spoke out against the act, there was minimal opposition in Congress, and both labor unions and the Ku Klux Klan supported the bill. When President Coolidge signed it into law, he declared, "America must be kept American."

Click and Explore

The Library of Congress's immigration collection (http://openstaxcollege.org/l/ 15Immigration) contains information on different immigrant groups, the timelines of their immigration, maps of their settlement routes, and the reasons they came. Click the images on the left navigation bar to learn about each group.

THE KU KLUX KLAN

The concern that a white, Protestant, Anglo-Saxon United States was under siege by throngs of undesirables was not exclusively directed at foreigners. The sense that the country was also facing a threat from within its borders and its own citizenry was also prevalent. This sense was clearly reflected in the popularity of the 1915 motion picture, D. W. Griffith's *The Birth of a Nation* (**Figure 3.10**). Based on *The Clansman*, a 1915 novel by Thomas Dixon, the film offers a racist, white-centric view of the Reconstruction Era. The film depicts noble white southerners made helpless by northern carpetbaggers who empower freed slaves to abuse white men and violate women. The heroes of the film were the Ku Klux Klan, who saved the whites, the South, and the nation. While the film was reviled by many African Americans and the NAACP for its historical inaccuracies and its maligning of freed slaves, it was celebrated by many whites who accepted the historical revisionism as an accurate portrayal of Reconstruction Era oppression. After viewing the film, President Wilson reportedly remarked, "It is like writing history with lightning, and my only regret is that it is all so terribly true."

Figure 3.10 A theatrical release poster for *The Birth of a Nation*, in 1915. The film glorified the role of the Ku Klux Klan in quelling the threat of black power during Reconstruction.

DEFINING "AMERICAN"

✪ *Artistic License and the Censor*

In a letter dated April 17, 1915, Mary Childs Nerney, a secretary of the NAACP, wrote to a local censor to request that certain scenes be cut from *The Birth of a Nation*.

> My dear Mr. Packard:
> I am utterly disgusted with the situation in regard to "The Birth of a Nation." As you will read in the next number of the Crisis, we have fought it at every possible point. In spite of the promise of the Mayor [of Chicago] to cut out the two objectionable scenes in the second part, which show a white girl committing suicide to escape from a Negro pursuer, and a mulatto politician trying to force marriage upon the daughter of his white benefactor, these two scenes still form the motif of the really unimportant incidents, of which I enclose a list. I have seen the thing four times and am positive that nothing more will be done about it. Jane Addams saw it when it was in its worst form in New York. I know of no one else from Chicago who saw it. I enclose Miss Addam's opinion.
> When we took the thing before the Police Magistrate he told us that he could do nothing about it unless it [led] to a breach of the peace. Some kind of demonstration began in the Liberty Theatre Wednesday night but the colored people took absolutely no part in it, and the only man arrested was a white man. This, of course, is exactly what Littleton, counsel for the producer, Griffith, held in the Magistrates' Court when we have our hearing and claimed that it might lead to a breach of the peace.
> Frankly, I do not think you can do one single thing. It has been to me a most liberal education and I purposely am through. The harm it is doing the colored people cannot be estimated. I hear echoes of it wherever I go and have no doubt that this was in the mind of the people who are producing it. Their profits here are something like $14,000 a day and their expenses about $400. I have ceased to worry about it, and if I seem disinterested, kindly remember that we have put six weeks of constant effort of this thing and have gotten nowhere.
> Sincerely yours,
> —Mary Childs Nerney, Secretary, NAACP

On what grounds does Nerney request censorship? What efforts to get the movie shut down did she describe?

The Ku Klux Klan, which had been dormant since the end of Reconstruction in 1877, experienced a resurgence of attention following the popularity of the film. Just months after the film's release, a second incarnation of the Klan was established at Stone Mountain, Georgia, under the leadership of William Simmons. This new Klan now publicly eschewed violence and received mainstream support. Its embrace of Protestantism, anti-Catholicism, and anti-Semitism, and its appeals for stricter immigration policies, gained the group a level of acceptance by nativists with similar prejudices. The group was not merely a male organization: The ranks of the Klan also included many women, with chapters of its women's auxiliary in locations across the country. These women's groups were active in a number of reform-minded activities, such as advocating for prohibition and the distribution of Bibles at public schools. But they also participated in more expressly Klan activities like burning crosses and the public denunciation of Catholics and Jews (**Figure 3.11**). By 1924, this **Second Ku Klux Klan** had six million members in the South, West, and, particularly, the Midwest—more Americans than there were in the nation's labor unions at the time. While the organization publicly abstained from violence, its member continued to employ intimidation, violence, and terrorism against its victims, particularly in the South.

Figure 3.11 In this 1921 image from the *Denver News*, three Ku Klux Klan members (two women and one man) stand in front of a burning cross.

The Klan's newfound popularity proved to be fairly short-lived. Several states effectively combatted the power and influence of the Klan through anti-masking legislation, that is, laws that barred the wearing of masks publicly. As the organization faced a series of public scandals, such as when the Grand Dragon of Indiana was convicted of murdering a white schoolteacher, prominent citizens became less likely to openly express their support for the group without a shield of anonymity. More importantly, influential people and citizen groups explicitly condemned the Klan. Reinhold Niebuhr, a popular Protestant minister and conservative intellectual in Detroit, admonished the group for its ostensibly Protestant zealotry and anti-Catholicism. Jewish organizations, especially the Anti-Defamation League, which had been founded just a couple of years before the reemergence of the Klan, amplified Jewish discontent at being the focus of Klan attention. And the NAACP, which had actively sought to ban the film *The Birth of a Nation*, worked to lobby congress and educate the public on lynchings. Ultimately, however, it was the Great Depression that put an end to the Klan. As dues-paying members dwindled, the Klan lost its organizational power and sunk into irrelevance until the 1950s.

FAITH, FUNDAMENTALISM, AND SCIENCE

The sense of degeneration that the Klan and anxiety over mass immigration prompted in the minds of many Americans was in part a response to the process of postwar urbanization. Cities were swiftly becoming centers of opportunity, but the growth of cities, especially the growth of immigrant populations in those cities, sharpened rural discontent over the perception of rapid cultural change. As more of the population flocked to cities for jobs and quality of life, many left behind in rural areas felt that their way of life was being threatened. To rural Americans, the ways of the city seemed sinful and profligate. Urbanites, for their part, viewed rural Americans as hayseeds who were hopelessly behind the times.

In this urban/rural conflict, Tennessee lawmakers drew a battle line over the issue of evolution and its contradiction of the accepted, biblical explanation of history. Charles Darwin had first published his theory of natural selection in 1859, and by the 1920s, many standard textbooks contained information about Darwin's theory of evolution. Fundamentalist Protestants targeted evolution as representative of all that was wrong with urban society. Tennessee's Butler Act made it illegal "to teach any theory that denies the story of the Divine Creation of man as taught in the Bible, and to teach instead that man has descended from a lower order of animals."

The American Civil Liberties Union (ACLU) hoped to challenge the Butler Act as an infringement of the freedom of speech. As a defendant, the ACLU enlisted teacher and coach John Scopes, who suggested that he may have taught evolution while substituting for an ill biology teacher. Town leaders in Dayton,

Tennessee, for their part, sensed an opportunity to promote their town, which had lost more than one-third of its population, and welcomed the ACLU to stage a test case against the Butler Act. The ACLU and the town got their wish as the **Scopes Monkey Trial**, as the newspapers publicized it, quickly turned into a carnival that captured the attention of the country and epitomized the nation's urban/rural divide (**Figure 3.12**).

Figure 3.12 During the Scopes Monkey Trial, supporters of the Butler Act read literature at the headquarters of the Anti-Evolution League in Dayton, Tennessee.

Fundamentalist champion William Jennings Bryan argued the case for the prosecution. Bryan was a three-time presidential candidate and Woodrow Wilson's Secretary of State until 1915, at which point he began preaching across the country about the spread of secularism and the declining role of religion in education. He was known for offering $100 to anyone who would admit to being descended from an ape. Clarence Darrow, a prominent lawyer and outspoken agnostic, led the defense team. His statement that, "Scopes isn't on trial, civilization is on trial. No man's belief will be safe if they win," struck a chord in society.

The outcome of the trial, in which Scopes was found guilty and fined $100, was never really in question, as Scopes himself had confessed to violating the law. Nevertheless, the trial itself proved to be high drama. The drama only escalated when Darrow made the unusual choice of calling Bryan as an expert witness on the Bible. Knowing of Bryan's convictions of a literal interpretation of the Bible, Darrow peppered him with a series of questions designed to ridicule such a belief. The result was that those who approved of the teaching of evolution saw Bryan as foolish, whereas many rural Americans considered the cross-examination an attack on the Bible and their faith.

DEFINING "AMERICAN"

✪ *H. L. Mencken on the Scopes Trial*

H. L. Mencken covered the trial for Baltimore's The Evening Sun. One of most popular writers of social satire of his age, Mencken was very critical of the South, the trial, and especially Bryan. He coined the terms "monkey trial "and "Bible belt." In the excerpt below, Mencken reflects on the trial's outcome and its overall importance for the United States.

> The Scopes trial, from the start, has been carried on in a manner exactly fitted to the anti-evolution law and the simian imbecility under it. There hasn't been the slightest pretense to decorum. The rustic judge, a candidate for re-election, has postured the yokels like a clown in a ten-cent side show, and almost every word he has uttered has been an undisguised appeal to their prejudices and superstitions. The chief prosecuting attorney, beginning like a competent lawyer and a man of self-respect, ended like a convert at a Billy Sunday revival. It fell to him, finally, to make a clear and astounding statement of theory of justice prevailing under fundamentalism. What he said, in brief, was that a man accused of infidelity had no rights whatever under Tennessee law. . . .
>
> Darrow has lost this case. It was lost long before he came to Dayton. But it seems to me that he has nevertheless performed a great public service by fighting it to a finish and in a perfectly serious way. Let no one mistake it for comedy, farcical though it may be in all its details. It serves notice on the country that Neanderthal man is organizing in these forlorn backwaters of the land, led by a fanatic, rid of sense and devoid of conscience. Tennessee, challenging him too timorously and too late, now sees its courts converted into camp meetings and its Bill of Rights made a mock of by its sworn officers of the law. There are other States that had better look to their arsenals before the Hun is at their gates.
>
> —H. L. Mencken, *The Evening Sun*, July 18, 1925

How does Mencken characterize Judge Raulston? About what threat is Mencken warning America?

Indicative of the revival of Protestant fundamentalism and the rejection of evolution among rural and white Americans was the rise of Billy Sunday. As a young man, Sunday had gained fame as a baseball player with exceptional skill and speed. Later, he found even more celebrity as the nation's most revered evangelist, drawing huge crowds at camp meetings around the country. He was one of the most influential evangelists of the time and had access to some of the wealthiest and most powerful families in the country (**Figure 3.13**). Sunday rallied many Americans around "old-time" fundamentalist religion and garnered support for prohibition. Recognizing Sunday's popular appeal, Bryan attempted to bring him to Dayton for the Scopes trial, although Sunday politely refused.

Figure 3.13 Billy Sunday, one of the most influential evangelists of his day, leaves the White House on February 20, 1922 (a). Aimee Semple McPherson, shown here preaching at the Angelus Temple in 1923 (b), founded the Foursquare Church. (credit a: modification of work by Library of Congress)

Even more spectacular than the rise of Billy Sunday was the popularity of Aimee Semple McPherson, a Canadian Pentecostal preacher whose Foursquare Church in Los Angeles catered to the large community of midwestern transplants and newcomers to California (**Figure 3.13**). Although her message promoted the fundamental truths of the Bible, her style was anything but old fashioned. Dressed in tight-fitting clothes and wearing makeup, she held radio-broadcast services in large venues that resembled concert halls and staged spectacular faith-healing performances. Blending Hollywood style and modern technology with a message of fundamentalist Christianity, McPherson exemplified the contradictions of the decade well before public revelations about her scandalous love affair cost her much of her status and following.

3.3 A New Generation

By the end of this section, you will be able to:
- Explain the factors that shaped the new morality and the changing role of women in the United States during the 1920s
- Describe the "new Negro" and the influence of the Harlem Renaissance
- Analyze the effects of prohibition on American society and culture
- Describe the character and main authors of the Lost Generation

The 1920s was a time of dramatic change in the United States. Many young people, especially those living in big cities, embraced a new morality that was much more permissive than that of previous generations. They listened to jazz music, especially in the nightclubs of Harlem. Although prohibition outlawed alcohol, criminal bootlegging and importing businesses thrived. The decade was not a pleasure cruise for everyone, however; in the wake of the Great War, many were left awaiting the promise of a new generation.

A NEW MORALITY

Many Americans were disillusioned in the post-World War I era, and their reactions took many forms. Rebellious American youth, in particular, adjusted to the changes by embracing a **new morality** that was far more permissive than the social mores of their parents. Many young women of the era shed their mother's morality and adopted the dress and mannerisms of a **flapper**, the Jazz Age female stereotype, seeking the endless party. Flappers wore shorter skirts, shorter hair, and more makeup, and they drank and smoked with the boys (**Figure 3.14**). Flappers' dresses emphasized straight lines from the shoulders to the knees, minimizing breasts and curves while highlighting legs and ankles. The male equivalent of a flapper was a "sheik," although that term has not remained as strong in the American vernacular. At the time, however, many of these fads became a type of conformity, especially among college-aged youths, with the signature bob haircut of the flapper becoming almost universal—in both the United States and overseas.

Figure 3.14 The flapper look, seen here in "Flapper" by Ellen Pyle for the cover of *The Saturday Evening Post* in February 1922, was a national craze in American cities during the 1920s.

As men and women pushed social and cultural boundaries in the Jazz Age, sexual mores changed and social customs grew more permissive. "Petting parties" or "necking parties" became the rage on college campuses. Psychologist Sigmund Freud and British "sexologist" Havelock Ellis emphasized that sex was a natural and pleasurable part of the human experience. Margaret Sanger, the founder of Planned Parenthood, launched an information campaign on birth control to give women a choice in the realm in which suffrage had changed little—the family. The popularization of contraception and the private space that the automobile offered to teenagers and unwed couples also contributed to changes in sexual behavior.

Flappers and sheiks also took their cues from the high-flying romances they saw on movie screens and confessions in movie magazines of immorality on movie sets. Movie posters promised: "Brilliant men, beautiful jazz babies, champagne baths, midnight revels, petting parties in the purple dawn, all ending in one terrific smashing climax that makes you gasp." And "neckers, petters, white kisses, red kisses, pleasure-mad daughters, sensation-craving mothers . . . the truth: bold, naked, sensational."

Click and Explore

Could you go "on a toot" with flappers and sheiks? Improve your chances with this collection (http://openstaxcollege.org/l/15JazzSlang) of Jazz Age slang.

New dances and new music—especially jazz—also characterized the Jazz Age. Born out of the African American community, jazz was a uniquely American music. The innovative sound emerged from a number of different communities and from a number of different musical traditions such as blues and ragtime. By the 1920s, jazz had spread from African American clubs in New Orleans and Chicago to reach greater popularity in New York and abroad. One New York jazz establishment, the Cotton Club, became particularly famous and attracted large audiences of hip, young, and white flappers and sheiks to see black entertainers play jazz (**Figure 3.15**).

Figure 3.15 Black jazz bands such as the King and Carter Jazzing Orchestra, photographed in 1921 by Robert Runyon, were immensely popular among white urbanites in the 1920s.

THE "NEW WOMAN"

The Jazz Age and the proliferation of the flapper lifestyle of the 1920s should not be seen merely as the product of postwar disillusionment and newfound prosperity. Rather, the search for new styles of dress and new forms of entertainment like jazz was part of a larger women's rights movement. The early 1920s, especially with the ratification of the Nineteenth Amendment guaranteeing full voting rights to women, was a period that witnessed the expansion of women's political power. The public flaunting of social and sexual norms by flappers represented an attempt to match gains in political equality with gains in the social sphere. Women were increasingly leaving the Victorian era norms of the previous generation behind, as they broadened the concept of women's liberation to include new forms of social expression such as dance, fashion, women's clubs, and forays into college and the professions.

Nor did the struggle for women's rights through the promotion and passage of legislation cease in the 1920s. In 1921, Congress passed the Promotion of the Welfare and Hygiene of Maternity and Infancy Act, also known as the Sheppard-Towner Act, which earmarked $1.25 million for well-baby clinics and educational programs, as well as nursing. This funding dramatically reduced the rate of infant mortality.

Two years later, in 1923, Alice Paul drafted and promoted an Equal Rights Amendment (ERA) that promised to end all sex discrimination by guaranteeing that "Men and women shall have equal rights throughout the United States and every place subject to its jurisdiction."

Yet, ironically, at precisely the time when the Progressive movement was achieving its long-sought-after goals, the movement itself was losing steam and the Progressive Era was coming to a close. As the heat of Progressive politics grew less intense, voter participation from both sexes declined over the course of the 1920s. After the passage of the Nineteenth Amendment, many women believed that they had accomplished their goals and dropped out of the movement. As a result, the proposed ERA stalled (the ERA eventually passed Congress almost fifty years later in 1972, but then failed to win ratification by a sufficient number of states), and, by the end of the 1920s, Congress even allowed funding for the Sheppard-Towner Act to lapse.

The growing lethargy toward women's rights was happening at a time when an increasing number of women were working for wages in the U.S. economy—not only in domestic service, but in retail, healthcare and education, offices, and manufacturing. Beginning in the 1920s, women's participation in the labor force increased steadily. However, most were paid less than men for the same type of work based on the rationale that they did not have to support a family. While the employment of single and unmarried women had largely won social acceptance, married women often suffered the stigma that they were working for pin money—frivolous additional discretionary income.

THE HARLEM RENAISSANCE AND THE NEW NEGRO

It wasn't only women who found new forms of expression in the 1920s. African Americans were also expanding their horizons and embracing the concept of the "new Negro." The decade witnessed the continued Great Migration of African Americans to the North, with over half a million fleeing the strict Jim Crow laws of the South. Life in the northern states, as many African Americans discovered, was hardly free of discrimination and segregation. Even without Jim Crow, businesses, property owners, employers, and private citizens typically practiced *de facto* segregation, which could be quite stifling and oppressive. Nonetheless, many southern blacks continued to move north into segregated neighborhoods that were already bursting at the seams, because the North, at the very least, offered two tickets toward black progress: schools and the vote. The black population of New York City doubled during the decade. As a result, Harlem, a neighborhood at the northern end of Manhattan, became a center for Afro-centric art, music, poetry, and politics. Political expression in the Harlem of the 1920s ran the gamut, as some leaders advocated a return to Africa, while others fought for inclusion and integration.

Revived by the wartime migration and fired up by the white violence of the postwar riots, urban blacks developed a strong cultural expression in the 1920s that came to be known as the Harlem Renaissance. In this rediscovery of black culture, African American artists and writers formulated an independent black culture and encouraged racial pride, rejecting any emulation of white American culture. Claude McKay's poem "If We Must Die" called on African Americans to start fighting back in the wake of the Red Summer riots of 1919 (discussed in a previous chapter, **Figure 3.16**). Langston Hughes, often nicknamed the "poet laureate" of the movement, invoked sacrifice and the just cause of civil rights in "The Colored Soldier," while another author of the movement, Zora Neale Hurston, celebrated the life and dialect of rural blacks in a fictional, all-black town in Florida. Hurston's *Their Eyes Were Watching God* was only published posthumously in 1937.

Figure 3.16 The Jamaican-born poet and novelist Claude McKay articulated the new sense of self and urban community of African Americans during the Harlem Renaissance. Although centered in the Harlem neighborhood of Manhattan, this cultural movement emerged in urban centers throughout the Northeast and Midwest.

The new Negro found political expression in a political ideology that celebrated African Americans distinct national identity. This **Negro nationalism**, as some referred to it, proposed that African Americans had a distinct and separate national heritage that should inspire pride and a sense of community. An early proponent of such nationalism was W. E. B. Du Bois. One of the founders of the NAACP, a brilliant writer and scholar, and the first African American to earn a Ph.D. from Harvard, Du Bois openly rejected assumptions of white supremacy. His conception of Negro nationalism encouraged Africans to work together in support of their own interests, promoted the elevation of black literature and cultural expression, and, most famously, embraced the African continent as the true homeland of all ethnic Africans—a concept known as Pan-Africanism.

Taking Negro nationalism to a new level was Marcus Garvey. Like many black Americans, the Jamaican immigrant had become utterly disillusioned with the prospect of overcoming white racism in the United States in the wake of the postwar riots and promoted a "Back to Africa" movement. To return African Americans to a presumably more welcoming home in Africa, Garvey founded the Black Star Steamship Line. He also started the United Negro Improvement Association (UNIA), which attracted thousands of primarily lower-income working people. UNIA members wore colorful uniforms and promoted the doctrine of a "negritude" that reversed the color hierarchy of white supremacy, prizing blackness and identifying light skin as a mark of inferiority. Intellectual leaders like Du Bois, whose lighter skin put him low on Garvey's social order, considered the UNIA leader a charlatan. Garvey was eventually imprisoned for mail fraud and then deported, but his legacy set the stage for Malcolm X and the Black Power movement of the 1960s.

PROHIBITION

At precisely the same time that African Americans and women were experimenting with new forms of social expression, the country as a whole was undergoing a process of austere and dramatic social reform in the form of alcohol prohibition. After decades of organizing to reduce or end the consumption of alcohol in the United States, temperance groups and the Anti-Saloon League finally succeeded in pushing through the Eighteenth Amendment in 1919, which banned the manufacture, sale, and transportation of intoxicating liquors (**Figure 3.17**). The law proved difficult to enforce, as illegal alcohol soon poured in from Canada and the Caribbean, and rural Americans resorted to home-brewed "moonshine." The   result was an eroding of respect for law and order, as many people continued to drink illegal liquor. Rather than bringing about an age of sobriety, as Progressive reformers had hoped, it gave rise to a new subculture that included illegal importers, interstate smuggling (or **bootlegging**), clandestine saloons referred to as "speakeasies," hipflasks, cocktail parties, and the organized crime of trafficking liquor.

(a)   (b)

Figure 3.17 While forces of law and order confiscated and discarded alcohol when they found it (a), consumers found ingenious ways of hiding liquor during prohibition, such as this cane that served as a flask (b).

Prohibition also revealed deep political divisions in the nation. The Democratic Party found itself deeply divided between urban, northern "wets" who hated the idea of abstinence, and rural, southern "dries" who favored the amendment. This divided the party and opened the door for the Republican Party to gain ascendancy in the 1920s. All politicians, including Woodrow Wilson, Herbert Hoover, Robert La Follette, and Franklin D. Roosevelt, equivocated in their support for the law. Publicly, they catered to the Anti-Saloon League; however, they failed to provide funding for enforcement.

Prohibition sparked a rise in organized crime. "Scarface" Al Capone (**Figure 3.18**) ran an extensive bootlegging and criminal operation known as the Chicago Outfit or Chicago mafia. By 1927, Capone's organization included a number of illegal activities including bootlegging, prostitution, gambling, loan sharking, and even murder. His operation was earning him more than $100 million annually, and many local police were on his payroll. Although he did not have a monopoly on crime, his organizational structure was better than many other criminals of his era. His liquor trafficking business and his Chicago soup kitchens during the Great Depression led some Americans to liken Capone to a modern-day Robin Hood. Still, Capone was eventually imprisoned for eleven years for tax evasion, including a stint in California's notorious Alcatraz prison.

Figure 3.18 Al Capone, pictured here in his U.S. Department of Justice mug shot, was convicted of tax fraud and sent to prison in 1931.

THE LOST GENERATION

As the country struggled with the effects and side-effects of prohibition, many young intellectuals endeavored to come to grips with a lingering sense of disillusionment. World War I, fundamentalism, and the Red Scare—a pervasive American fear of Communist infiltrators prompted by the success of the Bolshevik Revolution—all left their mark on these intellectuals. Known as the **Lost Generation**, writers like F. Scott Fitzgerald, Ernest Hemingway, Sinclair Lewis, Edith Wharton, and John Dos Passos expressed their hopelessness and despair by skewering the middle class in their work. They felt alienated from society, so they tried to escape (some literally) to criticize it. Many lived an **expatriate** life in Paris for the decade, although others went to Rome or Berlin.

The Lost Generation writer that best exemplifies the mood of the 1920s was F. Scott Fitzgerald, now considered one of the most influential writers of the twentieth century. His debut novel, *This Side of Paradise*, describes a generation of youth "grown up to find all gods dead, all wars fought, all faith in man shaken." *The Great Gatsby*, published in 1925, exposed the doom that always follows the fun, fast-lived life. Fitzgerald depicted the modern millionaire Jay Gatsby living a profligate life: unscrupulous, coarse, and in love with another man's wife. Both Fitzgerald and his wife Zelda lived this life as well, squandering the money he made from his writing.

MY STORY

☯ *F. Scott Fitzgerald on the 1920s*

In the 1920s, Fitzgerald was one of the most celebrated authors of his day, publishing *This Side of Paradise*, *The Beautiful and Damned*, and *The Great Gatsby* in quick succession. However, his profligate lifestyle with his wife Zelda sapped their funds, and Fitzgerald had to struggle to maintain their lavish lifestyle. Below is an excerpt from "The Crack-Up," a personal essay by Fitzgerald originally published in *Esquire* in which he describes his "good life" during the 1920s.

> It seemed a romantic business to be a successful literary man—you were not ever going to be as famous as a movie star but what note you had was probably longer-lived; you were never going to have the power of a man of strong political or religious convictions but you were certainly more independent. Of course within the practice of your trade you were forever unsatisfied—but I, for one, would not have chosen any other.
>
> As the Twenties passed, with my own twenties marching a little ahead of them, my two juvenile regrets—at not being big enough (or good enough) to play football in college, and at not getting overseas during the war—resolved themselves into childish waking dreams of imaginary heroism that were good enough to go to sleep on in restless nights. The big problems of life seemed to solve themselves, and if the business of fixing them was difficult, it made one too tired to think of more general problems.
>
> —F. Scott Fitzgerald, "The Crack-Up," 1936

How does Fitzgerald describe his life in the 1920s? How did his interpretation reflect the reality of the decade?

Equally idiosyncratic and disillusioned was writer Ernest Hemingway (**Figure 3.19**). He lived a peripatetic and adventurous lifestyle in Europe, Cuba, and Africa, working as an ambulance driver in Italy during World War I and traveling to Spain in the 1930s to cover the civil war there. His experiences of war and tragedy stuck with him, emerging in colorful scenes in his novels *The Sun Also Rises* (1926), *A Farewell to Arms* (1929), and *For Whom the Bell Tolls* (1940). In 1952, his novella, *The Old Man and the Sea*, won the Pulitzer Prize. Two years later, he won the Nobel Prize in Literature for this book and his overall influence on contemporary style.

Figure 3.19 Ernest Hemingway was one of the most prominent members of the Lost Generation who went to live as expatriates in Europe during the 1920s.

Click and Explore

Listen to an **audio** (http://openstaxcollege.org/l/15Hemingway) of Hemingway's Nobel Prize acceptance speech.

Not all Lost Generation writers were like Fitzgerald or Hemingway. The writing of Sinclair Lewis, rather than expressing a defined disillusionment, was more influenced by the Progressivism of the previous generation. In *Babbitt* (1922), he examined the "sheep following the herd" mentality that conformity promoted. He satirized American middle-class life as pleasure seeking and mindless. Similarly, writer Edith Wharton celebrated life in old New York, a vanished society, in *The Age of Innocence*, in 1920. Wharton came from a very wealthy, socialite family in New York, where she was educated by tutors and never attended college. She lived for many years in Europe; during the Great War, she worked in Paris helping women establish businesses.

3.4 Republican Ascendancy: Politics in the 1920s

By the end of this section, you will be able to:
- Discuss Warren G. Harding's strengths and weaknesses as president
- Explain how Calvin Coolidge was able to defeat the Democratic Party
- Explain what Calvin Coolidge meant by "the business of America is business"

The election of 1920 saw the weakening of the Democratic Party. The death of Theodore Roosevelt and Woodrow Wilson's ill health meant the passing of a generation of Progressive leaders. The waning of the Red Scare took with it the last vestiges of Progressive zeal, and Wilson's support of the League of Nations turned Irish and German immigrants against the Democrats. Americans were tired of reform, tired of witch hunts, and were more than ready for a return to "normalcy."

Above all, the 1920s signaled a return to a pro-business government—almost a return to the laissez-faire politics of the Gilded Age of the late nineteenth century. Calvin Coolidge's statement that "the chief business of the American people is business," often rendered as "the business of America is business" became the dominant attitude.

WARREN HARDING AND THE RETURN TO NORMALCY

In the election of 1920, professional Republicans were eager to nominate a man whom they could manage and control. Warren G. Harding, a senator from Ohio, represented just such a man (**Figure 3.20**). Before his nomination, Harding stated, "America's present need is not heroics but healing; not nostrums but normalcy; not revolution but restoration." Harding was genial and affable, but not everyone appreciated his speeches; Democratic presidential-hopeful William Gibbs McAdoo described Harding's speeches as "an army of pompous phrases moving across the landscape in search of an idea." H. L. Mencken, the great social critic of the 1920s, wrote of Harding's speaking, "It drags itself out of the dark abysm of pish, and crawls insanely up to the top-most pinnacle of posh. It is rumble and bumble. It is flap and doodle. It is balder and dash."

Harding was known for enjoying golf, alcohol, and poker (not necessarily in that order). Although his critics depicted him as weak, lazy, or incompetent, he was actually quite shrewd and politically astute. Together with his running mate, Calvin Coolidge, the governor of Massachusetts, they attracted the votes of many Americans who sought Harding's promised **return to normalcy**. In the election, Harding defeated Governor James Cox of Ohio by the greatest majority in the history of two-party politics: 61 percent of the popular vote.

(a)   (b)

Figure 3.20 Warren Harding (a) poses on the campaign trail in 1920. His running mate, Calvin Coolidge (b), would go on to become president in 1923, when Harding died suddenly while touring the United States.

Harding's cabinet reflected his pro-business agenda. Herbert Hoover, a millionaire mechanical engineer and miner, became his Secretary of Commerce. Hoover had served as head of the relief effort for Belgium during World War I and helped to feed those in Russia and Germany after the war ended. He was a very effective administrator, seeking to limit inefficiency in the government and promoting partnerships between government and businesses. Harding's Secretary of the Treasury, Andrew Mellon, was also a pro-business multimillionaire with a fortune built in banking and aluminum. Even more so than Hoover, Mellon entered public service with a strong sense that government should run as efficiently as any business, famously writing that "the Government is just a business, and can and should be run on business principles."

Consistent with his principles of running government with business-like efficiency, Harding proposed and signed into law tax rate cuts as well as the country's first formal budgeting process, which created a presidential budget director and required that the president submit an annual budget to Congress. These policies helped to reduce the debt that the United States had incurred during World War I. However, as Europe began to recover, U.S. exports to the continent dwindled. In an effort to protect U.S. agriculture and other businesses threatened by lower-priced imports, Harding pushed through the Emergency Tariff of 1921. This defensive tariff had the effect of increasing American purchasing power, although it also inflated the prices of many goods.

In the area of foreign policy, Harding worked to preserve the peace through international cooperation and the reduction of armaments around the world. Despite the refusal of the U.S. Senate to ratify the Treaty of Versailles, Harding was able to work with Germany and Austria to secure a formal peace. He convened a conference in Washington that brought world leaders together to agree on reducing the threat of future wars by reducing armaments. Out of these negotiations came a number of treaties designed to foster cooperation in the Far East, reduce the size of navies around the world, and establish guidelines for submarine usage. These agreements ultimately fell apart in the 1930s, as the world descended into war again. But, at the time, they were seen as a promising path to maintaining the peace.

Despite these developments, the Harding administration has gone down in history as one that was especially ridden with scandal. While Harding was personally honest, he surrounded himself with politicians who weren't. Harding made the mistake of often turning to unscrupulous advisors or even his "Ohio Gang" of drinking and poker buddies for advice and guidance. And, as he himself recognized, this group tended to cause him grief. "I have no trouble with my enemies," he once commented. "I can take care of my enemies in a fight. But my friends, my goddamned friends, they're the ones who keep me walking the floor at nights!"

The scandals mounted quickly. From 1920 to 1923, Secretary of the Interior Albert B. Fall was involved in a scam that became known as the **Teapot Dome scandal**. Fall had leased navy reserves in Teapot Dome, Wyoming, and two other sites in California to private oil companies without opening the bidding to other companies. In exchange, the companies gave him $300,000 in cash and bonds, as well as a herd of cattle for his ranch. Fall was convicted of accepting bribes from the oil companies; he was fined $100,000 and sentenced to a year in prison. It was the first time that a cabinet official had received such a sentence.

In 1923, Harding also learned that the head of the Veterans' Bureau, Colonel Charles Forbes, had absconded with most of the $250 million set aside for extravagant bureau functions. Harding allowed Forbes to resign and leave the country; however, after the president died, Forbes returned and was tried, convicted, and sentenced to two years in Leavenworth prison.

Although the Harding presidency had a number of large successes and variety of dark scandals, it ended before the first term was up. In July 1923, while traveling in Seattle, the president suffered a heart attack. On August 2, in his weakened condition, he suffered a stroke and died in San Francisco, leaving the presidency to his vice president, Calvin Coolidge. As for Harding, few presidents were so deeply mourned by the populace. His kindly nature and ability to poke fun at himself endeared him to the public.

Click and Explore

Listen to some of Harding's speeches (http://openstaxcollege.org/l/15Harding) at The University of Virginia's Miller Center's website.

A MAN OF FEW WORDS

Coolidge ended the scandals, but did little beyond that. Walter Lippman wrote in 1926 that "Mr. Coolidge's genius for inactivity is developed to a very high point. It is a grim, determined, alert inactivity, which keeps Mr. Coolidge occupied constantly."

Coolidge had a strong belief in the Puritan work ethic: Work hard, save your money, keep your mouth shut and listen, and good things will happen to you. Known as "Silent Cal," his clean image seemed capable of cleaning up scandals left by Harding. Republicans—and the nation—now had a president who combined a preference for normalcy with the respectability and honesty that was absent from the Harding administration.

Coolidge's first term was devoted to eliminating the taint of scandal that Harding had brought to the White House. Domestically, Coolidge adhered to the creed: "The business of America is business." He stood in awe of Andrew Mellon and followed his fiscal policies, which made him the only president to turn a legitimate profit in the White House. Coolidge believed the rich were worthy of their property and that poverty was the wage of sin. Most importantly, Coolidge believed that since only the rich best understood their own interests, the government should let businessmen handle their own affairs with as little federal intervention as possible. Coolidge was quoted as saying, "The man who builds a factory builds a temple. The man who works there worships there."

Thus, silence and inactivity became the dominant characteristics of the Coolidge presidency. Coolidge's legendary reserve was famous in Washington society. Contemporaries told a possibly apocryphal story of how, at a dinner party at the White House, a woman bet her friends that she could get Coolidge to say more than three words. He looked at her and said, "you lose."

The 1924 election saw Coolidge win easily over the divided Democrats, who fought over their nomination. Southerners wanted to nominate pro-prohibition, pro-Klan, anti-immigrant candidate William G. McAdoo. The eastern establishment wanted Alfred E. Smith, a Catholic, urban, and anti-prohibition candidate. After many battles, they compromised on corporation lawyer John W. Davis. Midwesterner Robert M. La Follette, promoted by farmers, socialists, and labor unions, attempted to resurrect the Progressive Party. Coolidge easily beat both candidates.

THE ELECTION OF 1928

This cultural battle between the forces of reaction and rebellion appeared to culminate with the election of 1928, the height of Republican ascendancy. On August 2, 1927, Coolidge announced that he would not be participating in the 1928 election; "I choose not to run," was his comment (**Figure 3.21**). Republicans promoted the heir apparent, Secretary of Commerce Herbert Hoover. The Democrats nominated Governor Alfred E. Smith of New York. Smith represented everything that small-town, rural America hated: He was Irish, Catholic, anti-prohibition, and a big-city politician. He was very flamboyant and outspoken, which also did not go over well with many Americans.

Figure 3.21 In this cartoon, Clifford Berryman lampoons Coolidge's laid-back attitude as he chooses "not to run" in 1928.

Republican prosperity carried the day once again, and Hoover won easily with twenty-one million votes over Al Smith's fifteen million. The stock market continued to rise, and prosperity was the watchword of the day. Many Americans who had not done so before invested in the market, believing that the prosperous times would continue.

As Hoover came into office, Americans had every reason to believe that prosperity would continue forever. In less than a year, however, the bubble would burst, and a harsh reality would take its place.

CHAPTER 4

Brother, Can You Spare a Dime? The Great Depression, 1929-1932

Figure 4.1 In 1935, American photographer Berenice Abbott photographed these shanties, which the unemployed in Lower Manhattan built during the depths of the Great Depression. (credit: modification of work by Works Progress Administration)

Chapter Outline

4.1 The Stock Market Crash of 1929
4.2 President Hoover's Response
4.3 The Depths of the Great Depression
4.4 Assessing the Hoover Years on the Eve of the New Deal

Introduction

On March 4, 1929, at his presidential inauguration, Herbert Hoover stated, "I have no fears for the future of our country. It is bright with hope." Most Americans shared his optimism. They believed that the prosperity of the 1920s would continue, and that the country was moving closer to a land of abundance for all. Little could Hoover imagine that barely a year into his presidency, shantytowns known as "Hoovervilles" would emerge on the fringes of most major cities (**Figure 4.1**), newspapers covering the homeless would be called "Hoover blankets," and pants pockets, turned inside-out to show their emptiness, would become "Hoover flags."

The stock market crash of October 1929 set the Great Depression into motion, but other factors were at the root of the problem, propelled onward by a series of both human-made and natural catastrophes. Anticipating a short downturn and living under an ethos of free enterprise and individualism, Americans suffered mightily in the first years of the Depression. As conditions worsened and the government failed to act, they grew increasingly desperate for change. While Hoover could not be blamed for the Great Depression, his failure to address the nation's hardships would remain his legacy.

4.1 The Stock Market Crash of 1929

By the end of this section, you will be able to:
- Identify the causes of the stock market crash of 1929
- Assess the underlying weaknesses in the economy that resulted in America's spiraling from prosperity to depression so quickly
- Explain how a stock market crash might contribute to a nationwide economic disaster

Herbert Hoover became president at a time of ongoing prosperity in the country. Americans hoped he would continue to lead the country through still more economic growth, and neither he nor the country was ready for the unraveling that followed. But Hoover's moderate policies, based upon a strongly held belief in the spirit of American individualism, were not enough to stem the ever-growing problems, and the economy slipped further and further into the Great Depression.

While it is misleading to view the stock market crash of 1929 as the sole cause of the Great Depression, the dramatic events of that October did play a role in the downward spiral of the American economy. The crash, which took place less than a year after Hoover was inaugurated, was the most extreme sign of the economy's weakness. Multiple factors contributed to the crash, which in turn caused a consumer panic that drove the economy even further downhill, in ways that neither Hoover nor the financial industry was able to restrain. Hoover, like many others at the time, thought and hoped that the country would right itself with limited government intervention. This was not the case, however, and millions of Americans sank into grinding poverty.

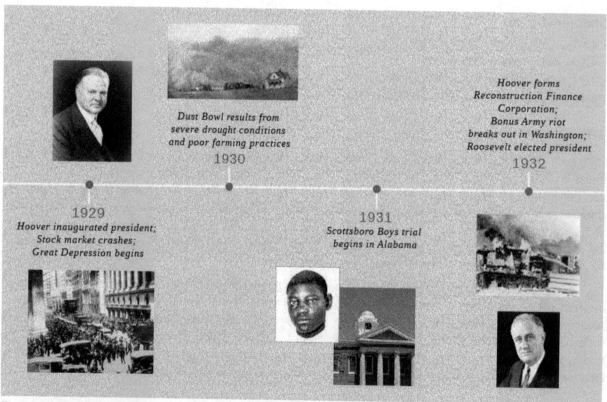

Figure 4.2 (credit "courthouse": modification of work by National Oceanic and Atmospheric Administration)

THE EARLY DAYS OF HOOVER'S PRESIDENCY

Upon his inauguration, President Hoover set forth an agenda that he hoped would continue the "Coolidge prosperity" of the previous administration. While accepting the Republican Party's presidential nomination in 1928, Hoover commented, "Given the chance to go forward with the policies of the last eight years, we shall soon with the help of God be in sight of the day when poverty will be banished from this nation forever." In the spirit of normalcy that defined the Republican ascendancy of the 1920s, Hoover planned to immediately overhaul federal regulations with the intention of allowing the nation's economy to grow unfettered by any controls. The role of the government, he contended, should be to create a partnership with the American people, in which the latter would rise (or fall) on their own merits and abilities. He felt the less government intervention in their lives, the better.

Yet, to listen to Hoover's later reflections on Franklin Roosevelt's first term in office, one could easily mistake his vision for America for the one held by his successor. Speaking in 1936 before an audience in Denver, Colorado, he acknowledged that it was always his intent as president to ensure "a nation built of home owners and farm owners. We want to see more and more of them insured against death and accident, unemployment and old age," he declared. "We want them all secure." [1] Such humanitarianism was not uncommon to Hoover. Throughout his early career in public service, he was committed to relief for people around the world. In 1900, he coordinated relief efforts for foreign nationals trapped in China during the Boxer Rebellion. At the outset of World War I, he led the food relief effort in Europe, specifically helping millions of Belgians who faced German forces. President Woodrow Wilson subsequently appointed him head of the U.S. Food Administration to coordinate rationing efforts in America as well as to secure essential food items for the Allied forces and citizens in Europe.

Hoover's first months in office hinted at the reformist, humanitarian spirit that he had displayed throughout his career. He continued the civil service reform of the early twentieth century by expanding opportunities for employment throughout the federal government. In response to the Teapot Dome Affair, which had occurred during the Harding administration, he invalidated several private oil leases on public lands. He directed the Department of Justice, through its Bureau of Investigation, to crack down on organized crime, resulting in the arrest and imprisonment of Al Capone. By the summer of 1929, he had signed into law the creation of a Federal Farm Board to help farmers with government price supports, expanded tax cuts across all income classes, and set aside federal funds to clean up slums in major American cities. To directly assist several overlooked populations, he created the Veterans Administration and expanded veterans' hospitals, established the Federal Bureau of Prisons to oversee incarceration conditions nationwide, and reorganized the Bureau of Indian Affairs to further protect Native Americans. Just prior to the stock market crash, he even proposed the creation of an old-age pension program, promising fifty dollars monthly to all Americans over the age of sixty-five—a proposal remarkably similar to the social security benefit that would become a hallmark of Roosevelt's subsequent New Deal programs. As the summer of 1929 came to a close, Hoover remained a popular successor to Calvin "Silent Cal" Coolidge, and all signs pointed to a highly successful administration.

THE GREAT CRASH

The promise of the Hoover administration was cut short when the stock market lost almost one-half its value in the fall of 1929, plunging many Americans into financial ruin. However, as a singular event, the stock market crash itself did not cause the Great Depression that followed. In fact, only approximately 10 percent of American households held stock investments and speculated in the market; yet nearly a third would lose their lifelong savings and jobs in the ensuing depression. The connection between the crash and the subsequent decade of hardship was complex, involving underlying weaknesses in the economy that many policymakers had long ignored.

---

1. Herbert Hoover, address delivered in Denver, Colorado, 30 October 1936, compiled in Hoover, *Addresses Upon the American Road, 1933-1938* (New York, 1938), p. 216. This particular quotation is frequently misidentified as part of Hoover's inaugural address in 1932.

What Was the Crash?

To understand the crash, it is useful to address the decade that preceded it. The prosperous 1920s ushered in a feeling of euphoria among middle-class and wealthy Americans, and people began to speculate on wilder investments. The government was a willing partner in this endeavor: The Federal Reserve followed a brief postwar recession in 1920–1921 with a policy of setting interest rates artificially low, as well as easing the reserve requirements on the nation's largest banks. As a result, the money supply in the U.S. increased by nearly 60 percent, which convinced even more Americans of the safety of investing in questionable schemes. They felt that prosperity was boundless and that extreme risks were likely tickets to wealth. Named for Charles Ponzi, the original "Ponzi schemes" emerged early in the 1920s to encourage novice investors to divert funds to unfounded ventures, which in reality simply used new investors' funds to pay off older investors as the schemes grew in size. **Speculation**, where investors purchased into high-risk schemes that they hoped would pay off quickly, became the norm. Several banks, including deposit institutions that originally avoided investment loans, began to offer easy credit, allowing people to invest, even when they lacked the money to do so. An example of this mindset was the Florida land boom of the 1920s: Real estate developers touted Florida as a tropical paradise and investors went all in, buying land they had never seen with money they didn't have and selling it for even higher prices.

AMERICANA

⊕ *Selling Optimism and Risk*

Advertising offers a useful window into the popular perceptions and beliefs of an era. By seeing how businesses were presenting their goods to consumers, it is possible to sense the hopes and aspirations of people at that moment in history. Maybe companies are selling patriotism or pride in technological advances. Maybe they are pushing idealized views of parenthood or safety. In the 1920s, advertisers were selling opportunity and euphoria, further feeding the notions of many Americans that prosperity would never end.

In the decade before the Great Depression, the optimism of the American public was seemingly boundless. Advertisements from that era show large new cars, timesaving labor devices, and, of course, land. This advertisement for California real estate illustrates how realtors in the West, much like the ongoing Florida land boom, used a combination of the hard sell and easy credit (Figure 4.3). "Buy now!!" the ad shouts. "You are sure to make money on these." In great numbers, people did. With easy access to credit and hard-pushing advertisements like this one, many felt that they could not afford to miss out on such an opportunity. Unfortunately, overspeculation in California and hurricanes along the Gulf Coast and in Florida conspired to burst this land bubble, and would-be millionaires were left with nothing but the ads that once pulled them in.

Figure 4.3 This real estate advertisement from Los Angeles illustrates the hard-sell techniques and easy credit offered to those who wished to buy in. Unfortunately, the opportunities being promoted with these techniques were of little value, and many lost their investments. (credit: "army.arch"/Flickr)

The Florida land boom went bust in 1925–1926. A combination of negative press about the speculative nature of the boom, IRS investigations into the questionable financial practices of several land brokers, and a railroad embargo that limited the delivery of construction supplies into the region significantly hampered investor interest. The subsequent Great Miami Hurricane of 1926 drove most land developers into outright bankruptcy. However, speculation continued throughout the decade, this time in the stock market. Buyers purchased stock "on margin"—buying for a small down payment with borrowed money, with the intention of quickly selling at a much higher price before the remaining payment came due— which worked well as long as prices continued to rise. Speculators were aided by retail stock brokerage firms, which catered to average investors anxious to play the market but lacking direct ties to investment banking houses or larger brokerage firms. When prices began to fluctuate in the summer of 1929, investors sought excuses to continue their speculation. When fluctuations turned to outright and steady losses, everyone started to sell. As September began to unfold, the Dow Jones Industrial Average peaked at a value of 381 points, or roughly ten times the stock market's value, at the start of the 1920s.

Several warning signs portended the impending crash but went unheeded by Americans still giddy over the potential fortunes that speculation might promise. A brief downturn in the market on September 18, 1929, raised questions among more-seasoned investment bankers, leading some to predict an end to high stock values, but did little to stem the tide of investment. Even the collapse of the London Stock Exchange on September 20 failed to fully curtail the optimism of American investors. However, when the New York Stock Exchange lost 11 percent of its value on October 24—often referred to as "Black Thursday"—key American investors sat up and took notice. In an effort to forestall a much-feared panic, leading banks, including Chase National, National City, J.P. Morgan, and others, conspired to purchase large amounts of blue chip stocks (including U.S. Steel) in order to keep the prices artificially high. Even that effort failed in the growing wave of stock sales. Nevertheless, Hoover delivered a radio address on Friday in which he assured the American people, "The fundamental business of the country . . . is on a sound and prosperous basis."

As newspapers across the country began to cover the story in earnest, investors anxiously awaited the start of the following week. When the Dow Jones Industrial Average lost another 13 percent of its value on Monday morning, many knew the end of stock market speculation was near. The evening before the infamous crash was ominous. Jonathan Leonard, a newspaper reporter who regularly covered the stock market beat, wrote of how Wall Street "lit up like a Christmas tree." Brokers and businessmen who feared the worst the next day crowded into restaurants and speakeasies (a place where alcoholic beverages were illegally sold). After a night of heavy drinking, they retreated to nearby hotels or flop-houses (cheap boarding houses), all of which were overbooked, and awaited sunrise. Children from nearby slums and tenement districts played stickball in the streets of the financial district, using wads of ticker tape for balls. Although they all awoke to newspapers filled with predictions of a financial turnaround, as well as technical reasons why the decline might be short-lived, the crash on Tuesday morning, October 29, caught few by surprise.

No one even heard the opening bell on Wall Street that day, as shouts of "Sell! Sell!" drowned it out. In the first three minutes alone, nearly three million shares of stock, accounting for $2 million of wealth, changed hands. The volume of Western Union telegrams tripled, and telephone lines could not meet the demand, as investors sought any means available to dump their stock immediately. Rumors spread of investors jumping from their office windows. Fistfights broke out on the trading floor, where one broker fainted from physical exhaustion. Stock trades happened at such a furious pace that runners had nowhere to store the trade slips, and so they resorted to stuffing them into trash cans. Although the stock exchange's board of governors briefly considered closing the exchange early, they subsequently chose to let the market run its course, lest the American public panic even further at the thought of closure. When the final bell rang, errand boys spent hours sweeping up tons of paper, tickertape, and sales slips. Among the more curious finds in the rubbish were torn suit coats, crumpled eyeglasses, and one broker's artificial leg. Outside a nearby brokerage house, a policeman allegedly found a discarded birdcage with a live parrot squawking, "More margin! More margin!"

On **Black Tuesday**, October 29, stock holders traded over sixteen million shares and lost over $14 billion in wealth in a single day. To put this in context, a trading day of three million shares was considered a busy day on the stock market. People unloaded their stock as quickly as they could, never minding the loss. Banks, facing debt and seeking to protect their own assets, demanded payment for the loans they had provided to individual investors. Those individuals who could not afford to pay found their stocks sold immediately and their life savings wiped out in minutes, yet their debt to the bank still remained (**Figure 4.4**).

Figure 4.4 October 29, 1929, or Black Tuesday, witnessed thousands of people racing to Wall Street discount brokerages and markets to sell their stocks. Prices plummeted throughout the day, eventually leading to a complete stock market crash.

The financial outcome of the crash was devastating. Between September 1 and November 30, 1929, the stock market lost over one-half its value, dropping from $64 billion to approximately $30 billion. Any effort to stem the tide was, as one historian noted, tantamount to bailing Niagara Falls with a bucket. The crash affected many more than the relatively few Americans who invested in the stock market. While only 10 percent of households had investments, over 90 percent of all banks had invested in the stock market. Many banks failed due to their dwindling cash reserves. This was in part due to the Federal Reserve lowering the limits of cash reserves that banks were traditionally required to hold in their vaults, as well as the fact that many banks invested in the stock market themselves. Eventually, thousands of banks closed their doors after losing all of their assets, leaving their customers penniless. While a few savvy investors got out at the right time and eventually made fortunes buying up discarded stock, those success stories were rare. Housewives who speculated with grocery money, bookkeepers who embezzled company funds hoping to strike it rich and pay the funds back before getting caught, and bankers who used customer deposits to follow speculative trends all lost. While the stock market crash was the trigger, the lack of appropriate economic and banking safeguards, along with a public psyche that pursued wealth and prosperity at all costs, allowed this event to spiral downward into a depression.

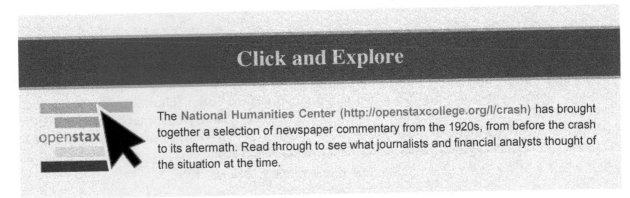

Click and Explore

The **National Humanities Center** (http://openstaxcollege.org/l/crash) has brought together a selection of newspaper commentary from the 1920s, from before the crash to its aftermath. Read through to see what journalists and financial analysts thought of the situation at the time.

Causes of the Crash

The crash of 1929 did not occur in a vacuum, nor did it cause the Great Depression. Rather, it was a tipping point where the underlying weaknesses in the economy, specifically in the nation's banking system, came to the fore. It also represented both the end of an era characterized by blind faith in American exceptionalism and the beginning of one in which citizens began increasingly to question some long-held American values. A number of factors played a role in bringing the stock market to this point and contributed to the downward trend in the market, which continued well into the 1930s. In addition to the Federal Reserve's questionable policies and misguided banking practices, three primary reasons for the collapse of the stock market were international economic woes, poor income distribution, and the psychology of public confidence.

After World War I, both America's allies and the defeated nations of Germany and Austria contended with disastrous economies. The Allies owed large amounts of money to U.S. banks, which had advanced them money during the war effort. Unable to repay these debts, the Allies looked to reparations from Germany and Austria to help. The economies of those countries, however, were struggling badly, and they could not pay their reparations, despite the loans that the U.S. provided to assist with their payments. The U.S. government refused to forgive these loans, and American banks were in the position of extending additional private loans to foreign governments, who used them to repay their debts to the U.S. government, essentially shifting their obligations to private banks. When other countries began to default on this second wave of private bank loans, still more strain was placed on U.S. banks, which soon sought to liquidate these loans at the first sign of a stock market crisis.

Poor income distribution among Americans compounded the problem. A strong stock market relies on today's buyers becoming tomorrow's sellers, and therefore it must always have an influx of new buyers. In the 1920s, this was not the case. Eighty percent of American families had virtually no savings, and only one-half to 1 percent of Americans controlled over a third of the wealth. This scenario meant that there were no new buyers coming into the marketplace, and nowhere for sellers to unload their stock as the speculation came to a close. In addition, the vast majority of Americans with limited savings lost their accounts as local banks closed, and likewise lost their jobs as investment in business and industry came to a screeching halt.

Finally, one of the most important factors in the crash was the contagion effect of panic. For much of the 1920s, the public felt confident that prosperity would continue forever, and therefore, in a self-fulfilling cycle, the market continued to grow. But once the panic began, it spread quickly and with the same cyclical results; people were worried that the market was going down, they sold their stock, and the market continued to drop. This was partly due to Americans' inability to weather market volatility, given the limited cash surpluses they had on hand, as well as their psychological concern that economic recovery might never happen.

IN THE AFTERMATH OF THE CRASH

After the crash, Hoover announced that the economy was "fundamentally sound." On the last day of trading in 1929, the New York Stock Exchange held its annual wild and lavish party, complete with confetti, musicians, and illegal alcohol. The U.S. Department of Labor predicted that 1930 would be "a splendid employment year." These sentiments were not as baseless as it may seem in hindsight. Historically, markets cycled up and down, and periods of growth were often followed by downturns that corrected themselves. But this time, there was no market correction; rather, the abrupt shock of the crash was followed by an even more devastating depression. Investors, along with the general public, withdrew their money from banks by the thousands, fearing the banks would go under. The more people pulled out their money in **bank runs**, the closer the banks came to insolvency (**Figure 4.5**).

Figure 4.5 As the financial markets collapsed, hurting the banks that had gambled with their holdings, people began to fear that the money they had in the bank would be lost. This began bank runs across the country, a period of still more panic, where people pulled their money out of banks to keep it hidden at home.

The contagion effect of the crash grew quickly. With investors losing billions of dollars, they invested very little in new or expanded businesses. At this time, two industries had the greatest impact on the country's economic future in terms of investment, potential growth, and employment: automotive and construction. After the crash, both were hit hard. In November 1929, fewer cars were built than in any other month since November 1919. Even before the crash, widespread saturation of the market meant that few Americans bought them, leading to a slowdown. Afterward, very few could afford them. By 1933, Stutz, Locomobile, Durant, Franklin, Deusenberg, and Pierce-Arrow automobiles, all luxury models, were largely unavailable; production had ground to a halt. They would not be made again until 1949. In construction, the drop-off was even more dramatic. It would be another thirty years before a new hotel or theater was built in New York City. The Empire State Building itself stood half empty for years after being completed in 1931.

The damage to major industries led to, and reflected, limited purchasing by both consumers and businesses. Even those Americans who continued to make a modest income during the Great Depression lost the drive for conspicuous consumption that they exhibited in the 1920s. People with less money to buy goods could not help businesses grow; in turn, businesses with no market for their products could not hire workers or purchase raw materials. Employers began to lay off workers. The country's gross national product declined by over 25 percent within a year, and wages and salaries declined by $4 billion. Unemployment tripled, from 1.5 million at the end of 1929 to 4.5 million by the end of 1930. By mid-1930, the slide into economic chaos had begun but was nowhere near complete.

THE NEW REALITY FOR AMERICANS

For most Americans, the crash affected daily life in myriad ways. In the immediate aftermath, there was a run on the banks, where citizens took their money out, if they could get it, and hid their savings under mattresses, in bookshelves, or anywhere else they felt was safe. Some went so far as to exchange their dollars for gold and ship it out of the country. A number of banks failed outright, and others, in their attempts to stay solvent, called in loans that people could not afford to repay. Working-class Americans saw their wages drop: Even Henry Ford, the champion of a high minimum wage, began lowering wages by as much as a dollar a day. Southern cotton planters paid workers only twenty cents for every one hundred pounds of cotton picked, meaning that the *strongest* picker might earn sixty cents for a fourteen-hour day of work. Cities struggled to collect property taxes and subsequently laid off teachers and police.

The new hardships that people faced were not always immediately apparent; many communities felt the changes but could not necessarily look out their windows and see anything different. Men who lost their jobs didn't stand on street corners begging; they disappeared. They might be found keeping warm by a trashcan bonfire or picking through garbage at dawn, but mostly, they stayed out of public view. As the effects of the crash continued, however, the results became more evident. Those living in cities grew accustomed to seeing long breadlines of unemployed men waiting for a meal (**Figure 4.6**). Companies fired workers and tore down employee housing to avoid paying property taxes. The landscape of the country had changed.

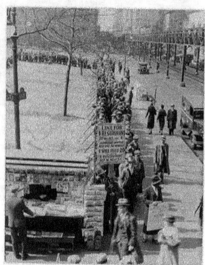

Figure 4.6 As the Great Depression set in, thousands of unemployed men lined up in cities around the country, waiting for a free meal or a hot cup of coffee.

The hardships of the Great Depression threw family life into disarray. Both marriage and birth rates declined in the decade after the crash. The most vulnerable members of society—children, women, minorities, and the working class—struggled the most. Parents often sent children out to beg for food at restaurants and stores to save themselves from the disgrace of begging. Many children dropped out of school, and even fewer went to college. Childhood, as it had existed in the prosperous twenties, was over. And yet, for many children living in rural areas where the affluence of the previous decade was not fully developed, the Depression was not viewed as a great challenge. School continued. Play was simple and enjoyed. Families adapted by growing more in gardens, canning, and preserving, wasting little food if any. Home-sewn clothing became the norm as the decade progressed, as did creative methods of shoe repair with cardboard soles. Yet, one always knew of stories of the "other" families who suffered more, including those living in cardboard boxes or caves. By one estimate, as many as 200,000 children moved about the country as vagrants due to familial disintegration.

Women's lives, too, were profoundly affected. Some wives and mothers sought employment to make ends meet, an undertaking that was often met with strong resistance from husbands and potential employers. Many men derided and criticized women who worked, feeling that jobs should go to unemployed men. Some campaigned to keep companies from hiring married women, and an increasing number of school districts expanded the long-held practice of banning the hiring of married female teachers. Despite the pushback, women entered the workforce in increasing numbers, from ten million at the start of the Depression to nearly thirteen million by the end of the 1930s. This increase took place in spite of the twenty-six states that passed a variety of laws to prohibit the employment of married women. Several women found employment in the emerging pink collar occupations, viewed as traditional women's work, including jobs as telephone operators, social workers, and secretaries. Others took jobs as maids and housecleaners, working for those fortunate few who had maintained their wealth.

White women's forays into domestic service came at the expense of minority women, who had even fewer employment options. Unsurprisingly, African American men and women experienced unemployment, and the grinding poverty that followed, at double and triple the rates of their white counterparts. By 1932, unemployment among African Americans reached near 50 percent. In rural areas, where large numbers of African Americans continued to live despite the Great Migration of 1910–1930, depression-era life represented an intensified version of the poverty that they traditionally experienced. Subsistence farming allowed many African Americans who lost either their land or jobs working for white landholders to survive, but their hardships increased. Life for African Americans in urban settings was equally trying, with blacks and working-class whites living in close proximity and competing for scarce jobs and resources.

Life for all rural Americans was difficult. Farmers largely did not experience the widespread prosperity of the 1920s. Although continued advancements in farming techniques and agricultural machinery led to increased agricultural production, decreasing demand (particularly in the previous markets created by World War I) steadily drove down commodity prices. As a result, farmers could barely pay the debt they owed on machinery and land mortgages, and even then could do so only as a result of generous lines of credit from banks. While factory workers may have lost their jobs and savings in the crash, many farmers also lost their homes, due to the thousands of farm foreclosures sought by desperate bankers. Between 1930 and 1935, nearly 750,000 family farms disappeared through foreclosure or bankruptcy. Even for those who managed to keep their farms, there was little market for their crops. Unemployed workers had less money to spend on food, and when they did purchase goods, the market excess had driven prices so low that farmers could barely piece together a living. A now-famous example of the farmer's plight is that, when the price of coal began to exceed that of corn, farmers would simply burn corn to stay warm in the winter.

As the effects of the Great Depression worsened, wealthier Americans had particular concern for "the deserving poor"—those who had lost all of their money due to no fault of their own. This concept gained greater attention beginning in the Progressive Era of the late nineteenth and early twentieth centuries, when early social reformers sought to improve the quality of life for all Americans by addressing the poverty that was becoming more prevalent, particularly in emerging urban areas. By the time of the Great Depression, social reformers and humanitarian agencies had determined that the "deserving poor" belonged to a different category from those who had speculated and lost. However, the sheer volume of Americans who fell into this group meant that charitable assistance could not begin to reach them all. Some fifteen million "deserving poor," or a full one-third of the labor force, were struggling by 1932. The country had no mechanism or system in place to help so many; however, Hoover remained adamant that such relief should rest in the hands of private agencies, not with the federal government (**Figure 4.7**).

Figure 4.7 In the early 1930s, without significant government relief programs, many people in urban centers relied on private agencies for assistance. In New York City, St. Peter's Mission distributed bread, soup, and canned goods to large numbers of the unemployed and others in need.

Unable to receive aid from the government, Americans thus turned to private charities; churches, synagogues, and other religious organizations; and state aid. But these organizations were not prepared to deal with the scope of the problem. Private aid organizations showed declining assets as well during the Depression, with fewer Americans possessing the ability to donate to such charities. Likewise, state governments were particularly ill-equipped. Governor Franklin D. Roosevelt was the first to institute a Department of Welfare in New York in 1929. City governments had equally little to offer. In New York City in 1932, family allowances were $2.39 per week, and only one-half of the families who qualified actually received them. In Detroit, allowances fell to fifteen cents a day per person, and eventually ran out completely. In most cases, relief was only in the form of food and fuel; organizations provided nothing in the way of rent, shelter, medical care, clothing, or other necessities. There was no infrastructure to support the elderly, who were the most vulnerable, and this population largely depended on their adult children to support them, adding to families' burdens (**Figure 4.8**).

Figure 4.8 Because there was no infrastructure to support them should they become unemployed or destitute, the elderly were extremely vulnerable during the Great Depression. As the depression continued, the results of this tenuous situation became more evident, as shown in this photo of a vacant storefront in San Francisco, captured by Dorothea Lange in 1935.

During this time, local community groups, such as police and teachers, worked to help the neediest. New York City police, for example, began contributing 1 percent of their salaries to start a food fund that was geared to help those found starving on the streets. In 1932, New York City schoolteachers also joined forces to try to help; they contributed as much as $250,000 per month from their own salaries to help needy children. Chicago teachers did the same, feeding some eleven thousand students out of their own pockets in 1931, despite the fact that many of them had not been paid a salary in months. These noble efforts, however, failed to fully address the level of desperation that the American public was facing.

4.2 President Hoover's Response

By the end of this section, you will be able to:
- Explain Herbert Hoover's responses to the Great Depression and how they reflected his political philosophy
- Identify the local, city, and state efforts to combat the Great Depression
- Analyze the frustration and anger that a majority of Americans directed at Herbert Hoover

President Hoover was unprepared for the scope of the depression crisis, and his limited response did not begin to help the millions of Americans in need. The steps he took were very much in keeping with his philosophy of limited government, a philosophy that many had shared with him until the upheavals of the Great Depression made it clear that a more direct government response was required. But Hoover was stubborn in his refusal to give "handouts," as he saw direct government aid. He called for a spirit of volunteerism among America's businesses, asking them to keep workers employed, and he exhorted the American people to tighten their belts and make do in the spirit of "rugged individualism." While Hoover's philosophy and his appeal to the country were very much in keeping with his character, it was not enough to keep the economy from plummeting further into economic chaos.

The steps Hoover did ultimately take were too little, too late. He created programs for putting people back to work and helping beleaguered local and state charities with aid. But the programs were small in scale and highly specific as to who could benefit, and they only touched a small percentage of those in need. As the situation worsened, the public grew increasingly unhappy with Hoover. He left office with one of the lowest approval ratings of any president in history.

THE INITIAL REACTION

In the immediate aftermath of Black Tuesday, Hoover sought to reassure Americans that all was well. Reading his words after the fact, it is easy to find fault. In 1929 he said, "Any lack of confidence in the economic future or the strength of business in the United States is foolish." In 1930, he stated, "The worst is behind us." In 1931, he pledged federal aid should he ever witness starvation in the country; but as of that date, he had yet to see such need in America, despite the very real evidence that children and the elderly were starving to death. Yet Hoover was neither intentionally blind nor unsympathetic. He simply held fast to a belief system that did not change as the realities of the Great Depression set in.

Hoover believed strongly in the ethos of **American individualism**: that hard work brought its own rewards. His life story testified to that belief. Hoover was born into poverty, made his way through college at Stanford University, and eventually made his fortune as an engineer. This experience, as well as his extensive travels in China and throughout Europe, shaped his fundamental conviction that the very existence of American civilization depended upon the moral fiber of its citizens, as evidenced by their ability to overcome all hardships through individual effort and resolve. The idea of government handouts to Americans was repellant to him. Whereas Europeans might need assistance, such as his hunger relief work in Belgium during and after World War I, he believed the American character to be different. In a 1931 radio address, he said, "The spread of government destroys initiative and thus destroys character."

Likewise, Hoover was not completely unaware of the potential harm that wild stock speculation might create if left unchecked. As secretary of commerce, Hoover often warned President Coolidge of the dangers that such speculation engendered. In the weeks before his inauguration, he offered many interviews to newspapers and magazines, urging Americans to curtail their rampant stock investments, and even encouraged the Federal Reserve to raise the discount rate to make it more costly for local banks to lend money to potential speculators. However, fearful of creating a panic, Hoover never issued a stern warning to discourage Americans from such investments. Neither Hoover, nor any other politician of that day, ever gave serious thought to outright government regulation of the stock market. This was even true in his personal choices, as Hoover often lamented poor stock advice he had once offered to a friend. When the stock nose-dived, Hoover bought the shares from his friend to assuage his guilt, vowing never again to advise anyone on matters of investment.

In keeping with these principles, Hoover's response to the crash focused on two very common American traditions: He asked individuals to tighten their belts and work harder, and he asked the business community to voluntarily help sustain the economy by retaining workers and continuing production. He immediately summoned a conference of leading industrialists to meet in Washington, DC, urging them to maintain their current wages while America rode out this brief economic panic. The crash, he assured business leaders, was not part of a greater downturn; they had nothing to worry about. Similar meetings with utility companies and railroad executives elicited promises for billions of dollars in new construction projects, while labor leaders agreed to withhold demands for wage increases and workers continued to labor. Hoover also persuaded Congress to pass a $160 million tax cut to bolster American incomes, leading many to conclude that the president was doing all he could to stem the tide of the panic. In April 1930, the *New York Times* editorial board concluded that "No one in his place could have done more."

However, these modest steps were not enough. By late 1931, when it became clear that the economy would not improve on its own, Hoover recognized the need for some government intervention. He created the President's Emergency Committee for Employment (PECE), later renamed the President's Organization of Unemployment Relief (POUR). In keeping with Hoover's distaste of what he viewed as handouts, this organization did *not* provide direct federal relief to people in need. Instead, it assisted state and private relief agencies, such as the Red Cross, Salvation Army, YMCA, and Community Chest. Hoover also strongly urged people of means to donate funds to help the poor, and he himself gave significant private donations to worthy causes. But these private efforts could not alleviate the widespread effects of poverty.

Congress pushed for a more direct government response to the hardship. In 1930–1931, it attempted to pass a $60 million bill to provide relief to drought victims by allowing them access to food, fertilizer, and animal feed. Hoover stood fast in his refusal to provide food, resisting any element of direct relief. The final bill of $47 million provided for everything *except* food but did not come close to adequately addressing the crisis. Again in 1931, Congress proposed the Federal Emergency Relief Bill, which would have provided $375 million to states to help provide food, clothing, and shelter to the homeless. But Hoover opposed the bill, stating that it ruined the balance of power between states and the federal government, and in February 1932, it was defeated by fourteen votes.

However, the president's adamant opposition to direct-relief federal government programs should not be viewed as one of indifference or uncaring toward the suffering American people. His personal sympathy for those in need was boundless. Hoover was one of only two presidents to reject his salary for the office he held. Throughout the Great Depression, he donated an average of $25,000 annually to various relief organizations to assist in their efforts. Furthermore, he helped to raise $500,000 in private funds to support the White House Conference on Child Health and Welfare in 1930. Rather than indifference or heartlessness, Hoover's steadfast adherence to a philosophy of individualism as the path toward long-term American recovery explained many of his policy decisions. "A voluntary deed," he repeatedly commented, "is infinitely more precious to our national ideal and spirit than a thousand-fold poured from the Treasury."

As conditions worsened, however, Hoover eventually relaxed his opposition to federal relief and formed the Reconstruction Finance Corporation (RFC) in 1932, in part because it was an election year and Hoover hoped to keep his office. Although not a form of direct relief to the American people in greatest need, the RFC was much larger in scope than any preceding effort, setting aside $2 billion in taxpayer money to rescue banks, credit unions, and insurance companies. The goal was to boost confidence in the nation's financial institutions by ensuring that they were on solid footing. This model was flawed on a number of levels. First, the program only lent money to banks with sufficient collateral, which meant that most of the aid went to large banks. In fact, of the first $61 million loaned, $41 million went to just three banks. Small town and rural banks got almost nothing. Furthermore, at this time, confidence in financial institutions was not the primary concern of most Americans. They needed food and jobs. Many had no money to put into the banks, no matter how confident they were that the banks were safe.

Hoover's other attempt at federal assistance also occurred in 1932, when he endorsed a bill by Senator Robert Wagner of New York. This was the Emergency Relief and Construction Act. This act authorized the RFC to expand beyond loans to financial institutions and allotted $1.5 billion to states to fund local public works projects. This program failed to deliver the kind of help needed, however, as Hoover severely limited the types of projects it could fund to those that were ultimately self-paying (such as toll bridges and public housing) and those that required skilled workers. While well intended, these programs maintained the status quo, and there was still no direct federal relief to the individuals who so desperately needed it.

PUBLIC REACTION TO HOOVER

Hoover's steadfast resistance to government aid cost him the reelection and has placed him squarely at the forefront of the most unpopular presidents, according to public opinion, in modern American history. His name became synonymous with the poverty of the era: "Hoovervilles" became the common name for homeless shantytowns (**Figure 4.9**) and "Hoover blankets" for the newspapers that the homeless used to keep warm. A "Hoover flag" was a pants pocket—empty of all money—turned inside out. By the 1932 election, hitchhikers held up signs reading: "If you don't give me a ride, I'll vote for Hoover." Americans did not necessarily believe that Hoover caused the Great Depression. Their anger stemmed instead from what appeared to be a willful refusal to help regular citizens with direct aid that might allow them to recover from the crisis.

(a)   (b)

Figure 4.9 Hoover became one of the least popular presidents in history. "Hoovervilles," or shantytowns, were a negative reminder of his role in the nation's financial crisis. This family (a) lived in a "Hooverville" in Elm Grove, Oklahoma. This shanty (b) was one of many making up a "Hooverville" in the Portland, Oregon area. (credit: modification of work by United States Farm Security Administration)

FRUSTRATION AND PROTEST: A BAD SITUATION GROWS WORSE FOR HOOVER

Desperation and frustration often create emotional responses, and the Great Depression was no exception. Throughout 1931–1932, companies trying to stay afloat sharply cut worker wages, and, in response, workers protested in increasingly bitter strikes. As the Depression unfolded, over 80 percent of automotive workers lost their jobs. Even the typically prosperous Ford Motor Company laid off two-thirds of its workforce.

In 1932, a major strike at the Ford Motor Company factory near Detroit resulted in over sixty injuries and four deaths. Often referred to as the Ford Hunger March, the event unfolded as a planned demonstration among unemployed Ford workers who, to protest their desperate situation, marched nine miles from Detroit to the company's River Rouge plant in Dearborn. At the Dearborn city limits, local police launched tear gas at the roughly three thousand protestors, who responded by throwing stones and clods of dirt. When they finally reached the gates of the plant, protestors faced more police and firemen, as well as private security guards. As the firemen turned hoses onto the protestors, the police and security guards opened fire. In addition to those killed and injured, police arrested fifty protestors. One week later, sixty thousand mourners attended the public funerals of the four victims of what many protesters labeled police brutality. The event set the tone for worsening labor relations in the U.S.

Farmers also organized and protested, often violently. The most notable example was the Farm Holiday Association. Led by Milo Reno, this organization held significant sway among farmers in Iowa, Nebraska, Wisconsin, Minnesota, and the Dakotas. Although they never comprised a majority of farmers in any of these states, their public actions drew press attention nationwide. Among their demands, the association sought a federal government plan to set agricultural prices artificially high enough to cover the farmers' costs, as well as a government commitment to sell any farm surpluses on the world market. To achieve their goals, the group called for farm holidays, during which farmers would neither sell their produce nor purchase any other goods until the government met their demands. However, the greatest strength of the association came from the unexpected and seldom-planned actions of its members, which included barricading roads into markets, attacking nonmember farmers, and destroying their produce. Some members even raided small town stores, destroying produce on the shelves. Members also engaged in "penny auctions," bidding pennies on foreclosed farm land and threatening any potential buyers with bodily harm if they competed in the sale. Once they won the auction, the association returned the land to the original owner. In Iowa, farmers threatened to hang a local judge if he signed any more farm foreclosures. At least one death occurred as a direct result of these protests before they waned following the election of Franklin Roosevelt.

One of the most notable protest movements occurred toward the end of Hoover's presidency and centered on the Bonus Expeditionary Force, or **Bonus Army**, in the spring of 1932. In this protest, approximately fifteen thousand World War I veterans marched on Washington to demand early payment of their veteran bonuses, which were not due to be paid until 1945. The group camped out in vacant federal buildings and set up camps in Anacostia Flats near the Capitol building (**Figure 4.10**).

Figure 4.10 In the spring of 1932, World War I veterans marched on Washington and set up camps in Anacostia Flats, remaining there for weeks. (credit: Library of Congress)

Many veterans remained in the city in protest for nearly two months, although the U.S. Senate officially rejected their request in July. By the middle of that month, Hoover wanted them gone. He ordered the police to empty the buildings and clear out the camps, and in the exchange that followed, police fired into the crowd, killing two veterans. Fearing an armed uprising, Hoover then ordered General Douglas MacArthur, along with his aides, Dwight Eisenhower and George Patton, to forcibly remove the veterans from Anacostia Flats. The ensuing raid proved catastrophic, as the military burned down the shantytown and injured dozens of people, including a twelve-week-old infant who was killed when accidentally struck by a tear gas canister (**Figure 4.11**).

Figure 4.11 When the U.S. Senate denied early payment of their veteran bonuses, and Hoover ordered their makeshift camps cleared, the Bonus Army protest turned violent, cementing Hoover's demise as a president. (credit: U.S. Department of Defense)

As Americans bore witness to photographs and newsreels of the U.S. Army forcibly removing veterans, Hoover's popularity plummeted even further. By the summer of 1932, he was largely a defeated man. His pessimism and failure mirrored that of the nation's citizens. America was a country in desperate need: in need of a charismatic leader to restore public confidence as well as provide concrete solutions to pull the economy out of the Great Depression.

Click and Explore

Whether he truly believed it or simply thought the American people wanted to hear it, Hoover continued to state publicly that the country was getting back on track. Listen as he speaks about the "Success of Recovery" (http://openstaxcollege.org/l/recovery) at a campaign stop in Detroit, Michigan on October 22, 1932.

4.3 The Depths of the Great Depression

By the end of this section, you will be able to:
- Identify the challenges that everyday Americans faced as a result of the Great Depression and analyze the government's initial unwillingness to provide assistance
- Explain the particular challenges that African Americans faced during the crisis
- Identify the unique challenges that farmers in the Great Plains faced during this period

From industrial strongholds to the rural Great Plains, from factory workers to farmers, the Great Depression affected millions. In cities, as industry slowed, then sometimes stopped altogether, workers lost jobs and joined breadlines, or sought out other charitable efforts. With limited government relief efforts, private charities tried to help, but they were unable to match the pace of demand. In rural areas, farmers suffered still more. In some parts of the country, prices for crops dropped so precipitously that farmers could not earn enough to pay their mortgages, losing their farms to foreclosure. In the Great Plains, one of the worst droughts in history left the land barren and unfit for growing even minimal food to live on.

The country's most vulnerable populations, such as children, the elderly, and those subject to discrimination, like African Americans, were the hardest hit. Most white Americans felt entitled to what few jobs were available, leaving African Americans unable to find work, even in the jobs once considered their domain. In all, the economic misery was unprecedented in the country's history.

STARVING TO DEATH

By the end of 1932, the Great Depression had affected some sixty million people, most of whom wealthier Americans perceived as the "deserving poor." Yet, at the time, federal efforts to help those in need were extremely limited, and national charities had neither the capacity nor the will to elicit the large-scale response required to address the problem. The American Red Cross did exist, but Chairman John Barton Payne contended that unemployment was not an "Act of God" but rather an "Act of Man," and therefore refused to get involved in widespread direct relief efforts. Clubs like the Elks tried to provide food, as did small groups of individually organized college students. Religious organizations remained on the front lines, offering food and shelter. In larger cities, breadlines and soup lines became a common sight. At one count in 1932, there were as many as eighty-two breadlines in New York City.

Despite these efforts, however, people were destitute and ultimately starving. Families would first run through any savings, if they were lucky enough to have any. Then, the few who had insurance would cash out their policies. Cash surrender payments of individual insurance policies tripled in the first three years of the Great Depression, with insurance companies issuing total payments in excess of $1.2 billion in 1932 alone. When those funds were depleted, people would borrow from family and friends, and when they could get no more, they would simply stop paying rent or mortgage payments. When evicted, they would move in with relatives, whose own situation was likely only a step or two behind. The added burden of additional people would speed along that family's demise, and the cycle would continue. This situation spiraled downward, and did so quickly. Even as late as 1939, over 60 percent of rural households, and 82 percent of farm families, were classified as "impoverished." In larger urban areas, unemployment levels exceeded the national average, with over half a million unemployed workers in Chicago, and nearly a million in New York City. Breadlines and soup kitchens were packed, serving as many as eighty-five thousand meals daily in New York City alone. Over fifty thousand New York citizens were homeless by the end of 1932.

Children, in particular, felt the brunt of poverty. Many in coastal cities would roam the docks in search of spoiled vegetables to bring home. Elsewhere, children begged at the doors of more well-off neighbors, hoping for stale bread, table scraps, or raw potato peelings. Said one childhood survivor of the Great Depression, "You get used to hunger. After the first few days it doesn't even hurt; you just get weak." In 1931 alone, there were at least twenty documented cases of starvation; in 1934, that number grew to 110. In rural areas where such documentation was lacking, the number was likely far higher. And while the middle class did not suffer from starvation, they experienced hunger as well.

By the time Hoover left office in 1933, the poor survived not on relief efforts, but because they had learned to be poor. A family with little food would stay in bed to save fuel and avoid burning calories. People began eating parts of animals that had normally been considered waste. They scavenged for scrap wood to burn in the furnace, and when electricity was turned off, it was not uncommon to try and tap into a neighbor's wire. Family members swapped clothes; sisters might take turns going to church in the one dress they owned. As one girl in a mountain town told her teacher, who had said to go home and get food, "I can't. It's my sister's turn to eat."

Click and Explore

For his book on the Great Depression, *Hard Times*, author Studs Terkel interviewed hundreds of Americans from across the country. He subsequently selected over seventy interviews to air on a radio show that was based in Chicago. Visit Studs **Terkel: Conversations with America (http://openstaxcollege.org/l/hardtimes)** to listen to those interviews, during which participants reflect on their personal hardships as well as on national events during the Great Depression.

BLACK AND POOR: AFRICAN AMERICANS AND THE GREAT DEPRESSION

Most African Americans did not participate in the land boom and stock market speculation that preceded the crash, but that did not stop the effects of the Great Depression from hitting them particularly hard. Subject to continuing racial discrimination, blacks nationwide fared even worse than their hard-hit white counterparts. As the prices for cotton and other agricultural products plummeted, farm owners paid workers less or simply laid them off. Landlords evicted sharecroppers, and even those who owned their land outright had to abandon it when there was no way to earn any income.

In cities, African Americans fared no better. Unemployment was rampant, and many whites felt that any available jobs belonged to whites first. In some Northern cities, whites would conspire to have African American workers fired to allow white workers access to their jobs. Even jobs traditionally held by black workers, such as household servants or janitors, were now going to whites. By 1932, approximately one-half of all black Americans were unemployed. Racial violence also began to rise. In the South, lynching became more common again, with twenty-eight documented lynchings in 1933, compared to eight in 1932. Since communities were preoccupied with their own hardships, and organizing civil rights efforts was a long, difficult process, many resigned themselves to, or even ignored, this culture of racism and violence. Occasionally, however, an incident was notorious enough to gain national attention.

One such incident was the case of the **Scottsboro Boys (Figure 4.12)**. In 1931, nine black boys, who had been riding the rails, were arrested for vagrancy and disorderly conduct after an altercation with some white travelers on the train. Two young white women, who had been dressed as boys and traveling with a group of white boys, came forward and said that the black boys had raped them. The case, which was tried in Scottsboro, Alabama, reignited decades of racial hatred and illustrated the injustice of the court system. Despite significant evidence that the women had not been raped at all, along with one of the women subsequently recanting her testimony, the all-white jury quickly convicted the boys and sentenced all but one of them to death. The verdict broke through the veil of indifference toward the plight of African Americans, and protests erupted among newspaper editors, academics, and social reformers in the North. The Communist Party of the United States offered to handle the case and sought retrial; the NAACP later joined in this effort. In all, the case was tried three separate times. The series of trials and retrials, appeals, and overturned convictions shone a spotlight on a system that provided poor legal counsel and relied on all-white juries. In October 1932, the U.S. Supreme Court agreed with the Communist Party's defense attorneys that the defendants had been denied adequate legal representation at the original trial, and that due process as provided by the Fourteenth Amendment had been denied as a result of the exclusion of any potential black jurors. Eventually, most of the accused received lengthy prison terms and subsequent parole, but avoided the death penalty. The Scottsboro case ultimately laid some of the early groundwork for the modern American civil rights movement. Alabama granted posthumous pardons to all defendants in 2013.

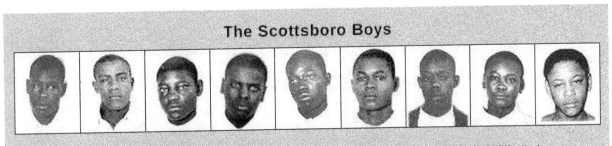

The Scottsboro Boys

Left to right: Clarence Norris, Charlie Weems, Haywood Patterson, Ozie Powell, Willie Roberson, Eugene Williams, Olen Montgomery, Andy Wright, Roy Wright

Figure 4.12 The trial and conviction of nine African American boys in Scottsboro, Alabama, illustrated the numerous injustices of the American court system. Despite being falsely accused, the boys received lengthy prison terms and were not officially pardoned by the State of Alabama until 2013.

Click and Explore

Read **Voices from Scottsboro** (http://openstaxcollege.org/l/scottsboro) for the perspectives of both participants and spectators in the Scottsboro case, from the initial trial to the moment, in 1976, when one of the women sued for slander.

ENVIRONMENTAL CATASTROPHE MEETS ECONOMIC HARDSHIP: THE DUST BOWL

Despite the widely held belief that rural Americans suffered less in the Great Depression due to their ability to at least grow their own food, this was not the case. Farmers, ranchers, and their families suffered more than any group other than African Americans during the Depression.

From the turn of the century through much of World War I, farmers in the Great Plains experienced prosperity due to unusually good growing conditions, high commodity prices, and generous government farming policies that led to a rush for land. As the federal government continued to purchase all excess produce for the war effort, farmers and ranchers fell into several bad practices, including mortgaging their farms and borrowing money against future production in order to expand. However, after the war, prosperity rapidly dwindled, particularly during the recession of 1921. Seeking to recoup their losses through economies of scale in which they would expand their production even further to take full advantage of their available land and machinery, farmers plowed under native grasses to plant acre after acre of wheat, with little regard for the long-term repercussions to the soil. Regardless of these misguided efforts, commodity prices continued to drop, finally plummeting in 1929, when the price of wheat dropped from two dollars to forty cents per bushel.

Exacerbating the problem was a massive drought that began in 1931 and lasted for eight terrible years. Dust storms roiled through the Great Plains, creating huge, choking clouds that piled up in doorways and filtered into homes through closed windows. Even more quickly than it had boomed, the land of agricultural opportunity went bust, due to widespread overproduction and overuse of the land, as well as to the harsh weather conditions that followed, resulting in the creation of the **Dust Bowl** (Figure 4.13).

Figure 4.13 The dust storms that blew through the Great Plains were epic in scale. Drifts of dirt piled up against doors and windows. People wore goggles and tied rags over their mouths to keep the dust out. (credit: U.S. National Oceanic and Atmospheric Administration)

Livestock died, or had to be sold, as there was no money for feed. Crops intended to feed the family withered and died in the drought. Terrifying dust storms became more and more frequent, as "black blizzards" of dirt blew across the landscape and created a new illness known as "dust pneumonia." In 1935 alone, over 850 million tons of topsoil blew away. To put this number in perspective, geologists estimate that it takes the earth five hundred years to naturally regenerate one inch of topsoil; yet, just one significant dust storm could destroy a similar amount. In their desperation to get more from the land, farmers had stripped it of the delicate balance that kept it healthy. Unaware of the consequences, they had moved away from such traditional practices as crop rotation and allowing land to regain its strength by permitting it to lie fallow between plantings, working the land to death.

For farmers, the results were catastrophic. Unlike most factory workers in the cities, in most cases, farmers lost their homes when they lost their livelihood. Most farms and ranches were originally mortgaged to small country banks that understood the dynamics of farming, but as these banks failed, they often sold rural mortgages to larger eastern banks that were less concerned with the specifics of farm life. With the effects of the drought and low commodity prices, farmers could not pay their local banks, which in turn lacked funds to pay the large urban banks. Ultimately, the large banks foreclosed on the farms, often swallowing up the small country banks in the process. It is worth noting that of the five thousand banks that closed between 1930 and 1932, over 75 percent were country banks in locations with populations under 2,500. Given this dynamic, it is easy to see why farmers in the Great Plains remained wary of big city bankers.

For farmers who survived the initial crash, the situation worsened, particularly in the Great Plains where years of overproduction and rapidly declining commodity prices took their toll. Prices continued to decline, and as farmers tried to stay afloat, they produced still more crops, which drove prices even lower. Farms failed at an astounding rate, and farmers sold out at rock-bottom prices. One farm in Shelby, Nebraska was mortgaged at $4,100 and sold for $49.50. One-fourth of the entire state of Mississippi was auctioned off *in a single day* at a foreclosure auction in April 1932.

Not all farmers tried to keep their land. Many, especially those who had arrived only recently, in an attempt to capitalize on the earlier prosperity, simply walked away (**Figure 4.14**). In hard-hit Oklahoma, thousands of farmers packed up what they could and walked or drove away from the land they thought would be their future. They, along with other displaced farmers from throughout the Great Plains, became known as Okies. Okies were an emblem of the failure of the American breadbasket to deliver on its promise, and their story was made famous in John Steinbeck's novel, *The Grapes of Wrath*.

Figure 4.14 As the Dust Bowl continued in the Great Plains, many had to abandon their land and equipment, as captured in this image from 1936, taken in Dallas, South Dakota. (credit: United States Department of Agriculture)

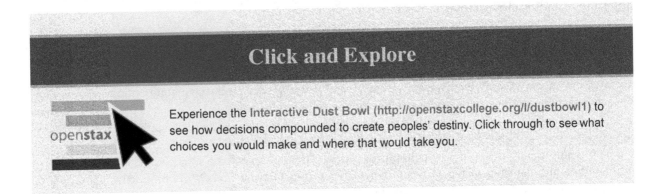

Click and Explore

Experience the Interactive Dust Bowl (http://openstaxcollege.org/l/dustbowl1) to see how decisions compounded to create peoples' destiny. Click through to see what choices you would make and where that would take you.

MY STORY

☼ *Caroline Henderson on the Dust Bowl*

Now we are facing a fourth year of failure. There can be no wheat for us in 1935 in spite of all our careful and expensive work in preparing ground, sowing and re-sowing our allocated acreage. Native grass pastures are permanently damaged, in many cases hopelessly ruined, smothered under by drifted sand. Fences are buried under banks of thistles and hard packed earth or undermined by the eroding action of the wind and lying flat on the ground. Less traveled roads are impassable, covered deep under by sand or the finer silt-like loam. Orchards, groves and hedge-rows cultivated for many years with patient care are dead or dying . . . Impossible it seems not to grieve that the work of hands should prove so perishable.
—Caroline Henderson, Shelton, Oklahoma, 1935

Much like other farm families whose livelihoods were destroyed by the Dust Bowl, Caroline Henderson describes a level of hardship that many Americans living in Depression-ravaged cities could never understand. Despite their hard work, millions of Americans were losing both their produce and their homes, sometimes in as little as forty-eight hours, to environmental catastrophes. Lacking any other explanation, many began to question what they had done to incur God's wrath. Note in particular Henderson's references to "dead," "dying," and "perishable," and contrast those terms with her depiction of the "careful and expensive work" undertaken by their own hands. Many simply could not understand how such a catastrophe could have occurred.

CHANGING VALUES, CHANGING CULTURE

In the decades before the Great Depression, and particularly in the 1920s, American culture largely reflected the values of individualism, self-reliance, and material success through competition. Novels like F. Scott Fitzgerald's *The Great Gatsby* and Sinclair Lewis's *Babbit* portrayed wealth and the self-made man in America, albeit in a critical fashion. In film, many silent movies, such as Charlie Chaplin's *The Gold Rush*, depicted the rags-to-riches fable that Americans so loved. With the shift in U.S. fortunes, however, came a shift in values, and with it, a new cultural reflection. The arts revealed a new emphasis on the welfare of the whole and the importance of community in preserving family life. While box office sales briefly declined at the beginning of the Depression, they quickly rebounded. Movies offered a way for Americans to think of better times, and people were willing to pay twenty-five cents for a chance to escape, at least for a few hours.

Even more than escapism, other films at the close of the decade reflected on the sense of community and family values that Americans struggled to maintain throughout the entire Depression. John Ford's screen version of Steinbeck's *The Grapes of Wrath* came out in 1940, portraying the haunting story of the Joad family's exodus from their Oklahoma farm to California in search of a better life. Their journey leads them to realize that they need to join a larger social movement—communism—dedicated to bettering the lives of all people. Tom Joad says, "Well, maybe it's like Casy says, a fella ain't got a soul of his own, but on'y a piece of a soul—the one big soul that belongs to ever'body." The greater lesson learned was one of the strength of community in the face of individual adversity.

Another trope was that of the hard-working everyman against greedy banks and corporations. This was perhaps best portrayed in the movies of Frank Capra, whose *Mr. Smith Goes to Washington* was emblematic of his work. In this 1939 film, Jimmy Stewart plays a legislator sent to Washington to finish out the term of a deceased senator. While there, he fights corruption to ensure the construction of a boy's camp in his hometown rather than a dam project that would only serve to line the pockets of a few. He ultimately engages in a two-day filibuster, standing up to the power players to do what's right. The Depression era was a favorite of Capra's to depict in his films, including *It's a Wonderful Life*, released in 1946. In this film, Jimmy Stewart runs a family-owned savings and loan, which at one point faces a bank run similar to those seen in 1929–1930. In the end, community support helps Stewart retain his business and home against the unscrupulous actions of a wealthy banker who sought to bring ruin to his family.

AMERICANA

◌ *"Brother, Can You Spare a Dime?"*

They used to tell me I was building a dream, and so I followed the mob
When there was earth to plow or guns to bear, I was always there, right on the job
They used to tell me I was building a dream, with peace and glory ahead
Why should I be standing in line, just waiting for bread?
Once I built a railroad, I made it run, made it race against time
Once I built a railroad, now it's done, Brother, can you spare a dime?
Once I built a tower up to the sun, brick and rivet and lime
Once I built a tower, now it's done, Brother, can you spare a dime?
—Jay Gorney and "Yip" Harburg

"Brother, Can You Spare a Dime?" first appeared in 1932, written for the Broadway musical *New Americana* by Jay Gorney, a composer who based the song's music on a Russian lullaby, and Edgar Yipsel "Yip" Harburg, a lyricist who would go on to win an Academy Award for the song "Over the Rainbow" from *The Wizard of Oz* (1939).

With its lyrics speaking to the plight of the common man during the Great Depression and the refrain appealing to the same sense of community later found in the films of Frank Capra, "Brother, Can You Spare a Dime?" quickly became the *de facto* anthem of the Great Depression. Recordings by Bing Crosby, Al Jolson, and Rudy Vallee all enjoyed tremendous popularity in the 1930s.

Click and Explore

For more on "Brother Can You Spare a Dime?" and the Great Depression, visit ArtsEdge (http://openstaxcollege.org/l/sparedime) to explore the Kennedy Center's digital resources and learn the "Story Behind the Song."

Finally, there was a great deal of pure escapism in the popular culture of the Depression. Even the songs found in films reminded many viewers of the bygone days of prosperity and happiness, from Al Dubin and Henry Warren's hit "We're in the Money" to the popular "Happy Days are Here Again." The latter eventually became the theme song of Franklin Roosevelt's 1932 presidential campaign. People wanted to forget their worries and enjoy the madcap antics of the Marx Brothers, the youthful charm of Shirley Temple, the dazzling dances of Fred Astaire and Ginger Rogers (**Figure 4.15**), or the comforting morals of the *Andy Hardy* series. The Hardy series—nine films in all, produced by MGM from 1936 to 1940—starred Judy Garland and Mickey Rooney, and all followed the adventures of a small-town judge and his son. No matter what the challenge, it was never so big that it could not be solved with a musical production put on by the neighborhood kids, bringing together friends and family members in a warm display of community values.

Figure 4.15 *Flying Down to Rio* (1933) was the first motion picture to feature the immensely popular dance duo of Fred Astaire and Ginger Rogers. The pair would go on to star in nine more Hollywood musicals throughout the 1930s and 1940s.

All of these movies reinforced traditional American values, which suffered during these hard times, in part due to declining marriage and birth rates, and increased domestic violence. At the same time, however, they reflected an increased interest in sex and sexuality. While the birth rate was dropping, surveys in *Fortune* magazine in 1936–1937 found that two-thirds of college students favored birth control, and that 50 percent of men and 25 percent of women admitted to premarital sex, continuing a trend among younger Americans that had begun to emerge in the 1920s. Contraceptive sales soared during the decade, and again, culture reflected this shift. Blonde bombshell Mae West was famous for her sexual innuendoes, and her flirtatious persona was hugely popular, although it got her banned on radio broadcasts throughout the Midwest. Whether West or Garland, Chaplin or Stewart, American film continued to be a barometer of American values, and their challenges, through the decade.

4.4 Assessing the Hoover Years on the Eve of the New Deal

By the end of this section, you will be able to:
- Identify the successes and failures of Herbert Hoover's presidency
- Determine the fairness and accuracy of assessments of Hoover's presidency

As so much of the Hoover presidency is circumscribed by the onset of the Great Depression, one must be careful in assessing his successes and failures, so as not to attribute all blame to Hoover. Given the suffering that many Americans endured between the fall of 1929 and Franklin Roosevelt's inauguration in the spring of 1933, it is easy to lay much of the blame at Hoover's doorstep (**Figure 4.16**). However, the extent to which Hoover was constrained by the economic circumstances unfolding well before he assumed office offers a few mitigating factors. Put simply, Hoover did not cause the stock market crash. However, his stubborn adherence to a questionable belief in "American individualism," despite mounting evidence that people were starving, requires that some blame be attributed to his policies (or lack thereof) for the depth and length of the Depression. Yet, Hoover's presidency was much more than simply combating the Depression. To assess the extent of his inability to provide meaningful national leadership through the darkest months of the Depression, his other policies require consideration.

Figure 4.16 Herbert Hoover (left) had the misfortune to be a president elected in prosperity and subsequently tasked with leading the country through the Great Depression. His unwillingness to face the harsh realities of widespread unemployment, farm foreclosures, business failures, and bank closings made him a deeply unpopular president, and he lost the 1932 election in a landslide to Franklin D. Roosevelt (right). (credit: Architect of the Capitol)

HOOVER'S FOREIGN POLICY

Although it was a relatively quiet period for U.S. diplomacy, Hoover did help to usher in a period of positive relations, specifically with several Latin American neighbors. This would establish the basis for Franklin Roosevelt's "Good Neighbor" policy. Following a goodwill tour of Central American countries immediately following his election in 1928, Hoover shaped the subsequent **Clark Memorandum**—released in 1930—which largely repudiated the previous Roosevelt Corollary, establishing a basis for unlimited American military intervention throughout Latin America. To the contrary, through the memorandum, Hoover asserted that greater emphasis should be placed upon the older Monroe Doctrine, in which the U.S. pledged assistance to her Latin American neighbors should any European powers interfere in Western Hemisphere affairs. Hoover further strengthened relations to the south by withdrawing American troops from Haiti and Nicaragua. Additionally, he outlined with Secretary of State Henry Stimson the Hoover-Stimson Doctrine, which announced that the United States would never recognize claims to territories seized by force (a direct response to the recent Japanese invasion of Manchuria).

Other diplomatic overtures met with less success for Hoover. Most notably, in an effort to support the American economy during the early stages of the Depression, the president signed into law the **Smoot-Hawley Tariff** in 1930. The law, which raised tariffs on thousands of imports, was intended to increase sales of American-made goods, but predictably angered foreign trade partners who in turn raised their tariffs on American imports, thus shrinking international trade and closing additional markets to desperate American manufacturers. As a result, the global depression worsened further. A similar attempt to spur the world economy, known as the Hoover Moratorium, likewise met with great opposition and little economic benefit. Issued in 1931, the moratorium called for a halt to World War I reparations to be paid by Germany to France, as well as forgiveness of Allied war debts to the U.S.

HOOVER AND CIVIL RIGHTS

Holding true to his belief in individualism, Hoover saw little need for significant civil rights legislation during his presidency, including any overtures from the NAACP to endorse federal anti-lynching legislation. He felt African Americans would benefit more from education and assimilation than from federal legislation or programs; yet he failed to recognize that, at this time in history, federal legislation and programs were required to ensure equal opportunities.

Hoover did give special attention to the improvement of Native American conditions, beginning with his selection of Charles Curtis as his vice-presidential running mate in the 1928 election. Curtis, of the Kaw Tribe, became the country's first Native American to hold so high an elected office. Hoover subsequently appointed Charles Rhoads as the new commissioner of the Bureau of Indian Affairs and advocated, with Rhoads' assistance, for Native American self-sufficiency and full assimilation as Americans under the Indian Citizenship Act of 1924. During Hoover's presidency, federal expenditures for Native American schools and health care doubled.

Click and Explore

Cartoons, especially political cartoons, provide a window into the frustrations and worries of an age. Browse the political cartoons at The Changing Face of Herbert Hoover (http://openstaxcollege.org/l/hoover) to better understand the historical context of Herbert Hoover's presidency.

A FINAL ASSESSMENT

Herbert Hoover's presidency, embarked upon with much promise following his election in November 1928, produced a legacy of mixed reactions. Some Americans blamed him for all of the economic and social woes from which they suffered for the next decade; all blamed him for simply not responding to their needs. As contemporary commentator and actor Will Rogers said at the time, "If an American was lucky enough to find an apple to eat in the Depression and bit into it only to find a worm, they would blame Hoover for the worm." Likewise, subsequent public opinion polls of presidential popularity, as well as polls of professional historians, routinely rate Hoover in the bottom seven of all U.S. presidents in terms of overall success.

However, Hoover the president was a product of his time. Americans sought a president in 1928 who would continue the policies of normalcy with which many associated the prosperity they enjoyed. They wanted a president who would forego government interference and allow industrial capitalism to grow unfettered. Hoover, from his days as the secretary of commerce, was the ideal candidate. In fact, he was *too* ideal when the Great Depression actually hit. Holding steadfast to his philosophy of "American individualism," Hoover proved largely incapable of shifting into economic crisis mode when Americans came to realize that prosperity could not last forever. Desperate to help, but unwilling to compromise on his philosophy, Hoover could not manage a comprehensive solution to the worldwide depression that few foresaw. Only when reelection was less than a year away did a reluctant Hoover initiate significant policies, but even then, they did not provide direct relief. By the start of 1932, unemployment hovered near 25 percent, and thousands of banks and factories were closing their doors. Combined with Hoover's ill-timed response to the Bonus Army crisis, his political fate was sealed. Americans would look to the next president for a solution. "Democracy is a harsh employer," Hoover concluded, as he awaited all but certain defeat in the November election of 1932 (**Figure 4.17**).

Figure 4.17 By the election of 1932, Hoover (left) knew that he was beaten. In photos from this time, he tends to appear grim-faced and downtrodden.

CHAPTER 5

Franklin Roosevelt and the New Deal, 1932-1941

Figure 5.1 President Roosevelt's Federal One Project allowed thousands of artists to create public art. This initiative was a response to the Great Depression as part of the Works Project Administration, and much of the public art in cities today date from this era. *New Deal* by Charles Wells can be found in the Clarkson S. Fisher Federal Building and U.S. Courthouse in Trenton, New Jersey. (credit: modification of work by Library of Congress)

Chapter Outline

5.1 The Rise of Franklin Roosevelt
5.2 The First New Deal
5.3 The Second New Deal

Introduction

The election of President Franklin Delano Roosevelt signaled both immediate relief for the American public as well as a permanent shift in the role of the federal government in guiding the economy and providing direct assistance to the people, albeit through expensive programs that made extensive budget deficits commonplace. For many, the immediate relief was, at a minimum, psychological: Herbert Hoover was gone, and the situation could not grow worse under Roosevelt. But as his New Deal unfolded, Americans learned more about the fundamental changes their new president brought with him to the Oval Office. In the span of little more than one hundred days, the country witnessed a wave of legislation never seen before or since.

Roosevelt understood the need to "save the patient," to borrow a medical phrase he often employed, as well as to "cure the ill." This meant both creating jobs, through such programs as the Works Progress Administration, which provided employment to over eight million Americans (**Figure 5.1**), as well as reconfiguring the structure of the American economy. In pursuit of these two goals, Americans re-elected Roosevelt for three additional terms in the White House and became full partners in the reshaping of their country.

5.1 The Rise of Franklin Roosevelt

By the end of this section, you should be able to:
- Describe the events of the 1932 presidential election and identify the characteristics that made Franklin Roosevelt a desirable candidate
- Explain why Congress amended the U.S. Constitution to reduce the period of time between presidential elections and inaugurations

Franklin Roosevelt was part of the political establishment and the wealthy elite, but in the 1932 presidential campaign, he did not want to be perceived that way. Roosevelt felt that the country needed sweeping change, and he ran a campaign intended to convince the American people that he could deliver that change. It was not the specifics of his campaign promises that were different; in fact, he gave very few details and likely did not yet have a clear idea of how he would raise the country out of the Great Depression. But he campaigned tirelessly, talking to thousands of people, appearing at his party's national convention, and striving to show the public that he was a different breed of politician. As Hoover grew more morose and physically unwell in the face of the campaign, Roosevelt thrived. He was elected in a landslide by a country ready for the change he had promised.

THE ELECTION OF FRANKLIN ROOSEVELT

By the 1932 presidential election, Hoover's popularity was at an all-time low. Despite his efforts to address the hardships that many Americans faced, his ineffectual response to the Great Depression left Americans angry and ready for change. Franklin Roosevelt, though born to wealth and educated at the best schools, offered the change people sought. His experience in politics had previously included a seat in the New York State legislature, a vice-presidential nomination, and a stint as governor of New York. During the latter, he introduced many state-level reforms that later formed the basis of his New Deal as well as worked with several advisors who later formed the **Brains Trust** that advised his federal agenda.

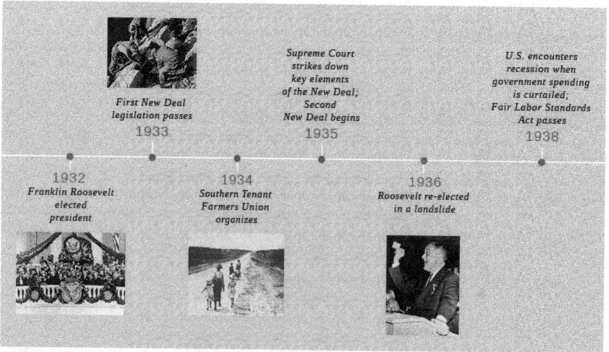

Figure 5.2

Roosevelt exuded confidence, which the American public desperately wished to see in their leader (**Figure 5.3**). And, despite his affluence, Americans felt that he could relate to their suffering due to his own physical hardships; he had been struck with polio a decade earlier and was essentially paralyzed from the waist down for the remainder of his life. Roosevelt understood that the public sympathized with his ailment; he likewise developed a genuine empathy for public suffering as a result of his illness. However, he never wanted to be photographed in his wheelchair or appear infirm in any way, for fear that the public's sympathy would transform into concern over his physical ability to discharge the duties of the Oval Office.

Figure 5.3 Franklin Roosevelt brought a new feeling of optimism and possibility to a country that was beaten down by hardship. His enthusiasm was in counterpoint to Herbert Hoover's discouraging last year in office.

Roosevelt also recognized the need to convey to the voting public that he was not simply another member of the political aristocracy. At a time when the country not only faced its most severe economic challenges to date, but Americans began to question some of the fundamental principles of capitalism and democracy, Roosevelt sought to show that he was different—that he could defy expectations—and through his actions could find creative solutions to address the nation's problems while restoring public confidence in fundamental American values. As a result, he not only was the first presidential candidate to appear in person at a national political convention to accept his party's nomination but also flew there through terrible weather from New York to Chicago in order to do so—a risky venture in what was still the early stages of flight as public transportation. At the Democratic National Convention in 1932, he coined the famous phrase: "I pledge myself to a new deal for the American people." The New Deal did not yet exist, but to the American people, any positive and optimistic response to the Great Depression was a welcome one.

Hoover assumed at first that Roosevelt would be easy to defeat, confident that he could never carry the eastern states and the business vote. He was sorely mistaken. Everywhere he went, Hoover was met with antagonism; anti-Hoover signs and protests were the norm. Hoover's public persona declined rapidly. Many news accounts reported that he seemed physically unwell, with an ashen face and shaking hands. Often, he seemed as though he would faint, and an aide constantly remained nearby with a chair in case he fell. In contrast, Roosevelt thrived on the campaign. He commented, "I have looked into the faces of thousands of Americans, and they have the frightened look of lost children."

The election results that November were never really in question: With three million more people voting than in 1928, Roosevelt won by a popular count of twenty-three million to fifteen million. He carried all but six states while winning over 57 percent of the popular vote. Whether they voted due to animosity towards Hoover for his relative inactivity, or out of hope for what Roosevelt would accomplish, the American public committed themselves to a new vision. Historians identify this election as the beginning of a new Democratic coalition, bringing together African Americans, other ethnic minorities, and organized labor as a voting bloc upon whom the party would rely for many of its electoral victories over the next fifty years. Unlike some European nations where similar challenges caused democratic constitutions to crumble and give way to radical ideologies and authoritarian governments, the Roosevelt administration changed the nation's economic fortunes with reforms, preserved the constitution, and expanded rather than limited the reach of democratic principles into the market economy. As a result, radical alternatives, such as the Fascist movement or Communist Party, remained on the margins of the nation's political culture.

THE INTERREGNUM

After the landslide election, the country—and Hoover—had to endure the **interregnum**, the difficult four months between the election and President Roosevelt's inauguration in March 1933. Congress did not pass a single significant piece of legislation during this period, although Hoover spent much of the time trying to get Roosevelt to commit publicly to a legislative agenda of Hoover's choosing. Roosevelt remained gracious but refused to begin his administration as the incumbent's advisor without any legal authority necessary to change policy. Unwilling to tie himself to Hoover's legacy of failed policies, Roosevelt kept quiet when Hoover supported the passage of a national sales tax. Meanwhile, the country suffered from Hoover's inability to further drive a legislative agenda through Congress. It was the worst winter since the beginning of the Great Depression, and the banking sector once again suffered another round of panics. While Roosevelt kept his distance from the final tremors of the Hoover administration, the country continued to suffer in wait. In part as a response to the challenges of this time, the U.S. Constitution was subsequently amended to reduce the period from election to inauguration to the now-commonplace two months.

Any ideas that Roosevelt held almost did not come to fruition, thanks to a would-be assassin's bullet. On February 15, 1933, after delivering a speech from his open car in Miami's Bayfront Park, local Italian bricklayer Giuseppe Zangara emerged from a crowd of well-wishers to fire six shots from his revolver. Although Roosevelt emerged from the assassination attempt unscathed, Zangara wounded five individuals that day, including Chicago Mayor Tony Cermak, who attended the speech in the hopes of resolving any long-standing differences with the president-elect. Roosevelt and his driver immediately rushed Cermak to the hospital where he died three days later. Roosevelt's calm and collected response to the event reassured many Americans of his ability to lead the nation through the challenges they faced. All that awaited was Roosevelt's inauguration before his ideas would unfold to the expectant public.

So what was Roosevelt's plan? Before he took office, it seems likely that he was not entirely sure. Certain elements were known: He believed in positive government action to solve the Depression; he believed in federal relief, public works, social security, and unemployment insurance; he wanted to restore public confidence in banks; he wanted stronger government regulation of the economy; and he wanted to directly help farmers. But how to take action on these beliefs was more in question. A month before his inauguration, he said to his advisors, "Let's concentrate upon one thing: Save the people and the nation, and if we have to change our minds twice every day to accomplish that end, we should do it."

Unlike Hoover, who professed an ideology of "American individualism," an adherence that rendered him largely incapable of widespread action, Roosevelt remained pragmatic and open-minded to possible solutions. To assist in formulating a variety of relief and recovery programs, Roosevelt turned to a group of men who had previously orchestrated his election campaign and victory. Collectively known as the "Brains Trust" (a phrase coined by a *New York Times* reporter to describe the multiple "brains" on Roosevelt's advisory team), the group most notably included Rexford Tugwell, Raymond Moley, and Adolph Berle. Moley, credited with bringing the group into existence, was a government professor who advocated for a new national tax policy to help the nation recover from its economic woes. Tugwell, who eventually focused his energy on the country's agricultural problems, saw an increased role for the federal government in setting wages and prices across the economy. Berle was a mediating influence, who often advised against a centrally controlled economy, but did see the role that the federal government could play in mediating the stark cycles of prosperity and depression that, if left unchecked, could result in the very situation in which the country presently found itself. Together, these men, along with others, advised

Roosevelt through the earliest days of the New Deal and helped to craft significant legislative programs for congressional review and approval.

INAUGURATION DAY: A NEW BEGINNING

March 4, 1933, dawned gray and rainy. Roosevelt rode in an open car along with outgoing president Hoover, facing the public, as he made his way to the U.S. Capitol. Hoover's mood was somber, still personally angry over his defeat in the general election the previous November; he refused to crack a smile at all during the ride among the crowd, despite Roosevelt's urging to the contrary. At the ceremony, Roosevelt rose with the aid of leg braces equipped under his specially tailored trousers and placed his hand on a Dutch family Bible as he took his solemn oath. At that very moment, the rain stopped and the sun began to shine directly on the platform, and those present would later claim that it was as though God himself was shining down on Roosevelt and the American people in that moment (**Figure 5.4**).

Figure 5.4 Roosevelt's inauguration was truly a day of new beginnings for the country. The sun breaking through the clouds as he was being sworn in became a metaphor for the hope that people felt at his presidency.

Bathed in the sunlight, Roosevelt delivered one of the most famous and oft-quoted inaugural addresses in history. He encouraged Americans to work with him to find solutions to the nation's problems and not to be paralyzed by fear into inaction. Borrowing a wartime analogy provided by Moley, who served as his speechwriter at the time, Roosevelt called upon all Americans to assemble and fight an essential battle against the forces of economic depression. He famously stated, "The only thing we have to fear is fear itself." Upon hearing his inaugural address, one observer in the crowd later commented, "Any man who can talk like that in times like these is worth every ounce of support a true American has." To borrow the popular song title of the day, "happy days were here again." Foregoing the traditional inaugural parties, the new president immediately returned to the White House to begin his work to save the nation.

Click and Explore

Visit the American Presidency Project (http://openstaxcollege.org/l/fdraug) to listen to Roosevelt's first inaugural speech and identify ways he conveyed optimism and a spirit of community to his listeners.

5.2 The First New Deal

By the end of this section, you should be able to:
- Identify the key pieces of legislation included in Roosevelt's "First New Deal"
- Assess the strengths, weaknesses, and general effectiveness of the First New Deal
- Explain Roosevelt's overall vision for addressing the structural problems in the U.S. economy

Much like a surgeon assessing the condition of an emergency room patient, Roosevelt began his administration with a broad, if not specific, strategy in mind: a combination of relief and recovery programs designed to first save the patient (in this case, the American people), and then to find a long-term cure (reform through federal regulation of the economy). What later became known as the "First New Deal" ushered in a wave of legislative activity seldom before seen in the history of the country. By the close of 1933, in an effort to stem the crisis, Congress had passed over fifteen significant pieces of legislation—many of the circulated bills allegedly still wet with ink from the printing presses as members voted upon them. Most bills could be grouped around issues of relief, recovery, and reform. At the outset of the First New Deal, specific goals included 1) bank reform; 2) job creation; 3) economic regulation; and 4) regional planning.

REFORM: THE BANKING CRISIS

When Roosevelt took office, he faced one of the worst moments in the country's banking history. States were in disarray. New York and Illinois had ordered the closure of their banks in the hopes of avoiding further "bank runs," which occurred when hundreds (if not thousands) of individuals ran to their banks to withdraw all of their savings. In all, over five thousand banks had been shuttered. Within forty-eight hours of his inauguration, Roosevelt proclaimed an official bank holiday and called Congress into a special session to address the crisis. The resulting Emergency Banking Act of 1933 was signed into law on March 9, 1933, a scant eight hours after Congress first saw it. The law officially took the country off the gold standard, a restrictive practice that, although conservative and traditionally viewed as safe, severely limited the circulation of paper money. Those who held gold were told to sell it to the U.S. Treasury for a discounted rate of a little over twenty dollars per ounce. Furthermore, dollar bills were no longer redeemable in gold. The law also gave the comptroller of currency the power to reorganize all national banks faced with insolvency, a level of federal oversight seldom seen prior to the Great Depression. Between March 11 and March 14, auditors from the Reconstruction Finance Corporation, the Treasury Department, and other federal agencies swept through the country, examining each bank. By March 15, 70 percent of the banks were declared solvent and allowed to reopen.

On March 12, the day before the banks were set to reopen, Roosevelt held his first "fireside chat" (**Figure 5.5**). In this initial radio address to the American people, he explained what the bank examiners had been doing over the previous week. He assured people that any bank open the next day had the federal government's stamp of approval. The combination of his reassuring manner and the promise that the government was addressing the problems worked wonders in changing the popular mindset. Just as the culture of panic had contributed to the country's downward spiral after the crash, so did this confidence-inducing move help to build it back up. Consumer confidence returned, and within weeks, close to $1 billion in cash and gold had been brought out from under mattresses and hidden bookshelves, and re-deposited in the nation's banks. The immediate crisis had been quelled, and the public was ready to believe in their new president.

Figure 5.5 Roosevelt's "fireside chats" provided an opportunity for him to speak directly to the American people, and the people were happy to listen. These radio addresses, commemorated at the Franklin D. Roosevelt Memorial in Washington, DC, with this bronze sculpture by George Segal, contributed to Roosevelt's tremendous popularity. (credit: Koshy Koshy)

DEFINING "AMERICAN"

✿ *The Power of Hearth and Home*

Fireside chats—Roosevelt's weekly radio addresses—underscored Roosevelt's savvy in understanding how best to reach people. Using simple terms and a reassuring tone, he invoked a family patriarch sitting by the fire, explaining to those who trusted him how he was working to help them. It is worth noting how he explained complex financial concepts quite simply, but at the same time, complimented the American people on their "intelligent support." One of his fireside chats is provided below:

> I recognize that the many proclamations from State capitols and from Washington, the legislation, the Treasury regulations, etc., couched for the most part in banking and legal terms, should be explained for the benefit of the average citizen. I owe this in particular because of the fortitude and good temper with which everybody has accepted the inconvenience and hardships of the banking holiday. I know that when you understand what we in Washington have been about I shall continue to have your cooperation as fully as I have had your sympathy and help during the past week. . . .

> The success of our whole great national program depends, of course, upon the cooperation of the public—on its intelligent support and use of a reliable system. . . . After all, there is an element in the readjustment of our financial system more important than currency, more important than gold, and that is the confidence of the people. Confidence and courage are the essentials of success in carrying out our plan. You people must have faith; you must not be stampeded by rumors or guesses. Let us unite in banishing fear. We have provided the machinery to restore our financial system; it is up to you to support and make it work. It is your problem no less than it is mine. Together we cannot fail.

> —Franklin D. Roosevelt, March 12, 1933

A huge part of Roosevelt's success in turning around the country can be seen in his addresses like these: He built support and galvanized the public. Ironically, Roosevelt, the man who famously said we have nothing to fear but fear itself, had a significant fear: fire. Being paralyzed with polio, he was very afraid of being left near a fireplace. But he knew the power of the hearth and home, and drew on this mental image to help the public view him the way that he hoped to be seen.

Click and Explore

Visit the American Presidency Project (http://openstaxcollege.org/l/fireside) to listen to one of Roosevelt's fireside chats. What kind of feeling does his language and demeanor evoke?

In June 1933, Roosevelt replaced the Emergency Banking Act with the more permanent Glass-Steagall Banking Act. This law prohibited commercial banks from engaging in investment banking, therefore stopping the practice of banks speculating in the stock market with deposits. This law also created the Federal Deposit Insurance Corporation, or FDIC, which insured personal bank deposits up to $2,500. Other measures designed to boost confidence in the overall economy beyond the banking system included passage of the Economy Act, which fulfilled Roosevelt's campaign pledge to reduce government spending by reducing salaries, including his own and those of the Congress. He also signed into law the Securities Act, which required full disclosure to the federal government from all corporations and investment banks that wanted to market stocks and bonds. Roosevelt also sought new revenue through the Beer Tax. As the Twenty-First Amendment, which would repeal the Eighteenth Amendment establishing Prohibition, moved towards ratification, this law authorized the manufacture of 3.2 percent beer and levied a tax on it.

THE FIRST HUNDRED DAYS

In his first hundred days in office, the new president pushed forward an unprecedented number of new bills, all geared towards stabilizing the economy, providing relief to individuals, creating jobs, and helping businesses. A sympathetic Democrat-controlled Congress helped propel his agenda forward.

Relief: Employment for the Masses

Even as he worked to rebuild the economy, Roosevelt recognized that the unemployed millions required jobs more quickly than the economy could provide. In a push to create new jobs, Roosevelt signed the Wagner-Peyser Act, creating the United States Employment Service, which promised states matching funds if they created local employment opportunities. He also authorized $500 million in direct grants through the Federal Emergency Relief Act (FERA). This money went directly to states to infuse relief agencies with the much-needed resources to help the nearly fifteen million unemployed. These two bills illustrate Roosevelt's dual purposes of providing short-term emergency help and building employment opportunities that would strengthen the economy in the long term.

Roosevelt was aware of the need for immediate help, but he mostly wanted to create more jobs. FERA overseer Harry Hopkins, who later was in charge of the Civil Works Administration (CWA), shared this sentiment. With Hopkins at its helm, the CWA, founded in early 1933, went on to put millions of men and women to work. At its peak, there were some four million Americans repairing bridges, building roads and airports, and undertaking other public projects. Another work program was the **Civilian Conservation Corps** Relief Act (CCC). The CCC provided government jobs for young men aged fourteen to twenty-four who came from relief families. They would earn thirty dollars per month planting trees, fighting forest fires, and refurbishing historic sites and parks, building an infrastructure that families would continue to enjoy for generations to come. Within the first two months, the CCC employed its first 250,000 men and eventually established about twenty-five hundred camps (**Figure 5.6**).

Figure 5.6 The CCC put hundreds of thousands of men to work on environmental projects around the country. Some call it the beginning of the modern environmentalist movement in the United States.

The various programs that made up the First New Deal are listed in the table below (**Table 5.1**).

Table 5.1 Key Programs from the First New Deal

New Deal Legislation	Years Enacted	Brief Description
Agricultural Adjustment Administration	1933–1935	Farm program designed to raise process by curtailing production
Civil Works Administration	1933–1934	Temporary job relief program
Civilian Conservation Corps	1933–1942	Employed young men to work in rural areas
Farm Credit Administration	1933–today	Low interest mortgages for farm owners
Federal Deposit Insurance Corporation	1933–today	Insure private bank deposits
Federal Emergency Relief Act	1933	Direct monetary relief to poor unemployed Americans
Glass-Steagall Act	1933	Regulate investment banking
Homeowners Loan Corporation	1933–1951	Government mortgages that allowed people to keep their homes
Indian Reorganization Act	1933	Abandoned federal policy of assimilation
National Recovery Administration	1933–1935	Industries agree to codes of fair practice to set price, wage, production levels
Public Works Administration	1933–1938	Large public works projects
Resettlement Administration	1933–1935	Resettles poor tenant farmers
Securities Act of 1933	1933–today	Created SEC; regulates stock transactions
Tennessee Valley Authority	1933–today	Regional development program; brought electrification to the valley

The final element of Roosevelt's efforts to provide relief to those in desperate straits was the Home Owners' Refinancing Act. Created by the Home Owners' Loan Corporation (HOLC), the program rescued homeowners from foreclosure by refinancing their mortgages. Not only did this save the homes of countless homeowners, but it also saved many of the small banks who owned the original mortgages by relieving them of that responsibility. Later New Deal legislation created the Federal Housing Authority, which eventually standardized the thirty-year mortgage and promoted the housing boom of the post-World War II era. A similar program, created through the Emergency Farm Mortgage Act and Farm Credit Act, provided the same service for farm mortgages.

Click and Explore

In this American Experience (http://openstaxcollege.org/l/Maher) interview, Neil Maher, author of *Nature's New Deal: The Civilian Conservation Corps and Roots of the Modern Environmental Movement*, provides a comprehensive look into what the CCC offered the country—and the president—on issues as diverse as economics, race, and recreation.

Rescuing Farms and Factories

While much of the legislation of the first hundred days focused on immediate relief and job creation through federal programs, Roosevelt was committed to addressing the underlying problems inherent in the American economy. In his efforts to do so, he created two of the most significant pieces of New Deal legislation: the Agricultural Adjustment Act (AAA) and the National Industry Recovery Act (NIRA).

Farms around the country were suffering, but from different causes. In the Great Plains, drought conditions meant that little was growing at all, while in the South, bumper crops and low prices meant that farmers could not sell their goods at prices that could sustain them. The AAA offered some direct relief: Farmers received $4.5 million through relief payments. But the larger part of the program paid southern farmers to reduce their production: Wheat, cotton, corn, hogs, tobacco, rice, and milk farmers were all eligible. Passed into law on May 12, 1933, it was designed to boost prices to a level that would alleviate rural poverty and restore profitability to American agriculture. These price increases would be achieved by encouraging farmers to limit production in order to increase demand while receiving cash payments in return. Corn producers would receive thirty cents per bushel for corn they did not grow. Hog farmers would get five dollars per head for hogs not raised. The program would be financed by a tax on processing plants, passed on to consumers in the form of higher prices.

This was a bold attempt to help farmers address the systemic problems of overproduction and lower commodity prices. Despite previous efforts to regulate farming through subsidies, never before had the federal government intervened on this scale; the notion of paying farmers *not* to produce crops was unheard of. One significant problem, however, was that, in some cases, there was already an excess of crops, in particular, cotton and hogs, which clogged the marketplace. A bumper crop in 1933, combined with the slow implementation of the AAA, led the government to order the plowing under of ten million acres of cotton, and the butchering of six million baby pigs and 200,000 sows. Although it worked to some degree—the price of cotton increased from six to twelve cents per pound—this move was deeply problematic. Critics saw it as the ultimate example of corrupt capitalism: a government destroying food, while its citizens were starving, in order to drive up prices.

Another problem plaguing this relief effort was the disparity between large commercial farms, which received the largest payments and set the quotas, and the small family farms that felt no relief. Large farms often cut production by laying off sharecroppers or evicting tenant farmers, making the program even worse for them than for small farm owners. Their frustration led to the creation of the Southern Tenant Farmers Union (STFU), an interracial organization that sought to gain government relief for these most disenfranchised of farmers. The STFU organized, protested, and won its members some wage increases through the mid-1930s, but the overall plight of these workers remained dismal. As a result, many of them followed the thousands of Dust Bowl refugees to California (**Figure 5.7**).

Figure 5.7 Sharecroppers and tenant farmers suffered enormously during the Great Depression. The STFU was created to help alleviate this suffering, but many farmers ending up taking to the road, along with other Dust Bowl refugees, on their way to California.

AMERICANA

⊙ *Labor Songs and the Southern Tenant Farmers Union*

> And if the growers get in the way, we're gonna roll right over them
> We're gonna roll right over them, we're gonna roll right over them
> And if the growers get in the way, we're gonna roll right over them
> We're gonna roll this union on
> —John Handcox, "Roll the Union On"

"Mean Things Happening in This Land," "Roll the Union On," and "Strike in Arkansas" are just a few of the folk songs written by John Handcox. A union organizer and STFU member, Handcox became the voice of the worker's struggle, writing dozens of songs that have continued to be sung by labor activists and folk singers over the years. Handcox joined the STFU in 1935, and used his songs to rally others, stating, "I found out singing was more inspiring than talking . . . to get the attention of the people."

Racially integrated and with active women members, the STFU was ahead of its time. Although criticized by other union leaders for its relationship with the Communist Party in creating the "Popular Front" for labor activism in 1934, the STFU succeeded in organizing strikes and bringing national attention to the issues that tenant farmers faced. While the programs Roosevelt put in place did not do enough to help these farmers, the STFU—and Handcox's music—remains a relevant part of the country's labor movement.

The AAA did succeed on some fronts. By the spring of 1934, farmers had formed over four thousand local committees, with more than three million farmers agreeing to participate. They signed individual contracts agreeing to take land out of production in return for government payments, and checks began to arrive by the end of 1934. For some farmers, especially those with large farms, the program spelled relief.

While Roosevelt hoped the AAA would help farms and farmers, he also sought aid for the beleaguered manufacturing sector. The Emergency Railroad Transportation Act created a national railroad office to encourage cooperation among different railroad companies, hoping to shore up an industry essential to the stability of the manufacturing sector, but one that had been devastated by mismanagement. More importantly, the NIRA suspended antitrust laws and allowed businesses and industries to work together in order to establish codes of fair competition, including issues of price setting and minimum wages. New Deal officials believed that allowing these collaborations would help industries stabilize prices   and production levels in the face of competitive overproduction and declining profits; however, at the same time, many felt it important to protect workers from potentially unfair agreements.

A new government agency, the National Recovery Administration (NRA), was central to this plan, and mandated that businesses accept a code that included minimum wages and maximum work hours. In order to protect workers from potentially unfair agreements among factory owners, every industry had its own "code of fair practice" that included workers' rights to organize and use collective bargaining to ensure that wages rose with prices (**Figure 5.8**). Headed by General Hugh S. Johnson, the NRA worked to create over five hundred different codes for different industries. The administration of such a complex plan naturally created its own problems. While codes for key industries such as automotive and steel made sense, Johnson pushed to create similar codes for dog food manufacturers, those who made shoulder pads for women's clothing, and even burlesque shows (regulating the number of strippers in any one show).

(a)   (b)

Figure 5.8 Consumers were encouraged to buy from companies displaying the Blue Eagle (a), the logo signifying compliance with the new NRA regulations. With talons gripping a gear, representing industry, and lightning bolts, representing power, the eagle (b) was intended to be a symbol of economic recovery.

The NIRA also created the Public Works Administration (PWA). The PWA set aside $3.3 billion to build public projects such as highways, federal buildings, and military bases. Although this program suffered from political squabbles over appropriations for projects in various congressional districts, as well as significant underfunding of public housing projects, it ultimately offered some of the most lasting benefits of the NIRA. Secretary of the Interior Harold Ickes ran the program, which completed over thirty-four thousand projects, including the Golden Gate Bridge in San Francisco and the Queens-Midtown Tunnel in New York. Between 1933 and 1939, the PWA accounted for the construction of over one-third of all new hospitals and 70 percent of all new public schools in the country.

Another challenge faced by the NRA was that the provision granting workers the right to organize appeared to others as a mandate to do so. In previously unorganized industries, such as oil and gas, rubber, and service occupations, workers now sought groups that would assist in their organization, bolstered by the encouragement they now felt from the government. The Communist Party took advantage of the opportunity to assist in the hope of creating widespread protests against the American industrial structure. The number of strikes nationwide doubled between 1932 and 1934, with over 1.5 million workers going on strike in 1934 alone, often in protests that culminated in bloodshed. A strike at the Auto-Lite plant in Toledo, Ohio, that summer resulted in ten thousand workers from other factories joining in sympathy with their fellow workers to attack potential strike-breakers with stones and bricks. Simultaneously in

Minneapolis, a teamsters strike resulted in frequent, bloody confrontations between workers and police, leading the governor to contemplate declaring martial law before the companies agreed to negotiate better wages and conditions for the workers. Finally, a San Francisco strike among 14,000 longshoremen closed the city's waterfront and eventually led to a city-wide general strike of over 130,000 workers, essentially paralyzing the city. Clashes between workers, and police and National Guardsmen left many strikers bloodied, and at least two dead.

Although Roosevelt's relief efforts provided jobs to many and benefitted communities with the construction of several essential building projects, the violence that erupted amid clashes between organized labor and factories backed by police and the authorities exposed a fundamental flaw in the president's approach. Immediate relief did not address long-existing, inherent class inequities that left workers exposed to poor working conditions, low wages, long hours, and little protection. For many workers, life on the job was not much better than life as an unemployed American. Employment programs may have put men back to work and provided much needed relief, but the fundamental flaws in the system required additional attention—attention that Roosevelt was unable to pay in the early days of the New Deal. Critics were plentiful, and the president would be forced to address them in the years ahead.

Regional Planning

Regionally, Roosevelt's work was most famously seen in the **Tennessee Valley Authority** (TVA) (**Figure 5.9**), a federal agency tasked with the job of planning and developing the area through flood control, reforestation, and hydroelectric power. Employing several thousand Americans on a project that Roosevelt envisioned as a template for future regional redevelopment, the TVA revitalized a river valley that landowners had badly over-farmed, leaving behind eroded soil that lacked essential nutrients for future farming. Under the direction of David Lilienthal, beginning in 1933, the TVA workers erected a series of dams to harness the Tennessee River in the creation of much-needed hydroelectric power. The arrival of both electric lighting and machinery to the region eased the lives of the people who lived there, as well as encouraged industrial growth. The TVA also included an educational component, teaching farmers important lessons about crop rotation, soil replenishment, fertilizing, and reforestation.

Figure 5.9 The TVA helped a struggling part of the country through the creation of jobs, and flood control and reforestation programs. The Wilson Dam, shown here, is one of nine TVA dams on the Tennessee River. (credit: United States Geological Survey)

The TVA was not without its critics, however, most notably among the fifteen thousand families who were displaced due to the massive construction projects. Although eventually the project benefited farmers with the introduction of new farming and fertilizing techniques, as well as the added benefit of electric power, many local citizens were initially mistrustful of the TVA and the federal government's agenda. Likewise, as with several other New Deal programs, women did not directly benefit from these employment opportunities, as they were explicitly excluded for the benefit of men who most Americans still considered the family's primary breadwinner. However, with the arrival of electricity came new industrial ventures, including several textile mills up and down the valley, several of which offered employment to women. Throughout his presidency, Roosevelt frequently pointed to the TVA as one of the glowing accomplishments of the New Deal and its ability to bring together the machinery of the federal government along with private interests to revitalize a regional economy. Just months before his death in 1945, he continued to speak of the possibility of creating other regional authorities throughout the country.

ASSESSING THE FIRST NEW DEAL

While many were pleased with the president's bold plans, there were numerous critics of the New Deal, discussed in the following section. The New Deal was far from perfect, but Roosevelt's quickly implemented policies reversed the economy's long slide. It put new capital into ailing banks. It rescued homeowners and farmers from foreclosure and helped people keep their homes. It offered some direct relief to the unemployed poor. It gave new incentives to farmers and industry alike, and put people back to work in an effort to both create jobs and boost consumer spending. The total number of working Americans rose from twenty-four to twenty-seven million between 1933 and 1935, in contrast to the seven-million-worker decline during the Hoover administration. Perhaps most importantly, the First New Deal changed the pervasive pessimism that had held the country in its grip since the end of 1929. For the first time in years, people had hope.

It was the hard work of Roosevelt's advisors—the "Brains Trust" of scholars and thinkers from leading universities—as well as Congress and the American public who helped the New Deal succeed as well as it did. Ironically, it was the American people's volunteer spirit, so extolled by Hoover, that Roosevelt was able to harness. The first hundred days of his administration was not a master plan that Roosevelt dreamed up and executed on his own. In fact, it was not a master plan at all, but rather a series of, at times, disjointed efforts made from different assumptions. But after taking office and analyzing the crisis, Roosevelt and his advisors did feel that they had a larger sense of what had caused the Great Depression and thus attempted a variety of solutions to fix it. They believed that it was caused by abuses on the part of a small group of bankers and businessmen, aided by Republican policies that built wealth for a few at the expense of many. The answer, they felt, was to root out these abuses through banking reform, as well as adjust production and consumption of both farm and industrial goods. This adjustment would come about by increasing the purchasing power of everyday people, as well as through regulatory policies like the NRA and AAA. While it may seem counterintuitive to raise crop prices and set prices on industrial goods, Roosevelt's advisors sought to halt the deflationary spiral and economic uncertainty that had prevented businesses from committing to investments and consumers from parting with their money.

5.3 The Second New Deal

By the end of this section, you should be able to:
- Identify key pieces of legislation from the Second New Deal
- Assess the entire New Deal, especially in terms of its impact on women, African Americans, and Native Americans

Roosevelt won his second term in a landslide, but that did not mean he was immune to criticism. His critics came from both the left and the right, with conservatives deeply concerned over his expansion of government spending and power, and liberals angered that he had not done more to help those still struggling. Adding to Roosevelt's challenges, the Supreme Court struck down several key elements of the First New Deal, angering Roosevelt and spurring him to try and stack the courts in his second term. Still, he entered his new term with the unequivocal support of the voting public, and he wasted no time beginning the second phase of his economic plan. While the First New Deal focused largely on stemming the immediate suffering of the American people, the Second New Deal put in place legislation that changed America's social safety net for good.

CHALLENGES FROM CRITICS ON ALL SIDES

While many people supported Roosevelt, especially in the first few years of his presidency, the New Deal did receive significant criticism, both from conservatives who felt that it was a radical agenda to ruin the country's model of free enterprise, and from liberals who felt that it did not provide enough help to those who needed it most (**Figure 5.10**).

Figure 5.10 Roosevelt used previously unheard of levels of government power in his attempt to push the country out of the Great Depression, as artist Joseph Parrish depicts here in this 1937 *Chicago Tribune* cartoon. While critics on the left felt that he had not done enough, critics on the right felt that his use of power was frighteningly close to fascism and socialism.

Industrialists and wealthy Americans led the conservative criticism against the president. Whether attacking his character or simply stating that he was moving away from American values toward fascism and socialism, they sought to undermine his power and popularity. Most notably, the American Liberty League—comprised largely of conservative Democrats who lamented the excesses of several of Roosevelt's New Deal programs—labeled the AAA as fascist and proclaimed later New Deal programs to be key threats to the very nature of democracy. Additional criticism came from the National Association of Manufacturers, which urged businessmen to outright ignore portions of the NRA that promoted collective bargaining, as well as subsequent labor protection legislation. In 1935, the U.S. Supreme Court dealt the most crushing blow to Roosevelt's vision, striking down several key pieces of the New Deal as unconstitutional. They found that both the AAA and the NIRA overreached federal authority. The negation of some of his most ambitious economic recovery efforts frustrated Roosevelt greatly, but he was powerless to stop it at this juncture.

Meanwhile, others felt that Roosevelt had not done enough. Dr. Francis E. Townsend of California was one who felt that Roosevelt had failed to adequately address the country's tremendous problems.   Townsend, who was a retired dentist, proposed an expansive pension plan for the elderly. The Townsend Plan, as it was known, gained a great deal of popularity: It recommended paying every citizen over sixty who retired from work the sum of $200 per month, provided they spend it in thirty days. Another figure who gained national attention was Father Charles Coughlin. He was a "radio priest" from Michigan who, although he initially supported the New Deal, subsequently argued that Roosevelt stopped far too short in his defense of labor, monetary reform, and the nationalization of key industries. The president's plan, he proclaimed, was inadequate. He created the National Union for Social Justice and used his weekly radio show to gain followers.

A more direct political threat to Roosevelt came from muckraker Upton Sinclair, who pursued the California governorship in 1934 through a campaign based upon criticism of the New Deal's shortcomings. In his "End Poverty in California" program, Sinclair called for a progressive income tax, a pension program for the elderly, and state seizure of factories and farms where property taxes remained unpaid. The state would then offer jobs to the unemployed to work those farms and factories in a cooperative mode. Although Sinclair lost the election to his Republican opponent, he did draw local and national attention to several of his ideas.

The biggest threat to the president, however, came from corrupt but beloved Louisiana senator Huey "Kingfish" Long (**Figure 5.11**). His disapproval of Roosevelt came in part from his own ambitions for higher office; Long stated that the president was not doing enough to help people and proposed his own Share Our Wealth program. Under this plan, Long recommended the liquidation of all large personal fortunes in order to fund direct payments to less fortunate Americans. He foresaw giving $5,000 to every family, $2,500 to every worker, as well as a series of elderly pensions and education funds. Despite his questionable math, which numerous economists quickly pointed out rendered his program unworkable, by 1935, Long had a significant following of over four million people. If he had not been assassinated by the son-in-law of a local political rival, he may well have been a contender against Roosevelt for the 1936 presidential nomination.

Figure 5.11 Huey P. Long was a charismatic populist and governor of Louisiana from 1928 to 1932. In 1932, he became a member of the U.S. Senate and would have been a serious rival for Roosevelt in the 1936 presidential election if his life had not been cut short by an assassin's bullet.

ANSWERING THE CHALLENGE

Roosevelt recognized that some of the criticisms of the New Deal were valid. Although he was still reeling from the Supreme Court's invalidation of key statutes, he decided to face his re-election bid in 1936 by unveiling another wave of legislation that he dubbed the Second New Deal. In the first week of June 1935, Roosevelt called congressional leaders into the White House and gave them a list of "must-pass" legislation that he wanted before they adjourned for the summer. Whereas the policies of the first hundred days may have shored up public confidence and stopped the most drastic of the problems, the second hundred days changed the face of America for the next sixty years.

The Banking Act of 1935 was the most far-reaching revision of banking laws since the creation of the Federal Reserve System in 1914. Previously, regional reserve banks, particularly the New York Reserve Bank—controlled by the powerful Morgan and Rockefeller families—had dominated policy-making at the Federal Reserve. Under the new system, there would be a seven-member board of governors to oversee regional banks. They would have control over reserve requirements, discount rates, board member selection, and more. Not surprisingly, this new board kept initial interest rates quite low, allowing the federal government to borrow billions of dollars of additional cash to fund major relief and recovery programs.

In 1935, Congress also passed the Emergency Relief Appropriation Act, which authorized the single largest expenditure at that time in the country's history: $4.8 billion. Almost one-third of those funds were invested in a new relief agency, the **Works Progress Administration** (WPA). Harry Hopkins, formerly head of the CWA, took on the WPA and ran it until 1943. In that time, the program provided employment relief to over eight million Americans, or approximately 20 percent of the country's workforce. The WPA funded the construction of more than 2,500 hospitals, 5,900 schools, 570,000 miles of road, and more. The WPA also created the Federal One Project, which employed approximately forty thousand artists in theater, art, music, and writing. They produced state murals, guidebooks, concerts, and drama performances all around the country (**Figure 5.12**). Additionally, the project funded the collection of oral histories, including those of former slaves, which provided a valuable addition to the nation's understanding of slave life. Finally, the WPA also included the National Youth Administration (NYA), which provided work-study jobs to over 500,000 college students and four million high school students.

Figure 5.12 Painted by artists funded by the Federal One Project, this section of *Ohio*, a mural located in the Bellevue, Ohio post office, illustrates a busy industrial scene. Artists painted the communities where they lived, thus creating visions of farms, factories, urban life, harvest celebrations, and more that still reflect the life and work of that era. (credit: Works Progress Administration)

Click and Explore

openstax

Browse the *Born in Slavery* collection (http://openstaxcollege.org/l/slavery) to examine personal accounts of former slaves, recorded between 1936 and 1938, as part of the Federal Writers' Project of the WPA.

With the implementation of the Second New Deal, Roosevelt also created the country's present-day social safety net. The **Social Security** Act established programs intended to help the most vulnerable: the elderly, the unemployed, the disabled, and the young. It included a pension fund for all retired people—except domestic workers and farmers, which therefore left many women and African Americans beyond the scope of its benefits—over the age of sixty-five, to be paid through a payroll tax on both employee and employer. Related to this act, Congress also passed a law on unemployment insurance, to be funded by a tax on employers, and programs for unwed mothers, as well as for those who were blind, deaf, or disabled. It is worth noting that some elements of these reforms were pulled from Roosevelt detractors Coughlin and Townsend; the popularity of their movements gave the president more leverage to push forward this type of legislation.

To the benefit of industrial workers, Roosevelt signed into law the Wagner Act, also known as the National Labor Relations Act. The protections previously afforded to workers under the NIRA were inadvertently lost when the Supreme Court struck down the original law due to larger regulatory concerns, leaving workers vulnerable. Roosevelt sought to salvage this important piece of labor legislation, doing so with the Wagner Act. The act created the National Labor Relations Board (NLRB) to once again protect American workers' right to unionize and bargain collectively, as well as to provide a federal vehicle for labor grievances to be heard. Although roundly criticized by the Republican Party and factory owners, the Wagner Act withstood several challenges and eventually received constitutional sanction by the U.S. Supreme Court in 1937. The law received the strong support of John L. Lewis and the Congress of Industrial Organizations who had long sought government protection of industrial unionism, from the time they split from the American Federation of Labor in 1935 over disputes on whether to organize workers along craft or industrial lines. Following passage of the law, Lewis began a widespread publicity campaign urging industrial workers to join "the president's union." The relationship was mutually beneficial to Roosevelt, who subsequently received the endorsement of Lewis's United Mine Workers union in the 1936 presidential election, along with a sizeable $500,000 campaign contribution. The Wagner Act permanently established government-secured workers' rights and protections from their employers, and it marked the beginning of labor's political support for the Democratic Party.

The various programs that made up the Second New Deal are listed in the table below (**Table 5.2**).

Table 5.2 Key Programs from the Second New Deal

New Deal Legislation	Years Enacted	Brief Description
Fair Labor Standards Act	1938–today	Established minimum wage and forty-hour workweek
Farm Security Administration	1935–today	Provides poor farmers with education and economic support programs
Federal Crop Insurance Corporation	1938–today	Insures crops and livestock against loss of revenue
National Labor Relations Act	1935–today	Recognized right of workers to unionize & collectively bargain
National Youth Administration	1935–1939 (part of WPA)	Part-time employment for college and high school students
Rural Electrification Administration	1935–today	Provides public utilities to rural areas
Social Security Act	1935–today	Aid to retirees, unemployed, disabled

Table 5.2 Key Programs from the Second New Deal

New Deal Legislation	Years Enacted	Brief Description
Surplus Commodities Program	1936–today	Provides food to the poor (still exists in Food Stamps program)
Works Progress Administration	1935–1943	Jobs program (including artists and youth)

THE FINAL PIECES

Roosevelt entered the 1936 presidential election on a wave of popularity, and he beat Republican opponent Alf Landon by a nearly unanimous Electoral College vote of 523 to 8. Believing it to be his moment of strongest public support, Roosevelt chose to exact a measure of revenge against the U.S. Supreme Court for challenging his programs and to pressure them against challenging his more recent Second New Deal provisions. To this end, Roosevelt created the informally named "**Supreme Court Packing Plan**" and tried to pack the court in his favor by expanding the number of justices and adding new ones who supported his views. His plan was to add one justice for every current justice over the age of seventy who refused to step down. This would have allowed him to add six more justices, expanding the bench from nine to fifteen. Opposition was quick and thorough from both the Supreme Court and Congress, as well as from his own party. The subsequent retirement of Justice Van Devanter from the court, as well as the sudden death of Senator Joe T. Robinson, who championed Roosevelt's plan before the Senate, all but signaled Roosevelt's defeat. However, although he never received the support to make these changes, Roosevelt appeared to succeed in politically intimidating the current justices into supporting his newer programs, and they upheld both the Wagner Act and the Social Security Act. Never again during his presidency would the Supreme Court strike down any significant elements of his New Deal.

Roosevelt was not as successful in addressing the nation's growing deficit. When he entered the presidency in 1933, Roosevelt did so with traditionally held fiscal beliefs, including the importance of a balanced budget in order to maintain public confidence in federal government operations. However, the severe economic conditions of the depression quickly convinced the president of the importance of government spending to create jobs and relief for the American people. As he commented to a crowd in Pittsburgh in 1936, "To balance our budget in 1933 or 1934 or 1935 would have been a crime against the American people. To do so . . . we should have had to set our face against human suffering with callous indifference. When Americans suffered, we refused to pass by on the other side. Humanity came first." However, after his successful re-election, Roosevelt anticipated that the economy would recover enough by late 1936 that he could curtail spending by 1937. This reduction in spending, he hoped, would curb the deficit. As the early months of 1937 unfolded, Roosevelt's hopes seemed supported by the most recent economic snapshot of the country. Production, wages, and profits had all returned to pre-1929 levels, while unemployment was at its lowest rate in the decade, down from 25 percent to 14 percent. But no sooner did Roosevelt cut spending when a recession hit. Two million Americans were newly out of work as unemployment quickly rose by 5 percent and industrial production declined by a third. Breadlines began to build again, while banks prepared to close.

Historians continue to debate the causes of this recession within a depression. Some believe the fear of increased taxes forced factory owners to curtail planned expansion; others blame the Federal Reserve for tightening the nation's money supply. Roosevelt, however, blamed the downturn on his decision to significantly curtail federal government spending in job relief programs such as the WPA. Several of his closest advisors, including Harry Hopkins, Henry Wallace, and others, urged him to adopt the new economic theory espoused by British economic John Maynard Keynes, who argued that deficit spending was necessary in advanced capitalist economies in order to maintain employment and stimulate consumer spending. Convinced of the necessity of such an approach, Roosevelt asked Congress in the spring of 1938 for additional emergency relief spending. Congress immediately authorized $33 billion for PWA and WPA work projects. Although World War II would provide the final impetus for lasting economic recovery, Roosevelt's willingness to adapt in 1938 avoided another disaster.

Roosevelt signed the last substantial piece of New Deal legislation in the summer of 1938. The Fair Labor Standards Act established a federal minimum wage—at the time, forty cents per hour—a maximum workweek of forty hours (with an opportunity for four additional hours of work at overtime wages), and prohibited child labor for those under age sixteen. Roosevelt was unaware that the war would soon dominate his legacy, but this proved to be his last major piece of economic legislation in a presidency that changed the fabric of the country forever.

IN THE FINAL ANALYSIS

The legacy of the New Deal is in part seen in the vast increase in national power: The federal government accepted responsibility for the nation's economic stability and prosperity. In retrospect, the majority of historians and economists judge it to have been a tremendous success. The New Deal not only established minimum standards for wages, working conditions, and overall welfare, it also allowed millions of Americans to hold onto their homes, farms, and savings. It laid the groundwork for an agenda of expanded federal government influence over the economy that continued through President Harry Truman's "Fair Deal" in the 1950s and President Lyndon Johnson's call for a "Great Society" in the 1960s. The New Deal state that embraced its responsibility for the citizens' welfare and proved willing to use its power and resources to spread the nation's prosperity lasted well into the 1980s, and many of its tenets persist today. Many would also agree that the postwar economic stability of the 1950s found its roots in the stabilizing influences introduced by social security, the job stability that union contracts provided, and federal housing mortgage programs introduced in the New Deal. The environment of the American West in particular, benefited from New Deal projects such as the Soil Conservation program.

Still, Roosevelt's programs also had their critics. Following the conservative rise initiated by presidential candidate Barry Goldwater in 1964, and most often associated with the Ronald Reagan era of the 1980s, critics of the welfare state pointed to Roosevelt's presidency as the start of a slippery slope towards entitlement and the destruction of the individualist spirit upon which the United States had presumably developed in the nineteenth and early twentieth centuries. Although the growth of the GDP between 1934 and 1940 approached an average of 7.5 percent—higher than in any other peacetime period in U.S. history, critics of the New Deal point out that unemployment still hovered around 15 percent in 1940. While the New Deal resulted in some environmental improvements, it also inaugurated a number of massive infrastructural projects, such as the Grand Coulee Dam on the Columbia River, that came with grave environmental consequences. And other shortcomings of the New Deal were obvious and deliberate at the time.

African Americans under the New Deal

Critics point out that not all Americans benefited from the New Deal. African Americans in particular were left out, with overt discrimination in hiring practices within the federal job programs, such as the CCC, CWA, and WPA. The NRA was oftentimes criticized as the "Negro Run Around" or "Negroes Ruined Again" program. As well, the AAA left tenant farmers and sharecroppers, many of whom were black, with no support. Even Social Security originally excluded domestic workers, a primary source of employment for African American women. Facing such criticism early in his administration, Roosevelt undertook some efforts to ensure a measure of equality in hiring practices for the relief agencies, and opportunities began to present themselves by 1935. The WPA eventually employed 350,000 African Americans annually, accounting for nearly 15 percent of its workforce. By the close of the CCC in 1938, this program had employed over 300,000 African Americans, increasing the black percentage of its workforce from 3 percent at the outset to nearly 11 percent at its close. Likewise, in 1934, the PWA began to require that all government projects under its purview hire African Americans using a quota that reflected their percentage of the local population being served. Additionally, among several important WPA projects, the Federal One Project included a literacy program that eventually reached over one million African American children, helping them learn how to read and write.

On the issue of race relations themselves, Roosevelt has a mixed legacy. Within his White House, Roosevelt had a number of African American appointees, although most were in minor positions. Unofficially, Roosevelt relied upon advice from the Federal Council on Negro Affairs, also known as his "Black Cabinet." This group included a young Harvard economist, Dr. Robert Weaver, who subsequently became the nation's first black cabinet secretary in 1966, as President Lyndon Johnson's Secretary of Housing and Urban Development. Aubrey Williams, the director of the NYA, hired more black administrators than any other federal agency, and appointed them to oversee projects throughout the country. One key figure in the NYA was Mary McLeod Bethune (**Figure 5.13**), a prominent African American educator tapped by Roosevelt to act as the director of the NYA's Division of Negro Affairs. Bethune had been a spokesperson and an educator for years; with this role, she became one of the president's foremost African American advisors. During his presidency, Roosevelt became the first to appoint a black federal judge, as well as the first commander-in-chief to promote an African American to brigadier general. Most notably, he became the first president to publicly speak against lynching as a "vile form of collective murder."

Figure 5.13 This photo of Eleanor Roosevelt and Mary McLeod Bethune (second from left) was taken at the opening of Midway Hall, a federal building to house female African American government workers. Bethune was sometimes criticized for working with those in power, but her willingness to build alliances contributed to success in raising money and support for her causes.

MY STORY

✪ *Mary McLeod Bethune on Racial Justice*

Democracy is for me, and for twelve million black Americans, a goal towards which our nation is marching. It is a dream and an ideal in whose ultimate realization we have a deep and abiding faith. For me, it is based on Christianity, in which we confidently entrust our destiny as a people. Under God's guidance in this great democracy, we are rising out of the darkness of slavery into the light of freedom. Here my race has been afforded [the] opportunity to advance from a people 80 percent illiterate to a people 80 percent literate; from abject poverty to the ownership and operation of a million farms and 750,000 homes; from total disfranchisement to participation in government; from the status of chattels to recognized contributors to the American culture.

When Mary McLeod Bethune spoke these words, she spoke on behalf of a race of American citizens for whom the Great Depression was much more than economic hardship. For African Americans, the Depression once again exposed the racism and inequality that gripped the nation economically, socially, and politically. Her work as a member of President Franklin Roosevelt's unofficial "Black Cabinet" as well as the Director of the Division of Negro Affairs for the NYA, presented her an opportunity to advance African American causes on all fronts—but especially in the area of black literacy. As part of the larger WPA, she also influenced employment programs in the arts and public work sectors, and routinely had the president's ear on matters related to racial justice.

Click and Explore

Listen to this audio clip (http://openstaxcollege.org/l/bethune) of Eleanor Roosevelt interviewing Mary McLeod Bethune. By listening to her talking to Bethune and offering up her support, it becomes clear how compelling the immensely popular first lady was when speaking about programs of close personal interest to her. How do you think this would have been received by Roosevelt's supporters?

However, despite these efforts, Roosevelt also understood the precariousness of his political position. In order to maintain a coalition of Democrats to support his larger relief and recovery efforts, Roosevelt could not afford to alienate Southern Democrats who might easily bolt should he openly advocate for civil rights. While he spoke about the importance of anti-lynching legislation, he never formally pushed Congress to propose such a law. He did publicly support the abolition of the poll tax, which Congress eventually accomplished in 1941. Likewise, although agency directors adopted changes to ensure job opportunities for African Americans at the federal level, at the local level, few advancements were made, and African Americans remained at the back of the employment lines. Despite such failures, however, Roosevelt deserves credit for acknowledging the importance of race relations and civil rights. At the federal level, more than any of his predecessors since the Civil War, Roosevelt remained aware of the role that the federal government can play in initiating important discussions about civil rights, as well as encouraging the development of a new cadre of civil rights leaders.

Although unable to bring about sweeping civil rights reforms for African Americans in the early stages of his administration, Roosevelt was able to work with Congress to significantly improve the lives of Indians. In 1934, he signed into law the Indian Reorganization Act (sometimes referred to as the "Indian New Deal"). This law formally abandoned the assimilationist policies set forth in the Dawes Severalty Act of

1887. Rather than forcing Indians to adapt to American culture, the new program encouraged them to develop forms of local self-government, as well as to preserve their artifacts and heritage. John Collier, the Commissioner on Indian Bureau Affairs from 1933 to 1945, championed this legislation and saw it as an opportunity to correct past injustices that land allotment and assimilation had wrought upon Indians. Although the re-establishment of communal tribal lands would prove to be difficult, Collier used this law to convince federal officials to return nearly two million acres of government-held land to various tribes in order to move the process along. Although subsequent legislation later circumscribed the degree to which tribes were allowed to self-govern on reservations, Collier's work is still viewed as a significant step in improving race relations with Indians and preserving their heritage.

Women and the New Deal

For women, Roosevelt's policies and practices had a similarly mixed effect. Wage discrimination in federal jobs programs was rampant, and relief policies encouraged women to remain home and leave jobs open for men. This belief was well in line with the gender norms of the day. Several federal relief programs specifically forbade husbands and wives' both drawing jobs or relief from the same agency. The WPA became the first specific New Deal agency to openly hire women—specifically widows, single women, and the wives of disabled husbands. While they did not take part in construction projects, these women did undertake sewing projects to provide blankets and clothing to hospitals and relief agencies. Likewise, several women took part in the various Federal One art projects. Despite the obvious gender limitations, many women strongly supported Roosevelt's New Deal, as much for its direct relief handouts for women as for its employment opportunities for men. One such woman was Mary (Molly) Dewson. A longtime activist in the women's suffrage movement, Dewson worked for women's rights and ultimately rose to be the Director of the Women's Division of the Democratic Party. Dewson and Mary McLeod Bethune, the national champion of African American education and literacy who rose to the level of Director of the Division of Negro Affairs for the NYA, understood the limitations of the New Deal, but also the opportunities for advancement it presented during very trying times. Rather than lamenting what Roosevelt could not or would not do, they felt, and perhaps rightly so, that Roosevelt would do more than most to help women and African Americans achieve a piece of the new America he was building.

Among the few, but notable, women who directly impacted Roosevelt's policies was Frances Perkins, who as Secretary of Labor was the first female member of any presidential cabinet, and First Lady Eleanor Roosevelt, who was a strong and public advocate for social causes. Perkins, one of only two original Cabinet members to stay with Roosevelt for his entire presidency, was directly involved in the administration of the CCC, PWA, NRA, and the Social Security Act. Among several important measures, she took greatest pleasure in championing minimum wage statutes as well as the penultimate piece of New Deal legislation, the Fair Labor Standards Act. Roosevelt came to trust Perkins' advice with few questions or concerns, and steadfastly supported her work through the end of his life (**Figure 5.14**).

(a)   (b)

Figure 5.14 After leaving her post as head of the Women's Division of the Democratic Party, Molly Dewson (a) later accepted an appointment to the Social Security Board, working with fellow board members Arthur J. Altmeyer and George E. Bigge, shown here in 1937. Another influential advisor to President Franklin Roosevelt was Frances Perkins (b), who, as U.S. Secretary of Labor, graced the cover of *Time* magazine on August 14, 1933.

DEFINING "AMERICAN"

✸ *Molly Dewson and Women Democrats*

In her effort to get President Roosevelt re-elected in 1936, Dewson commented, "We don't make the old-fashioned plea to the women that our nominee is charming, and all that. We appeal to the intelligence of the country's women. Ours were economic issues and we found the women ready to listen."

As head of the Women's Division of the Democratic National Committee (DNC) in 1932, Molly Dewson proved to be an influential supporter of President Franklin Roosevelt and one of his key advisors regarding issues pertaining to women's rights. Agreeing with First Lady Eleanor Roosevelt that "Women must learn to play the games as men do," Dewson worked diligently in her position with the DNC to ensure that women could serve as delegates and alternates to the national conventions. Her approach, and her realization that women were intelligent enough to make rational choices, greatly appealed to Roosevelt. Her methods were perhaps not too different from his own, as he spoke to the public through his fireside chats. Dewson's impressive organizational skills on behalf of the party earned her the nickname "the little general" from President Roosevelt.

However, Eleanor Roosevelt, more so than any other individual, came to represent the strongest influence upon the president; and she used her unique position to champion several causes for women, African Americans, and the rural poor (**Figure 5.15**). She married Franklin Roosevelt, who was her fifth cousin, in 1905 and subsequently had six children, one of whom died at only seven months old. A strong supporter of her husband's political ambitions, Eleanor campaigned by his side through the failed vice-presidential bid in 1920 and on his behalf after he was diagnosed with polio in 1921. When she discovered letters of her husband's affair with her social secretary, Lucy Mercer, the marriage became less one of romance and more one of a political partnership that would continue—strained at times—until the president's death in 1945.

Figure 5.15 Eleanor Roosevelt travelled the country to promote New Deal programs. Here she visits a WPA nursery school in Des Moines, Iowa, on June 8, 1936. (credit: FDR Presidential Library & Museum)

Historians agree that the first lady used her presence in the White House, in addition to the leverage of her failed marriage and knowledge of her husband's infidelities, to her advantage. She promoted several causes that the president himself would have had difficulty championing at the time. From newspaper and magazine articles she authored, to a busy travel schedule that saw her regularly cross the country, the first lady sought to remind Americans that their plight was foremost on the minds of all working in the White House. Eleanor was so active in her public appearances that, by 1940, she began holding regular press conferences to answer reporters' questions. Among her first substantial projects was the creation of Arthurdale—a resettlement community for displaced coal miners in West Virginia. Although the planned community became less of an administration priority as the years progressed (eventually folding in 1940), for seven years, Eleanor remained committed to its success as a model of assistance for the rural poor.

Exposed to issues of racial segregation in the Arthurdale experiment, Eleanor subsequently supported many civil rights causes through the remainder of the Roosevelt presidency. When it further became clear that racial discrimination was rampant in the administration of virtually all New Deal job programs—especially in the southern states—she continued to pressure her husband for remedies. In 1934, she openly lobbied for passage of the federal anti-lynching bill that the president privately supported but could not politically endorse. Despite the subsequent failure of the Senate to pass such legislation, Eleanor succeeded in arranging a meeting between her husband and then-NAACP president Walter White to discuss anti-lynching and other pertinent calls for civil rights legislation.

White was only one of Eleanor's African American guests to the White House. Breaking with precedent, and much to the disdain of many White House officials, the first lady routinely invited prominent African Americans to dine with her and the president. Most notably, when the Daughters of the American Revolution (DAR) refused to permit internationally renowned black opera contralto Marian Anderson to sing in Constitution Hall, Eleanor resigned her membership in the DAR and arranged for Anderson to sing at a public concert on the steps of the Lincoln Memorial, followed by her appearance at a state dinner at the White House in honor of the king and queen of England. With regard to race relations in particular, Eleanor Roosevelt was able to accomplish what her husband—for delicate political reasons—could not: become the administration's face for civil rights.

CHAPTER 6

Fighting the Good Fight in World War II, 1941-1945

Figure 6.1 During World War II, American propaganda was used to drum up patriotism and support for the war effort. This poster shows the grit and determination of infantrymen in the face of enemy fire.

Chapter Outline

6.1 The Origins of War: Europe, Asia, and the United States
6.2 The Home Front
6.3 Victory in the European Theater
6.4 The Pacific Theater and the Atomic Bomb

Introduction

World War II awakened the sleeping giant of the United States from the lingering effects of the Great Depression. Although the country had not entirely disengaged itself from foreign affairs following World War I, it had remained largely divorced from events occurring in Europe until the late 1930s. World War II forced the United States to involve itself once again in European affairs. It also helped to relieve the unemployment of the 1930s and stir industrial growth. The propaganda poster above (**Figure 6.1**) was part of a concerted effort to get Americans to see themselves as citizens of a strong, unified country, dedicated to the protection of freedom and democracy. However, the war that unified many Americans also brought to the fore many of the nation's racial and ethnic divisions, both on the frontlines—where military units, such as the one depicted in this poster, were segregated by race—and on the home front. Yet, the war also created new opportunities for ethnic minorities and women, which, in postwar America, would contribute to their demand for greater rights.

6.1 The Origins of War: Europe, Asia, and the United States

By the end of this section, you will be able to:
- Explain the factors in Europe that gave rise to Fascism and Nazism
- Discuss the events in Europe and Asia that led to the start of the war
- Identify the early steps taken by President Franklin D. Roosevelt to increase American aid to nations fighting totalitarianism while maintaining neutrality

The years between the First and Second World Wars were politically and economically tumultuous for the United States and especially for the world. The Russian Revolution of 1917, Germany's defeat in World War I, and the subsequent Treaty of Versailles had broken up the Austro-Hungarian, German, and Russian empires and significantly redrew the map of Europe. President Woodrow Wilson had wished to make World War I the "war to end all wars" and hoped that his new paradigm of "collective security" in international relations, as actualized through the League of Nations, would limit power struggles among the nations of the world. However, during the next two decades, America's attention turned away from global politics and toward its own needs. At the same time, much of the world was dealing with economic and political crises, and different types of totalitarian regimes began to take hold in Europe. In Asia, an ascendant Japan began to expand its borders. Although the United States remained focused on the economic challenges of the Great Depression as World War II approached, ultimately it became clear that American involvement in the fight against Nazi Germany and Japan was in the nation's interest.

ISOLATION

While during the 1920s and 1930s there were Americans who favored active engagement in Europe, most Americans, including many prominent politicians, were leery of getting too involved in European affairs or accepting commitments to other nations that might restrict America's ability to act independently, keeping with the isolationist tradition. Although the United States continued to intervene in the affairs

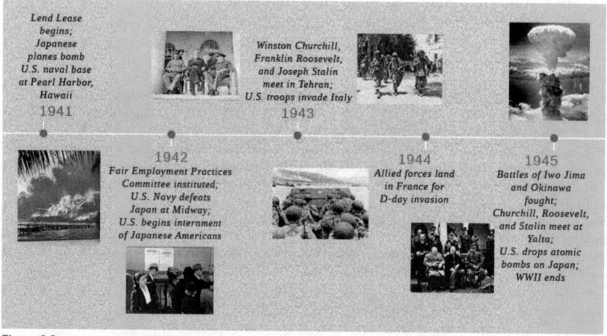

Figure 6.2

of countries in the Western Hemisphere during this period, the general mood in America was to avoid becoming involved in any crises that might lead the nation into another global conflict.

Despite its largely noninterventionist foreign policy, the United States did nevertheless take steps to try to lessen the chances of war and cut its defense spending at the same time. President Warren G. Harding's administration participated in the Washington Naval Conference of 1921–1922, which reduced the size of the navies of the nine signatory nations. In addition, the Four Power Treaty, signed by the United States, Great Britain, France, and Japan in 1921, committed the signatories to eschewing any territorial expansion in Asia. In 1928, the United States and fourteen other nations signed the Kellogg-Briand Pact, declaring war an international crime. Despite hopes that such agreements would lead to a more peaceful world—far more nations signed on to the agreement in later years—they failed because none of them committed any of the nations to take action in the event of treaty violations.

THE MARCH TOWARD WAR

While the United States focused on domestic issues, economic depression and political instability were growing in Europe. During the 1920s, the international financial system was propped up largely by American loans to foreign countries. The crash of 1929, when the U.S. stock market plummeted and American capital dried up, set in motion a series of financial chain reactions that contributed significantly to a global downward economic spiral. Around the world, industrialized economies faced significant problems of economic depression and worker unemployment.

Totalitarianism in Europe

Many European countries had been suffering even before the Great Depression began. A postwar recession and the continuation of wartime inflation had hurt many economies, as did a decrease in agricultural prices, which made it harder for farmers to buy manufactured goods or pay off loans to banks. In such an unstable environment, Benito Mussolini capitalized on the frustrations of the Italian people who felt betrayed by the Versailles Treaty. In 1919, Mussolini created the *Fasci Italiani di Combattimento* (Italian Combat Squadron). The organization's main tenets of **Fascism** called for a totalitarian form of government and a heightened focus on national unity, militarism, social Darwinism, and loyalty to the state. With the support of major Italian industrialists and the king, who saw Fascism as a bulwark against growing Socialist and Communist movements, Mussolini became prime minister in 1922. Between 1925 and 1927, Mussolini transformed the nation into a single party state and removed all restraints on his power.

In Germany, a similar pattern led to the rise of the totalitarian National Socialist Party. Political fragmentation through the 1920s accentuated the severe economic problems facing the country. As a result, the German Communist Party began to grow in strength, frightening many wealthy and middle-class Germans. In addition, the terms of the Treaty of Versailles had given rise to a deep-seated resentment of the victorious Allies. It was in such an environment that Adolf Hitler's anti-Communist National Socialist Party—the Nazis—was born.

The Nazis gained numerous followers during the Great Depression, which hurt Germany tremendously, plunging it further into economic crisis. By 1932, nearly 30 percent of the German labor force was unemployed. Not surprisingly, the political mood was angry and sullen. Hitler, a World War I veteran, promised to return Germany to greatness. By the beginning of 1933, the Nazis had become the largest party in the German legislature. Germany's president, Paul von Hindenburg, at the urging of large industrialists who feared a Communist uprising, appointed Hitler to the position of prime minister in January 1933. In the elections that took place the next month, the Nazis passed the Enabling Act, which gave Hitler the power to make all laws for the next four years. Hitler thus effectively became the dictator of Germany and remained so long after the four-year term passed. Like Italy, Germany had become a one-party totalitarian state (**Figure 6.3**). Nazi Germany was an anti-Semitic nation, and in 1935, the Nuremberg Laws deprived Jews, whom Hitler blamed for Germany's downfall, of German citizenship and the rights thereof.

(a)   (b)

Figure 6.3 Italian Fascists under the dictatorial leadership of Benito Mussolini (a, center) and German National Socialist Party leader and dictator Adolf Hitler (b) systematically dismantled democratic institutions and pushed military buildups, racial supremacy, and an aggressive nationalism in the 1920s and early 1930s.

Once in power, Hitler began to rebuild German military might. He commenced his program by withdrawing Germany from the League of Nations in October 1933. In 1936, in accordance with his promise to restore German greatness, Hitler dispatched military units into the Rhineland, on the border with France, which was an act contrary to the provisions of the Versailles Treaty. In March 1938, claiming that he sought only to reunite ethnic Germans within the borders of one country, Hitler invaded Austria. At a conference in Munich later that year, Great Britain's prime minister, Neville Chamberlain, and France's prime minister, Édouard Daladier, agreed to the partial dismemberment of Czechoslovakia and the occupation of the Sudetenland (a region with a sizable German population) by German troops (**Figure 6.4**). This Munich Pact offered a policy of **appeasement**, in the hope that German expansionist appetites could be satisfied without war. But not long after the agreement, Germany occupied the rest of Czechoslovakia as well.

Figure 6.4 Prime Minister Neville Chamberlain arrives home in England bearing the Munich Pact agreement. The jubilant Chamberlain proclaimed that the agreement meant "peace in our time."

In the Soviet Union, Premier Joseph Stalin, observing Hitler's actions and listening to his public pronouncements, realized that Poland, part of which had once belonged to Germany and was home to people of German ancestry, was most likely next. Although fiercely opposed to Hitler, Stalin, sobered by the French and British betrayal of Czechoslovakia and unprepared for a major war, decided the best way to protect the Soviet Union, and gain additional territory, was to come to some accommodation with the German dictator. In August 1939, Germany and the Soviet Union essentially agreed to divide Poland between them and not make war upon one another.

Japan

Militaristic politicians also took control of Japan in the 1930s. The Japanese had worked assiduously for decades to modernize, build their strength, and become a prosperous, respected nation. The sentiment in Japan was decidedly pro-capitalist, and the Japanese militarists were fiercely supportive of a capitalist economy. They viewed with great concern the rise of Communism in the Soviet Union and in particular China, where the issue was fueling a civil war, and feared that the Soviet Union would make inroads in Asia by assisting China's Communists. The Japanese militarists thus found a common ideological enemy with Fascism and National Socialism, which had based their rise to power on anti-Communist sentiments. In 1936, Japan and Germany signed the Anti-Comintern Pact, pledging mutual assistance in defending themselves against the Comintern, the international agency created by the Soviet Union to promote worldwide Communist revolution. In 1937, Italy joined the pact, essentially creating the foundation of what became the military alliance of the Axis powers.

Like its European allies, Japan was intent upon creating an empire for itself. In 1931, it created a new nation, a puppet state called Manchukuo, which had been cobbled together from the three northernmost provinces of China. Although the League of Nations formally protested Japan's seizure of Chinese territory in 1931 and 1932, it did nothing else. In 1937, a clash between Japanese and Chinese troops, known as the Marco Polo Bridge Incident, led to a full-scale invasion of China by the Japanese. By the end of the year, the Chinese had suffered some serious defeats. In Nanjing, then called Nanking by Westerners, Japanese soldiers systematically raped Chinese women and massacred hundreds of thousands of civilians, leading to international outcry. Public sentiment against Japan in the United States reached new heights. Members of Protestant churches that were involved in missionary work in China were particularly outraged, as were Chinese Americans. A troop of Chinese American Boy Scouts in New York City's Chinatown defied Boy Scout policy and marched in protest against Japanese aggression.

FROM NEUTRALITY TO ENGAGEMENT

President Franklin Roosevelt was aware of the challenges facing the targets of Nazi aggression in Europe and Japanese aggression in Asia. Although he hoped to offer U.S. support, Congress's commitment to nonintervention was difficult to overcome. Such a policy in regards to Europe was strongly encouraged by Senator Gerald P. Nye of North Dakota. Nye claimed that the United States had been tricked into participating in World War I by a group of industrialists and bankers who sought to gain from the country's participation in the war. The United States, Nye urged, should not be drawn again into an international dispute over matters that did not concern it. His sentiments were shared by other noninterventionists in Congress (**Figure 6.5**).

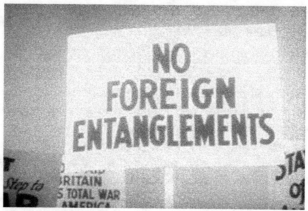

Figure 6.5 This protest sign shows the unwillingness of many Americans to become involved in a foreign war. A reluctance to intervene in events outside of the Western Hemisphere had characterized American foreign policy since the administration of George Washington. World War I had been an exception that many American politicians regretted making.

Roosevelt's willingness to accede to the demands of the noninterventionists led him even to refuse assistance to those fleeing Nazi Germany. Although Roosevelt was aware of Nazi persecution of the Jews, he did little to aid them. In a symbolic act of support, he withdrew the American ambassador to Germany in 1938. He did not press for a relaxation of immigration quotas that would have allowed more refugees to enter the country, however. In 1939, he refused to support a bill that would have admitted twenty thousand Jewish refugee children to the United States. Again in 1939, when German refugees aboard the SS *St. Louis*, most of them Jews, were refused permission to land in Cuba and turned to the United States for help, the U.S. State Department informed them that immigration quotas for Germany had already been filled. Once again, Roosevelt did not intervene, because he feared that nativists in Congress might smear him as a friend of Jews.

To ensure that the United States did not get drawn into another war, Congress passed a series of Neutrality Acts in the second half of the 1930s. The Neutrality Act of 1935 banned the sale of armaments to warring nations. The following year, another Neutrality Act prohibited loaning money to belligerent countries. The last piece of legislation, the Neutrality Act of 1937, forbade the transportation of weapons or passengers to belligerent nations on board American ships and also prohibited American citizens from traveling on board the ships of nations at war.

Once all-out war began between Japan and China in 1937, Roosevelt sought ways to help the Chinese that did not violate U.S. law. Since Japan did not formally declare war on China, a state of belligerency did not technically exist. Therefore, under the terms of the Neutrality Acts, America was not prevented from transporting goods to China. In 1940, the president of China, Chiang Kai-shek, was able to prevail upon Roosevelt to ship to China one hundred P-40 fighter planes and to allow American volunteers, who technically became members of the Chinese Air Force, to fly them.

War Begins in Europe

In 1938, the agreement reached at the Munich Conference failed to satisfy Hitler—in fact, the refusal of Britain and France to go to war over the issue infuriated the German dictator. In May of the next year, Germany and Italy formalized their military alliance with the "Pact of Steel." On September 1, 1939, Hitler unleashed his Blitzkrieg, or "lightning war," against Poland, using swift, surprise attacks combining infantry, tanks, and aircraft to quickly overwhelm the enemy. Britain and France had already learned from Munich that Hitler could not be trusted and that his territorial demands were insatiable. On September 3, 1939, they declared war on Germany, and the European phase of World War II began. Responding to the German invasion of Poland, Roosevelt worked with Congress to alter the Neutrality Laws to permit a policy of "Cash and Carry" in munitions for Britain and France. The legislation, passed and signed by

Roosevelt in November 1939, permitted belligerents to purchase war **materiel** if they could pay cash for it and arrange for its transportation on board their own ships.

When the Germans commenced their spring offensive in 1940, they defeated France in six weeks with a highly mobile and quick invasion of France, Belgium, Luxembourg, and the Netherlands. In the Far East, Japan took advantage of France's surrender to Germany to occupy French Indochina. In response, beginning with the Export Control Act in July 1940, the United States began to embargo the shipment of various materials to Japan, starting first with aviation gasoline and machine tools, and proceeding to scrap iron and steel.

The Atlantic Charter

Following the surrender of France, the Battle of Britain began, as Germany proceeded to try to bomb England into submission. As the battle raged in the skies over Great Britain throughout the summer and autumn of 1940 (**Figure 6.6**), Roosevelt became increasingly concerned over England's ability to hold out against the German juggernaut. In June 1941, Hitler broke the nonaggression pact with the Soviet Union that had given him the backing to ravage Poland and marched his armies deep into Soviet territory, where they would kill Red Army regulars and civilians by the millions until their advances were stalled in the devastating one-year battle over Stalingrad two years later.

Click and Explore

Listen to the BBC's archived reports (http://openstaxcollege.org/l/15BattleBrit) of the Battle of Britain, including Winston Churchill's "Finest Hour" speech.

In August 1941, Roosevelt met with the British prime minister, Winston Churchill, off the coast of Newfoundland, Canada. At this meeting, the two leaders drafted the Atlantic Charter, the blueprint of Anglo-American cooperation during World War II. The charter stated that the United States and Britain sought no territory from the conflict. It proclaimed that citizens of all countries should be given the right of self-determination, self-government should be restored in places where it had been eliminated, and trade barriers should be lowered. Further, the charter mandated freedom of the seas, renounced the use of force to settle international disputes, and called for postwar disarmament.

Figure 6.6 London and other major British cities suffered extensive damaged from the bombing raids of the Battle of Britain. Over one million London houses were destroyed or damaged during "The Blitz" and almost twenty thousand Londoners were killed.

In March 1941, concerns over Britain's ability to defend itself also influenced Congress to authorize a policy of Lend Lease, a practice by which the United States could sell, lease, or transfer armaments to any nation deemed important to the defense of the United States. Lend Lease effectively ended the policy of nonintervention and dissolved America's pretense of being a neutral nation. The program ran from 1941 to 1945, and distributed some $45 billion worth of weaponry and supplies to Britain, the Soviet Union, China, and other allies.

A Date Which Will Live in Infamy

By the second half of 1941, Japan was feeling the pressure of the American embargo. As it could no longer buy strategic material from the United States, the Japanese were determined to obtain a sufficient supply of oil by taking control of the Dutch East Indies. However, they realized that such an action might increase the possibility of American intervention, since the Philippines, a U.S. territory, lay on the direct route that oil tankers would have to take to reach Japan from Indonesia. Japanese leaders thus attempted to secure a diplomatic solution by negotiating with the United States while also authorizing the navy to plan for war. The Japanese government also decided that if no peaceful resolution could be reached by the end of November 1941, then the nation would have to go to war against the United States.

The American final counterproposal to various offers by Japan was for the Japanese to completely withdraw, without any conditions, from China and enter into nonaggression pacts with all the Pacific powers. Japan found that proposal unacceptable but delayed its rejection for as long as possible. Then, at 7:48 a.m. on Sunday, December 7, the Japanese attacked the U.S. Pacific fleet at anchor in Pearl Harbor, Hawaii (**Figure 6.7**). They launched two waves of attacks from six aircraft carriers that had snuck into the central Pacific without being detected. The attacks brought some 353 fighters, bombers, and torpedo bombers down on the unprepared fleet. The Japanese hit all eight battleships in the harbor and sank four of them. They also damaged several cruisers and destroyers. On the ground, nearly two hundred aircraft were destroyed, and twenty-four hundred servicemen were killed. Another eleven hundred were wounded. Japanese losses were minimal. The strike was part of a more concerted campaign by the Japanese to gain territory. They subsequently attacked Hong Kong, Malaysia, Singapore, Guam, Wake Island, and the Philippines.

Figure 6.7 This famous shot captured the explosion of the USS *Shaw* after the Japanese bombed Pearl Harbor. While American losses were significant, the Japanese lost only twenty-nine planes and five miniature submarines.

Whatever reluctance to engage in conflict the American people had had before December 7, 1941, quickly evaporated. Americans' incredulity that Japan would take such a radical step quickly turned to a fiery anger, especially as the attack took place while Japanese diplomats in Washington were still negotiating a possible settlement. President Roosevelt, referring to the day of the attack as "a date which will live in infamy," asked Congress for a declaration of war, which it delivered to Japan on December 8. On December 11, Germany and Italy declared war on the United States in accordance with their alliance with Japan. Against its wishes, the United States had become part of the European conflict.

Click and Explore

You can listen to Franklin Roosevelt's speech to Congress (http://openstaxcollege.org/l/15FDRWar) seeking a Declaration of War at this archive of presidential recordings.

6.2 The Home Front

By the end of this section, you will be able to:
- Describe the steps taken by the United States to prepare for war
- Describe how the war changed employment patterns in the United States
- Discuss the contributions of civilians on the home front, especially women, to the war effort
- Analyze how the war affected race relations in the United States

The impact of the war on the United States was nowhere near as devastating as it was in Europe and the Pacific, where the battles were waged, but it still profoundly changed everyday life for all Americans.

On the positive side, the war effort finally and definitively ended the economic depression that had been plaguing the country since 1929. It also called upon Americans to unite behind the war effort and give of their money, their time, and their effort, as they sacrificed at home to assure success abroad. The upheaval caused by white men leaving for war meant that for many disenfranchised groups, such as women and African Americans, there were new opportunities in employment and wage earning. Still, fear and racism drove cracks in the nation's unified facade.

MOBILIZING A NATION

Although the United States had sought to avoid armed conflict, the country was not entirely unprepared for war. Production of armaments had increased since 1939, when, as a result of Congress's authorization of the Cash and Carry policy, contracts for weapons had begun to trickle into American factories. War production increased further following the passage of Lend Lease in 1941. However, when the United States entered the war, the majority of American factories were still engaged in civilian production, and many doubted that American businesses would be sufficiently motivated to convert their factories to wartime production.

Just a few years earlier, Roosevelt had been frustrated and impatient with business leaders when they failed to fully support the New Deal, but enlisting industrialists in the nation's crusade was necessary if the United States was to produce enough armaments to win the war. To encourage cooperation, the government agreed to assume all costs of development and production, and also guarantee a profit on the sale of what was produced. This arrangement resulted in 233 to 350 percent increases in profits over what the same businesses had been able to achieve from 1937 to 1940. In terms of dollars earned, corporate profits rose from $6.4 billion in 1940 to nearly $11 billion in 1944. As the country switched to wartime production, the top one hundred U.S. corporations received approximately 70 percent of government contracts; big businesses prospered.

In addition to gearing up industry to fight the war, the country also needed to build an army. A peacetime draft, the first in American history, had been established in September 1940, but the initial draftees were to serve for only one year, a length of time that was later extended. Furthermore, Congress had specified that no more than 900,000 men could receive military training at any one time. By December 1941, the United States had only one division completely ready to be deployed. Military planners estimated that it might take nine million men to secure victory. A massive draft program was required to expand the nation's military forces. Over the course of the war, approximately fifty million men registered for the draft; ten million were subsequently inducted into the service.

Approximately 2.5 million African Americans registered for the draft, and 1 million of them subsequently served. Initially, African American soldiers, who served in segregated units, had been used as support troops and not been sent into combat. By the end of the war, however, manpower needs resulted in African American recruits serving in the infantry and flying planes. The Tuskegee Institute in Alabama had instituted a civilian pilot training program for aspiring African American pilots. When the war began, the Department of War absorbed the program and adapted it to train combat pilots. First Lady Eleanor Roosevelt demonstrated both her commitment to African Americans and the war effort by visiting Tuskegee in 1941, shortly after the unit had been organized. To encourage the military to give the airmen a chance to serve in actual combat, she insisted on taking a ride in a plane flown by an African American pilot to demonstrate the Tuskegee Airmen's skill (**Figure 6.8**). When the Tuskegee Airmen did get their opportunity to serve in combat, they did so with distinction.

Figure 6.8 First Lady Eleanor Roosevelt insisted on flying with an African American pilot to help fight racism in the military. The First Lady was famous for her support of civil rights.

In addition, forty-four thousand Native Americans served in all theaters of the war. In some of the Pacific campaigns, Native Americans made distinct and unique contributions to Allied victories. Navajo marines served in communications units, exchanging information over radios using codes based on their native language, which the Japanese were unable to comprehend or to crack. They became known as code talkers and participated in the battles of Guadalcanal, Iwo Jima, Peleliu, and Tarawa. A smaller number of Comanche code talkers performed a similar function in the European theater.

While millions of Americans heeded the rallying cry for patriotism and service, there were those who, for various reasons, did not accept the call. Before the war began, American Peace Mobilization had campaigned against American involvement in the European conflict as had the noninterventionist America First organization. Both groups ended their opposition, however, at the time of the German invasion of the Soviet Union and the Japanese attack on Pearl Harbor, respectively. Nevertheless, during the war, some seventy-two thousand men registered as **conscientious objectors** (COs), and fifty-two thousand were granted that status. Of that fifty-two thousand, some accepted noncombat roles in the military, whereas others accepted unpaid work in civilian work camps. Many belonged to pacifist religious sects such as the Quakers or Mennonites. They were willing to serve their country, but they refused to kill. COs suffered public condemnation for disloyalty, and family members often turned against them. Strangers assaulted them. A portion of the town of Plymouth, NH, was destroyed by fire because the residents did not want to call upon the services of the COs trained as firemen at a nearby camp. Only a very small number of men evaded the draft completely.

Most Americans, however, were willing to serve, and they required a competent officer corps. The very same day that Germany invaded Poland in 1939, President Roosevelt promoted George C. Marshall, a veteran of World War I and an expert at training officers, from a one-star general to a four-star general, and gave him the responsibility of serving as Army Chief of Staff. The desire to create a command staff that could win the army's confidence no doubt contributed to the rather meteoric rise of Dwight D. Eisenhower (**Figure 6.9**). During World War I, Eisenhower had been assigned to organize America's new tank corps, and, although he never saw combat during the war, he demonstrated excellent organizational skills. When the United States entered World War II, Eisenhower was appointed commander of the General European Theater of Operations in June 1942.

Figure 6.9 Dwight D. Eisenhower rose quickly through the ranks to become commander of the European Theater of Operations by June 1942.

MY STORY

⊙ *General Eisenhower on Winning a War*

Promoted to the level of one-star general just before the attack on Pearl Harbor, Dwight D. Eisenhower had never held an active command position above the level of a battalion and was not considered a potential commander of major military operations. However, after he was assigned to the General Staff in Washington, DC, he quickly rose through the ranks and, by late 1942, was appointed commander of the North African campaign.

Excerpts from General Eisenhower's diary reveal his dedication to the war effort. He continued to work despite suffering a great personal loss.

> March 9, 1942
> General McNaughton (commanding Canadians in Britain) came to see me. He believes in attacking in Europe (thank God). He's over here in an effort to speed up landing craft production and cargo ships. Has some d good ideas. Sent him to see Somervell and Admiral Land. How I hope he can do something on landing craft.
>
> March 10, 1942
> Father dies this morning. Nothing I can do but send a wire.
> One thing that might help win this war is to get someone to shoot [Admiral] King. He's the antithesis of cooperation, a deliberately rude person, which means he's a mental bully. He became Commander in Chief of the fleet some time ago. Today he takes over, also Stark's job as chief of naval operations. It's a good thing to get rid of the double head in the navy, and of course Stark was just a nice old lady, but this fellow is going to cause a blow-up sooner or later, I'll bet a cookie.
> Gradually some of the people with whom I have to deal are coming to agree with me that there are just three "musts" for the Allies this year: hold open the line to England and support her as necessary, keep Russia in the war as an active participant; hold the India-Middle East buttress between Japs and Germans. All this assumes the safety from major attack of North America, Hawaii, and Caribbean area.
> We lost eight cargo ships yesterday. That we must stop, because any effort we make depends upon sea communication.
>
> March 11, 1942
> I have felt terribly. I should like so much to be with my Mother these few days. But we're at war. And war is not soft, it has no time to indulge even the deepest and most sacred emotions. I loved my Dad. I think my Mother the finest person I've ever known. She has been the inspiration for Dad's life and a true helpmeet in every sense of the word.
> I'm quitting work now, 7:30 p.m. I haven't the heart to go on tonight.
> —Dwight D. Eisenhower, *The Eisenhower Diaries*

What does Eisenhower identify as the most important steps to take to win the war?

EMPLOYMENT AND MIGRATION PATTERNS IN THE UNITED STATES

Even before the official beginning of the war, the country started to prepare. In August 1940, Congress created the Defense Plant Corporation, which had built 344 plants in the West by 1945, and had funneled over $1.8 billion into the economies of western states. After Pearl Harbor, as American military strategists began to plan counterattacks and campaigns against the Axis powers, California became a training ground. Troops trained there for tank warfare and amphibious assaults as well as desert campaigns—since the first assault against the Axis powers was planned for North Africa.

As thousands of Americans swarmed to the West Coast to take jobs in defense plants and shipyards, cities like Richmond, California, and nearby Oakland, expanded quickly. Richmond grew from a city of 20,000 people to 100,000 in only three years. Almost overnight, the population of California skyrocketed. African Americans moved out of the rural South into northern or West Coast cities to provide the muscle and skill to build the machines of war. Building on earlier waves of African American migration after the Civil

War and during World War I, the demographics of the nation changed with the growing urbanization of the African American population. Women also relocated to either follow their husbands to military bases or take jobs in the defense industry, as the total mobilization of the national economy began to tap into previously underemployed populations.

Roosevelt and his administration already had experience in establishing government controls and taking the initiative in economic matters during the Depression. In April 1941, Roosevelt created the Office of Price Administration (OPA), and, once the United States entered the war, the OPA regulated prices and attempted to combat inflation. The OPA ultimately had the power to set ceiling prices for all goods, except agricultural commodities, and to ration a long list of items. During the war, major labor unions pledged not to strike in order to prevent disruptions in production; in return, the government encouraged businesses to recognize unions and promised to help workers bargain for better wages.

As in World War I, the government turned to bond drives to finance the war. Millions of Americans purchased more than $185 billion worth of war bonds. Children purchased Victory Stamps and exchanged full stamp booklets for bonds. The federal government also instituted the current tax-withholding system to ensure collection of taxes. Finally, the government once again urged Americans to plant victory gardens, using marketing campaigns and celebrities to promote the idea (**Figure 6.10**). Americans responded eagerly, planting gardens in their backyards and vacant lots.

 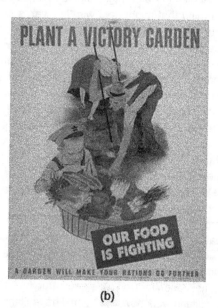

(a)   (b)

Figure 6.10 Wartime rationing meant that Americans had to do without many everyday items and learn to grow their own produce in order to allow the country's food supply to go to the troops.

The federal government also instituted rationing to ensure that America's fighting men were well fed. Civilians were issued ration booklets, books of coupons that enabled them to buy limited amounts of meat, coffee, butter, sugar, and other foods. Wartime cookbooks were produced, such as the Betty Crocker cookbook *Your Share*, telling housewives how to prepare tasty meals without scarce food items. Other items were rationed as well, including shoes, liquor, cigarettes, and gasoline. With a few exceptions, such as doctors, Americans were allowed to drive their automobiles only on certain days of the week. Most Americans complied with these regulations, but some illegally bought and sold rationed goods on the black market.

Click and Explore

View an excerpt from a PBS documentary on rationing (http://openstaxcollege.org/l/15Rationing) during World War II.

Civilians on the home front also recycled, conserved, and participated in scrap drives to collect items needed for the production of war materiel. Housewives saved cooking fats, needed to produce explosives. Children collected scrap metal, paper, rubber, silk, nylon, and old rags. Some children sacrificed beloved metal toys in order to "win the war." Civilian volunteers, trained to recognize enemy aircraft, watched the skies along the coasts and on the borders.

WOMEN IN THE WAR: ROSIE THE RIVETER AND BEYOND

As in the previous war, the gap in the labor force created by departing soldiers meant opportunities for women. In particular, World War II led many to take jobs in defense plants and factories around the country. For many women, these jobs provided unprecedented opportunities to move into occupations previously thought of as exclusive to men, especially the aircraft industry, where a majority of workers were composed of women by 1943. Most women in the labor force did not work in the defense industry, however. The majority took over other factory jobs that had been held by men. Many took positions in offices as well. As white women, many of whom had been in the workforce before the war, moved into these more highly paid positions, African American women, most of whom had previously been limited to domestic service, took over white women's lower-paying positions in factories; some were also hired by defense plants, however. Although women often earned more money than ever before, it was still far less than men received for doing the same jobs. Nevertheless, many achieved a degree of financial self-reliance that was enticing. By 1944, as many as 33 percent of the women working in the defense industries were mothers and worked "double-day" shifts—one at the plant and one at home.

Still, there was some resistance to women going to work in such a male-dominated environment. In order to recruit women for factory jobs, the government created a propaganda campaign centered on a now-iconic figure known as **Rosie the Riveter** (Figure 6.11). Rosie, who was a composite based on several real women, was most famously depicted by American illustrator Norman Rockwell. Rosie was tough yet feminine. To reassure men that the demands of war would not make women too masculine, some factories gave female employees lessons in how to apply makeup, and cosmetics were never rationed during the war. Elizabeth Arden even created a special red lipstick for use by women reservists in the Marine Corps.

(a)   (b)

Figure 6.11 "Rosie the Riveter" became a generic term for all women working in the defense industry. Although the Rosie depicted on posters was white, many of the real Rosies were African American, such as this woman who poses atop an airplane at the Lockheed Aircraft Corporation in Burbank, California (a), and Anna Bland, a worker at the Richmond Shipyards (b).

Although many saw the entry of women into the workforce as a positive thing, they also acknowledged that working women, especially mothers, faced great challenges. To try to address the dual role of women as workers and mothers, Eleanor Roosevelt urged her husband to approve the first U.S. government childcare facilities under the Community Facilities Act of 1942. Eventually, seven centers, servicing 105,000 children, were built. The First Lady also urged industry leaders like Henry Kaiser to build model childcare facilities for their workers. Still, these efforts did not meet the full need for childcare for working mothers.

The lack of childcare facilities meant that many children had to fend for themselves after school, and some had to assume responsibility for housework and the care of younger siblings. Some mothers took younger children to work with them and left them locked in their cars during the workday. Police and social workers also reported an increase in juvenile delinquency during the war. New York City saw its average number of juvenile cases balloon from 9,500 in the prewar years to 11,200 during the war. In San Diego, delinquency rates for girls, including sexual misbehavior, shot up by 355 percent. It is unclear whether more juveniles were actually engaging in delinquent behavior; the police may simply have become more vigilant during wartime and arrested youngsters for activities that would have gone overlooked before the war. In any event, law enforcement and juvenile courts attributed the perceived increase to a lack of supervision by working mothers.

Tens of thousands of women served in the war effort more directly. Approximately 350,000 joined the military. They worked as nurses, drove trucks, repaired airplanes, and performed clerical work to free up men for combat. Those who joined the Women's Airforce Service Pilots (WASPs) flew planes from the factories to military bases. Some of these women were killed in combat and captured as prisoners of war. Over sixteen hundred of the women nurses received various decorations for courage under fire. Many women also flocked to work in a variety of civil service jobs. Others worked as chemists and engineers, developing weapons for the war. This included thousands of women who were recruited to work on the Manhattan Project, developing the atomic bomb.

THE CULTURE OF WAR: ENTERTAINERS AND THE WAR EFFORT

During the Great Depression, movies had served as a welcome diversion from the difficulties of everyday life, and during the war, this held still truer. By 1941, there were more movie theaters than banks in the United States. In the 1930s, newsreels, which were shown in movie theaters before feature films, had informed the American public of what was happening elsewhere in the world. This interest grew once American armies began to engage the enemy. Many informational documentaries about the war were also shown in movie theaters. The most famous were those in the *Why We Fight* series, filmed by Hollywood director Frank Capra. During the war, Americans flocked to the movies not only to learn what was happening to the troops overseas but also to be distracted from the fears and hardships of wartime by cartoons, dramas, and comedies. By 1945, movie attendance had reached an all-time high.

Click and Explore

This link shows newsreel footage of a raid (http://openstaxcollege.org/l/15Tarawa) on Tarawa Island. This footage was shown in movie theaters around the country.

Many feature films were patriotic stories that showed the day's biggest stars as soldiers fighting the nefarious German and Japanese enemy. During the war years, there was a consistent supply of patriotic movies, with actors glorifying and inspiring America's fighting men. John Wayne, who had become a star in the 1930s, appeared in many war-themed movies, including *The Fighting Seabees* and *Back to Bataan*.

Besides appearing in patriotic movies, many male entertainers temporarily gave up their careers to serve in the armed forces (**Figure 6.12**). Jimmy Stewart served in the Army Air Force and appeared in a short film entitled *Winning Your Wings* that encouraged young men to enlist. Tyrone Power joined the U.S. Marines. Female entertainers did their part as well. Rita Hayworth and Marlene Dietrich entertained the troops. African American singer and dancer Josephine Baker entertained Allied troops in North Africa and also carried secret messages for the French Resistance. Actress Carole Lombard was killed in a plane crash while returning home from a rally where she had sold war bonds.

(a)   (b)

Figure 6.12 General George Marshall awards Frank Capra the Distinguished Service Cross in 1945 (a), in recognition of the important contribution that Capra's films made to the war effort. Jimmy Stewart was awarded numerous commendations for his military service, including the French Croix de Guerre (b).

DEFINING "AMERICAN"

✪ *The Meaning of Democracy*

E. B. White was one of the most famous writers of the twentieth century. During the 1940s, he was known for the articles that he contributed to *The New Yorker* and the column that he wrote for *Harper's Magazine*. Today, he is remembered for his children's books *Stuart Little* and *Charlotte's Web*, and for his collaboration with William Strunk, Jr., *The Elements of Style*, a guide to writing. In 1943, he wrote a definition of democracy as an example of what Americans hoped that they were fighting for.

> We received a letter from the Writer's War Board the other day asking for a statement on 'The Meaning of Democracy.' It presumably is our duty to comply with such a request, and it is certainly our pleasure. Surely the Board knows what democracy is. It is the line that forms on the right. It is the 'don't' in don't shove. It is the hole in the stuffed shirt through which the sawdust slowly trickles; it is the dent in the high hat. Democracy is the recurrent suspicion that more than half of the people are right more than half of the time. It is the feeling of privacy in the voting booths, the feeling of communion in the libraries, the feeling of vitality everywhere. Democracy is a letter to the editor. Democracy is the score at the beginning of the ninth. It is an idea that hasn't been disproved yet, a song the words of which have not gone bad. It is the mustard on the hot dog and the cream in the rationed coffee. Democracy is a request from a War Board, in the middle of the morning in the middle of a war, wanting to know what democracy is.

Do you agree with this definition of democracy? Would you change anything to make it more contemporary?

SOCIAL TENSIONS ON THE HOME FRONT

The need for Americans to come together, whether in Hollywood, the defense industries, or the military, to support the war effort encouraged feelings of unity among the American population. However, the desire for unity did not always mean that Americans of color were treated as equals or even tolerated, despite their proclamations of patriotism and their willingness to join in the effort to defeat America's enemies in Europe and Asia. For African Americans, Mexican Americans, and especially for Japanese Americans, feelings of patriotism and willingness to serve one's country both at home and abroad was not enough to guarantee equal treatment by white Americans or to prevent the U.S. government from regarding them as the enemy.

African Americans and Double V

The African American community had, at the outset of the war, forged some promising relationships with the Roosevelt administration through civil rights activist Mary McLeod Bethune and Roosevelt's "Black Cabinet" of African American advisors. Through the intervention of Eleanor Roosevelt, Bethune was appointed to the advisory council set up by the War Department Women's Interest Section. In this position, Bethune was able to organize the first officer candidate school for women and enable African American women to become officers in the Women's Auxiliary Corps.

As the U.S. economy revived as a result of government defense contracts, African Americans wanted to ensure that their service to the country earned them better opportunities and more equal treatment. Accordingly, in 1942, after African American labor leader A. Philip Randolph pressured Roosevelt with a threatened "March on Washington," the president created, by Executive Order 8802, the Fair Employment Practices Committee. The purpose of this committee was to see that there was no discrimination in the defense industries. While they were effective in forcing defense contractors, such as the DuPont Corporation, to hire African Americans, they were not able to force corporations to place African Americans in well-paid positions. For example, at DuPont's plutonium production plant in Hanford,

Washington, African Americans were hired as low-paid construction workers but not as laboratory technicians.

During the war, the Congress of Racial Equality (CORE), founded by James Farmer in 1942, used peaceful civil disobedience in the form of sit-ins to desegregate certain public spaces in Washington, DC, and elsewhere, as its contribution to the war effort. Members of CORE sought support for their movement by stating that one of their goals was to deprive the enemy of the ability to generate anti-American propaganda by accusing the United States of racism. After all, they argued, if the United States were going to denounce Germany and Japan for abusing human rights, the country should itself be as exemplary as possible. Indeed, CORE's actions were in keeping with the goals of the **Double V campaign** that was begun in 1942 by the *Pittsburgh Courier*, the largest African American newspaper at the time (**Figure 6.13**). The campaign called upon African Americans to accomplish the two "Vs": victory over America's foreign enemies and victory over racism in the United States.

Figure 6.13 During World War II, African Americans volunteered for government work just as white Americans did. These Washington, DC, residents have become civil defense workers as part of the Double V campaign that called for victory at home and abroad.

Despite the willingness of African Americans to fight for the United States, racial tensions often erupted in violence, as the geographic relocation necessitated by the war brought African Americans into closer contact with whites. There were race riots in Detroit, Harlem, and Beaumont, Texas, in which white residents responded with sometimes deadly violence to their new black coworkers or neighbors. There were also racial incidents at or near several military bases in the South. Incidents of African American soldiers being harassed or assaulted occurred at Fort Benning, Georgia; Fort Jackson, South Carolina; Alexandria, Louisiana; Fayetteville, Arkansas; and Tampa, Florida. African American leaders such as James Farmer and Walter White, the executive secretary of the NAACP since 1931, were asked by General Eisenhower to investigate complaints of the mistreatment of African American servicemen while on active duty. They prepared a fourteen-point memorandum on how to improve conditions for African Americans in the service, sowing some of the seeds of the postwar civil rights movement during the war years.

The Zoot Suit Riots

Mexican Americans also encountered racial prejudice. The Mexican American population in Southern California grew during World War II due to the increased use of Mexican agricultural workers in the fields to replace the white workers who had left for better paying jobs in the defense industries. The United States and Mexican governments instituted the "bracero" program on August 4, 1942, which sought to address the needs of California growers for manual labor to increase food production during wartime. The result was the immigration of thousands of impoverished Mexicans into the United States to work as *braceros*, or manual laborers.

Forced by racial discrimination to live in the barrios of East Los Angeles, many Mexican American youths sought to create their own identity and began to adopt a distinctive style of dress known as **zoot suits**, which were also popular among many young African American men. The zoot suits, which required large amounts of cloth to produce, violated wartime regulations that restricted the amount of cloth that could be used in civilian garments. Among the charges leveled at young Mexican Americans was that they were un-American and unpatriotic; wearing zoot suits was seen as evidence of this. Many native-born Americans also denounced Mexican American men for being unwilling to serve in the military, even though some 350,000 Mexican Americans either volunteered to serve or were drafted into the armed services. In the summer of 1943, "zoot-suit riots" occurred in Los Angeles when carloads of white sailors, encouraged by other white civilians, stripped and beat a group of young men wearing the distinctive form of dress. In retaliation, young Mexican American men attacked and beat up sailors. The response was swift and severe, as sailors and civilians went on a spree attacking young Mexican Americans on the streets, in bars, and in movie theaters. More than one hundred people were injured.

Internment

Japanese Americans also suffered from discrimination. The Japanese attack on Pearl Harbor unleashed a cascade of racist assumptions about Japanese immigrants and Japanese Americans in the United States that culminated in the relocation and **internment** of 120,000 people of Japanese ancestry, 66 percent of whom had been born in the United States. **Executive Order 9066**, signed by Roosevelt on February 19, 1942, gave the army power to remove people from "military areas" to prevent sabotage or espionage. The army then used this authority to relocate people of Japanese ancestry living along the Pacific coast of Washington, Oregon, and California, as well as in parts of Arizona, to internment camps in the American interior. Although a study commissioned earlier by Roosevelt indicated that there was little danger of disloyalty on the part of West Coast Japanese, fears of sabotage, perhaps spurred by the attempted rescue of a Japanese airman shot down at Pearl Harbor by Japanese living in Hawaii, and racist sentiments led Roosevelt to act. Ironically, Japanese in Hawaii were not interned. Although characterized afterwards as America's worst wartime mistake by Eugene V. Rostow in the September 1945 edition of *Harper's Magazine*, the government's actions were in keeping with decades of anti-Asian sentiment on the West Coast.

After the order went into effect, Lt. General John L. DeWitt, in charge of the Western Defense command, ordered approximately 127,000 Japanese and Japanese Americans—roughly 90 percent of those of Japanese ethnicity living in the United States—to assembly centers where they were transferred to hastily prepared camps in the interior of California, Arizona, Colorado, Utah, Idaho, Wyoming, and Arkansas (**Figure 6.14**). Those who were sent to the camps reported that the experience was deeply traumatic. Families were sometimes separated. People could only bring a few of their belongings and had to abandon the rest of their possessions. The camps themselves were dismal and overcrowded. Despite the hardships, the Japanese attempted to build communities in the camps and resume "normal" life. Adults participated in camp government and worked at a variety of jobs. Children attended school, played basketball against local teams, and organized Boy Scout units. Nevertheless, they were imprisoned, and minor infractions, such as wandering too near the camp gate or barbed wire fences while on an evening stroll, could meet with severe consequences. Some sixteen thousand Germans, including some from Latin America, and German Americans were also placed in internment camps, as were 2,373 persons of Italian ancestry. However, unlike the case with Japanese Americans, they represented only a tiny percentage of the members of these ethnic groups living in the country. Most of these people were innocent of any wrongdoing, but some Germans were members of the Nazi party. No interned Japanese Americans were found guilty of sabotage or espionage.

Figure 6.14 Japanese Americans standing in line in front of a poster detailing internment orders in California.

Despite being singled out for special treatment, many Japanese Americans sought to enlist, but draft boards commonly classified them as 4-C: undesirable aliens. However, as the war ground on, some were reclassified as eligible for service. In total, nearly thirty-three thousand Japanese Americans served in the military during the war. Of particular note was the 442nd Regimental Combat Team, nicknamed the "Go For Broke," which finished the war as the most decorated unit in U.S. military history given its size and length of service. While their successes, and the successes of the African American pilots, were lauded, the country and the military still struggled to contend with its own racial tensions, even as the soldiers in Europe faced the brutality of Nazi Germany.

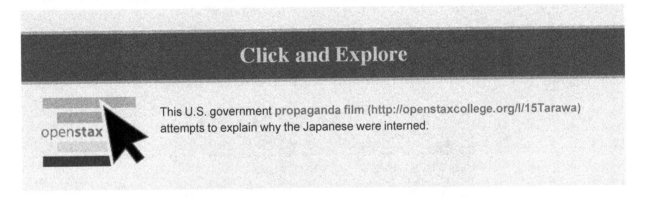

Click and Explore

This U.S. government propaganda film (http://openstaxcollege.org/l/15Tarawa) attempts to explain why the Japanese were interned.

6.3 Victory in the European Theater

By the end of this section, you will be able to:
- Identify the major battles of the European theater
- Analyze the goals and results of the major wartime summit meetings

Despite the fact that a Japanese attack in the Pacific was the tripwire for America's entrance into the war, Roosevelt had been concerned about Great Britain since the beginning of the Battle of Britain. Roosevelt viewed Germany as the greater threat to freedom. Hence, he leaned towards a "Europe First" strategy, even before the United States became an active belligerent. That meant that the United States would concentrate the majority of its resources and energies in achieving a victory over Germany first and then focus on defeating Japan. Within Europe, Churchill and Roosevelt were committed to saving Britain   and acted with this goal in mind, often ignoring the needs of the Soviet Union. As Roosevelt imagined an "empire-free" postwar world, in keeping with the goals of the Atlantic Charter, he could also envision the United States becoming the preeminent world power economically, politically, and militarily.

WARTIME DIPLOMACY

Franklin Roosevelt entered World War II with an eye toward a new postwar world, one where the United States would succeed Britain as the leader of Western capitalist democracies, replacing the old British imperial system with one based on free trade and decolonization. The goals of the Atlantic Charter had explicitly included self-determination, self-government, and free trade. In 1941, although Roosevelt had yet to meet Soviet premier Joseph Stalin, he had confidence that he could forge a positive relationship with him, a confidence that Churchill believed was born of naiveté. These allied leaders, known as the **Big Three**, thrown together by the necessity to defeat common enemies, took steps towards working in concert despite their differences.

Through a series of wartime conferences, Roosevelt and the other global leaders sought to come up with a strategy to both defeat the Germans and bolster relationships among allies. In January 1943, at Casablanca, Morocco, Churchill convinced Roosevelt to delay an invasion of France in favor of an invasion of Sicily (**Figure 6.15**). It was also at this conference that Roosevelt enunciated the doctrine of "unconditional surrender." Roosevelt agreed to demand an unconditional surrender from Germany and Japan to assure the Soviet Union that the United States would not negotiate a separate peace and prepare the former belligerents for a thorough and permanent transformation after the war. Roosevelt thought that announcing this as a specific war aim would discourage any nation or leader from seeking any negotiated armistice that would hinder efforts to reform and transform the defeated nations. Stalin, who was not at the conference, affirmed the concept of unconditional surrender when asked to do so. However, he was dismayed over the delay in establishing a "second front" along which the Americans and British would directly engage German forces in western Europe. A western front, brought about through an invasion across the English Channel, which Stalin had been demanding since 1941, offered the best means of drawing Germany away from the east. At a meeting in Tehran, Iran, also in November 1943, Churchill, Roosevelt, and Stalin met to finalize plans for a cross-channel invasion.

Figure 6.15 Prime Minister Winston Churchill and President Roosevelt met together multiple times during the war. One such conference was located in Casablanca, Morocco, in January 1943.

THE INVASION OF EUROPE

Preparing to engage the Nazis in Europe, the United States landed in North Africa in 1942. The Axis campaigns in North Africa had begun when Italy declared war on England in June 1940, and British forces had invaded the Italian colony of Libya. The Italians had responded with a counteroffensive that penetrated into Egypt, only to be defeated by the British again. In response, Hitler dispatched the Afrika Korps under General Erwin Rommel, and the outcome of the situation was in doubt until shortly before American forces joined the British.

Although the Allied campaign secured control of the southern Mediterranean and preserved Egypt and the Suez Canal for the British, Stalin and the Soviets were still engaging hundreds of German divisions in bitter struggles at Stalingrad and Leningrad. The invasion of North Africa did nothing to draw German troops away from the Soviet Union. An invasion of Europe by way of Italy, which is what the British and American campaign in North Africa laid the ground for, pulled a few German divisions away from their Russian targets. But while Stalin urged his allies to invade France, British and American troops pursued the defeat of Mussolini's Italy. This choice greatly frustrated Stalin, who felt that British interests were taking precedence over the agony that the Soviet Union was enduring at the hands of the invading German army. However, Churchill saw Italy as the vulnerable underbelly of Europe and believed that Italian support for Mussolini was waning, suggesting that victory there might be relatively easy. Moreover, Churchill pointed out that if Italy were taken out of the war, then the Allies would control the Mediterranean, offering the Allies easier shipping access to both the Soviet Union and the British Far Eastern colonies.

D-Day

A direct assault on Nazi Germany's "Fortress Europe" was still necessary for final victory. On June 6, 1944, the second front became a reality when Allied forces stormed the beaches of northern France on **D-day**. Beginning at 6:30 a.m., some twenty-four thousand British, Canadian, and American troops waded ashore along a fifty-mile piece of the Normandy coast (**Figure 6.16**). Well over a million troops would follow their lead. German forces on the hills and cliffs above shot at them, and once they reached the beach, they encountered barbed wire and land mines. More than ten thousand Allied soldiers were wounded or killed during the assault. Following the establishment of beachheads at Normandy, it took months of difficult fighting before Paris was liberated on August 20, 1944. The invasion did succeed in diverting German forces from the eastern front to the western front, relieving some of the pressure on Stalin's troops. By that time, however, Russian forces had already defeated the German army at Stalingrad, an event that many consider the turning point of the war in Europe, and begun to push the Germans out of the Soviet Union.

Figure 6.16 U.S. troops in a military landing craft approach the beach code-named "Omaha" on June 6, 1944. More than ten thousand soldiers were killed or wounded during the D-day assault along the coast of Normandy, France.

Nazi Germany was not ready to surrender, however. On December 16, in a surprise move, the Germans threw nearly a quarter-million men at the Western Allies in an attempt to divide their armies and encircle major elements of the American forces. The struggle, known as the Battle of the Bulge, raged until the end of January. Some ninety thousand Americans were killed, wounded, or lost in action. Nevertheless, the Germans were turned back, and Hitler's forces were so spent that they could never again mount offensive operations.

Confronting the Holocaust

The Holocaust, Hitler's plan to kill the Jews of Europe, had begun as early as 1933, with the construction of Dachau, the first of more than forty thousand camps for incarcerating Jews, submitting them to forced labor, or exterminating them. Eventually, six extermination camps were established between 1941 and 1945 in Polish territory. Jewish men, women, and children from throughout Europe were transported to these camps in Germany and other areas under Nazi control. Although the majority of the people in the camps were Jews, the Nazis sent Roma (gypsies), gays and lesbians, Jehovah's Witnesses, and political opponents to the camps as well. Some prisoners were put to work at hard labor; many of them subsequently died of disease or starvation. Most of those sent to the extermination camps were killed upon arrival with poisoned gas. Ultimately, some eleven million people died in the camps. As Soviet troops began to advance from the east and U.S. forces from the west, camp guards attempted to hide the evidence of their crimes by destroying records and camp buildings, and marching surviving prisoners away from the sites (**Figure 6.17**).

Figure 6.17 A U.S. senator, and member of a congressional committee investigating Nazi atrocities, views the evidence first hand at Buchenwald concentration camp near Weimar, Germany, in the summer of 1945.

MY STORY

✪ *Felix L. Sparks on the Liberation of Dachau*

The horrors of the concentration camps remained with the soldiers who liberated them long after the war had ended. Below is an excerpt of the recollection of one soldier.

> Our first experience with the camp came as a traumatic shock. The first evidence of the horrors to come was a string of forty railway cars on a railway spur leading into the camp. Each car was filled with emaciated human corpses, both men and women. A hasty search by the stunned infantry soldiers revealed no signs of life among the hundreds of still bodies, over two thousand in all.
>
> It was in this atmosphere of human depravity, degradation and death that the soldiers of my battalion then entered the camp itself. Almost all of the SS command guarding the camp had fled before our arrival, leaving behind about two hundred lower ranking members of the command. There was some sporadic firing of weapons. As we approached the confinement area, the scene numbed my senses. Dante's Inferno seemed pale compared to the real hell of Dachau. A row of small cement structures near the prison entrance contained a coal-fired crematorium, a gas chamber, and rooms piled high with naked and emaciated corpses. As I turned to look over the prison yard with un-believing eyes, I saw a large number of dead inmates lying where they has fallen in the last few hours or days before our arrival. Since all of the bodies were in various stages of decomposition, the stench of death was overpowering. The men of the 45th Infantry Division were hardened combat veterans. We had been in combat almost two years at that point. While we were accustomed to death, we were not able to comprehend the type of death that we encountered at Dachau.
>
> —Felix L. Sparks, remarks at the U.S. Holocaust Museum, May 8, 1995

Click and Explore

Listen to the **accounts of Holocaust survivors** (http://openstaxcollege.org/l/ 15Holocaust) by clicking on "Listen Now" below the name of the person whose story you wish to hear.

YALTA AND PREPARING FOR VICTORY

The last time the Big Three met was in early February 1945 at Yalta in the Soviet Union. Roosevelt was sick, and Stalin's armies were pushing the German army back towards Berlin from the east. Churchill and Roosevelt thus had to accept a number of compromises that strengthened Stalin's position in eastern Europe. In particular, they agreed to allow the Communist government installed by the Soviet Union in Poland to remain in power until free elections took place. For his part, Stalin reaffirmed his commitment, first voiced at Tehran, to enter the war against Japan following the surrender of Germany (**Figure 6.18**). He also agreed that the Soviet Union would participate in the United Nations, a new peacekeeping body intended to replace the League of Nations. The Big Three left Yalta with many details remaining unclear, planning to finalize plans for the treatment of Germany and the shape of postwar Europe at a later conference. However, Roosevelt did not live to attend the next meeting. He died on April 12, 1945, and Harry S. Truman became president.

Figure 6.18 Prime Minister Winston Churchill, President Franklin Roosevelt, and Premier Joseph Stalin made final plans for the defeat of Nazi Germany at Yalta in February 1945.

By April 1945, Soviet forces had reached Berlin, and both the U.S. and British Allies were pushing up against Germany's last defenses in the western part of the nation. Hitler committed suicide on April 30, 1945. On May 8, 1945, Germany surrendered. The war in Europe was over, and the Allies and liberated regions celebrated the end of the long ordeal. Germany was thoroughly defeated; its industries and cities were badly damaged.

The victorious Allies set about determining what to do to rebuild Europe at the Potsdam Summit Conference in July 1945. Attending the conference were Stalin, Truman, and Churchill, now the outgoing prime minister, as well as the new British prime minister, Clement Atlee. Plans to divide Germany and Austria, and their capital cities, into four zones—to be occupied by the British, French, Americans, and Soviets—a subject discussed at Yalta, were finalized. In addition, the Allies agreed to dismantle Germany's heavy industry in order to make it impossible for the country to produce more armaments.

6.4 The Pacific Theater and the Atomic Bomb

By the end of this section, you will be able to:
- Discuss the strategy employed against the Japanese and some of the significant battles of the Pacific campaign
- Describe the effects of the atomic bombs on Hiroshima and Nagasaki
- Analyze the decision to drop atomic bombs on Japan

Japanese forces won a series of early victories against Allied forces from December 1941 to May 1942. They seized Guam and Wake Island from the United States, and streamed through Malaysia and Thailand into the Philippines and through the Dutch East Indies. By February 1942, they were threatening Australia. The Allies turned the tide in May and June 1942, at the Battle of Coral Sea and the Battle of Midway. The Battle of Midway witnessed the first Japanese naval defeat since the nineteenth century. Shortly after the American victory, U.S. forces invaded Guadalcanal and New Guinea. Slowly, throughout 1943, the United States engaged in a campaign of "island hopping," gradually moving across the Pacific to Japan. In 1944, the United States, seized Saipan and won the Battle of the Philippine Sea. Progressively, American forces drew closer to the strategically important targets of Iwo Jima and Okinawa.

THE PACIFIC CAMPAIGN

During the 1930s, Americans had caught glimpses of Japanese armies in action and grew increasingly sympathetic towards war-torn China. Stories of Japanese atrocities bordering on genocide and the shock of the attack on Pearl Harbor intensified racial animosity toward the Japanese. Wartime propaganda portrayed Japanese soldiers as uncivilized and barbaric, sometimes even inhuman (**Figure 6.19**), unlike America's German foes. Admiral William Halsey spoke for many Americans when he urged them to "Kill Japs! Kill Japs! Kill more Japs!" Stories of the dispiriting defeats at Bataan and the Japanese capture of the Philippines at Corregidor in 1942 revealed the Japanese cruelty and mistreatment of Americans. The "Bataan Death March," during which as many as 650 American and 10,000 Filipino prisoners of war died, intensified anti-Japanese feelings. Kamikaze attacks that took place towards the end of the war were regarded as proof of the irrationality of Japanese martial values and mindless loyalty to Emperor Hirohito.

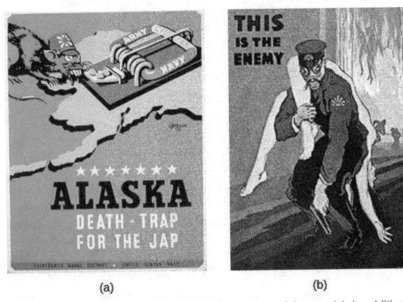

(a)   (b)

Figure 6.19 Anti-Japanese propaganda often portrayed the Japanese as inhuman (a). In addition to emphasizing the supposed apish features of the Japanese (b), this poster depicts the victim as a white woman, undoubtedly to increase American horror even more.

Despite the Allies' Europe First strategy, American forces took the resources that they could assemble and swung into action as quickly as they could to blunt the Japanese advance. Infuriated by stories of defeat at the hands of the allegedly racially inferior Japanese, many high-ranking American military leaders demanded that greater attention be paid to the Pacific campaign. Rather than simply wait for the invasion of France to begin, naval and army officers such as General Douglas MacArthur argued that American resources should be deployed in the Pacific to reclaim territory seized by Japan.

In the Pacific, MacArthur and the Allied forces pursued an island hopping strategy that bypassed certain island strongholds held by the Japanese that were of little or no strategic value. By seizing locations from which Japanese communications and transportation routes could be disrupted or destroyed, the Allies advanced towards Japan without engaging the thousands of Japanese stationed on garrisoned islands. The goal was to advance American air strength close enough to Japan proper to achieve air superiority over the home islands; the nation could then be bombed into submission or at least weakened in preparation for an amphibious assault. By February 1945, American forces had reached the island of Iwo Jima (**Figure 6.20**). Iwo Jima was originally meant to serve as a forward air base for fighter planes, providing cover for long-distance bombing raids on Japan. Two months later, an even larger engagement, the hardest fought and bloodiest battle of the Pacific theater, took place as American forces invaded Okinawa. The battle raged from April 1945 well into July 1945; the island was finally secured at the cost of seventeen thousand American soldiers killed and thirty-six thousand wounded. Japanese forces lost over 100,000 troops. Perhaps as many as 150,000 civilians perished as well.

Figure 6.20 American forces come ashore on Iwo Jima. Their vehicles had difficulty moving on the beach's volcanic sands. Troops endured shelling by Japanese troops on Mount Suribachi, the mountain in the background.

DROPPING THE ATOMIC BOMB

All belligerents in World War II sought to develop powerful and devastating weaponry. As early as 1939, German scientists had discovered how to split uranium atoms, the technology that would ultimately allow for the creation of the atomic bomb. Albert Einstein, who had emigrated to the United States in 1933 to escape the Nazis, urged President Roosevelt to launch an American atomic research project, and Roosevelt agreed to do so, with reservations. In late 1941, the program received its code name: the **Manhattan Project**. Located at Los Alamos, New Mexico, the Manhattan Project ultimately employed 150,000 people and cost some $2 billion. In July 1945, the project's scientists successfully tested the first atomic bomb.

In the spring of 1945, the military began to prepare for the possible use of an atomic bomb by choosing appropriate targets. Suspecting that the immediate bomb blast would extend over one mile and secondary effects would include fire damage, a compact city of significant military value with densely built frame buildings seemed to be the best target. Eventually, the city of Hiroshima, the headquarters of the Japanese Second Army, and the communications and supply hub for all of southern Japan, was chosen. The city of Kokura was chosen as the primary target of the second bomb, and Nagasaki, an industrial center producing war materiel and the largest seaport in southern Japan, was selected as a secondary target.

The *Enola Gay*, a B-29 bomber named after its pilot's mother, dropped an atomic bomb known as "Little Boy" on Hiroshima at 8:15 a.m. A huge mushroom cloud rose above the city. Survivors sitting down for breakfast or preparing to go to school recalled seeing a bright light and then being blown across the room. The immense heat of the blast melted stone and metal, and ignited fires throughout the city. One man later recalled watching his mother and brother burn to death as fire consumed their home. A female survivor, a child at the time of the attack, remembered finding the body of her mother, which had been reduced to ashes and fell apart as she touched it. Two-thirds of the buildings in Hiroshima were destroyed. Within an hour after the bombing, radioactive "black rain" began to fall. Approximately seventy thousand people died in the original blast. The same number would later die of radiation poisoning. When Japan refused to surrender, a second atomic bomb, named Fat Man, was dropped on Nagasaki on August 9, 1945. At least sixty thousand people were killed at Nagasaki. Kokura, the primary target, had been shrouded in clouds on that morning and thus had escaped destruction. It is impossible to say with certainty how many died in the two attacks; the heat of the bomb blasts incinerated or vaporized many of the victims (**Figure 6.21**).

(a)   (b)

Figure 6.21 According to estimates, the atomic bombs dropped on Hiroshima and Nagasaki (a) together killed anywhere from 125,000 to over 250,000 people. The so-called Genbaku (A-Bomb) Dome, now the Hiroshima Peace Memorial, was the only building left standing near the Hiroshima bomb's hypocenter (b).

The decision to use nuclear weapons is widely debated. Why exactly did the United States deploy an atomic bomb? The fierce resistance that the Japanese forces mounted during their early campaigns led American planners to believe that any invasion of the Japanese home islands would be exceedingly bloody. According to some estimates, as many as 250,000 Americans might die in securing a final victory. Such considerations undoubtedly influenced President Truman's decision. Truman, who had not known about the Manhattan Project until Roosevelt's death, also may not have realized how truly destructive it was. Indeed, some of the scientists who had built the bomb were surprised by its power. One question that has not been fully answered is why the United States dropped the second bomb on Nagasaki. As some scholars have noted, if Truman's intention was to eliminate the need for a home island invasion, he could have given Japan more time to respond after bombing Hiroshima. He did not, however. The second bombing may have been intended to send a message to Stalin, who was becoming intransigent regarding postwar Europe. If it is indeed true that Truman had political motivations for using the bombs, then the destruction of Nagasaki might have been the first salvo of the Cold War with the Soviet Union. And yet, other historians have pointed out that the war had unleashed such massive atrocities against civilians by all belligerents—the United States included—that by the summer of 1945, the president no longer needed any particular reason to use his entire nuclear arsenal.

THE WAR ENDS

Whatever the true reasons for their use, the bombs had the desired effect of getting Japan to surrender. Even before the atomic attacks, the conventional bombings of Japan, the defeat of its forces in the field, and the entry of the Soviet Union into the war had convinced the Imperial Council that they had to end the war. They had hoped to negotiate the terms of the peace, but Emperor Hirohito intervened after the destruction of Nagasaki and accepted unconditional surrender. Although many Japanese shuddered at the humiliation of defeat, most were relieved that the war was over. Japan's industries and cities had been thoroughly destroyed, and the immediate future looked bleak as they awaited their fate at the hands of the American occupation forces.

The victors had yet another nation to rebuild and reform, but the war was finally over. Following the surrender, the Japanese colony of Korea was divided along the thirty-eighth parallel; the Soviet Union was given control of the northern half and the United States was given control of the southern portion. In Europe, as had been agreed upon at a meeting of the Allies in Potsdam in the summer of 1945, Germany was divided into four occupation zones that would be controlled by Britain, France, the Soviet Union, and the United States, respectively. The city of Berlin was similarly split into four. Plans were made to prosecute war criminals in both Japan and Germany. In October 1945, the United Nations was created. People around the world celebrated the end of the conflict, but America's use of atomic bombs and disagreements between the United States and the Soviet Union at Yalta and Potsdam would contribute to ongoing instability in the postwar world.

CHAPTER 7

Post-War Prosperity and Cold War Fears, 1945-1960

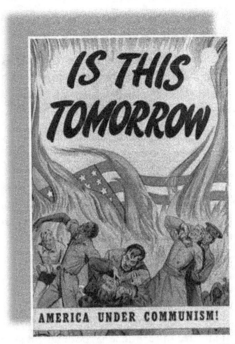

Figure 7.1 *Is This Tomorrow?* warned Americans about the potential horrors of living under a Communist dictatorship. Postwar propaganda such as this comic book, the cover of which showed invading Russians attacking Americans and the U.S. flag in flames, served to drum up fear during the Cold War.

Chapter Outline

Introduction

Is This Tomorrow? (**Figure 7.1**), a 1947 comic book, highlights one way that the federal government and some Americans revived popular sentiment in opposition to Communism. The United States and the Soviet Union, allies during World War II, had different visions for the postwar world. As Joseph Stalin, premier of the Soviet Union, tightened his grip on the countries of Eastern Europe, Americans began to fear that it was his goal to spread the Communist revolution throughout the world and make newly independent nations puppets of the Soviet Union. To enlist as many Americans as possible in the fight against Soviet domination, the U.S. government and purveyors of popular culture churned out propaganda intended to convince average citizens of the dangers posed by the Soviet Union. Artwork such as the cover of *Is This Tomorrow?*, which depicts Russians attacking Americans, including a struggling woman and an African American veteran still wearing his uniform, played upon postwar fears of Communism and of a future war with the Soviet Union. These fears dominated American life following World War II and affected foreign policy, military strategy, urban planning, popular culture, and the civil rights movement.

7.1 The Challenges of Peacetime

By the end of this section, you will be able to:
- Identify the issues that the nation faced during demobilization
- Explain the goals and objectives of the Truman administration
- Evaluate the actions taken by the U.S. government to address the concerns of returning veterans

The decade and a half immediately following the end of World War II was one in which middle- and working-class Americans hoped for a better life than the one they lived before the war. These hopes were tainted by fears of economic hardship, as many who experienced the Great Depression feared a return to economic decline. Others clamored for the opportunity to spend the savings they had accumulated through long hours on the job during the war when consumer goods were rarely available.

African Americans who had served in the armed forces and worked in the defense industry did not wish to return to "normal." Instead, they wanted the same rights and opportunities that other Americans had. Still other citizens were less concerned with the economy or civil rights; instead, they looked with suspicion at the Soviet presence in Eastern Europe. What would happen now that the United States and the Soviet Union were no longer allies, and the other nations that had long helped maintain a balance of power were left seriously damaged by the war? Harry Truman, president for less than a year when the war ended, was charged with addressing all of these concerns and giving the American people a "fair deal."

DEMOBILIZATION AND THE RETURN TO CIVILIAN LIFE

The most immediate task to be completed after World War II was demobilizing the military and reintegrating the veterans into civilian life. In response to popular pressure and concerns over the budget, the United States sought to demobilize its armed forces as quickly as possible. Many servicemen, labeled the "Ohio boys" (Over the Hill in October), threatened to vote Republican if they were not home by

Figure 7.2 (credit: "1953": modification of work by Library of Congress)

Christmas 1946. Understandably, this placed a great deal of pressure on the still-inexperienced president to shrink the size of the U.S. military.

Not everyone wanted the government to reduce America's military might, however. Secretary of the Navy James Forrestal and Secretary of War Robert P. Patterson warned Truman in October 1945 that an overly rapid demobilization jeopardized the nation's strategic position in the world. While Truman agreed with their assessment, he felt powerless to put a halt to demobilization. In response to mounting political pressure, the government reduced the size of the U.S. military from a high of 12 million in June 1945 to 1.5 million in June 1947—still more troops than the nation ever had in arms during peacetime. Soldiers and sailors were not the only ones dismissed from service. As the war drew to a close, millions of women working the jobs of men who had gone off to fight were dismissed by their employers, often because the demand for war materiel had declined and because government propaganda encouraged them to go home to make way for the returning troops. While most women workers surveyed at the end of the war wished to keep their jobs (75–90 percent, depending on the study), many did in fact leave them. Nevertheless, throughout the late 1940s and the 1950s, women continued to make up approximately one-third of the U.S. labor force.

Readjustment to postwar life was difficult for the returning troops. The U.S. Army estimated that as many of 20 percent of its casualties were psychological. Although many eagerly awaited their return to civilian status, others feared that they would not be able to resume a humdrum existence after the experience of fighting on the front lines. Veterans also worried that they wouldn't find work and that civilian defense workers were better positioned to take advantage of the new jobs opening up in the peacetime economy. Some felt that their wives and children would not welcome their presence, and some children did indeed resent the return of fathers who threatened to disrupt the mother-child household. Those on the home front worried as well. Doctors warned fiancées, wives, and mothers that soldiers might return with psychological problems that would make them difficult to live with.

The GI Bill of Rights

Well before the end of the war, Congress had passed one of the most significant and far-reaching pieces of legislation to ease veterans' transition into civilian life: the Servicemen's Readjustment Act, also known as the **GI Bill** (**Figure 7.3**). Every honorably discharged veteran who had seen active duty, but not necessarily combat, was eligible to receive a year's worth of unemployment compensation. This provision not only calmed veterans' fears regarding their ability to support themselves, but it also prevented large numbers of men—as well as some women—from suddenly entering a job market that did not have enough positions for them. Another way that the GI Bill averted a glut in the labor market was by giving returning veterans the opportunity to pursue an education; it paid for tuition at a college or vocational school, and gave them a stipend to live on while they completed their studies.

Figure 7.3 President Franklin D. Roosevelt signed the Servicemen's Readjustment Act, or GI Bill, on June 22, 1944, just weeks after the Allied invasion of Normandy, France, and more than a year before the end of the war.

The result was a dramatic increase in the number of students—especially male ones—enrolled in American colleges and universities. In 1940, only 5.5 percent of American men had a college degree. By 1950, that percentage had increased to 7.3 percent, as more than two million servicemen took advantage of the benefits offered by the GI Bill to complete college. The numbers continued to grow throughout the 1950s. Upon graduation, these men were prepared for skilled blue-collar or white-collar jobs that paved the way for many to enter the middle class. The creation of a well-educated, skilled labor force helped the U.S. economy as well. Other benefits offered by the GI Bill included low-interest loans to purchase homes or start small businesses.

However, not all veterans were able to take advantage of the GI Bill. African American veterans could use their educational benefits only to attend schools that accepted black students. The approximately nine thousand servicemen and women who were dishonorably discharged because they were gay or lesbian were ineligible for GI Bill benefits. Benefits for some Mexican American veterans, mainly in Texas, were also denied or delayed.

The Return of the Japanese

While most veterans received assistance to help in their adjustment to postwar life, others returned home to an uncertain future without the promise of government aid to help them resume their prewar lives. Japanese Americans from the West Coast who had been interned during the war also confronted the task of rebuilding their lives. In December 1944, Franklin Roosevelt had declared an end to the forced relocation of Japanese Americans, and as of January 1945, they were free to return to their homes. In many areas, however, neighbors clung to their prejudices and denounced those of Japanese descent as disloyal and dangerous. These feelings had been worsened by wartime propaganda, which often featured horrific accounts of Japanese mistreatment of prisoners, and by the statements of military officers to the effect that the Japanese were inherently savage. Facing such animosity, many Japanese American families chose to move elsewhere. Those who did return often found that in their absence, "friends" and neighbors had sold possessions that had been left with them for safekeeping. Many homes had been vandalized and farms destroyed. When Japanese Americans reopened their businesses, former customers sometimes boycotted them.

Click and Explore

For more on the experiences of Japanese Americans (http://openstaxcollege.org/l/15JapaneseOR) after internment, read about their return to communities in Oregon after World War II.

THE FAIR DEAL

Early in his presidency, Truman sought to build on the promises of Roosevelt's New Deal. Besides demobilizing the armed forces and preparing for the homecoming of servicemen and women, he also had to guide the nation through the process of returning to a peacetime economy. To this end, he proposed an ambitious program of social legislation that included establishing a federal minimum wage, expanding Social Security and public housing, and prohibiting child labor. Wartime price controls were retained for some items but removed from others, like meat. In his 1949 inaugural address, Truman referred to his programs as the "**Fair Deal**," a nod to his predecessor's New Deal. He wanted the Fair Deal to include Americans of color and became the first president to address the National Association for the Advancement of Colored People (NAACP). He also took decisive steps towards extending civil rights to African Americans by establishing, by executive order in December 1946, a Presidential Committee on Civil Rights to investigate racial discrimination in the United States. Truman also desegregated the armed forces, again by executive order, in July 1948, overriding many objections that the military was no place for social experimentation.

Congress, however, which was dominated by Republicans and southern conservative Democrats, refused to pass more "radical" pieces of legislation, such as a bill providing for national healthcare. The American Medical Association spent some $1.5 million to defeat Truman's healthcare proposal, which it sought to discredit as socialized medicine in order to appeal to Americans' fear of Communism. The same Congress also refused to make lynching a federal crime or outlaw the poll tax that reduced the access of poor Americans to the ballot box. Congress also rejected a bill that would have made Roosevelt's Fair Employment Practices Committee, which prohibited racial discrimination by companies doing business with the federal government, permanent. At the same time, they passed many conservative pieces of legislation. For example, the Taft-Hartley Act, which limited the power of unions, became law despite Truman's veto.

7.2 The Cold War

By the end of this section, you will be able to:
* Explain how and why the Cold War emerged in the wake of World War II
* Describe the steps taken by the U.S. government to oppose Communist expansion in Europe and Asia
* Discuss the government's efforts to root out Communist influences in the United States

As World War II drew to a close, the alliance that had made the United States and the Soviet Union partners in their defeat of the Axis powers—Germany, Italy, and Japan—began to fall apart. Both sides realized that their visions for the future of Europe and the world were incompatible. Joseph Stalin, the premier of the Soviet Union, wished to retain hold of Eastern Europe and establish Communist, pro-Soviet governments there, in an effort to both expand Soviet influence and protect the Soviet Union from future invasions. He also sought to bring Communist revolution to Asia and to developing nations elsewhere in the world. The United States wanted to expand its influence as well by protecting or installing democratic governments throughout the world. It sought to combat the influence of the Soviet Union by forming alliances with Asian, African, and Latin American nations, and by helping these countries to establish or expand prosperous, free-market economies. The end of the war left the industrialized nations of Europe and Asia physically devastated and economically exhausted by years of invasion, battle, and bombardment. With Great Britain, France, Germany, Italy, Japan, and China reduced to shadows of their former selves, the United States and the Soviet Union emerged as the last two superpowers and quickly found themselves locked in a contest for military, economic, social, technological, and ideological supremacy.

FROM ISOLATIONISM TO ENGAGEMENT

The United States had a long history of avoiding foreign alliances that might require the commitment of its troops abroad. However, in accepting the realities of the post-World War II world, in which traditional powers like Great Britain or France were no longer strong enough to police the globe, the United States realized that it would have to make a permanent change in its foreign policy, shifting from relative isolation to active engagement.

On assuming the office of president upon the death of Franklin Roosevelt, Harry Truman was already troubled by Soviet actions in Europe. He disliked the concessions made by Roosevelt at Yalta, which had allowed the Soviet Union to install a Communist government in Poland. At the Potsdam conference, held from July 17 to August 2, 1945, Truman also opposed Stalin's plans to demand large reparations from Germany. He feared the burden that this would impose on Germany might lead to another cycle of German rearmament and aggression—a fear based on that nation's development after World War I (**Figure 7.4**).

Figure 7.4 At the postwar conference in Potsdam, Germany, Harry Truman stands between Joseph Stalin (right) and Clement Atlee (left). Atlee became prime minister of Great Britain, replacing Winston Churchill, while the conference was taking place.

Although the United States and the Soviet Union did finally reach an agreement at Potsdam, this was the final occasion on which they cooperated for quite some time. Each remained convinced that its own economic and political systems were superior to the other's, and the two superpowers quickly found themselves drawn into conflict. The decades-long struggle between them for technological and ideological supremacy became known as the **Cold War**. So called because it did not include direct military confrontation between Soviet and U.S. troops, the Cold War was fought with a variety of other weapons: espionage and surveillance, political assassinations, propaganda, and the formation of alliances with other nations. It also became an arms race, as both countries competed to build the greatest stockpile of nuclear weapons, and proxy wars were fought on their behalf, primarily by the citizens of poorer nations, such as Korea and Vietnam.

CONTAINMENT ABROAD

In February 1946, George Kennan, a State Department official stationed at the U.S. embassy in Moscow, sent an eight-thousand-word message to Washington, DC. In what became known as the "Long Telegram," Kennan maintained that Soviet leaders believed that the only way to protect the Soviet Union was to destroy "rival" nations and their influence over weaker nations. According to Kennan, the Soviet Union was not so much a revolutionary regime as a totalitarian bureaucracy that was unable to accept the prospect of a peaceful coexistence of the United States and itself. He advised that the best way to thwart Soviet plans for the world was to contain Soviet influence—primarily through economic policy—to those places where it already existed and prevent its political expansion into new areas. This strategy, which came to be known as the policy of **containment**, formed the basis for U.S. foreign policy and military decision making for more than thirty years.

As Communist governments came to power elsewhere in the world, American policymakers extended their strategy of containment to what became known as the **domino theory** under the Eisenhower administration: Neighbors to Communist nations, so was the assumption, were likely to succumb to the same allegedly dangerous and infectious ideology. Like dominos toppling one another, entire regions would eventually be controlled by the Soviets. The demand for anti-Communist containment appeared as early as March 1946 in a speech by Winston Churchill, in which he referred to an **Iron Curtain** that divided Europe into the "free" West and the Communist East controlled by the Soviet Union.

The commitment to containing Soviet expansion made necessary the ability to mount a strong military offense and defense. In pursuit of this goal, the U.S. military was reorganized under the National Security Act of 1947. This act streamlined the government in matters of security by creating the National Security Council and establishing the Central Intelligence Agency (CIA) to conduct surveillance and espionage in foreign nations. It also created the Department of the Air Force, which was combined with the Departments of the Army and Navy in 1949 to form one Department of Defense.

The Truman Doctrine

In Europe, the end of World War II witnessed the rise of a number of internal struggles for control of countries that had been occupied by Nazi Germany. Great Britain occupied Greece as the Nazi regime there collapsed. The British aided the authoritarian government of Greece in its battles against Greek Communists. In March 1947, Great Britain announced that it could no longer afford the cost of supporting government military activities and withdrew from participation in the Greek civil war. Stepping into this power vacuum, the United States announced the Truman Doctrine, which offered support to Greece and Turkey in the form of financial assistance, weaponry, and troops to help train their militaries and bolster their governments against Communism. Eventually, the program was expanded to include any state trying to withstand a Communist takeover. The Truman Doctrine thus became a hallmark of U.S. Cold War policy.

DEFINING "AMERICAN"

⊙ *The Truman Doctrine*

In 1947, Great Britain, which had assumed responsibility for the disarming of German troops in Greece at the end of World War II, could no longer afford to provide financial support for the authoritarian Greek government, which was attempting to win a civil war against Greek leftist rebels. President Truman, unwilling to allow a Communist government to come to power there, requested Congress to provide funds for the government of Greece to continue its fight against the rebels. Truman also requested aid for the government of Turkey to fight the forces of Communism in that country. He said:

> At the present moment in world history nearly every nation must choose between alternative ways of life. The choice is too often not a free one.
> Should we fail to aid Greece and Turkey in this fateful hour, the effect will be far reaching to the West as well as to the East.
> The seeds of totalitarian regimes are nurtured by misery and want. They spread and grow in the evil soil of poverty and strife. They reach their full growth when the hope of a people for a better life has died. We must keep that hope alive.
> The free peoples of the world look to us for support in maintaining their freedoms.
> If we falter in our leadership, we may endanger the peace of the world—and we shall surely endanger the welfare of our own nation.
> Great responsibilities have been placed upon us by the swift movement of events.
> I am confident that the Congress will face these responsibilities squarely.

What role is Truman suggesting that the United States assume in the postwar world? Does the United States still assume this role?

The Marshall Plan

By 1946, the American economy was growing significantly. At the same time, the economic situation in Europe was disastrous. The war had turned much of Western Europe into a battlefield, and the rebuilding of factories, public transportation systems, and power stations progressed exceedingly slowly. Starvation loomed as a real possibility for many. As a result of these conditions, Communism was making significant inroads in both Italy and France. These concerns led Truman, along with Secretary of State George C. Marshall, to propose to Congress the European Recovery Program, popularly known as the **Marshall Plan**. Between its implantation in April 1948 and its termination in 1951, this program gave $13 billion in economic aid to European nations.

Truman's motivation was economic and political, as well as humanitarian. The plan stipulated that the European nations had to work together in order to receive aid, thus enforcing unity through enticement, while seeking to undercut the political popularity of French and Italian Communists and dissuading moderates from forming coalition governments with them. Likewise, much of the money had to be spent on American goods, boosting the postwar economy of the United States as well as the American cultural presence in Europe. Stalin regarded the program as a form of bribery. The Soviet Union refused to accept aid from the Marshall Plan, even though it could have done so, and forbade the Communist states of Eastern Europe to accept U.S. funds as well. Those states that did accept aid began to experience an economic recovery.

MY STORY

⚙ *George C. Marshall and the Nobel Peace Prize*

The youngest child of a Pennsylvania businessman and Democrat, George C. Marshall (Figure 7.5) chose a military career. He attended the Virginia Military Institute, was a veteran of World War I, and spent the rest of his life either in the military or otherwise in the service of his country, including as President Truman's Secretary of State. He was awarded the Nobel Peace Prize in 1953, the only soldier to ever receive that honor. Below is an excerpt of his remarks as he accepted the award.

Figure 7.5 During World War II, George C. Marshall was responsible for expanding the 189,000-member U.S. Army into a modern, fighting force of eight million by 1942. As Secretary of State under Truman, he proposed the European Recovery Program to aid European economies struggling after the war.

> There has been considerable comment over the awarding of the Nobel Peace Prize to a soldier. I am afraid this does not seem as remarkable to me as it quite evidently appears to others. I know a great deal of the horrors and tragedies of war. Today, as chairman of the American Battle Monuments Commission, it is my duty to supervise the construction and maintenance of military cemeteries in many countries overseas, particularly in Western Europe. The cost of war in human lives is constantly spread before me, written neatly in many ledgers whose columns are gravestones. I am deeply moved to find some means or method of avoiding another calamity of war. Almost daily I hear from the wives, or mothers, or families of the fallen. The tragedy of the aftermath is almost constantly before me.
>
> I share with you an active concern for some practical method for avoiding war. . . . A very strong military posture is vitally necessary today. How long it must continue I am not prepared to estimate, but I am sure that it is too narrow a basis on which to build a dependable, long-enduring peace. The guarantee for a long continued peace will depend on other factors in addition to a moderated military strength, and no less important. Perhaps the most important single factor will be a spiritual regeneration to develop goodwill, faith, and understanding among nations. Economic factors will undoubtedly play an important part. Agreements to secure a balance of power, however disagreeable they may seem, must likewise be considered. And with all these there must be wisdom and the will to act on that wisdom.

What steps did Marshall recommend be taken to maintain a lasting peace? To what extent have today's nations heeded his advice?

Showdown in Europe

The lack of consensus with the Soviets on the future of Germany led the United States, Great Britain, and France to support joining their respective occupation zones into a single, independent state. In December 1946, they took steps to do so, but the Soviet Union did not wish the western zones of the country to unify under a democratic, pro-capitalist government. The Soviet Union also feared the possibility of a unified West Berlin, located entirely within the Soviet sector. Three days after the western allies authorized the introduction of a new currency in Western Germany—the Deutsche Mark—Stalin ordered all land and water routes to the western zones of the city Berlin to be cut off in June 1948. Hoping to starve the western parts of the city into submission, the Berlin blockade was also a test of the emerging U.S. policy of containment.

Unwilling to abandon Berlin, the United States, Great Britain, and France began to deliver all needed supplies to West Berlin by air (**Figure 7.6**). In April 1949, the three countries joined Canada and eight Western European nations to form the North Atlantic Treaty Organization (NATO), an alliance pledging its members to mutual defense in the event of attack. On May 12, 1949, a year and approximately two million tons of supplies later, the Soviets admitted defeat and ended the blockade of Berlin. On May 23, the Federal Republic of Germany (FRG), consisting of the unified western zones and commonly referred to as West Germany, was formed. The Soviets responded by creating the German Democratic Republic, or East Germany, in October 1949.

(a) (b)

Figure 7.6 American C-47 transport planes (a) are loaded with staged supplies at a French airport before taking off for Berlin. Residents of Berlin wait for a U.S. plane (b) carrying needed supplies to land at Templehof Airport in the American sector of the city.

CONTAINMENT AT HOME

In 1949, two incidents severely disrupted American confidence in the ability of the United States to contain the spread of Communism and limit Soviet power in the world. First, on August 29, 1949, the Soviet Union exploded its first atomic bomb—no longer did the United States have a monopoly on nuclear power. A few months later, on October 1, 1949, Chinese Communist Party leader Mao Zedong announced the triumph of the Chinese Communists over their Nationalist foes in a civil war that had been raging since 1927. The Nationalist forces, under their leader Chiang Kai-shek, departed for Taiwan in December 1949.

Immediately, there were suspicions that spies had passed bomb-making secrets to the Soviets and that Communist sympathizers in the U.S. State Department had hidden information that might have enabled the United States to ward off the Communist victory in China. Indeed, in February 1950, Wisconsin senator Joseph McCarthy, a Republican, charged in a speech that the State Department was filled with Communists. Also in 1950, the imprisonment in Great Britain of Klaus Fuchs, a German-born physicist who had worked on the Manhattan Project and was then convicted of passing nuclear secrets to the Soviets, increased American fears. Information given by Fuchs to the British implicated a number of

American citizens as well. The most infamous trial of suspected American spies was that of Julius and Ethel Rosenberg, who were executed in June 1953 despite a lack of evidence against them. Several decades later, evidence was found that Julius, but not Ethel, had in fact given information to the Soviet Union.

Fears that Communists within the United States were jeopardizing the country's security had existed even before the victory of Mao Zedong and the arrest and conviction of the atomic spies. Roosevelt's New Deal and Truman's Fair Deal were often criticized as "socialist," which many mistakenly associated with Communism, and Democrats were often branded Communists by Republicans. In response, on March 21, 1947, Truman signed Executive Order 9835, which provided the Federal Bureau of Investigation with broad powers to investigate federal employees and identify potential security risks. State and municipal governments instituted their own loyalty boards to find and dismiss potentially disloyal workers.

In addition to loyalty review boards, the House Committee on Un-American Activities (HUAC), established in 1938 to investigate suspected Nazi sympathizers, after World War II also sought to root out suspected Communists in business, academia, and the media. HUAC was particularly interested in Hollywood because it feared that Communist sympathizers might use motion pictures as pro-Soviet propaganda. Witnesses were subpoenaed and required to testify before the committee; refusal could result in imprisonment. Those who invoked Fifth Amendment protections, or were otherwise suspected of Communist sympathies, often lost their jobs or found themselves on a **blacklist**, which prevented them from securing employment. Notable artists who were blacklisted in the 1940s and 1950s include composer Leonard Bernstein, novelist Dashiell Hammett, playwright and screenwriter Lillian Hellman, actor and singer Paul Robeson, and musician Artie Shaw.

TO THE TRENCHES AGAIN

Just as the U.S. government feared the possibility of Communist infiltration of the United States, so too was it alert for signs that Communist forces were on the move elsewhere. The Soviet Union had been granted control of the northern half of the Korean peninsula at the end of World War II, and the United States had control of the southern portion. The Soviets displayed little interest in extending its power into South Korea, and Stalin did not wish to risk confrontation with the United States over Korea. North Korea's leaders, however, wished to reunify the peninsula under Communist rule. In April 1950, Stalin finally gave permission to North Korea's leader Kim Il Sung to invade South Korea and provided the North Koreans with weapons and military advisors.

On June 25, 1950, troops of the North Korean People's Democratic Army crossed the thirty-eighth parallel, the border between North and South Korea. The first major test of the U.S. policy of containment in Asia had begun, for the domino theory held that a victory by North Korea might lead to further Communist expansion in Asia, in the virtual backyard of the United States' chief new ally in East Asia—Japan. The United Nations (UN), which had been established in 1945, was quick to react. On June 27, the UN Security Council denounced North Korea's actions and called upon UN members to help South Korea defeat the invading forces. As a permanent member of the Security Council, the Soviet Union could have vetoed the action, but it had boycotted UN meetings following the awarding of China's seat on the Security Council to Taiwan instead of to Mao Zedong's People's Republic of China.

On June 27, Truman ordered U.S. military forces into South Korea. They established a defensive line on the far southern part of the Korean peninsula near the town of Pusan. A U.S.-led invasion at Inchon on September 15 halted the North Korean advance and turned it into a retreat (**Figure 7.7**). As North Korean forces moved back across the thirty-eighth parallel, UN forces under the command of U.S. General Douglas MacArthur followed. MacArthur's goal was not only to drive the North Korean army out of South Korea but to destroy Communist North Korea as well. At this stage, he had the support of President Truman; however, as UN forces approached the Yalu River, the border between China and North Korea, MacArthur's and Truman's objectives diverged. Chinese premier Zhou Enlai, who had provided supplies and military advisors for North Korea before the conflict began, sent troops into battle to support North Korea and caught U.S. troops by surprise. Following a costly retreat from North Korea's Chosin Reservoir, a swift advance of Chinese and North Korean forces and another invasion of Seoul, MacArthur urged Truman to deploy nuclear weapons against China. Truman, however, did not wish to risk a broader war in Asia. MacArthur criticized Truman's decision and voiced his disagreement in a letter to a Republican congressman, who subsequently allowed the letter to become public. In April 1951, Truman accused MacArthur of insubordination and relieved him of his command. The Joint Chiefs of Staff agreed, calling the escalation MacArthur had called for "the wrong war, at the wrong place, at the wrong time, and with the wrong enemy." Nonetheless, the public gave MacArthur a hero's welcome in New York with the largest ticker tape parade in the nation's history.

Figure 7.7 After the initial invasion of South Korea by the North Korean People's Democratic Army, the United Nations established a defensive line in the southern part of the country. The landing at Inchon in September reversed the tide of the war and allowed UN forces under General Douglas MacArthur to retake the city of Seoul, which had fallen to North Korean troops in the early days of the war.

By July 1951, the UN forces had recovered from the setbacks earlier in the year and pushed North Korean and Chinese forces back across the thirty-eighth parallel, and peace talks began. However, combat raged on for more than two additional years. The primary source of contention was the fate of prisoners of war. The Chinese and North Koreans insisted that their prisoners be returned to them, but many of these men did not wish to be repatriated. Finally, an armistice agreement was signed on July 27, 1953. A border between North and South Korea, one quite close to the original thirty-eighth parallel line, was agreed upon. A demilitarized zone between the two nations was established, and both sides agreed that prisoners of war would be allowed to choose whether to be returned to their homelands. Five million people died in the three-year conflict. Of these, around 36,500 were U.S. soldiers; a majority were Korean civilians.

Click and Explore

Read firsthand accounts (http://openstaxcollege.org/l/15KOWar) of U.S. soldiers who served in Korea, including prisoners of war.

As the war in Korea came to an end, so did one of the most frightening anti-Communist campaigns in the United States. After charging the U.S. State Department with harboring Communists, Senator Joseph McCarthy had continued to make similar accusations against other government agencies. Prominent Republicans like Senator Robert Taft and Congressman Richard Nixon regarded McCarthy as an asset who targeted Democratic politicians, and they supported his actions. In 1953, as chair of the Senate Committee on Government Operations, McCarthy investigated the Voice of America, which broadcast news and pro-U.S. propaganda to foreign countries, and the State Department's overseas libraries. After an aborted effort to investigate Protestant clergy, McCarthy turned his attention to the U.S. Army. This proved to be the end of the senator's political career. From April to June 1954, the Army-McCarthy Hearings were televised, and the American public, able to witness his use of intimidation and innuendo firsthand, rejected McCarthy's approach to rooting out Communism in the United States (**Figure 7.8**). In December 1954, the U.S. Senate officially condemned his actions with a censure, ending his prospects for political leadership.

Figure 7.8 Senator Joseph McCarthy (left) consults with Roy Cohn (right) during the Army-McCarthy hearings. Cohn, a lawyer who worked for McCarthy, was responsible for investigating State Department libraries overseas for "subversive" books.

One particularly heinous aspect of the hunt for Communists in the United States, likened by playwright Arthur Miller to the witch hunts of old, was its effort to root out gay men and lesbians employed by the government. Many anti-Communists, including McCarthy, believed that gay men, referred to by Senator Everett Dirksen as "lavender lads," were morally weak and thus were particularly likely to betray their country. Many also believed that lesbians and gay men were prone to being blackmailed by Soviet agents because of their sexual orientation, which at the time was regarded by psychiatrists as a form of mental illness.

7.3 The American Dream

By the end of this section, you will be able to:
- Describe President Dwight D. Eisenhower's domestic and foreign policies
- Discuss gender roles in the 1950s
- Discuss the growth of the suburbs and the effect of suburbanization on American society

Against the backdrop of the Cold War, Americans dedicated themselves to building a peaceful and prosperous society after the deprivation and instability of the Great Depression and World War II. Dwight D. Eisenhower, the general who led the United States to victory in Europe in 1945, proved to be the perfect president for the new era. Lacking strong conservative positions, he steered a middle path between conservatism and liberalism, and presided over a peacetime decade of economic growth and social conformity. In foreign affairs, Eisenhower's New Look policy simultaneously expanded the nation's nuclear arsenal and prevented the expansion of the defense budget for conventional forces.

WE LIKE IKE

After Harry Truman declined to run again for the presidency, the election of 1952 emerged as a contest between the Democratic nominee, Illinois governor Adlai Stevenson, and Republican Dwight D. Eisenhower, who had directed American forces in Europe during World War II (**Figure 7.9**). Eisenhower campaigned largely on a promise to end the war in Korea, a conflict the public had grown weary of fighting. He also vowed to fight Communism both at home and abroad, a commitment he demonstrated by choosing as his running mate Richard M. Nixon, a congressman who had made a name for himself by pursuing Communists, notably former State Department employee and suspected Soviet agent Alger Hiss.

Figure 7.9 Dwight D. Eisenhower was the perfect presidential candidate in 1952. He had never before run for office or even cast a vote, and thus had no political record to be challenged or criticized.

In 1952, Eisenhower supporters enthusiastically proclaimed "We Like Ike," and Eisenhower defeated Stevenson by winning 54 percent of the popular vote and 87 percent of the electoral vote (**Figure 7.10**). When he assumed office in 1953, Eisenhower employed a leadership style he had developed during his years of military service. He was calm and willing to delegate authority regarding domestic affairs to his cabinet members, allowing him to focus his own efforts on foreign policy. Unlike many earlier presidents, such as Harry Truman, Eisenhower was largely nonpartisan and consistently sought a   middle ground between liberalism and conservatism. He strove to balance the federal budget, which appealed to conservative Republicans, but retained much of the New Deal and even expanded Social Security. He maintained high levels of defense spending but, in his farewell speech in 1961, warned about the growth of the **military-industrial complex**, the matrix of relationships between officials in the Department of Defense and executives in the defense industry who all benefited from increases in defense spending. He disliked the tactics of Joseph McCarthy but did not oppose him directly, preferring to remain above the fray. He saw himself as a leader called upon to do his best for his country, not as a politician engaged in a contest for advantage over rivals.

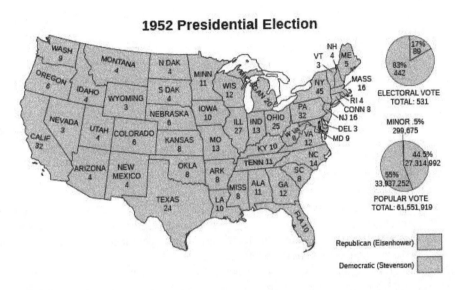

Figure 7.10 The above map shows the resounding victory of Dwight D. Eisenhower over Adlai Stevenson in the 1952 election. Stevenson carried only the South, where whites had voted for Democratic Party candidates since the time of the Civil War.

In keeping with his goal of a balanced budget, Eisenhower switched the emphasis in defense from larger conventional forces to greater stockpiles of nuclear weapons. His New Look strategy embraced nuclear **"massive retaliation,"** a plan for nuclear response to a first Soviet strike so devastating that the attackers would not be able to respond. Some labeled this approach "Mutually Assured Destruction" or MAD.

Part of preparing for a possible war with the Soviet Union was informing the American public what to do in the event of a nuclear attack. The government provided instructions for building and equipping bomb shelters in the basement or backyard, and some cities constructed municipal shelters. Schools purchased dog tags to help identify students in the aftermath of an attack and showed children instructional films telling them what to do if atomic bombs were dropped on the city where they lived.

☼ *"A Guide for Surviving Nuclear War"*

To prepare its citizens for the possibility of nuclear war, in 1950, the U.S. government published and distributed informative pamphlets such as "A Guide for Surviving Nuclear War" excerpted here.

> Just like fire bombs and ordinary high explosives, atomic weapons cause most of their death and damage by blast and heat. So first let's look at a few things you can do to escape these two dangers.
>
> Even if you have only a second's warning, there is one important thing you can do to lessen your chances of injury by blast: Fall flat on your face.
>
> More than half of all wounds are the result of being bodily tossed about or being struck by falling and flying objects. If you lie down flat, you are least likely to be thrown about. If you have time to pick a good spot, there is less chance of your being struck by flying glass and other things.
>
> If you are inside a building, the best place to flatten out is close against the cellar wall. If you haven't time to get down there, lie down along an inside wall, or duck under a bed or table. . .
>
> If caught out-of-doors, either drop down alongside the base of a good substantial building—avoid flimsy, wooden ones likely to be blown over on top of you—or else jump in any handy ditch or gutter.
>
> When you fall flat to protect yourself from a bombing, don't look up to see what is coming. Even during the daylight hours, the flash from a bursting A-bomb can cause several moments of blindness, if you're facing that way. To prevent it, bury your face in your arms and hold it there for 10 to 12 seconds after the explosion. . . .
>
> If you work in the open, always wear full-length, loose-fitting, light-colored clothes in time of emergency. Never go around with your sleeves rolled up. Always wear a hat—the brim could save you a serious face burn.

What do you think was the purpose of these directions? Do you think they could actually help people survive an atomic bomb blast? If not, why publish such booklets?

Click and Explore

View this short instructional film (http://openstaxcollege.org/l/15DuckCover) made in 1951 that teaches elementary school children what to do in the event an atomic bomb is dropped. Why do you think officials tried to convey the message that a nuclear attack was survivable?

Government and industry allocated enormous amounts of money to the research and development of more powerful weapons. This investment generated rapid strides in missile technology as well as increasingly sensitive radar. Computers that could react more quickly than humans and thereby shoot down speeding missiles were also investigated. Many scientists on both sides of the Cold War, including captured Germans such as rocket engineer Werner von Braun, worked on these devices. An early success for the West came in 1950, when Alan Turing, a British mathematician who had broken Germany's Enigma code during World War II, created a machine that mimicked human thought. His discoveries led scientists to consider the possibility of developing true artificial intelligence.

However, the United States often feared that the Soviets were making greater strides in developing technology with potential military applications. This was especially true following the Soviet Union's launch of *Sputnik* (**Figure 7.11**), the first manmade satellite, in October 1957. In September 1958, Congress passed the National Defense Education Act, which pumped over $775 million into educational programs over four years, especially those programs that focused on math and science. Congressional appropriations to the National Science Foundation also increased by $100 million in a single year, from $34 million in 1958 to $134 million in 1959. One consequence of this increased funding was the growth of science and engineering programs at American universities.

Figure 7.11 The launch of the Soviet satellite *Sputnik* frightened many in the United States, who feared that Soviet technology had surpassed their own. To calm these fears, Americans domesticated *Sputnik*, creating children's games based on it and using its shape as a decorative motif.

In the diplomatic sphere, Eisenhower pushed Secretary of State John Foster Dulles to take a firmer stance against the Soviets to reassure European allies of continued American support. At the same time, keenly sensing that the stalemate in Korea had cost Truman his popularity, Eisenhower worked to avoid being drawn into foreign wars. Thus, when the French found themselves fighting Vietnamese Communists for control of France's former colony of Indochina, Eisenhower provided money but not troops. Likewise, the United States took no steps when Hungary attempted to break away from Soviet domination in 1956. The United States also refused to be drawn in when Great Britain, France, and Israel invaded the Suez Canal Zone following Egypt's nationalization of the canal in 1956. Indeed, Eisenhower, wishing to avoid conflict with the Soviet Union, threatened to impose economic sanctions on the invading countries if they did not withdraw.

SUBURBANIZATION

Although the Eisenhower years were marked by fear of the Soviet Union and its military might, they were also a time of peace and prosperity. Even as many Americans remained mired in poverty, many others with limited economic opportunities, like African Americans or union workers, were better off financially in the 1950s and rose into the ranks of the middle class. Wishing to build the secure life that the Great Depression had deprived their parents of, young men and women married in record numbers and purchased homes where they could start families of their own. In 1940, the rate of homeownership in the United States was 43.6 percent. By 1960, it was almost 62 percent. Many of these newly purchased homes had been built in the new suburban areas that began to encircle American cities after the war. Although middle-class families had begun to move to the suburbs beginning in the nineteenth century, suburban growth accelerated rapidly after World War II.

Several factors contributed to this development. During World War II, the United States had suffered from a housing shortage, especially in cities with shipyards or large defense plants. Now that the war was over, real estate developers and contractors rushed to alleviate the scarcity. Unused land on the fringes of American cities provided the perfect place for new housing, which attracted not only the middle class, which had long sought homes outside the crowded cities, but also blue-collar workers who took advantage of the low-interest mortgages offered by the GI Bill.

An additional factor was the use of prefabricated construction techniques pioneered during World War II, which allowed houses complete with plumbing, electrical wiring, and appliances to be built and painted in a day. Employing these methods, developers built acres of inexpensive tract housing throughout the country. One of the first developers to take advantage of this method was William Levitt, who purchased farmland in Nassau County, Long Island, in 1947 and built thousands of prefabricated houses. The new community was named **Levittown**.

Levitt's houses cost only $8,000 and could be bought with little or no down payment. The first day they were offered for sale, more than one thousand were purchased. Levitt went on to build similar developments, also called Levittown, in New Jersey and Pennsylvania (**Figure 7.12**). As developers around the country rushed to emulate him, the name Levittown became synonymous with suburban tract housing, in which entire neighborhoods were built to either a single plan or a mere handful of designs. The houses were so similar that workers told of coming home late at night and walking into the wrong one. Levittown homes were similar in other ways as well; most were owned by white families. Levitt used restrictive language in his agreements with potential homeowners to ensure that only whites would live in his communities.

Figure 7.12 This aerial view of Levittown, Pennsylvania, reveals acres of standardized homes. The roads were curved to prevent cars from speeding through the residential community that was home to many young families.

In the decade between 1950 and 1960, the suburbs grew by 46 percent. The transition from urban to suburban life exerted profound effects on both the economy and society. For example, fifteen of the largest U.S. cities saw their tax bases shrink significantly in the postwar period, and the apportionment of seats in the House of Representatives shifted to the suburbs and away from urban areas.

The development of the suburbs also increased reliance on the automobile for transportation. Suburban men drove to work in nearby cities or, when possible, were driven to commuter rail stations by their wives. In the early years of suburban development, before schools, parks, and supermarkets were built, access to an automobile was crucial, and the pressure on families to purchase a second one was strong. As families rushed to purchase them, the annual production of passenger cars leaped from 2.2 million to 8 million between 1946 and 1955, and by 1960, about 20 percent of suburban families owned two cars. The growing number of cars on the road changed consumption patterns, and drive-in and drive-through convenience stores, restaurants, and movie theaters began to dot the landscape. The first McDonalds opened in San Bernardino, California, in 1954 to cater to drivers in a hurry.

As drivers jammed highways and small streets in record numbers, cities and states rushed to build additional roadways and ease congestion. To help finance these massive construction efforts, states began taxing gasoline, and the federal government provided hundreds of thousands of dollars for the construction of the interstate highway system (**Figure 7.13**). The resulting construction projects, designed to make it easier for suburbanites to commute to and from cities, often destroyed urban working-class neighborhoods. Increased funding for highway construction also left less money for public transportation, making it impossible for those who could not afford automobiles to live in the suburbs.

Figure 7.13 In the late 1940s, a network of newly constructed highways connected suburban Long Island with Manhattan. The nation's new road network also served a military purpose; interstate highways made it easier to deploy troops in the event of a national emergency.

THE ORGANIZATION MAN

As the government poured money into the defense industry and into universities that conducted research for the government, the economy boomed. The construction and automobile industries employed thousands, as did the industries they relied upon: steel, oil and gasoline refining, rubber, and lumber. As people moved into new homes, their purchases of appliances, carpeting, furniture, and home decorations spurred growth in other industries. The building of miles of roads also employed thousands. Unemployment was low, and wages for members of both the working and middle classes were high.

Following World War II, the majority of white Americans were members of the middle class, based on such criteria as education, income, and home ownership. Even most blue-collar families could afford such elements of a middle-class lifestyle as new cars, suburban homes, and regular vacations. Most African Americans, however, were not members of the middle class. In 1950, the median income for white families was $20,656, whereas for black families it was $11,203. By 1960, when the average white family earned $28,485 a year, blacks still lagged behind at $15,786; nevertheless, this represented a more than 40 percent increase in African American income in the space of a decade.

While working-class men found jobs in factories and on construction crews, those in the middle class often worked for corporations that, as a result of government spending, had grown substantially during World War II and were still getting larger. Such corporations, far too large to allow managers to form personal relationships with all of their subordinates, valued conformity to company rules and standards above all else. In his best-selling book *The Organization Man*, however, William H. Whyte criticized the notion that conformity was the best path to success and self-fulfillment.

Conformity was still the watchword of suburban life: Many neighborhoods had rules mandating what types of clotheslines could be used and prohibited residents from parking their cars on the street. Above all, conforming to societal norms meant marrying young and having children. In the post-World War II period, marriage rates rose; the average age at first marriage dropped to twenty-three for men and twenty for women. Between 1946 and 1964, married couples also gave birth to the largest generation in U.S. history to date; this **baby boom** resulted in the cohort known as the baby boomers. Conformity also required that the wives of both working- and middle-class men stay home and raise children instead of working for wages outside the home. Most conformed to this norm, at least while their children were young. Nevertheless, 40 percent of women with young children and half of women with older children sought at least part-time employment. They did so partly out of necessity and partly to pay for the new elements of "the good life"—second cars, vacations, and college education for their children.

The children born during the baby boom were members of a more privileged generation than their parents had been. Entire industries sprang up to cater to their need for clothing, toys, games, books, and breakfast cereals. For the first time in U.S. history, attending high school was an experience shared by the majority, regardless of race or region. As the baby boomers grew into adolescence, marketers realized that they not only controlled large amounts of disposable income earned at part-time jobs, but they exerted a great deal of influence over their parents' purchases as well. Madison Avenue began to appeal to teenage interests. Boys yearned for cars, and girls of all ethnicities wanted boyfriends who had them. New fashion magazines for adolescent girls, such as *Seventeen*, advertised the latest clothing and cosmetics, and teen romance magazines, like *Copper Romance*, a publication for young African American women, filled drugstore racks. The music and movie industries also altered their products to appeal to affluent adolescents who were growing tired of parental constraints.

7.4 Popular Culture and Mass Media

By the end of this section, you will be able to:
*   Describe Americans' different responses to rock and roll music
*   Discuss the way contemporary movies and television reflected postwar American society

With a greater generational consciousness than previous generations, the baby boomers sought to define and redefine their identities in numerous ways. Music, especially rock and roll, reflected their desire to rebel against adult authority. Other forms of popular culture, such as movies and television, sought to entertain, while reinforcing values such as religious faith, patriotism, and conformity to societal norms.

ROCKING AROUND THE CLOCK

In the late 1940s, some white country musicians began to experiment with the rhythms of the blues, a decades-old musical genre of rural southern blacks. This experimentation led to the creation of a new musical form known as rockabilly, and by the 1950s, rockabilly had developed into **rock and roll**. Rock and roll music celebrated themes such as young love and freedom from the oppression of middle-class society. It quickly grew in favor among American teens, thanks largely to the efforts of disc jockey Alan Freed, who named and popularized the music by playing it on the radio in Cleveland, where he also organized the first rock and roll concert, and later in New York.

The theme of rebellion against authority, present in many rock and roll songs, appealed to teens. In 1954, Bill Haley and His Comets provided youth with an anthem for their rebellion—"Rock Around the Clock" (**Figure 7.14**). The song, used in the 1955 movie *Blackboard Jungle* about a white teacher at a troubled inner-city high school, seemed to be calling for teens to declare their independence from adult control.

Figure 7.14 The band Bill Haley and His Comets (a) was among the first to launch the new genre of rock and roll. Their hit song "Rock Around the Clock" supposedly caused some teens to break into violent behavior when they heard it. Chuck Berry (b) was a performer who combined rhythm and blues and rock and roll. He dazzled crowds with guitar solos and electrifying performances.

Haley illustrated how white artists could take musical motifs from the African American community and achieve mainstream success. Teen heartthrob Elvis Presley rose to stardom doing the same. Thus, besides encouraging a feeling of youthful rebellion, rock and roll also began to tear down color barriers, as white youths sought out African American musicians such as Chuck Berry and Little Richard (**Figure 28.14**).

While youth had found an outlet for their feelings and concerns, parents were much less enthused about rock and roll and the values it seemed to promote. Many regarded the music as a threat to American values. When Elvis Presley appeared on *The Ed Sullivan Show*, a popular television variety program, the camera deliberately focused on his torso and did not show his swiveling hips or legs shaking in time to the music. Despite adults' dislike of the genre, or perhaps because of it, more than 68 percent of the music played on the radio in 1956 was rock and roll.

HOLLYWOOD ON THE DEFENSIVE

At first, Hollywood encountered difficulties in adjusting to the post-World War II environment. Although domestic audiences reached a record high in 1946 and the war's end meant expanding international markets too, the groundwork for the eventual dismantling of the traditional studio system was laid in 1948, with a landmark decision by the U.S. Supreme Court. Previously, film studios had owned their own movie theater chains in which they exhibited the films they produced; however, in *United States v. Paramount Pictures, Inc.*, this vertical integration of the industry—the complete control by one firm of the production, distribution, and exhibition of motion pictures—was deemed a violation of antitrust laws.

The HUAC hearings also targeted Hollywood. When Senator McCarthy called eleven "unfriendly witnesses" to testify before Congress about Communism in the film industry in October 1947, only playwright Bertolt Brecht answered questions. The other ten, who refused to testify, were cited for contempt of Congress on November 24. The next day, film executives declared that the so-called "Hollywood Ten" would no longer be employed in the industry until they had sworn they were not Communists (**Figure 7.15**). Eventually, more than three hundred actors, screenwriters, directors, musicians, and other entertainment professionals were placed on the industry blacklist. Some never worked in Hollywood again; others directed films or wrote screenplays under assumed names.

Figure 7.15 One of the original Hollywood Ten, director Edward Dmytryk publicly announced he had once been a Communist and, in April 1951, answered questions and "named names" before the House Committee on Un-American Activities.

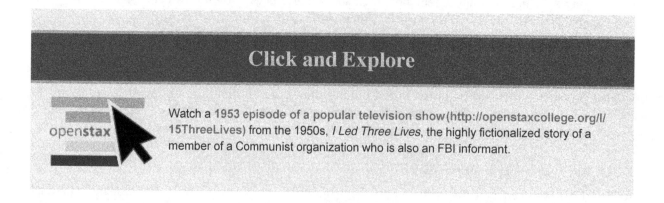

Click and Explore

Watch a 1953 episode of a popular television show (http://openstaxcollege.org/l/ 15ThreeLives) from the 1950s, *I Led Three Lives*, the highly fictionalized story of a member of a Communist organization who is also an FBI informant.

Hollywood reacted aggressively to these various challenges. Filmmakers tried new techniques, like CinemaScope and Cinerama, which allowed movies to be shown on large screens and in 3-D. Audiences were drawn to movies not because of gimmicks, however, but because of the stories they told. Dramas and romantic comedies continued to be popular fare for adults, and, to appeal to teens, studios produced large numbers of horror films and movies starring music idols such as Elvis. Many films took espionage, a timely topic, as their subject matter, and science fiction hits such as *Invasion of the Body Snatchers*, about a small town whose inhabitants fall prey to space aliens, played on audience fears of both Communist invasion and nuclear technology.

THE TRIUMPH OF TELEVISION

By far the greatest challenge to Hollywood, however, came from the relatively new medium of television. Although the technology had been developed in the late 1920s, through much of the 1940s, only a fairly small audience of the wealthy had access to it. As a result, programming was limited. With the post-World War II economic boom, all this changed. Where there had been only 178,000 televisions in homes in 1948, by 1955, over three-quarters of a million U.S. households, about half of all homes, had television (**Figure 7.16**).

Figure 7.16 An American family relaxes in front of their television set in 1958. Many gathered not only to watch the programming but also to eat dinner. The marketing of small folding tray tables and frozen "TV dinners" encouraged such behavior.

Various types of programs were broadcast on the handful of major networks: situation comedies, variety programs, game shows, soap operas, talk shows, medical dramas, adventure series, cartoons, and police procedurals. Many comedies presented an idealized image of white suburban family life: Happy housewife mothers, wise fathers, and mischievous but not dangerously rebellious children were constants on shows like *Leave It to Beaver* and *Father Knows Best* in the late 1950s. These shows also reinforced certain perspectives on the values of individualism and family—values that came to be redefined as "American" in opposition to alleged Communist collectivism. Westerns, which stressed unity in the face of danger and the ability to survive in hostile environments, were popular too. Programming designed specifically for children began to emerge with shows such as *Captain Kangaroo*, *Romper Room*, and *The Mickey Mouse Club* designed to appeal to members of the baby boom.

7.5 The African American Struggle for Civil Rights

By the end of this section, you will be able to:
- Explain how Presidents Truman and Eisenhower addressed civil rights issues
- Discuss efforts by African Americans to end discrimination and segregation
- Describe southern whites' response to the civil rights movement

In the aftermath of World War II, African Americans began to mount organized resistance to racially discriminatory policies in force throughout much of the United States. In the South, they used a combination of legal challenges and grassroots activism to begin dismantling the racial segregation that had stood for nearly a century following the end of Reconstruction. Community activists and civil rights leaders targeted racially discriminatory housing practices, segregated transportation, and legal requirements that African Americans and whites be educated separately. While many of these challenges were successful, life did not necessarily improve for African Americans. Hostile whites fought these changes in any way they could, including by resorting to violence.

EARLY VICTORIES

During World War II, many African Americans had supported the "Double-V Campaign," which called on them to defeat foreign enemies while simultaneously fighting against segregation and discrimination at home. After World War II ended, many returned home to discover that, despite their sacrifices, the United States was not willing to extend them any greater rights than they had enjoyed before the war. Particularly rankling was the fact that although African American veterans were legally entitled to draw benefits under the GI Bill, discriminatory practices prevented them from doing so. For example, many banks would not give them mortgages if they wished to buy homes in predominantly African American neighborhoods, which banks often considered too risky an investment. However, African Americans who attempted to purchase homes in white neighborhoods often found themselves unable to do so because of real estate covenants that prevented owners from selling their property to blacks. Indeed, when a black family purchased a Levittown house in 1957, they were subjected to harassment and threats of violence.

Click and Explore

For a look at the experiences of an African American family (http://openstaxcollege.org/l/15Levittown) that tried to move to a white suburban community, view the 1957 documentary *Crisis in Levittown*.

The postwar era, however, saw African Americans make greater use of the courts to defend their rights. In 1944, an African American woman, Irene Morgan, was arrested in Virginia for refusing to give up her seat on an interstate bus and sued to have her conviction overturned. In *Morgan v. the Commonwealth of Virginia* in 1946, the U.S. Supreme Court ruled that the conviction should be overturned because it violated the interstate commerce clause of the Constitution. This victory emboldened some civil rights activists to launch the Journey of Reconciliation, a bus trip taken by eight African American men and eight white men through the states of the Upper South to test the South's enforcement of the *Morgan* decision.

Other victories followed. In 1948, in *Shelley v. Kraemer*, the U.S. Supreme Court held that courts could not enforce real estate covenants that restricted the purchase or sale of property based on race. In 1950, the NAACP brought a case before the U.S. Supreme Court that they hoped would help to undermine the concept of "separate but equal" as espoused in the 1896 decision in *Plessy v. Ferguson*, which gave legal sanction to segregated school systems. *Sweatt v. Painter* was a case brought by Herman Marion Sweatt, who sued the University of Texas for denying him admission to its law school because state law prohibited integrated education. Texas attempted to form a separate law school for African Americans only, but in its decision on the case, the U.S. Supreme Court rejected this solution, holding that the separate school provided neither equal facilities nor "intangibles," such as the ability to form relationships with other future lawyers, that a professional school should provide.

Not all efforts to enact desegregation required the use of the courts, however. On April 15, 1947, Jackie Robinson started for the Brooklyn Dodgers, playing first base. He was the first African American to play baseball in the National League, breaking the color barrier. Although African Americans had their own baseball teams in the Negro Leagues, Robinson opened the gates for them to play in direct competition with white players in the major leagues. Other African American athletes also began to challenge the segregation of American sports. At the 1948 Summer Olympics, Alice Coachman, an African American, was the only American woman to take a gold medal in the games (**Figure 7.17**). These changes, while symbolically significant, were mere cracks in the wall of segregation.

(a)   (b)

Figure 7.17 Baseball legend Jackie Robinson (a) was active in the civil rights movement. He served on the NAACP's board of directors and helped to found an African American-owned bank. Alice Coachman (b), who competed in track and field at Tuskegee University, was the first black woman to win an Olympic gold medal.

DESEGREGATION AND INTEGRATION

Until 1954, racial segregation in education was not only legal but was required in seventeen states and permissible in several others (**Figure 7.18**). Utilizing evidence provided in sociological studies conducted by Kenneth Clark and Gunnar Myrdal, however, Thurgood Marshall, then chief counsel for the NAACP, successfully argued the landmark case *Brown v. Board of Education of Topeka, Kansas* before the U.S. Supreme Court led by Chief Justice Earl Warren. Marshall showed that the practice of segregation in public schools made African American students feel inferior. Even if the facilities provided were equal in nature, the Court noted in its decision, the very fact that some students were separated from others on the basis of their race made segregation unconstitutional.

U.S. School Segregation prior to *Brown v. Board of Education*

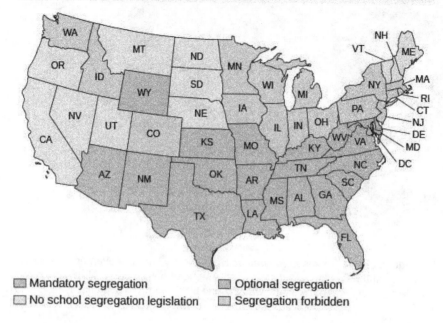

Mandatory segregation

No school segregation legislation

Optional segregation

Segregation forbidden

Figure 7.18 This map shows those states in which racial segregation in public education was required by law before the 1954 *Brown v. Board of Education* decision. In 1960, four years later, fewer than 10 percent of southern African American students attended the same schools as white students.

DEFINING "AMERICAN"

⊙ *Thurgood Marshall on Fighting Racism*

As a law student in 1933, Thurgood Marshall (Figure 7.19) was recruited by his mentor Charles Hamilton Houston to assist in gathering information for the defense of a black man in Virginia accused of killing two white women. His continued close association with Houston led Marshall to aggressively defend blacks in the court system and to use the courts as the weapon by which equal rights might be extracted from the U.S. Constitution and a white racist system. Houston also suggested that it would be important to establish legal precedents regarding the *Plessy v. Ferguson* ruling of separate but equal.

Figure 7.19 In 1956, NAACP leaders (from left to right) Henry L. Moon, Roy Wilkins, Herbert Hill, and Thurgood Marshall present a new poster in the campaign against southern white racism. Marshall successfully argued the landmark case *Brown v. Board of Education* (1954) before the U.S. Supreme Court and later became the court's first African American justice.

By 1938, Marshall had become "Mr. Civil Rights" and formally organized the NAACP's Legal Defense and Education Fund in 1940 to garner the resources to take on cases to break the racist justice system of America. A direct result of Marshall's energies and commitment was his 1940 victory in a Supreme Court case, *Chambers v. Florida*, which held that confessions obtained by violence and torture were inadmissible in a court of law. His most well-known case was *Brown v. Board of Education* in 1954, which held that state laws establishing separate public schools for black and white students were unconstitutional.

Later in life, Marshall reflected on his career fighting racism in a speech at Howard Law School in 1978:

> Be aware of that myth, that everything is going to be all right. Don't give in. I add that, because it seems to me, that what we need to do today is to refocus. Back in the 30s and 40s, we could go no place but to court. We knew then, the court was not the final solution. Many of us knew the final solution would have to be politics, if for no other reason, politics is cheaper than lawsuits. So now we have both. We have our legal arm, and we have our political arm. Let's use them both. And don't listen to this myth that it can be solved by either or that it has already been solved. Take it from me, it has not been solved.

When Marshall says that the problems of racism have not been solved, to what was he referring?

Plessy v. Fergusson had been overturned. The challenge now was to integrate schools. A year later, the U.S. Supreme Court ordered southern school systems to begin **desegregation** "with all deliberate speed." Some school districts voluntarily integrated their schools. For many other districts, however, "deliberate speed" was very, very slow.

It soon became clear that enforcing *Brown v. the Board of Education* would require presidential intervention. Eisenhower did not agree with the U.S. Supreme Court's decision and did not wish to force southern states to integrate their schools. However, as president, he was responsible for doing so. In 1957, Central High School in Little Rock, Arkansas, was forced to accept its first nine African American students, who became known as the **Little Rock Nine**. In response, Arkansas governor Orval Faubus called out the state National Guard to prevent the students from attending classes, removing the troops only after Eisenhower told him to do so. A subsequent attempt by the nine students to attend school resulted in mob violence. Eisenhower then placed the Arkansas National Guard under federal control and sent the U.S. Army's 101st airborne unit to escort the students to and from school as well as from class to class (**Figure 7.20**). This was the first time since the end of Reconstruction that federal troops once more protected the rights of African Americans in the South.

Figure 7.20 In 1957, U.S. soldiers from the 101st Airborne were called in to escort the Little Rock Nine into and around formerly all-white Central High School in Little Rock, Arkansas.

Throughout the course of the school year, the Little Rock Nine were insulted, harassed, and physically assaulted; nevertheless, they returned to school each day. At the end of the school year, the first African American student graduated from Central High. At the beginning of the 1958–1959 school year, Orval Faubus ordered all Little Rock's public schools closed. In the opinion of white segregationists, keeping all students out of school was preferable to having them attend integrated schools. In 1959, the U.S. Supreme Court ruled that the school had to be reopened and that the process of desegregation had to proceed.

WHITE RESPONSES

Efforts to desegregate public schools led to a backlash among most southern whites. Many greeted the *Brown* decision with horror; some World War II veterans questioned how the government they had fought for could betray them in such a fashion. Some white parents promptly withdrew their children from public schools and enrolled them in all-white private academies, many newly created for the sole purpose of keeping white children from attending integrated schools. Often, these "academies" held classes in neighbors' basements or living rooms.

Other white southerners turned to state legislatures or courts to solve the problem of school integration. Orders to integrate school districts were routinely challenged in court. When the lawsuits proved unsuccessful, many southern school districts responded by closing all public schools, as Orval Faubus had done after Central High School was integrated. One county in Virginia closed its public schools for five years rather than see them integrated. Besides suing school districts, many southern segregationists filed lawsuits against the NAACP, trying to bankrupt the organization. Many national politicians supported the segregationist efforts. In 1956, ninety-six members of Congress signed "The Southern Manifesto," in which they accused the U.S. Supreme Court of misusing its power and violating the principle of **states' rights**, which maintained that states had rights equal to those of the federal government.

Unfortunately, many white southern racists, frightened by challenges to the social order, responded with violence. When Little Rock's Central High School desegregated, an irate Ku Klux Klansman from a neighboring community sent a letter to the members of the city's school board in which he denounced them as Communists and threatened to kill them. White rage sometimes erupted into murder. In August 1955, both white and black Americans were shocked by the brutality of the murder of Emmett Till. Till, a fourteen-year-old boy from Chicago, had been vacationing with relatives in Mississippi. While visiting a white-owned store, he had made a remark to the white woman behind the counter. A few days later, the husband and brother-in-law of the woman came to the home of Till's relatives in the middle of the night and abducted the boy. Till's beaten and mutilated body was found in a nearby river three days later. Till's mother insisted on an open-casket funeral; she wished to use her son's body to reveal the brutality of southern racism. The murder of a child who had been guilty of no more than a casual remark captured the nation's attention, as did the acquittal of the two men who admitted killing him.

THE MONTGOMERY BUS BOYCOTT

One of those inspired by Till's death was Rosa Parks, an NAACP member from Montgomery, Alabama, who became the face of the 1955–1956 Montgomery Bus Boycott. City ordinances in Montgomery segregated the city's buses, forcing African American passengers to ride in the back section. They had to enter through the rear of the bus, could not share seats with white passengers, and, if the front of the bus was full and a white passenger requested an African American's seat, had to relinquish their place to the white rider. The bus company also refused to hire African American drivers even though most of the people who rode the buses were black.

On December 1, 1955, Rosa Parks refused to give her seat to a white man, and the Montgomery police arrested her. After being bailed out of jail, she decided to fight the laws requiring segregation in court. To support her, the Women's Political Council, a group of African American female activists, organized a boycott of Montgomery's buses. News of the boycott spread through newspaper notices and by word of mouth; ministers rallied their congregations to support the Women's Political Council. Their efforts were successful, and forty thousand African American riders did not take the bus on December 5, the first day of the boycott.

Other African American leaders within the city embraced the boycott and maintained it beyond December 5, Rosa Parks' court date. Among them was a young minister named Martin Luther King, Jr. For the next year, black Montgomery residents avoided the city's buses. Some organized carpools. Others paid for rides in African American-owned taxis, whose drivers reduced their fees. Most walked to and from school, work, and church for 381 days, the duration of the boycott. In June 1956, an Alabama federal court found the segregation ordinance unconstitutional. The city appealed, but the U.S. Supreme Court upheld the decision. The city's buses were desegregated.

CHAPTER 8

Contesting Futures: America in the 1960s

Figure 8.1 In Aaron Shikler's official portrait of *John Fitzgerald Kennedy* (1970), the president stands with arms folded, apparently deep in thought. The portrait was painted seven years after Kennedy's death, at the request of his widow, Jacqueline Kennedy Onassis. It depicts the president with his head down, because Shikler did not wish to paint the dead man's eyes.

Chapter Outline

8.1 The Kennedy Promise
8.2 Lyndon Johnson and the Great Society
8.3 The Civil Rights Movement Marches On
8.4 Challenging the Status Quo

Introduction

The 1960s was a decade of hope, change, and war that witnessed an important shift in American culture. Citizens from all walks of life sought to expand the meaning of the American promise. Their efforts helped unravel the national consensus and laid bare a far more fragmented society. As a result, men and women from all ethnic groups attempted to reform American society to make it more equitable. The United States also began to take unprecedented steps to exert what it believed to be a positive influence on the world. At the same time, the country's role in Vietnam revealed the limits of military power and the contradictions of U.S. foreign policy. The posthumous portrait of John F. Kennedy (**Figure 8.1**) captures this mix of the era's promise and defeat. His election encouraged many to work for a better future, not just for the middle class but for the marginalized as well. Kennedy's running mate, Lyndon B. Johnson, also envisioned a country characterized by the social and economic freedoms established during the New Deal years. Kennedy's assassination in 1963, and the assassinations five years later of Martin Luther King, Jr. and Robert F. Kennedy, made it dramatically clear that not all Americans shared this vision of a more inclusive democracy.

8.1 The Kennedy Promise

By the end of this section, you will be able to:
- Assess Kennedy's Cold War strategy
- Describe Kennedy's contribution to the civil rights movement

In the 1950s, President Dwight D. Eisenhower presided over a United States that prized conformity over change. Although change naturally occurred, as it does in every era, it was slow and greeted warily. By the 1960s, however, the pace of change had quickened and its scope broadened, as restive and energetic waves of World War II veterans and baby boomers of both sexes and all ethnicities began to make their influence felt politically, economically, and culturally. No one symbolized the hopes and energies of the new decade more than John Fitzgerald Kennedy, the nation's new, young, and seemingly healthful, president. Kennedy had emphasized the country's aspirations and challenges as a "new frontier" when accepting his party's nomination at the Democratic National Convention in Los Angeles, California.

THE NEW FRONTIER

The son of Joseph P. Kennedy, a wealthy Boston business owner and former ambassador to Great Britain, John F. Kennedy graduated from Harvard University and went on to serve in the U.S. House of Representatives in 1946. Even though he was young and inexperienced, his reputation as a war hero who had saved the crew of his PT boat after it was destroyed by the Japanese helped him to win election over more seasoned candidates, as did his father's fortune. In 1952, he was elected to the U.S. Senate for the first of two terms. For many, including Arthur M. Schlesinger, Jr., a historian and member of Kennedy's administration, Kennedy represented a bright, shining future in which the United States would lead the way in solving the most daunting problems facing the world.

Kennedy's popular reputation as a great politician undoubtedly owes much to the style and attitude he personified. He and his wife Jacqueline conveyed a sense of optimism and youthfulness. "Jackie" was an elegant first lady who wore designer dresses, served French food in the White House, and invited classical

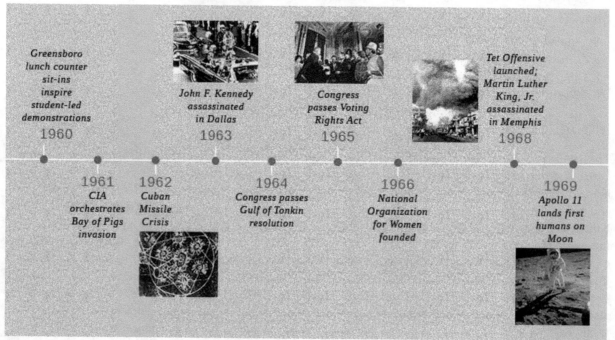

Figure 8.2

musicians to entertain at state functions. "Jack" Kennedy, or JFK, went sailing off the coast of his family's Cape Cod estate and socialized with celebrities (**Figure 8.3**). Few knew that behind Kennedy's healthful and sporty image was a gravely ill man whose wartime injuries caused him daily agony.

(a)   (b)

Figure 8.3 John F. Kennedy and first lady Jacqueline, shown here in the White House in 1962 (a) and watching the America's Cup race that same year (b), brought youth, glamour, and optimism to Washington, DC, and the nation.

Nowhere was Kennedy's style more evident than in the first televised presidential debate held on September 23, 1960, between him and his Republican opponent Vice President Richard M. Nixon. Seventy million viewers watched the debate on television; millions more heard it on the radio. Radio listeners judged Nixon the winner, whereas those who watched the debate on television believed the more telegenic Kennedy made the better showing.

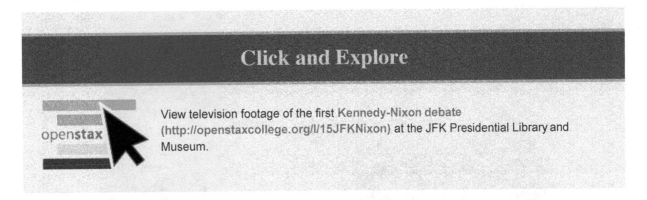

Click and Explore

View television footage of the first Kennedy-Nixon debate (http://openstaxcollege.org/l/15JFKNixon) at the JFK Presidential Library and Museum.

Kennedy did not appeal to all voters, however. Many feared that because he was Roman Catholic, his decisions would be influenced by the Pope. Even traditional Democratic supporters, like the head of the United Auto Workers, Walter Reuther, feared that a Catholic candidate would lose the support of Protestants. Many southern Democrats also disliked Kennedy because of his liberal position on civil rights. To shore up support for Kennedy in the South, Lyndon B. Johnson, the Protestant Texan who was Senate majority leader, was added to the Democratic ticket as the vice presidential candidate. In the end, Kennedy won the election by the closest margin since 1888, defeating Nixon with only 0.01 percent more of the record sixty-seven million votes cast. His victory in the Electoral College was greater: 303 electoral votes to Nixon's 219. Kennedy's win made him both the youngest man elected to the presidency and the first U.S. president born in the twentieth century.

Kennedy dedicated his inaugural address to the theme of a new future for the United States. "Ask not what your country can do for you; ask what you can do for your country," he challenged his fellow Americans. His lofty goals ranged from fighting poverty to winning the space race against the Soviet Union with a moon landing. He assembled an administration of energetic people assured of their ability to shape the future. Dean Rusk was named secretary of state. Robert McNamara, the former president of Ford Motor Company, became secretary of defense. Kennedy appointed his younger brother Robert as attorney general, much to the chagrin of many who viewed the appointment as a blatant example of nepotism.

Kennedy's domestic reform plans remained hampered, however, by his narrow victory and lack of support from members of his own party, especially southern Democrats. As a result, he remained hesitant to propose new civil rights legislation. His achievements came primarily in poverty relief and care for the disabled. Unemployment benefits were expanded, the food stamps program was piloted, and the school lunch program was extended to more students. In October 1963, the passage of the Mental Retardation Facilities and Community Mental Health Centers Construction Act increased support for public mental health services.

KENNEDY THE COLD WARRIOR

Kennedy focused most of his energies on foreign policy, an arena in which he had been interested since his college years and in which, like all presidents, he was less constrained by the dictates of Congress. Kennedy, who had promised in his inaugural address to protect the interests of the "free world," engaged in Cold War politics on a variety of fronts. For example, in response to the lead that the Soviets had taken in the space race when Yuri Gagarin became the first human to successfully orbit the earth, Kennedy urged Congress to not only put a man into space (**Figure 8.4**) but also land an American on the moon, a goal finally accomplished in 1969. This investment advanced a variety of military technologies, especially the nation's long-range missile capability, resulting in numerous profitable spin-offs for the aviation and communication industries. It also funded a growing middle class of government workers, engineers, and defense contractors in states ranging from California to Texas to Florida—a region that would come to be known as the Sun Belt—becoming a symbol of American technological superiority. At the same time, however, the use of massive federal resources for space technologies did not change the economic outlook for low-income communities and underprivileged regions.

Figure 8.4 On May 5, 1961, Alan Shepard became the first American to travel into space, as millions across the country watched the television coverage of his Apollo 11 mission, including Vice President Johnson, President Kennedy, and Jacqueline Kennedy in the White House. (credit: National Archives and Records Administration)

To counter Soviet influence in the developing world, Kennedy supported a variety of measures. One of these was the Alliance for Progress, which collaborated with the governments of Latin American countries to promote economic growth and social stability in nations whose populations might find themselves drawn to communism. Kennedy also established the Agency for International Development to oversee the distribution of foreign aid, and he founded the Peace Corps, which recruited idealistic young people to undertake humanitarian projects in Asia, Africa, and Latin America. He hoped that by augmenting the food supply and improving healthcare and education, the U.S. government could encourage developing nations to align themselves with the United States and reject Soviet or Chinese overtures. The first group of Peace Corps volunteers departed for the four corners of the globe in 1961, serving as an instrument of "soft power" in the Cold War.

Kennedy's various aid projects, like the Peace Corps, fit closely with his administration's **flexible response**, which Robert McNamara advocated as a better alternative to the all-or-nothing defensive strategy of mutually assured destruction favored during Eisenhower's presidency. The plan was to develop different strategies, tactics, and even military capabilities to respond more appropriately to small or medium-sized insurgencies, and political or diplomatic crises. One component of flexible response was the Green Berets, a U.S. Army Special Forces unit trained in **counterinsurgency**—the military suppression of rebel and nationalist groups in foreign nations. Much of the Kennedy administration's new approach to defense, however, remained focused on the ability and willingness of the United States to wage both conventional and nuclear warfare, and Kennedy continued to call for increases in the American nuclear arsenal.

Cuba

Kennedy's multifaceted approach to national defense is exemplified by his careful handling of the Communist government of Fidel Castro in Cuba. In January 1959, following the overthrow of the corrupt and dictatorial regime of Fulgencio Batista, Castro assumed leadership of the new Cuban government. The progressive reforms he began indicated that he favored Communism, and his pro-Soviet foreign policy frightened the Eisenhower administration, which asked the Central Intelligence Agency (CIA) to find a way to remove him from power. Rather than have the U.S. military invade the small island nation, less than one hundred miles from Florida, and risk the world's criticism, the CIA instead trained a small force of Cuban exiles for the job. After landing at the Bay of Pigs on the Cuban coast, these insurgents, the CIA believed, would inspire their countrymen to rise up and topple Castro's regime. The United States also promised air support for the invasion.

Kennedy agreed to support the previous administration's plans, and on April 17, 1961, approximately fourteen hundred Cuban exiles stormed ashore at the designated spot. However, Kennedy feared domestic criticism and worried about Soviet retaliation elsewhere in the world, such as Berlin. He cancelled the anticipated air support, which enabled the Cuban army to easily defeat the insurgents. The hoped-for uprising of the Cuban people also failed to occur. The surviving members of the exile army were taken into custody.

The Bay of Pigs invasion was a major foreign policy disaster for President Kennedy and highlighted Cuba's military vulnerability to the Castro administration. The following year, the Soviet Union sent troops and technicians to Cuba to strengthen its new ally against further U.S. military plots. Then, on October 14, U.S. spy planes took aerial photographs that confirmed the presence of long-range ballistic missile sites in Cuba. The United States was now within easy reach of Soviet nuclear warheads (**Figure 8.5**).

(a)   (b)

Figure 8.5 This low-level U.S. Navy photograph of San Cristobal, Cuba, clearly shows one of the sites built to launch intermediate-range missiles at the United States (a). As the date indicates, it was taken on the last day of the Cuban Missile Crisis. Following the crisis, Kennedy met with the reconnaissance pilots who flew the Cuban missions (b). credit a: modification of work by National Archives and Records Administration; credit b: modification of work by Central Intelligence Agency)

On October 22, Kennedy demanded that Soviet premier Nikita Khrushchev remove the missiles. He also ordered a **naval quarantine** placed around Cuba to prevent Soviet ships from approaching. Despite his use of the word "quarantine" instead of "blockade," for a blockade was considered an act of war, a potential war with the Soviet Union was nevertheless on the president's mind. As U.S. ships headed for Cuba, the army was told to prepare for war, and Kennedy appeared on national television to declare his intention to defend the Western Hemisphere from Soviet aggression.

The world held its breath awaiting the Soviet reply. Realizing how serious the United States was, Khrushchev sought a peaceful solution to the crisis, overruling those in his government who urged a harder stance. Behind the scenes, Robert Kennedy and Soviet ambassador Anatoly Dobrynin worked toward a compromise that would allow both superpowers to back down without either side's seeming intimidated by the other. On October 26, Khrushchev agreed to remove the Russian missiles in exchange for Kennedy's promise not to invade Cuba. On October 27, Kennedy's agreement was made public, and the crisis ended. Not made public, but nevertheless part of the agreement, was Kennedy's promise to remove U.S. warheads from Turkey, as close to Soviet targets as the Cuban missiles had been to American ones.

The showdown between the United States and the Soviet Union over Cuba's missiles had put the world on the brink of a nuclear war. Both sides already had long-range bombers with nuclear weapons airborne or ready for launch, and were only hours away from the first strike. In the long run, this nearly catastrophic example of nuclear brinksmanship ended up making the world safer. A telephone "hot line" was installed, linking Washington and Moscow to avert future crises, and in 1963, Kennedy and Khrushchev signed the Limited Test Ban Treaty, prohibiting tests of nuclear weapons in Earth's atmosphere.

Vietnam

Cuba was not the only arena in which the United States sought to contain the advance of Communism. In Indochina, nationalist independence movements, most notably Vietnam's Viet Minh under the leadership of Ho Chi Minh, had strong Communist sympathies. President Harry S. Truman had no love for France's colonial regime in Southeast Asia but did not want to risk the loyalty of its Western European ally against the Soviet Union. In 1950, the Truman administration sent a small military advisory group to Vietnam and provided financial aid to help France defeat the Viet Minh.

In 1954, Vietnamese forces finally defeated the French, and the country was temporarily divided at the seventeenth parallel. Ho Chi Minh and the Viet Minh controlled the North. In the South, the last Vietnamese emperor and ally to France, Bao Dai, named the French-educated, anti-Communist Ngo Dinh Diem as his prime minister. But Diem refused to abide by the Geneva Accords, the treaty ending the conflict that called for countrywide national elections in 1956, with the victor to rule a reunified nation. After a fraudulent election in the South in 1955, he ousted Bao Dai and proclaimed himself president of the Republic of Vietnam. He cancelled the 1956 elections in the South and began to round up Communists and supporters of Ho Chi Minh, who won the election in the North.

Realizing that Diem would never agree to the reunification of the country under Ho Chi Minh's leadership, the North Vietnamese began efforts to overthrow the government of the South by encouraging insurgents to attack South Vietnamese officials. By 1960, North Vietnam had also created the National Liberation Front (NLF) to resist Diem and carry out an insurgency in the South. The United States, fearing the spread of Communism under Ho Chi Minh, supported Diem, assuming he would create a democratic, pro-Western government in South Vietnam. However, Diem's oppressive and corrupt government made him a very unpopular ruler, particularly with farmers, students, and Buddhists, and many in the South actively assisted the NLF and North Vietnam in trying to overthrow his government.

When Kennedy took office, Diem's government was faltering. Continuing the policies of the Eisenhower administration, Kennedy supplied Diem with money and military advisors to prop up his government (**Figure 8.6**). By November 1963, there were sixteen thousand U.S. troops in Vietnam, training members of that country's special forces and flying air missions that dumped defoliant chemicals on the countryside to expose North Vietnamese and NLF forces and supply routes. A few weeks before Kennedy's own death, Diem and his brother Nhu were assassinated by South Vietnamese military officers after U.S. officials had indicated their support for a new regime.

Figure 8.6 Following the French retreat from Indochina, the United States stepped in to prevent what it believed was a building Communist threat in the region. Under President Kennedy's leadership, the United States sent thousands of military advisors to Vietnam. (credit: Abbie Rowe)

TENTATIVE STEPS TOWARD CIVIL RIGHTS

Cold War concerns, which guided U.S. policy in Cuba and Vietnam, also motivated the Kennedy administration's steps toward racial equality. Realizing that legal segregation and widespread discrimination hurt the country's chances of gaining allies in Africa, Asia, and Latin America, the federal government increased efforts to secure the civil rights of African Americans in the 1960s. During his presidential campaign, Kennedy had intimated his support for civil rights, and his efforts to secure the release of civil rights leader Martin Luther King, Jr., who was arrested following a demonstration, won him the African American vote. Lacking widespread backing in Congress, however, and anxious not to offend white southerners, Kennedy was cautious in assisting African Americans in their fight for full citizenship rights.

His strongest focus was on securing the voting rights of African Americans. Kennedy feared the loss of support from southern white Democrats and the impact a struggle over civil rights could have on his foreign policy agenda as well as on his reelection in 1964. But he thought voter registration drives far preferable to the boycotts, sit-ins, and integration marches that had generated such intense global media coverage in previous years. Encouraged by Congress's passage of the Civil Rights Act of 1960, which permitted federal courts to appoint referees to guarantee that qualified persons would be registered to vote, Kennedy focused on the passage of a constitutional amendment outlawing poll taxes, a tactic that southern states used to disenfranchise African American voters. Originally proposed by President Truman's Committee on Civil Rights, the idea had been largely forgotten during Eisenhower's time in office. Kennedy, however, revived it and convinced Spessard Holland, a conservative Florida senator, to introduce the proposed amendment in Congress. It passed both houses of Congress and was sent to the states for ratification in September 1962.

Kennedy also reacted to the demands of the civil rights movement for equality in education. For example, when African American student James Meredith, encouraged by Kennedy's speeches, attempted to enroll at the segregated University of Mississippi in 1962, riots broke out on campus (**Figure 8.7**). The president responded by sending the U.S. Army and National Guard to Oxford, Mississippi, to support the U.S. Marshals that his brother Robert, the attorney general, had dispatched.

Figure 8.7 Escorted by a U.S. marshal and the assistant attorney general for civil rights, James Meredith (center) enters the University of Mississippi over the riotous protests of white southerners. Meredith later attempted a "March against Fear" in 1966 to protest the inability of southern African Americans to vote. His walk ended when a passing motorist shot and wounded him. (credit: Library of Congress)

Following similar violence at the University of Alabama when two African American students, Vivian Malone and James Hood, attempted to enroll in 1963, Kennedy responded with a bill that would give the federal government greater power to enforce school desegregation, prohibit segregation in public accommodations, and outlaw discrimination in employment. Kennedy would not live to see his bill enacted; it would become law during Lyndon Johnson's administration as the 1964 Civil Rights Act.

TRAGEDY IN DALLAS

Although his stance on civil rights had won him support in the African American community and his steely performance during the Cuban Missile Crisis had led his overall popularity to surge, Kennedy understood that he had to solidify his base in the South to secure his reelection. On November 21, 1963, he accompanied Lyndon Johnson to Texas to rally his supporters. The next day, shots rang out as Kennedy's motorcade made its way through the streets of Dallas. Seriously injured, Kennedy was rushed to Parkland Hospital and pronounced dead.

The gunfire that killed Kennedy appeared to come from the upper stories of the Texas School Book Depository building; later that day, Lee Harvey Oswald, an employee at the depository and a trained sniper, was arrested (**Figure 8.8**). Two days later, while being transferred from Dallas police headquarters to the county jail, Oswald was shot and killed by Jack Ruby, a local nightclub owner who claimed he acted to avenge the president.

Figure 8.8 Lee Harvey Oswald (center) was arrested at the Texas Theatre in Dallas a few hours after shooting President Kennedy.

Almost immediately, rumors began to circulate regarding the Kennedy assassination, and conspiracy theorists, pointing to the unlikely coincidence of Oswald's murder a few days after Kennedy's, began to propose alternate theories about the events. To quiet the rumors and allay fears that the government was hiding evidence, Lyndon Johnson, Kennedy's successor, appointed a fact-finding commission headed by Earl Warren, chief justice of the U.S. Supreme Court, to examine all the evidence and render a verdict. The Warren Commission concluded that Lee Harvey Oswald had acted alone and there had been no conspiracy. The commission's ruling failed to satisfy many, and multiple theories have sprung up over time. No credible evidence has ever been uncovered, however, to prove either that someone other than Oswald murdered Kennedy or that Oswald acted with co-conspirators.

8.2 Lyndon Johnson and the Great Society

By the end of this section, you will be able to:
- Describe the major accomplishments of Lyndon Johnson's Great Society
- Identify the legal advances made in the area of civil rights
- Explain how Lyndon Johnson deepened the American commitment in Vietnam

On November 27, 1963, a few days after taking the oath of office, President Johnson addressed a joint session of Congress and vowed to accomplish the goals that John F. Kennedy had set and to expand the role of the federal government in securing economic opportunity and civil rights for all. Johnson brought to his presidency a vision of a **Great Society** in which everyone could share in the opportunities for a better life that the United States offered, and in which the words "liberty and justice for all" would have real meaning.

THE GREAT SOCIETY

In May 1964, in a speech at the University of Michigan, Lyndon Johnson described in detail his vision of the Great Society he planned to create (**Figure 8.9**). When the Eighty-Ninth Congress convened the following January, he and his supporters began their effort to turn the promise into reality. By combatting racial discrimination and attempting to eliminate poverty, the reforms of the Johnson administration changed the nation.

(a)   (b)

Figure 8.9 In a speech at the University of Michigan in Ann Arbor on May 22, 1964 (a), President Johnson announced some of his goals for the Great Society. These included rebuilding cities, preserving the natural environment, and improving education. Johnson signed the Elementary and Secondary Education Act in his hometown of Johnson City, Texas, alongside his childhood schoolteacher, Kate Deadrich Loney (b). (credit a: modification of work by Cecil Stoughton)

One of the chief pieces of legislation that Congress passed in 1965 was the Elementary and Secondary Education Act (**Figure 8.9**). Johnson, a former teacher, realized that a lack of education was the primary cause of poverty and other social problems. Educational reform was thus an important pillar of the society he hoped to build. This act provided increased federal funding to both elementary and secondary schools, allocating more than $1 billion for the purchase of books and library materials, and the creation of educational programs for disadvantaged children. The Higher Education Act, signed into law the same year, provided scholarships and low-interest loans for the poor, increased federal funding for colleges and universities, and created a corps of teachers to serve schools in impoverished areas.

Education was not the only area toward which Johnson directed his attention. Consumer protection laws were also passed that improved the safety of meat and poultry, placed warning labels on cigarette packages, required "truth in lending" by creditors, and set safety standards for motor vehicles. Funds were provided to improve public transportation and to fund high-speed mass transit. To protect the environment, the Johnson administration created laws protecting air and water quality, regulating the disposal of solid waste, preserving wilderness areas, and protecting endangered species. All of these laws fit within Johnson's plan to make the United States a better place to live. Perhaps influenced by Kennedy's commitment to the arts, Johnson also signed legislation creating the National Endowment for the Arts and the National Endowment for the Humanities, which provided funding for artists and scholars. The Public Broadcasting Act of 1967 authorized the creation of the private, not-for-profit Corporation for Public Broadcasting, which helped launch the Public Broadcasting Service (PBS) and National Public Radio (NPR) in 1970.

In 1965, the Johnson administration also encouraged Congress to pass the Immigration and Nationality Act, which essentially overturned legislation from the 1920s that had favored immigrants from western and northern Europe over those from eastern and southern Europe. The law lifted severe restrictions on immigration from Asia and gave preference to immigrants with family ties in the United States and immigrants with desirable skills. Although the measure seemed less significant than many of the other legislative victories of the Johnson administration at the time, it opened the door for a new era in immigration and made possible the formation of Asian and Latin American immigrant communities in the following decades.

While these laws touched on important aspects of the Great Society, the centerpiece of Johnson's plan was the eradication of poverty in the United States. The **war on poverty**, as he termed it, was fought on many fronts. The 1965 Housing and Urban Development Act offered grants to improve city housing and subsidized rents for the poor. The Model Cities program likewise provided money for urban development projects and the building of public housing.

The Economic Opportunity Act (EOA) of 1964 established and funded a variety of programs to assist the poor in finding jobs. The Office of Economic Opportunity (OEO), first administered by President Kennedy's brother-in-law Sargent Shriver, coordinated programs such as the Jobs Corps and the Neighborhood Youth Corps, which provided job training programs and work experience for the disadvantaged. Volunteers in Service to America recruited people to offer educational programs and other community services in poor areas, just as the Peace Corps did abroad. The Community Action Program, also under the OEO, funded local Community Action Agencies, organizations created and managed by residents of disadvantaged communities to improve their own lives and those of their neighbors. The Head Start program, intended to prepare low-income children for elementary school, was also under the OEO until it was transferred to Department of Health, Education, and Welfare in 1969.

The EOA fought rural poverty by providing low-interest loans to those wishing to improve their farms or start businesses (**Figure 8.10**). EOA funds were also used to provide housing and education for migrant farm workers. Other legislation created jobs in Appalachia, one of the poorest regions in the United States, and brought programs to Indian reservations. One of EOA's successes was the Rough Rock Demonstration School on the Navajo Reservation that, while respecting Navajo traditions and culture, also trained people for careers and jobs outside the reservation.

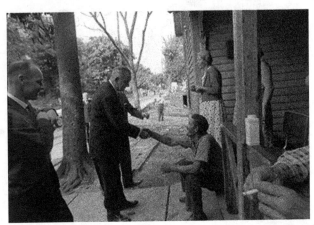

Figure 8.10 President Johnson visits a poor family in Appalachia in 1964. Government initiatives designed to combat poverty helped rural communities like this one by providing low-interest loans and housing. (credit: Cecil Stoughton)

The Johnson administration, realizing the nation's elderly were among its poorest and most disadvantaged citizens, passed the Social Security Act of 1965. The most profound change made by this act was the creation of Medicare, a program to pay the medical expenses of those over sixty-five. Although opposed by the American Medical Association, which feared the creation of a national healthcare system, the new program was supported by most citizens because it would benefit all social classes, not just the poor. The act and subsequent amendments to it also provided coverage for self-employed people in certain occupations and expanded the number of disabled who qualified for benefits. The following year, the Medicaid program allotted federal funds to pay for medical care for the poor.

JOHNSON'S COMMITMENT TO CIVIL RIGHTS

The eradication of poverty was matched in importance by the Great Society's advancement of civil rights. Indeed, the condition of the poor could not be alleviated if racial discrimination limited their access to jobs, education, and housing. Realizing this, Johnson drove the long-awaited civil rights act, proposed by Kennedy in June 1963 in the wake of riots at the University of Alabama, through Congress. Under

Kennedy's leadership, the bill had passed the House of Representatives but was stalled in the Senate by a filibuster. Johnson, a master politician, marshaled his considerable personal influence and memories of his fallen predecessor to break the filibuster. The Civil Rights Act of 1964, the most far-reaching civil rights act yet passed by Congress, banned discrimination in public accommodations, sought to aid schools in efforts to desegregate, and prohibited federal funding of programs that permitted racial segregation. Further, it barred discrimination in employment on the basis of race, color, national origin, religion, or gender, and established an Equal Employment Opportunity Commission.

Protecting African Americans' right to vote was as important as ending racial inequality in the United States. In January 1964, the Twenty-Fourth Amendment, prohibiting the imposition of poll taxes on voters, was finally ratified. Poverty would no longer serve as an obstacle to voting. Other impediments remained, however. Attempts to register southern African American voters encountered white resistance, and protests against this interference often met with violence. On March 7, 1965, a planned protest march from Selma, Alabama, to the state capitol in Montgomery, turned into "Bloody Sunday" when marchers crossing the Edmund Pettus Bridge encountered a cordon of state police, wielding batons and tear gas (**Figure 8.11**). Images of white brutality appeared on television screens throughout the nation and in newspapers around the world.

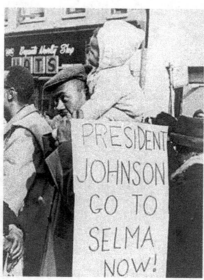

Figure 8.11 African American marchers in Selma, Alabama, were attacked by state police officers in 1965, and the resulting "Bloody Sunday" helped create support for the civil rights movement among northern whites. (credit: Library of Congress)

Deeply disturbed by the violence in Alabama and the refusal of Governor George Wallace to address it, Johnson introduced a bill in Congress that would remove obstacles for African American voters and lend federal support to their cause. His proposal, the Voting Rights Act of 1965, prohibited states and local governments from passing laws that discriminated against voters on the basis of race (**Figure 8.12**). Literacy tests and other barriers to voting that had kept ethnic minorities from the polls were thus outlawed. Following the passage of the act, a quarter of a million African Americans registered to vote, and by 1967, the majority of African Americans had done so. Johnson's final piece of civil rights legislation was the Civil Rights Act of 1968, which prohibited discrimination in housing on the basis of race, color, national origin, or religion.

(a)   (b)

Figure 8.12 The Voting Rights Act (a) was signed into law on August 6, 1965, in the presence of major figures of the civil rights movement, including Rosa Parks and Martin Luther King, Jr. (b).

INCREASED COMMITMENT IN VIETNAM

Building the Great Society had been Lyndon Johnson's biggest priority, and he effectively used his decades of experience in building legislative majorities in a style that ranged from diplomacy to quid pro quo deals to bullying. In the summer of 1964, he deployed these political skills to secure congressional approval for a new strategy in Vietnam—with fateful consequences.

President Johnson had never been the cold warrior Kennedy was, but believed that the credibility of the nation and his office depended on maintaining a foreign policy of containment. When, on August 2, the U.S. destroyer USS *Maddox* conducted an arguably provocative intelligence-gathering mission in the gulf of Tonkin, it reported an attack by North Vietnamese torpedo boats. Two days later, the *Maddox* was supposedly struck again, and a second ship, the USS *Turner Joy*, reported that it also had been fired upon. The North Vietnamese denied the second attack, and Johnson himself doubted the reliability of the crews' report. The National Security Agency has since revealed that the August 4 attacks did not occur. Relying on information available at the time, however, Secretary of Defense Robert McNamara reported to Congress that U.S. ships had been fired upon in international waters while conducting routine operations. On August 10, with only two dissenting votes, Congress passed the Gulf of Tonkin Resolution, giving President Johnson the authority to use military force in Vietnam without asking Congress for a declaration of war. The resolution dramatically increased the power of the U.S. president and transformed the American role in Vietnam from advisor to combatant.

In 1965, large-scale U.S. bombing of North Vietnam began. The intent of the campaign, which lasted three years under various names, was to force the North to end its support for the insurgency in the South. More than 200,000 U.S. combat troops were also sent to South Vietnam. At first, most of the American public supported the president's actions in Vietnam. Support began to ebb, however, as more troops were deployed. Frustrated by losses suffered by the South's Army of the Republic of Vietnam (ARVN), General William Westmoreland called for the United States to take more responsibility for fighting the war. By April 1966, more Americans were being killed in battle than ARVN troops. Johnson, however, maintained that the war could be won if the United States stayed the course, and in November 1967, Westmoreland proclaimed the end was in sight.

Click and Explore

To hear one soldier's story about his time in Vietnam, listen to Sergeant Charles G. Richardson's recollections (http://openstaxcollege.org/l/15VietnamVet) of his experience on the ground and his reflections on his military service.

Westmoreland's predictions were called into question, however, when in January 1968, the North Vietnamese launched their most aggressive assault on the South, deploying close to eighty-five thousand troops. During the Tet Offensive, as these attacks were known, nearly one hundred cities in the South were attacked, including the capital of Saigon (**Figure 8.13**). In heavy fighting, U.S. and South Vietnamese forces recaptured all the points taken by the enemy.

(a)   (b)

Figure 8.13 During the 1968 Tet Offensive, North Vietnamese and South Communist rebel armies known as Viet Cong attacked South Vietnamese and U.S. targets throughout Vietnam (a), with Saigon as the focus (b). Tet, the lunar New Year, was an important holiday in Vietnam and temporary ceasefires usually took place at this time. (credit a: modification of work by Central Intelligence Agency)

Although North Vietnamese forces suffered far more casualties than the roughly forty-one hundred U.S. soldiers killed, public opinion in the United States, fueled by graphic images provided in unprecedented media coverage, turned against the war. Disastrous surprise attacks like the Tet Offensive persuaded many that the war would not be over soon and raised doubts about whether Johnson's administration was telling the truth about the real state of affairs. In May 1968, with over 400,000 U.S. soldiers in Vietnam, Johnson began peace talks with the North.

It was too late to save Johnson himself, however. Many of the most outspoken critics of the war were Democratic politicians whose opposition began to erode unity within the party. Minnesota senator Eugene McCarthy, who had called for an end to the war and the withdrawal of troops from Vietnam, received nearly as many votes in the New Hampshire presidential primary as Johnson did, even though he had been expected to fare very poorly. McCarthy's success in New Hampshire encouraged Robert Kennedy to announce his candidacy as well. Johnson, suffering health problems and realizing his actions in Vietnam had hurt his public standing, announced that he would not seek reelection and withdrew from the 1968 presidential race.

THE END OF THE GREAT SOCIETY

Perhaps the greatest casualty of the nation's war in Vietnam was the Great Society. As the war escalated, the money spent to fund it also increased, leaving less to pay for the many social programs Johnson had created to lift Americans out of poverty. Johnson knew he could not achieve his Great Society while spending money to wage the war. He was unwilling to withdraw from Vietnam, however, for fear that the world would perceive this action as evidence of American failure and doubt the ability of the United States to carry out its responsibilities as a superpower.

Vietnam doomed the Great Society in other ways as well. Dreams of racial harmony suffered, as many African Americans, angered by the failure of Johnson's programs to alleviate severe poverty in the inner cities, rioted in frustration. Their anger was heightened by the fact that a disproportionate number of African Americans were fighting and dying in Vietnam. Nearly two-thirds of eligible African Americans were drafted, whereas draft deferments for college, exemptions for skilled workers in the military industrial complex, and officer training programs allowed white middle-class youth to either avoid the draft or volunteer for a military branch of their choice. As a result, less than one-third of white men were drafted.

Although the Great Society failed to eliminate suffering or increase civil rights to the extent that Johnson wished, it made a significant difference in people's lives. By the end of Johnson's administration, the percentage of people living below the poverty line had been cut nearly in half. While more people of color than whites continued to live in poverty, the percentage of poor African Americans had decreased dramatically. The creation of Medicare and Medicaid as well as the expansion of Social Security benefits and welfare payments improved the lives of many, while increased federal funding for education enabled more people to attend college than ever before. Conservative critics argued that, by expanding the responsibilities of the federal government to care for the poor, Johnson had hurt both taxpayers and the poor themselves. Aid to the poor, many maintained, would not only fail to solve the problem of poverty but would also encourage people to become dependent on government "handouts" and lose their desire and ability to care for themselves—an argument that many found intuitively compelling but which lacked conclusive evidence. These same critics also accused Johnson of saddling the United States with a large debt as a result of the deficit spending (funded by borrowing) in which he had engaged.

8.3 The Civil Rights Movement Marches On

By the end of this section, you will be able to:
- Explain the strategies of the African American civil rights movement in the 1960s
- Discuss the rise and philosophy of Black Power
- Identify achievements of the Mexican American civil rights movement in the 1960s

During the 1960s, the federal government, encouraged by both genuine concern for the dispossessed and the realities of the Cold War, had increased its efforts to protect civil rights and ensure equal economic and educational opportunities for all. However, most of the credit for progress toward racial equality in the Unites States lies with grassroots activists. Indeed, it was campaigns and demonstrations by ordinary people that spurred the federal government to action. Although the African American civil rights movement was the most prominent of the crusades for racial justice, other ethnic minorities also worked to seize their piece of the American dream during the promising years of the 1960s. Many were influenced by the African American cause and often used similar tactics.

CHANGE FROM THE BOTTOM UP

For many people inspired by the victories of *Brown v. Board of Education* and the Montgomery Bus Boycott, the glacial pace of progress in the segregated South was frustrating if not intolerable. In some places, such as Greensboro, North Carolina, local NAACP chapters had been influenced by whites who provided financing for the organization. This aid, together with the belief that more forceful efforts at reform would only increase white resistance, had persuaded some African American organizations to pursue a "politics of moderation" instead of attempting to radically alter the status quo. Martin Luther King Jr.'s inspirational appeal for peaceful change in the city of Greensboro in 1958, however, planted the seed for a more assertive civil rights movement.

On February 1, 1960, four sophomores at the North Carolina Agricultural & Technical College in Greensboro—Ezell Blair, Jr., Joseph McNeil, David Richmond, and Franklin McCain—entered the local Woolworth's and sat at the lunch counter. The lunch counter was segregated, and they were refused service as they knew they would be. They had specifically chosen Woolworth's, because it was a national chain and was thus believed to be especially vulnerable to negative publicity. Over the next few days, more protesters joined the four sophomores. Hostile whites responded with threats and taunted the students by pouring sugar and ketchup on their heads. The successful six-month-long Greensboro sit-in initiated the student phase of the African American civil rights movement and, within two months, the sit-in movement had spread to fifty-four cities in nine states (**Figure 8.14**).

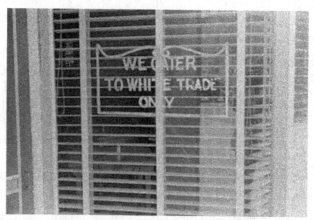

Figure 8.14 Businesses such as this one were among those that became targets of activists protesting segregation. Segregated businesses could be found throughout the United States; this one was located in Ohio. (credit: Library of Congress)

In the words of grassroots civil rights activist Ella Baker, the students at Woolworth's wanted more than a hamburger; the movement they helped launch was about empowerment. Baker pushed for a "participatory Democracy" that built on the grassroots campaigns of active citizens instead of deferring to the leadership of educated elites and experts. As a result of her actions, in April 1960, the Student Nonviolent Coordinating Committee (SNCC) formed to carry the battle forward. Within a year, more than one hundred cities had desegregated at least some public accommodations in response to student-led demonstrations. The sit-ins inspired other forms of nonviolent protest intended to desegregate public spaces. "Sleep-ins" occupied motel lobbies, "read-ins" filled public libraries, and churches became the sites of "pray-ins."

Students also took part in the 1961 "freedom rides" sponsored by the Congress of Racial Equality (CORE) and SNCC. The intent of the African American and white volunteers who undertook these bus rides south was to test enforcement of a U.S. Supreme Court decision prohibiting segregation on interstate transportation and to protest segregated waiting rooms in southern terminals. Departing Washington, DC, on May 4, the volunteers headed south on buses that challenged the seating order of Jim Crow segregation. Whites would ride in the back, African-Americans would sit in the front, and on other occasions, riders of different races would share the same bench seat. The freedom riders encountered little difficulty until they reached Rock Hill, South Carolina, where a mob severely beat John Lewis, a freedom rider who later became chairman of SNCC (**Figure 8.15**). The danger increased as the riders continued through Georgia into Alabama, where one of the two buses was firebombed outside the town of Anniston. The second group continued to Birmingham, where the riders were attacked by the Ku Klux Klan as they attempted to disembark at the city bus station. The remaining volunteers continued to Mississippi, where they were arrested when they attempted to desegregate the waiting rooms in the Jackson bus terminal.

Figure 8.15 Civil rights activists Bayard Rustin, Andrew Young, Rep. William Fitts Ryan, James Farmer, and John Lewis (l to r) in a newspaper photograph from 1965.

FREE BY '63 (OR '64 OR '65)

The grassroots efforts of people like the Freedom Riders to change discriminatory laws and longstanding racist traditions grew more widely known in the mid-1960s. The approaching centennial of Abraham Lincoln's Emancipation Proclamation spawned the slogan "Free by '63" among civil rights activists. As African Americans increased their calls for full rights for all Americans, many civil rights groups changed their tactics to reflect this new urgency.

Perhaps the most famous of the civil rights-era demonstrations was the March on Washington for Jobs and Freedom, held in August 1963, on the one hundredth anniversary of Abraham Lincoln's Emancipation Proclamation. Its purpose was to pressure President Kennedy to act on his promises regarding civil rights. The date was the eighth anniversary of the brutal racist murder of fourteen-year-old Emmett Till in Money, Mississippi. As the crowd gathered outside the Lincoln Memorial and spilled across the National Mall (**Figure 8.16**), Martin Luther King, Jr. delivered his most famous speech. In "I Have a Dream," King called for an end to racial injustice in the United States and envisioned a harmonious, integrated society. The speech marked the high point of the civil rights movement and established the legitimacy of its goals. However, it did not prevent white terrorism in the South, nor did it permanently sustain the tactics of nonviolent civil disobedience.

(a)   (b)

Figure 8.16 During the March on Washington for Jobs and Freedom (a), a huge crowd gathered on the National Mall (b) to hear the speakers. Although thousands attended, many of the march's organizers had hoped that enough people would come to Washington to shut down the city.

Other gatherings of civil rights activists ended tragically, and some demonstrations were intended to provoke a hostile response from whites and thus reveal the inhumanity of the Jim Crow laws and their supporters. In 1963, the Southern Christian Leadership Conference (SCLC) led by Martin Luther King, Jr. mounted protests in some 186 cities throughout the South. The campaign in Birmingham that began in April and extended into the fall of 1963 attracted the most notice, however, when a peaceful protest was met with violence by police, who attacked demonstrators, including children, with fire hoses and dogs. The world looked on in horror as innocent people were assaulted and thousands arrested. King himself was jailed on Easter Sunday, 1963, and, in response to the pleas of white clergymen for peace and patience, he penned one of the most significant documents of the struggle—"Letter from a Birmingham Jail." In the letter, King argued that African Americans had waited patiently for more than three hundred years to be given the rights that all human beings deserved; the time for waiting was over.

DEFINING "AMERICAN"

⚙ *Letter from a Birmingham Jail*

By 1963, Martin Luther King, Jr. had become one of the most prominent leaders of the civil rights movement, and he continued to espouse nonviolent civil disobedience as a way of registering African American resistance against unfair, discriminatory, and racist laws and behaviors. While the campaign in Birmingham began with an African American boycott of white businesses to end discrimination in employment practices and public segregation, it became a fight over free speech when King was arrested for violating a local injunction against demonstrations. King wrote his "Letter from a Birmingham Jail" in response to an op-ed by eight white Alabama clergymen who complained about the SCLC's fiery tactics and argued that social change needed to be pursued gradually. The letter criticizes those who did not support the cause of civil rights:

> In spite of my shattered dreams of the past, I came to Birmingham with the hope that the white religious leadership in the community would see the justice of our cause and, with deep moral concern, serve as the channel through which our just grievances could get to the power structure. I had hoped that each of you would understand. But again I have been disappointed. I have heard numerous religious leaders of the South call upon their worshippers to comply with a desegregation decision because it is the law, but I have longed to hear white ministers say follow this decree because integration is morally right and the Negro is your brother. In the midst of blatant injustices inflicted upon the Negro, I have watched white churches stand on the sideline and merely mouth pious irrelevancies and sanctimonious trivialities. In the midst of a mighty struggle to rid our nation of racial and economic injustice, I have heard so many ministers say, "Those are social issues with which the Gospel has no real concern," and I have watched so many churches commit themselves to a completely other-worldly religion which made a strange distinction between body and soul, the sacred and the secular.

Since its publication, the "Letter" has become one of the most cogent, impassioned, and succinct statements of the aspirations of the civil rights movement and the frustration over the glacial pace of progress in achieving justice and equality for all Americans.

What civil rights tactics raised the objections of the white clergymen King addressed in his letter? Why?

Some of the greatest violence during this era was aimed at those who attempted to register African Americans to vote. In 1964, SNCC, working with other civil rights groups, initiated its Mississippi Summer Project, also known as Freedom Summer. The purpose was to register African American voters in one of the most racist states in the nation. Volunteers also built "freedom schools" and community centers. SNCC invited hundreds of white middle-class students, mostly from the North, to help in the task. Many volunteers were harassed, beaten, and arrested, and African American homes and churches were burned. Three civil rights workers, James Chaney, Michael Schwerner, and Andrew Goodman, were killed by the Ku Klux Klan. That summer, civil rights activists Fannie Lou Hamer, Ella Baker, and Robert Parris Moses formally organized the Mississippi Freedom Democratic Party (MFDP) as an alternative to the all-white Mississippi Democratic Party. The Democratic National Convention's organizers, however, would allow only two MFDP delegates to be seated, and they were confined to the roles of nonvoting observers.

The vision of whites and African Americans working together peacefully to end racial injustice suffered a severe blow with the death of Martin Luther King, Jr. in Memphis, Tennessee, in April 1968. King had gone there to support sanitation workers trying to unionize. In the city, he found a divided civil rights movement; older activists who supported his policy of nonviolence were being challenged by younger African Americans who advocated a more militant approach. On April 4, King was shot and killed while standing on the balcony of his motel. Within hours, the nation's cities exploded with violence as angry African Americans, shocked by his murder, burned and looted inner-city neighborhoods across the country (**Figure 8.17**). While whites recoiled from news about the riots in fear and dismay, they also criticized African Americans for destroying their own neighborhoods; they did not realize that most of the violence was directed against businesses that were not owned by blacks and that treated African American customers with suspicion and hostility.

Figure 8.17 Many businesses, such as those in this neighborhood at the intersection of 7th and N Streets in NW, Washington, DC, were destroyed in riots that followed the assassination of Martin Luther King, Jr.

BLACK FRUSTRATION, BLACK POWER

The episodes of violence that accompanied Martin Luther King Jr.'s murder were but the latest in a string of urban riots that had shaken the United States since the mid-1960s. Between 1964 and 1968, there were 329 riots in 257 cities across the nation. In 1964, riots broke out in Harlem and other African American neighborhoods. In 1965, a traffic stop set in motion a chain of events that culminated in riots in Watts, an African American neighborhood in Los Angeles. Thousands of businesses were destroyed, and, by the time the violence ended, thirty-four people were dead, most of them African Americans killed by the Los Angeles police and the National Guard. More riots took place in 1966 and 1967.

Frustration and anger lay at the heart of these disruptions. Despite the programs of the Great Society, good healthcare, job opportunities, and safe housing were abysmally lacking in urban African American neighborhoods in cities throughout the country, including in the North and West, where discrimination was less overt but just as crippling. In the eyes of many rioters, the federal government either could not or would not end their suffering, and most existing civil rights groups and their leaders had been unable to achieve significant results toward racial justice and equality. Disillusioned, many African Americans turned to those with more radical ideas about how best to obtain equality and justice.

Click and Explore

Watch "Troops Patrol L.A." to see how the 1965 Watts Riots (http://openstaxcollege.org/l/15WattsRiot) were presented in newsreel footage of the day.

Within the chorus of voices calling for integration and legal equality were many that more stridently demanded empowerment and thus supported **Black Power**. Black Power meant a variety of things. One of the most famous users of the term was Stokely Carmichael, the chairman of SNCC, who later changed his name to Kwame Ture. For Carmichael, Black Power was the power of African Americans to unite as a political force and create their own institutions apart from white-dominated ones, an idea first suggested in the 1920s by political leader and orator Marcus Garvey. Like Garvey, Carmichael became an advocate of **black separatism**, arguing that African Americans should live apart from whites and solve their problems for themselves. In keeping with this philosophy, Carmichael expelled SNCC's white members. He left SNCC in 1967 and later joined the Black Panthers (see below).

Long before Carmichael began to call for separatism, the Nation of Islam, founded in 1930, had advocated the same thing. In the 1960s, its most famous member was Malcolm X, born Malcolm Little (**Figure 8.18**). The Nation of Islam advocated the separation of white Americans and African Americans because of a belief that African Americans could not thrive in an atmosphere of white racism. Indeed, in a 1963 interview, Malcolm X, discussing the teachings of the head of the Nation of Islam in America, Elijah Muhammad, referred to white people as "devils" more than a dozen times. Rejecting the nonviolent strategy of other civil rights activists, he maintained that violence in the face of violence was appropriate.

(a)   (b)

Figure 8.18 Stokely Carmichael (a), one of the most famous and outspoken advocates of Black Power, is surrounded by members of the media after speaking at Michigan State University in 1967. Malcolm X (b) was raised in a family influenced by Marcus Garvey and persecuted for its outspoken support of civil rights. While serving a stint in prison for armed robbery, he was introduced to and committed himself to the Nation of Islam. (credit b: modification of work by Library of Congress)

In 1964, after a trip to Africa, Malcolm X left the Nation of Islam to found the Organization of Afro-American Unity with the goal of achieving freedom, justice, and equality "by any means necessary." His views regarding black-white relations changed somewhat thereafter, but he remained fiercely committed to the cause of African American empowerment. On February 21, 1965, he was killed by members of the Nation of Islam. Stokely Carmichael later recalled that Malcolm X had provided an intellectual basis for Black Nationalism and given legitimacy to the use of violence in achieving the goals of Black Power.

DEFINING "AMERICAN"

⊙ *The New Negro*

In a roundtable conversation in October 1961, Malcolm X suggested that a "New Negro" was coming to the fore. The term and concept of a "New Negro" arose during the Harlem Renaissance of the 1920s and was revived during the civil rights movements of the 1960s.

> "I think there is a new so-called Negro. We don't recognize the term 'Negro' but I really believe that there's a new so-called Negro here in America. He not only is impatient. Not only is he dissatisfied, not only is he disillusioned, but he's getting very angry. And whereas the so-called Negro in the past was willing to sit around and wait for someone else to change his condition or correct his condition, there's a growing tendency on the part of a vast number of so-called Negroes today to take action themselves, not to sit and wait for someone else to correct the situation. This, in my opinion, is primarily what has produced this new Negro. He is not willing to wait. He thinks that what he wants is right, what he wants is just, and since these things are just and right, it's wrong to sit around and wait for someone else to correct a nasty condition when they get ready."

In what ways were Martin Luther King, Jr. and the members of SNCC "New Negroes?"

Unlike Stokely Carmichael and the Nation of Islam, most Black Power advocates did not believe African Americans needed to separate themselves from white society. The Black Panther Party, founded in 1966 in Oakland, California, by Bobby Seale and Huey Newton, believed African Americans were as much the victims of capitalism as of white racism. Accordingly, the group espoused Marxist teachings, and called for jobs, housing, and education, as well as protection from police brutality and exemption from military service in their Ten Point Program. The Black Panthers also patrolled the streets of African American neighborhoods to protect residents from police brutality, yet sometimes beat and murdered those who did not agree with their cause and tactics. Their militant attitude and advocacy of armed self-defense attracted many young men but also led to many encounters with the police, which sometimes included arrests and even shootouts, such as those that took place in Los Angeles, Chicago and Carbondale, Illinois.

The self-empowerment philosophy of Black Power influenced mainstream civil rights groups such as the National Economic Growth Reconstruction Organization (NEGRO), which sold bonds and operated a clothing factory and construction company in New York, and the Opportunities Industrialization Center in Philadelphia, which provided job training and placement—by 1969, it had branches in seventy cities. Black Power was also part of a much larger process of cultural change. The 1960s composed a decade not only of Black Power but also of **Black Pride**. African American abolitionist John S. Rock had coined the phrase "Black Is Beautiful" in 1858, but in the 1960s, it became an important part of efforts within the African American community to raise self-esteem and encourage pride in African ancestry. Black Pride urged African Americans to reclaim their African heritage and, to promote group solidarity, to substitute African and African-inspired cultural practices, such as handshakes, hairstyles, and dress, for white practices. One of the many cultural products of this movement was the popular television music program *Soul Train*, created by Don Cornelius in 1969, which celebrated black culture and aesthetics (**Figure 8.19**).

Figure 8.19 When the Jackson Five appeared on *Soul Train*, each of the five brothers sported a large afro, a symbol of Black Pride in the 1960s and 70s.

THE MEXICAN AMERICAN FIGHT FOR CIVIL RIGHTS

The African American bid for full citizenship was surely the most visible of the battles for civil rights taking place in the United States. However, other minority groups that had been legally discriminated against or otherwise denied access to economic and educational opportunities began to increase efforts to secure their rights in the 1960s. Like the African American movement, the Mexican American civil rights movement won its earliest victories in the federal courts. In 1947, in *Mendez v. Westminster*, the U.S. Court of Appeals for the Ninth Circuit ruled that segregating children of Hispanic descent was unconstitutional. In 1954, the same year as *Brown v. Board of Education*, Mexican Americans prevailed in *Hernandez v. Texas*, when the U.S. Supreme Court extended the protections of the Fourteenth Amendment to all ethnic groups in the United States.

The highest-profile struggle of the Mexican American civil rights movement was the fight that Caesar Chavez (**Figure 8.20**) and Dolores Huerta waged in the fields of California to organize migrant farm workers. In 1962, Chavez and Huerta founded the National Farm Workers Association (NFWA). In 1965, when Filipino grape pickers led by Filipino American Larry Itliong went on strike to call attention to their plight, Chavez lent his support. Workers organized by the NFWA also went on strike, and the two organizations merged to form the United Farm Workers. When Chavez asked American consumers to boycott grapes, politically conscious people around the country heeded his call, and many unionized longshoremen refused to unload grape shipments. In 1966, Chavez led striking workers to the state capitol in Sacramento, further publicizing the cause. Martin Luther King, Jr. telegraphed words of encouragement to Chavez, whom he called a "brother." The strike ended in 1970 when California farmers recognized the right of farm workers to unionize. However, the farm workers did not gain all they sought, and the larger struggle did not end.

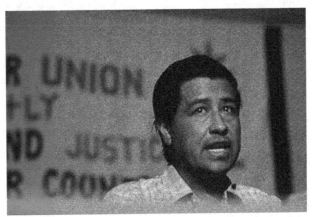

Figure 8.20 Cesar Chavez was influenced by the nonviolent philosophy of Indian nationalist Mahatma Gandhi. In 1968, he emulated Gandhi by engaging in a hunger strike.

The equivalent of the Black Power movement among Mexican Americans was the Chicano Movement. Proudly adopting a derogatory term for Mexican Americans, Chicano activists demanded increased political power for Mexican Americans, education that recognized their cultural heritage, and the restoration of lands taken from them at the end of the Mexican-American War in 1848. One of the founding members, Rodolfo "Corky" Gonzales, launched the Crusade for Justice in Denver in 1965, to provide jobs, legal services, and healthcare for Mexican Americans. From this movement arose La Raza Unida, a political party that attracted many Mexican American college students. Elsewhere, Reies López Tijerina fought for years to reclaim lost and illegally expropriated ancestral lands in New Mexico; he was one of the co-sponsors of the Poor People's March on Washington in 1967.

8.4 Challenging the Status Quo

By the end of this section, you will be able to:
- Describe the goals and activities of SDS, the Free Speech Movement, and the antiwar movement
- Explain the rise, goals, and activities of the women's movement

By the 1960s, a generation of white Americans raised in prosperity and steeped in the culture of conformity of the 1950s had come of age. However, many of these baby boomers (those born between 1946 and 1964) rejected the conformity and luxuries that their parents had provided. These young, middle-class Americans, especially those fortunate enough to attend college when many of their working-class and African American contemporaries were being sent to Vietnam, began to organize to fight for their own rights and end the war that was claiming the lives of so many.

THE NEW LEFT

By 1960, about one-third of the U.S. population was living in the suburbs; during the 1960s, the average family income rose by 33 percent. Material culture blossomed, and at the end of the decade, 70 percent of American families owned washing machines, 83 percent had refrigerators or freezers, and almost 80 percent had at least one car. Entertainment occupied a larger part of both working- and middle-class leisure hours. By 1960, American consumers were spending $85 billion a year on entertainment, double the spending of the preceding decade; by 1969, about 79 percent of American households had black-and-white televisions, and 31 percent could afford color sets. Movies and sports were regular aspects of the weekly routine, and the family vacation became an annual custom for both the middle and working class.

Meanwhile, baby boomers, many raised in this environment of affluence, streamed into universities across the nation in unprecedented numbers looking to "find" themselves. Instead, they found traditional systems that forced them to take required courses, confined them to rigid programs of study, and surrounded them with rules limiting what they could do in their free time. These young people were only too willing to take up Kennedy's call to action, and many did so by joining the civil rights movement. To them, it seemed only right for the children of the "greatest generation" to help those less privileged to fight battles for justice and equality. The more radical aligned themselves with the New Left, activists of the 1960s who rejected the staid liberalism of the Democratic Party. New Left organizations sought reform in areas such as civil rights and women's rights, campaigned for free speech and more liberal policies toward drug use, and condemned the war in Vietnam.

One of the most prominent New Left groups was Students for a Democratic Society (SDS). Organized in 1960, SDS held its first meeting at the University of Michigan, Ann Arbor. Its philosophy was expressed in its manifesto, the **Port Huron Statement**, written by Tom Hayden and adopted in 1962, affirming the group's dedication to fighting economic inequality and discrimination. It called for greater participation in the democratic process by ordinary people, advocated civil disobedience, and rejected the anti-Communist position held by most other groups committed to social reform in the United States.

Click and Explore

Read the full text of the **Port Huron Statement** (http://openstaxcollege.org/l/ **15PHStatement**) by Tom Hayden.

SDS members demanded that universities allow more student participation in university governance and shed their entanglements with the military-industrial complex. They sought to rouse the poor to political action to defeat poverty and racism. In the summer of 1964, a small group of SDS members moved into the uptown district of Chicago and tried to take on racism and poverty through community organization. Under the umbrella of their Economic Research and Action Project, they created JOIN (Jobs or Income Now) to address problems of urban poverty and resisted plans to displace the poor under the guise of urban renewal. They also called for police review boards to end police brutality, organized free breakfast programs, and started social and recreational clubs for neighborhood youth. Eventually, the movement fissured over whether to remain a campus-based student organization or a community-based development organization.

During the same time that SDS became active in Chicago, another student movement emerged on the West Coast, when actions by student activists at the University of California, Berkeley, led to the formation of Berkeley's Free Speech Movement in 1964. University rules prohibited the solicitation of funds for political causes by anyone other than members of the student Democratic and Republican organizations, and restricted advocacy of political causes on campus. In October 1964, when a student handing out literature for CORE refused to show campus police officers his student ID card, he was promptly arrested. Instantly, the campus police car was surrounded by angry students, who refused to let the vehicle move for thirty-two hours until the student was released. In December, students organized a massive sit-in to resolve the issue of political activities on campus. While unsuccessful in the short term, the movement inspired student activism on campuses throughout the country.

A target of many student groups was the war in Vietnam (**Figure 8.21**). In April 1965, SDS organized a march on Washington for peace; about twenty thousand people attended. That same week, the faculty at the University of Michigan suspended classes and conducted a 24-hour "teach-in" on the war. The idea quickly spread, and on May 15, the first national "teach-in" was held at 122 colleges and universities across the nation. Originally designed to be a debate on the pros and cons of the war, at Berkeley, the teach-ins became massive antiwar rallies. By the end of that year, there had been antiwar rallies in some sixty cities.

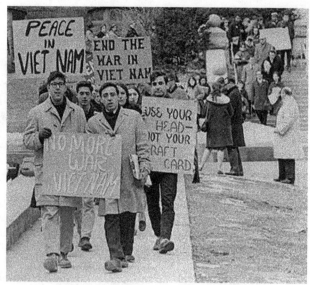

Figure 8.21 Students at the University of Wisconsin-Madison protested the war in Vietnam in 1965. Their actions were typical of many on college campuses across the country during the 1960s. (credit: "Yarnalgo"/Flickr)

AMERICANA

⊙ *Blue Jeans: The Uniform of Nonconformist Radicalism*

Overwhelmingly, young cultural warriors and social activists of the 1960s, trying to escape the shackles of what they perceived to be limits on their freedoms, adopted blue jeans as the uniform of their generation. Originally worn by manual laborers because of their near-indestructibility, blue jeans were commonly associated with cowboys, the quintessential icon of American independence. During the 1930s, jeans were adopted by a broader customer base as a result of the popularity of cowboy movies and dude ranch vacations. After World War II, Levi Strauss, their original manufacturer, began to market them east of the Mississippi, and competitors such as Wrangler and Lee fought for a share of the market. In the 1950s, youths testing the limits of middle-class conformity adopted them in imitation of movie stars like James Dean. By the 1960s, jeans became even more closely associated with youthful rebellion against tradition, a symbol available to everyone, rich and poor, black and white, men and women.

What other styles and behaviors of the 1960s expressed nonconformity, and how?

WOMEN'S RIGHTS

On the national scene, the civil rights movement was creating a climate of protest and claiming rights and new roles in society for people of color. Women played significant roles in organizations fighting for civil rights like SNCC and SDS. However, they often found that those organizations, enlightened as they might be about racial issues or the war in Vietnam, could still be influenced by patriarchal ideas of male superiority. Two members of SNCC, Casey Hayden and Mary King, presented some of their concerns about their organization's treatment of women in a document entitled "On the Position of Women in SNCC." Stokely Carmichael responded that the appropriate position for women in SNCC was "prone."

Just as the abolitionist movement made nineteenth-century women more aware of their lack of power and encouraged them to form the first women's rights movement, the protest movements of the 1960s inspired many white and middle-class women to create their own organized movement for greater rights. Not all were young women engaged in social protest. Many were older, married women who found the traditional roles of housewife and mother unfulfilling. In 1963, writer and feminist Betty Friedan published *The Feminine Mystique* in which she contested the post-World War II belief that it was women's destiny to marry and bear children. Friedan's book was a best-seller and began to raise the consciousness of many women who agreed that homemaking in the suburbs sapped them of their individualism and left them unsatisfied.

The Civil Rights Act of 1964, which prohibited discrimination in employment on the basis of race, color, national origin, and religion, also prohibited, in **Title VII**, discrimination on the basis of sex. Ironically, protection for women had been included at the suggestion of a Virginia congressman in an attempt to *prevent* the act's passage; his reasoning seemed to be that, while a white man might accept that African Americans needed and deserved protection from discrimination, the idea that women deserved equality with men would be far too radical for any of his male colleagues to contemplate. Nevertheless, the act passed, although the struggle to achieve equal pay for equal work continues today.

Medical science also contributed a tool to assist women in their liberation. In 1960, the U.S. Food and Drug Administration approved the birth control pill, freeing women from the restrictions of pregnancy and childbearing. Women who were able to limit, delay, and prevent reproduction were freer to work, attend college, and delay marriage. Within five years of the pill's approval, some six million women were using it.

The pill was the first medicine ever intended to be taken by people who were not sick. Even conservatives saw it as a possible means of making marriages stronger by removing the fear of an unwanted pregnancy and improving the health of women. Its opponents, however, argued that it would promote sexual promiscuity, undermine the institutions of marriage and the family, and destroy the moral code of the nation. By the early 1960s, thirty states had made it a criminal offense to sell contraceptive devices.

In 1966, the National Organization for Women (NOW) formed and proceeded to set an agenda for the feminist movement (**Figure 8.22**). Framed by a statement of purpose written by Friedan, the agenda began by proclaiming NOW's goal to make possible women's participation in all aspects of American life and to gain for them all the rights enjoyed by men. Among the specific goals was the passage of the Equal Rights Amendment (yet to be adopted).

Figure 8.22 Early members of NOW discuss the problems faced by American women. Betty Friedan is second from the left. (credit: Smithsonian Institution Archives)

More radical feminists, like their colleagues in other movements, were dissatisfied with merely redressing economic issues and devised their own brand of consciousness-raising events and symbolic attacks on women's oppression. The most famous of these was an event staged in September 1968 by New York Radical Women. Protesting stereotypical notions of femininity and rejecting traditional gender expectations, the group demonstrated at the Miss America Pageant in Atlantic City, New Jersey, to bring attention to the contest's—and society's—exploitation of women. The protestors crowned a sheep Miss America and then tossed instruments of women's oppression, including high-heeled shoes, curlers, girdles, and bras, into a "freedom trash can." News accounts famously, and incorrectly, described the protest as a "bra burning."

CHAPTER 9

Political Storms at Home and Abroad, 1968-1980

Figure 9.1 Pop artist Peter Max designed this postage stamp to commemorate Expo '74, a world's fair held in Spokane, Washington. The fair's theme was the natural environment. Unfortunately, and ironically, gasoline shortages prevented many from attending the exposition.

Chapter Outline

Introduction

From May 4 to November 4, 1974, a universal exposition was held in the city of Spokane, Washington. This world's fair, Expo '74, and the postage stamp issued to commemorate it, reflected many of the issues and interests of the 1970s (**Figure 9.1**). The stamp features psychedelic colors, and the character of the Cosmic Runner in the center wears bellbottoms, a popular fashion at the time. The theme of the fair was the environment, a subject beginning to be of great concern to people in the United States, especially the younger generation and those in the hippie counterculture. In the 1970s, the environment, social justice, distrust of the government, and a desire to end the war in Vietnam—the concerns and attitudes of younger people, women, gays and lesbians, and people of color—began to draw the attention of the mainstream as well.

9.1 Identity Politics in a Fractured Society

By the end of this section, you will be able to:
- Describe the counterculture of the 1960s
- Explain the origins of the American Indian Movement and its major activities
- Assess the significance of the gay rights and women's liberation movements

The political divisions that plagued the United States in the 1960s were reflected in the rise of **identity politics** in the 1970s. As people lost hope of reuniting as a society with common interests and goals, many focused on issues of significance to the subgroups to which they belonged, based on culture, ethnicity, sexual orientation, gender, and religion.

HIPPIES AND THE COUNTERCULTURE

In the late 1960s and early 1970s, many young people came to embrace a new wave of cultural dissent. The **counterculture** offered an alternative to the bland homogeneity of American middle-class life, patriarchal family structures, self-discipline, unquestioning patriotism, and the acquisition of property. In fact, there were many alternative cultures.

"Hippies" rejected the conventions of traditional society. Men sported beards and grew their hair long; both men and women wore clothing from non-Western cultures, defied their parents, rejected social etiquettes and manners, and turned to music as an expression of their sense of self. Casual sex between unmarried men and women was acceptable. Drug use, especially of marijuana and psychedelic drugs like LSD and peyote, was common. Most hippies were also deeply attracted to the ideas of peace and freedom. They protested the war in Vietnam and preached a doctrine of personal freedom to be and act as one wished.

Some hippies dropped out of mainstream society altogether and expressed their disillusionment with the cultural and spiritual limitations of American freedom. They joined communes, usually in rural areas,   to

Woodstock festival held
1969

Nixon goes to China
1972

Nixon resigns due to Watergate scandal
1974

Camp David Accords signed
1978

1968
Vietnamese massacred at My Lai; Richard Nixon elected president

1970
National Guard fires on students at Kent State University

1973
Roe v. Wade legalizes abortion nationally; Paris Peace Accords end U.S. role in Vietnam; OAPEC proclaims oil embargo

1976
Jimmy Carter elected president

1979
Iranian protesters storm U.S. Embassy in Tehran and take hostages

Figure 9.2

share a desire to live closer to nature, respect for the earth, a dislike of modern life, and a disdain for wealth and material goods. Many communes grew their own organic food. Others abolished the concept of private property, and all members shared willingly with one another. Some sought to abolish traditional ideas regarding love and marriage, and free love was practiced openly. One of the most famous communes was The Farm, established in Tennessee in 1971. Residents adopted a blend of Christian and Asian beliefs. They shared housing, owned no private property except tools and clothing, advocated nonviolence, and tried to live as one with nature, becoming vegetarians and avoiding the use of animal products. They smoked marijuana in an effort to reach a higher state of consciousness and to achieve a feeling of oneness and harmony.

Music, especially rock and folk music, occupied an important place in the counterculture. Concerts provided the opportunity to form seemingly impromptu communities to celebrate youth, rebellion, and individuality. In mid-August 1969, nearly 400,000 people attended a music festival in rural Bethel, New York, many for free (**Figure 9.3**). They jammed roads throughout the state, and thousands had to be turned around and sent home. Thirty-two acts performed for a crowd that partook freely of marijuana, LSD, and alcohol during the rainy three-day event that became known as Woodstock (after the nearby town) and became the cultural touchstone of a generation. No other event better symbolized the cultural independence and freedom of Americans coming of age in the 1960s.

Figure 9.3 The crowd at Woodstock greatly exceeded the fifty thousand expected. Mark Goff covered Woodstock as a young freelance reporter for *Kaleidoscope*, a Milwaukee-based alternative newspaper, and captured this image of Swami Satchidananda, who declared music "'the celestial sound that controls the whole universe" at the opening ceremony.

MY STORY

✪ Glenn Weiser on Attending Woodstock

On the way to Woodstock, Glenn Weiser remembers that the crowds were so large they essentially turned it into a free concert:

> As we got closer to the site [on Thursday, August 14, 1969] we heard that so many people had already arrived that the crowd had torn down the fences enclosing the festival grounds (in fact they were never put up to begin with). Everyone was being allowed in for free. . . .
>
> Early on Friday afternoon about a dozen of us got together and spread out some blankets on the grass at a spot about a third of the way up the hill on stage right and then dropped LSD. I took Orange Sunshine, a strong, clean dose in an orange tab that was perhaps the best street acid ever. Underground chemists in southern California had made millions of doses, and the nation was flooded with it that summer. We smoked some tasty black hashish to amuse ourselves while waiting for the acid to hit, and sat back to groove along with Richie Havens.
>
> In two hours we were all soaring, and everything was just fine. In fact, it couldn't have been better—there I was with my beautiful hometown friends, higher than a church steeple and listening to wonderful music in the cool summer weather of the Catskills. After all, the dirty little secret of the late '60s was that psychedelic drugs taken in a pleasant setting could be completely exhilarating.
> —Glenn Weiser, "Woodstock 1969 Remembered"

In this account, Glenn Weiser describes both the music and his drug use. What social trends did Woodstock reflect? How might the festival have influenced American culture and society, both aesthetically and behaviorally?

AMERICAN INDIAN PROTEST

As the young, primarily white men and women who became hippies strove to create new identities for themselves, they borrowed liberally from other cultures, including that of Native Americans. At the same time, many Indians were themselves seeking to maintain their culture or retrieve elements that had been lost. In 1968, a group of Indian activists, including Dennis Banks, George Mitchell, and Clyde Bellecourt, convened a gathering of two hundred people in Minneapolis, Minnesota, and formed the American Indian Movement (AIM) (**Figure 9.4**). The organizers were urban dwellers frustrated by decades of poverty and discrimination. In 1970, the average life expectancy of Indians was forty-six years compared to the national average of sixty-nine. The suicide rate was twice that of the general population, and the infant mortality rate was the highest in the country. Half of all Indians lived on reservations, where unemployment reached 50 percent. Among those in cities, 20 percent lived below the poverty line.

Figure 9.4 This teepee was erected on the National Mall near the Washington Monument as part of an AIM demonstration (a). Note that the AIM flag (b) combines an Indian silhouette with the peace sign, the ubiquitous symbol of the 1960s and '70s.

On November 20, 1969, a small group of Indian activists landed on Alcatraz Island (the former site of a notorious federal prison) in San Francisco Bay. They announced plans to build an American Indian cultural center, including a history museum, an ecology center, and a spiritual sanctuary. People on the mainland provided supplies by boat, and celebrities visited Alcatraz to publicize the cause. More people joined the occupiers until, at one point, they numbered about four hundred. From the beginning, the federal government negotiated with them to persuade them to leave. They were reluctant to accede, but over time, the occupiers began to drift away of their own accord. Government forces removed the final holdouts on June 11, 1971, nineteen months after the occupation began.

DEFINING "AMERICAN"

⊙ *Proclamation to the Great White Father and All His People*

In occupying Alcatraz Island, Indian activists sought to call attention to their grievances and expectations about what America should mean. At the beginning of the nineteen-month occupation, Mohawk Richard Oakes delivered the following proclamation:

> We, the native Americans, re-claim the land known as Alcatraz Island in the name of all American Indians by right of discovery.

> We wish to be fair and honorable in our dealings with the Caucasian inhabitants of this land, and hereby offer the following treaty:

> We will purchase said Alcatraz Island for twenty-four dollars ($24) in glass beads and red cloth, a precedent set by the white man's purchase of a similar island about 300 years ago. . . .

> We feel that this so-called Alcatraz Island is more than suitable for an Indian Reservation, as determined by the white man's own standards. By this we mean that this place resembles most Indian reservations in that:

> 1. It is isolated from modern facilities, and without adequate means of transportation.

> 2. It has no fresh running water.

> 3. It has inadequate sanitation facilities.

> 4. There are no oil or mineral rights.

> 5. There is no industry and so unemployment is very great.

> 6. There are no health care facilities.

> 7. The soil is rocky and non-productive; and the land does not support game.

> 8. There are no educational facilities.

> 9. The population has always exceeded the land base.

> 10. The population has always been held as prisoners and kept dependent upon others.

> Further, it would be fitting and symbolic that ships from all over the world, entering the Golden Gate, would first see Indian land, and thus be reminded of the true history of this nation. This tiny island would be a symbol of the great lands once ruled by free and noble Indians.

What does the Alcatraz Proclamation reveal about the Indian view of U.S. history?

Click and Explore

Listen to Richard Oakes, one of the leaders of the Alcatraz Island occupation, as he reads the Alcatraz Proclamation (http://openstaxcollege.org/l/15PHStatement1) aloud.

The next major demonstration came in 1972 when AIM members and others marched on Washington, DC—a journey they called the "Trail of Broken Treaties"—and occupied the offices of the Bureau of Indian Affairs (BIA). The group presented a list of demands, which included improved housing, education, and economic opportunities in Indian communities; the drafting of new treaties; the return of Indian lands; and protections for native religions and culture.

The most dramatic event staged by AIM was the occupation of the Indian community of Wounded Knee, South Dakota, in February 1973. Wounded Knee, on the Pine Ridge Indian Reservation, had historical significance: It was the site of an 1890 massacre of members of the Lakota tribe by the U.S. Army. AIM went to the reservation following the failure of a group of Oglala to impeach the tribal president Dick Wilson, whom they accused of corruption and the use of strong-arm tactics to silence critics. AIM used the occasion to criticize the U.S. government for failing to live up to its treaties with native peoples.

The federal government surrounded the area with U.S. marshals, FBI agents, and other law enforcement forces. A siege ensued that lasted seventy-one days, with frequent gunfire from both sides, wounding a U.S. marshal as well as an FBI agent, and killing two Indians. The government did very little to meet the protesters' demands. Two AIM leaders, Dennis Banks and Russell Means, were arrested, but charges were later dismissed. The Nixon administration had already halted the federal policy of termination and restored millions of acres to tribes. Increased funding for Indian education, healthcare, legal services, housing, and economic development followed, along with the hiring of more Indian employees in the BIA.

GAY RIGHTS

Combined with the sexual revolution and the feminist movement of the 1960s, the counterculture helped establish a climate that fostered the struggle for gay and lesbian rights. Many gay rights groups were founded in Los Angeles and San Francisco, cities that were administrative centers in the network of U.S. military installations and the places where many gay men suffered dishonorable discharges. The first postwar organization for homosexual civil rights, the Mattachine Society, was launched in Los Angeles in 1950. The first national organization for lesbians, the Daughters of Bilitis, was founded in San Francisco five years later. In 1966, the city became home to the world's first organization for transsexual people, the National Transsexual Counseling Unit, and in 1967, the Sexual Freedom League of San Francisco was born.

Through these organizations and others, gay and lesbian activists fought against the criminalization and discrimination of their sexual identities on a number of occasions throughout the 1960s, employing strategies of both protests and litigation. However, the most famous event in the gay rights movement took place not in San Francisco but in New York City. Early in the morning of June 28, 1969, police raided a Greenwich Village gay bar called the Stonewall Inn. Although such raids were common, the response of the Stonewall patrons was anything but. As the police prepared to arrest many of the customers, especially transsexuals and cross-dressers, who were particular targets for police harassment, a crowd began to gather. Angered by the brutal treatment of the prisoners, the crowd attacked. Beer bottles and bricks were thrown. The police barricaded themselves inside the bar and waited for reinforcements. The riot continued for several hours and resumed the following night. Shortly thereafter, the Gay Liberation Front and Gay Activists' Alliance were formed, and began to protest discrimination, homophobia, and violence against gay people, promoting gay liberation and gay pride.

With a call for gay men and women to "come out"—a consciousness-raising campaign that shared many principles with the counterculture, gay and lesbian communities moved from the urban underground into the political sphere. Gay rights activists protested strongly against the official position of the American Psychiatric Association (APA), which categorized homosexuality as a mental illness and often resulted in job loss, loss of custody, and other serious personal consequences. By 1974, the APA had ceased to classify homosexuality as a form of mental illness but continued to consider it a "sexual orientation disturbance." Nevertheless, in 1974, Kathy Kozachenko became the first openly lesbian woman voted into office in Ann Arbor, Michigan. In 1977, Harvey Milk became California's first openly gay man elected to public office, although his service on San Francisco's board of supervisors, along with that of San Francisco mayor George Moscone, was cut short by the bullet of disgruntled former city supervisor Dan White.

MAYBE NOT NOW

The feminist push for greater rights continued through the 1970s (**Figure 9.5**). The media often ridiculed feminists as "women's libbers" and focused on more radical organizations like W.I.T.C.H. (Women's International Terrorist Conspiracy from Hell), a loose association of activist groups. Many reporters stressed the most unusual goals of the most radical women—calls for the abolition of marriage and demands that manholes be renamed "personholes."

Figure 9.5 In 1970, supporters of equal rights for women marched in Washington, DC.

The majority of feminists, however, sought meaningful accomplishments. In the 1970s, they opened battered women's shelters and successfully fought for protection from employment discrimination for pregnant women, reform of rape laws (such as the abolition of laws requiring a witness to corroborate a woman's report of rape), criminalization of domestic violence, and funding for schools that sought to counter sexist stereotypes of women. In 1973, the U.S. Supreme Court in *Roe v. Wade* affirmed a number of state laws under which abortions obtained during the first three months of pregnancy were legal. This made a nontherapeutic abortion a legal medical procedure nationwide.

Many advances in women's rights were the result of women's greater engagement in politics. For example, Patsy Mink, the first Asian American woman elected to Congress, was the co-author of the Education Amendments Act of 1972, Title IX of which prohibits sex discrimination in education. Mink had been interested in fighting discrimination in education since her youth, when she opposed racial segregation in campus housing while a student at the University of Nebraska. She went to law school after being denied admission to medical school because of her gender. Like Mink, many other women sought and won political office, many with the help of the National Women's Political Caucus (NWPC). In 1971, the NWPC was formed by Bella Abzug, Gloria Steinem, Shirley Chisholm, and other leading feminists to encourage women's participation in political parties, elect women to office, and raise money for their campaigns (**Figure 9.6**).

(a)   (b)

Figure 9.6 Patsy Mink (a), a Japanese American from Hawaii, was the first Asian American woman elected to the House of Representatives. In her successful 1970 congressional campaign, Bella Abzug (b) declared, "This woman's place is in the House... the House of Representatives!"

The ultimate political goal of the National Organization for Women (NOW) was the passage of an Equal Rights Amendment (ERA). The amendment passed Congress in March 1972, and was sent to the states for ratification with a deadline of seven years for passage; if the amendment was not ratified by thirty-eight states by 1979, it would die. Twenty-two states ratified the ERA in 1972, and eight more in 1973. In the next two years, only four states voted for the amendment. In 1979, still four votes short, the amendment received a brief reprieve when Congress agreed to a three-year extension, but it never passed, as the result of the well-organized opposition of Christian and other socially conservative, grassroots organizations.

9.2 Coming Apart, Coming Together

By the end of this section, you will be able to:
* Explain the factors responsible for Richard Nixon's election in 1968
* Describe the splintering of the Democratic Party in 1968
* Discuss Richard Nixon's economic policies
* Discuss the major successes of Richard Nixon's foreign policy

The presidential election of 1968 revealed a rupture of the New Deal coalition that had come together under Franklin Roosevelt in the 1930s. The Democrats were divided by internal dissension over the Vietnam War, the civil rights movement, and the challenges of the New Left. Meanwhile, the Republican candidate, Richard Nixon, won voters in the South, Southwest, and northern suburbs by appealing to their anxieties about civil rights, women's rights, antiwar protests, and the counterculture taking place around them. Nixon spent his first term in office pushing measures that slowed the progress of civil rights and sought to restore economic stability. His greatest triumphs were in foreign policy. But his largest priority throughout his first term was his reelection in 1972.

THE "NEW NIXON"

The Republicans held their 1968 national convention from August 5–8 in Miami, Florida. Richard Nixon quickly emerged as the frontrunner for the nomination, ahead of Nelson Rockefeller and Ronald Reagan.

This success was not accidental: From 1962, when he lost his bid for the governorship of California, to 1968, Nixon had been collecting political credits by branding himself as a candidate who could appeal to mainstream voters and by tirelessly working for other Republican candidates. In 1964, for example, he vigorously supported Barry Goldwater's presidential bid and thus built good relationships with the new conservative movement in the Republican Party.

Although Goldwater lost the 1964 election, his vigorous rejection of New Deal state and social legislation, along with his support of states' rights, proved popular in the Deep South, which had resisted federal efforts at racial integration. Taking a lesson from Goldwater's experience, Nixon also employed a **southern strategy** in 1968. Denouncing segregation and the denial of the vote to African Americans, he nevertheless maintained that southern states be allowed to pursue racial equality at their own pace and criticized forced integration. Nixon thus garnered the support of South Carolina's senior senator and avid segregationist Strom Thurmond, which helped him win the Republican nomination on the first ballot.

Nixon also courted northern, blue-collar workers, whom he later called the **silent majority**, to acknowledge their belief that their voices were seldom heard. These voters feared the social changes taking place in the country: Antiwar protests challenged their own sense of patriotism and civic duty, whereas the recreational use of new drugs threatened their cherished principles of self-discipline, and urban riots invoked the specter of a racial reckoning. Government action on behalf of the marginalized raised the question of whether its traditional constituency—the white middle class—would lose its privileged place in American politics. Some felt left behind as the government turned to the problems of African Americans. Nixon's promises of stability and his emphasis on law and order appealed to them. He portrayed himself as a fervent patriot who would take a strong stand against racial unrest and antiwar protests. Nixon harshly critiqued Lyndon Johnson's Great Society, and he promised a secret plan to end the war in Vietnam honorably and bring home the troops. He also promised to reform the Supreme Court, which he contended had gone too far in "coddling criminals." Under Chief Justice Earl Warren, the court had used the due process and equal protection clauses of the Fourteenth Amendment to grant those accused under state law the ability to defend themselves and secure protections against unlawful search and seizure, cruel and unusual punishment, and self-incrimination.

Nixon had found the political capital that would ensure his victory in the suburbs, which produced more votes than either urban or rural areas. He championed "middle America," which was fed up with social convulsions, and called upon the country to come together. His running mate, Spiro T. Agnew, a former governor of Maryland, blasted the Democratic ticket as fiscally irresponsible and "soft on communism." Nixon and Agnew's message thus appealed to northern middle-class and blue-collar whites as well as southern whites who had fled to the suburbs in the wake of the Supreme Court's pro-integration decision in *Brown v. Board of Education* (**Figure 9.7**).

(a)   (b)

Figure 9.7 On the 1968 campaign trail, Richard Nixon flashes his famous "V for Victory" gesture (a). Nixon's strategy was to appeal to working- and middle-class suburbanites. This image of him in the White House bowling alley seems calculated to appeal to his core constituency (b).

DEMOCRATS IN DISARRAY

By contrast, in early 1968, the political constituency that Lyndon Johnson had cobbled together to win the presidency in 1964 seemed to be falling apart. When Eugene McCarthy, the Democratic senator from Minnesota, announced that he would challenge Johnson in the primaries in an explicitly antiwar campaign, Johnson was overwhelmingly favored by Democratic voters. But then the Tet Offensive in Vietnam exploded on American television screens on January 31, playing out on the nightly news for weeks. On February 27, Walter Cronkite, a highly respected television journalist, offered his opinion that the war in Vietnam was unwinnable. When the votes were counted in New Hampshire on March 12, McCarthy had won twenty of the state's twenty-four delegates.

McCarthy's popularity encouraged Robert (Bobby) Kennedy to also enter the race. Realizing that his war policies could unleash a divisive fight within his own party for the nomination, Johnson announced his withdrawal on March 31, fracturing the Democratic Party. One faction consisted of the traditional party leaders who appealed to unionized, blue-collar constituents and white ethnics (Americans with recent European immigrant backgrounds). This group fell in behind Johnson's vice president, Hubert H. Humphrey, who took up the mainstream party's torch almost immediately after Johnson's announcement. The second group consisted of idealistic young activists who had slogged through the snows of New Hampshire to give McCarthy a boost and saw themselves as the future of the Democratic Party. The third group, composed of Catholics, African Americans and other minorities, and some of the young, antiwar element, galvanized around Robert Kennedy (**Figure 9.8**). Finally, there were the southern Democrats, the **Dixiecrats**, who opposed the advances made by the civil rights movement. Some found themselves attracted to the Republican candidate Richard Nixon. Many others, however, supported the third-party candidacy of segregationist George C. Wallace, the former governor of Alabama. Wallace won close to ten million votes, which was 13.5 percent of all votes cast. He was particularly popular in the South, where he carried five states and received forty-six Electoral College votes.

Figure 9.8 In his brother's (John F. Kennedy's) administration, Robert (Bobby) Kennedy had served as attorney general and had spoken out about racial equality.

Kennedy and McCarthy fiercely contested the remaining primaries of the 1968 season. There were only fifteen at that time. McCarthy beat Kennedy handily in Wisconsin, Pennsylvania, and Massachusetts. Kennedy took Indiana and Nebraska before losing Oregon to McCarthy. Kennedy's only hope was that a strong enough showing in the California primary on June 4 might swing uncommitted delegates his way. He did manage to beat McCarthy, winning 46 percent of the vote to McCarthy's 42 percent, but it was a fruitless victory. As he attempted to exit the Ambassador Hotel in Los Angeles after his victory speech, Kennedy was shot; he died twenty-six hours later. His killer, Sirhan B. Sirhan, a Jordanian immigrant, had allegedly targeted him for advocating military support for Israel in its conflict with neighboring Arab states.

Going into the nominating convention in Chicago in 1968, Humphrey, who promised to pursue the "Politics of Joy," seemed clearly in command of the regular party apparatus. But the national debates over civil rights, student protests, and the Vietnam War had made 1968 a particularly anguished year, and many people felt anything but joyful. Some party factions hoped to make their voices heard; others wished to disrupt the convention altogether. Among them were antiwar protestors, hippies, and **Yippies**—members of the leftist, anarchistic Youth International Party organized by Jerry Rubin and Abbie Hoffman—who called for the establishment of a new nation consisting of cooperative institutions to replace those currently in existence. To demonstrate their contempt for "the establishment" and the proceedings inside the hall, the Yippies nominated a pig named Pigasus for president.

A chaotic scene developed inside the convention hall and outside at Grant Park, where the protesters camped. Chicago's mayor, Richard J. Daley, was anxious to demonstrate that he could maintain law and order, especially because several days of destructive rioting had followed the murder of Martin Luther King, Jr. earlier that year. He thus let loose a force of twelve thousand police officers, six thousand members of the Illinois National Guard, and six thousand U.S. Army soldiers. Television cameras caught what later became known as a "police riot": Armed officers made their way into crowds of law-abiding protesters, clubbing anyone they encountered and setting off tear gas canisters. The protesters fought back. Inside the convention hall, a Democratic senator from Connecticut called for adjournment, whereas other delegates insisted on proceeding. Ironically, Hubert Humphrey received the nomination and gave an acceptance speech in which he spoke in support of "law and order." When the convention ended, Rubin,

Hoffman, and five other protesters (called the "Chicago Seven") were placed on trial for inciting a riot (Figure 9.9).

(a)   (b)

Figure 9.9 Despite facing charges following events at the Democratic National Convention in Chicago, Abbie Hoffman continued to protest the war on campuses across the country, as here (a) at the University of Oklahoma. Jerry Rubin (b) visited the campus of the University of Buffalo in March 1970, just one month after his conviction in the Chicago Seven trial. (credit a: modification of work by Richard O. Barry)

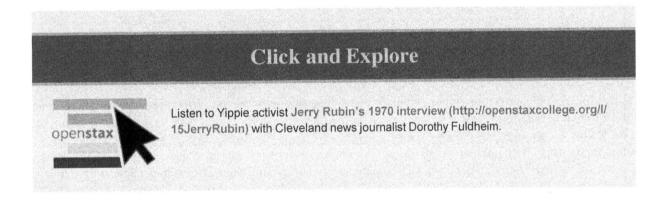

Click and Explore

Listen to Yippie activist Jerry Rubin's 1970 interview (http://openstaxcollege.org/l/15JerryRubin) with Cleveland news journalist Dorothy Fuldheim.

THE DOMESTIC NIXON

The images of violence and the impression of things spinning out of control seriously damaged Humphrey's chances for victory. Many liberals and young antiwar activists, disappointed by his selection over McCarthy and still shocked by the death of Robert Kennedy, did not vote for Humphrey. Others turned against him because of his failure to chastise the Chicago police for their violence. Some resented the fact that Humphrey had received 1,759 delegates on the first ballot at the convention, nearly three times the number won by McCarthy, even though in the primaries, he had received only 2 percent of the popular vote. Many loyal Democratic voters at home, shocked by the violence they saw on television, turned away from their party, which seemed to have attracted dangerous "radicals," and began to consider Nixon's promises of law and order.

As the Democratic Party collapsed, Nixon successfully campaigned for the votes of both working- and middle-class white Americans, winning the 1968 election. Although Humphrey received nearly the same percentage of the popular vote, Nixon easily won the Electoral College, gaining 301 votes to Humphrey's 191 and Wallace's 46.

Once elected, Nixon began to pursue a policy of deliberate neglect of the civil rights movement and the needs of ethnic minorities. For example, in 1969, for the first time in fifteen years, federal lawyers sided with the state of Mississippi when it sought to slow the pace of school desegregation. Similarly, Nixon consistently showed his opposition to busing to achieve racial desegregation. He saw that restricting African American activity was a way of undercutting a source of votes for the Democratic Party and sought to overhaul the provisions of the Voting Rights Act of 1965. In March 1970, he commented that he did not believe an "open" America had to be homogeneous or fully integrated, maintaining that it was "natural" for members of ethnic groups to live together in their own enclaves. In other policy areas, especially economic ones, Nixon was either moderate or supportive of the progress of African Americans; for example, he expanded affirmative action, a program begun during the Johnson administration to improve employment and educational opportunities for racial minorities.

Although Nixon always kept his eye on the political environment, the economy required attention. The nation had enjoyed seven years of expansion since 1961, but inflation (a general rise in prices) was threatening to constrict the purchasing power of the American consumer and therefore curtail economic expansion. Nixon tried to appeal to fiscal conservatives in the Republican Party, reach out to disaffected Democrats, and, at the same time, work with a Democratic Party-controlled Congress. As a result, Nixon's approach to the economy seemed erratic. Despite the heavy criticisms he had leveled against the Great Society, he embraced and expanded many of its features. In 1969, he signed a tax bill that eliminated the investment tax credit and moved some two million of the poorest people off the tax rolls altogether. He federalized the food stamp program and established national eligibility requirements, and signed into law the automatic adjustments for inflation of Social Security payments. On the other hand, he won the praise of conservatives with his "New Federalism"—drastically expanding the use of federal "block grants" to states to spend as they wished without strings attached.

By mid-1970, a recession was beginning and unemployment was 6.2 percent, twice the level under Johnson. After earlier efforts at controlling inflation with controlled federal spending—economists assumed that reduced federal spending and borrowing would curb the amount of money in circulation and stabilize prices—Nixon proposed a budget with an $11 billion deficit in 1971. The hope was that more federal funds in the economy would stimulate investment and job creation. When the unemployment rate refused to budge the following year, he proposed a budget with a $25 billion deficit. At the same time, he tried to fight continuing inflation by freezing wages and prices for ninety days, which proved to be only a temporary fix. The combination of unemployment and rising prices posed an unfamiliar challenge to economists whose fiscal policies of either expanding or contracting federal spending could only address one side of the problem at the cost of the other. This phenomenon of "**stagflation**"—a term that combined the economic conditions of stagnation and inflation—outlived the Nixon administration, enduring into the early 1980s.

The origins of the nation's new economic troubles were not just a matter of policy. Postwar industrial development in Asia and Western Europe—especially in Germany and Japan—had created serious competition to American businesses. By 1971, American appetites for imports left foreign central banks with billions of U.S. currency, which had been fixed to gold in the international monetary and trade agreement of Bretton Woods back in 1944. When foreign dollar holdings exceeded U.S. gold reserves in 1971, President Nixon allowed the dollar to flow freely against the price of gold. This caused an immediate 8 percent devaluation of the dollar, made American goods cheaper abroad, and stimulated exports. Nixon's move also marked the beginning of the end of the dollar's dominance in international trade.

The situation was made worse in October 1973, when Syria and Egypt jointly attacked Israel to recover territory that had been lost in 1967, starting the Yom Kippur War. The Soviet Union significantly aided its allies, Egypt and Syria, and the United States supported Israel, earning the enmity of Arab nations. In retaliation, the Organization of Arab Petroleum Exporting Countries (OAPEC) imposed an embargo on oil shipments to the United States from October 1973 to March 1974. The ensuing shortage of oil pushed its price from three dollars a barrel to twelve dollars a barrel. The average price of gasoline in the United States shot from thirty-eight cents a gallon before the embargo to fifty-five cents a gallon in June 1974, and the prices of other goods whose manufacture and transportation relied on oil or gas also rose and did not come down. The oil embargo had a lasting impact on the economy and underscored the nation's interdependency with international political and economic developments.

Faced with high fuel prices, American consumers panicked. Gas stations limited the amount customers could purchase and closed on Sundays as supplies ran low (**Figure 9.10**). To conserve oil, Congress reduced the speed limit on interstate highways to fifty-five miles per hour. People were asked to turn down their thermostats, and automobile manufacturers in Detroit explored the possibility of building more fuel-efficient cars. Even after the embargo ended, prices continued to rise, and by the end of the Nixon years in 1974, inflation had soared to 12.2 percent.

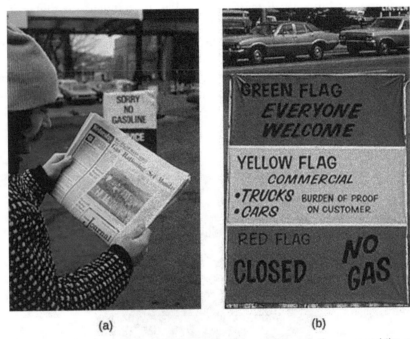

(a) (b)

Figure 9.10 The oil shortage triggered a rush to purchase gasoline, and gas stations around the country were choked with cars waiting to fill up. Eventually, fuel shortages caused gas stations to develop various ways to ration gasoline to their customers (a), such as the "flag policy" used by gas dealers in Oregon (b).

Although Nixon's economic and civil rights policies differed from those of his predecessors, in other areas, he followed their lead. President Kennedy had committed the nation to putting a man on the moon before the end of the decade. Nixon, like Johnson before him, supported significant budget allocations to the National Aeronautics and Space Administration (NASA) to achieve this goal. On July 20, 1969, hundreds of millions of people around the world watched as astronauts Neil Armstrong and Edwin "Buzz" Aldrin walked on the surface of the moon and planted the U.S. flag. Watching from the White House, President Nixon spoke to the astronauts via satellite phone. The entire project cost the American taxpayer some $25 billion, approximately 4 percent of the nation's gross national product, and was such a source of pride for the nation that the Soviet Union and China refused to televise it. Coming amid all the struggles and crises that the country was enduring, the moon landing gave citizens a sense of accomplishment that stood in stark contrast to the foreign policy failures, growing economic challenges, and escalating divisions at home.

NIXON THE DIPLOMAT

Despite the many domestic issues on Nixon's agenda, he prioritized foreign policy and clearly preferred bold and dramatic actions in that arena. Realizing that five major economic powers—the United States, Western Europe, the Soviet Union, China, and Japan—dominated world affairs, he sought opportunities for the United States to pit the others against each other. In 1969, he announced a new Cold War principle known as the Nixon Doctrine, a policy whereby the United States would continue to assist its allies but would not assume the responsibility of defending the entire non-Communist world. Other nations, like Japan, needed to assume more of the burden of defending themselves.

Playing what was later referred to as "the China card," Nixon abruptly reversed two decades of U.S. diplomatic sanctions and hostility to the Communist regime in the People's Republic of China, when he announced, in August 1971, that he would personally travel to Beijing and meet with China's leader, Chairman Mao Zedong, in February 1972 (**Figure 9.11**). Nixon hoped that opening up to the Chinese government would prompt its bitter rival, the Soviet Union, to compete for global influence and seek a more productive relationship with the United States. He also hoped that establishing a friendly relationship with China would isolate North Vietnam and ease a peace settlement, allowing the United States to extract its troops from the war honorably. Concurring that the Soviet Union should be restrained from making advances in Asia, Nixon and Chinese premier Zhou Enlai agreed to disagree on several issues and ended up signing a friendship treaty. They promised to work towards establishing trade between the two nations and to eventually establishing full diplomatic relations with each other.

Figure 9.11 President Nixon and First Lady Patricia Nixon visited the Great Wall on their 1972 trip to China. The Chinese showed them the sights and hosted a banquet for them in the Great Hall of the People. Nixon was the first U.S. president to visit China following the Communist victory in the civil war in 1949.

Continuing his strategy of pitting one Communist nation against another, in May 1972, Nixon made another newsworthy trip, traveling to Moscow to meet with the Soviet leader Leonid Brezhnev. The two discussed a policy of **détente**, a relaxation of tensions between their nations, and signed the Strategic Arms Limitation Treaty (SALT), which limited each side to deploying only two antiballistic missile systems. It also limited the number of nuclear missiles maintained by each country. In 1974, a protocol was signed that reduced antiballistic missile sites to one per country, since neither country had yet begun to build its second system. Moreover, the two sides signed agreements to allow scientific and technological exchanges, and promised to work towards a joint space mission.

9.3 Vietnam: The Downward Spiral

By the end of this section, you will be able to:
- Describe the events that fueled antiwar sentiment in the Vietnam era
- Explain Nixon's steps to withdraw the United States from the conflict in South Vietnam

As early as 1967, critics of the war in Vietnam had begun to call for the repeal of the Gulf of Tonkin Resolution, which gave President Johnson the authority to conduct military operations in Vietnam in defense of an ally, South Vietnam. Nixon initially opposed the repeal efforts, claiming that doing so might have consequences that reached far beyond Vietnam. Nevertheless, by 1969, he was beginning troop withdrawals from Vietnam while simultaneously looking for a "knockout blow" against the North Vietnamese. In sum, the Nixon administration was in need of an exit strategy.

The escalation of the war, however, made an easy withdrawal increasingly difficult. Officially, the United States was the ally and partner of the South Vietnamese, whose "hearts and minds" it was trying to win through a combination of military assistance and economic development. In reality, however, U.S. soldiers, who found themselves fighting in an inhospitable environment thousands of miles from home to protect people who often resented their presence and aided their enemies, came to regard the Vietnamese as backward, cowardly people and the government of South Vietnam as hopelessly inefficient and corrupt. Instead of winning "hearts and minds," U.S. warfare in Vietnam cost the lives and limbs of U.S. troops and millions of Vietnamese combatants and civilians (**Figure 9.12**).

Figure 9.12 U.S. soldiers in Hue in 1968 at during the Tet Offensive. The frustrating experience of fighting the seemingly unwinnable war left many soldiers, and the public in general, disillusioned with the government.

For their part, the North Vietnamese forces and the National Liberation Front in South Vietnam also used brutal tactics to terrorize and kill their opponents or effectively control their territory. Political assassinations and forced indoctrination were common. Captured U.S. soldiers frequently endured torture and imprisonment.

MY LAI

Racism on the part of some U.S. soldiers and a desire to retaliate against those they perceived to be responsible for harming U.S. troops affected the conduct of the war. A war correspondent who served in Vietnam noted, "In motivating the GI to fight by appealing to his racist feelings, the United States military discovered that it had liberated an emotion over which it was to lose control." It was not unusual for U.S. soldiers to evacuate and burn villages suspected of shielding Viet Cong fighters, both to deprive the enemy of potential support and to enact revenge for enemy brutality. Troops shot at farmers' water buffalo for target practice. American and South Vietnamese use of napalm, a jellied gasoline that sticks to the objects it burns, was common. Originally developed to burn down structures during World War II, in Vietnam, it was directed against human beings as well, as had occurred during the Korean War.

DEFINING "AMERICAN"

⊙ *Vietnam Veterans against the War Statement*

Many U.S. soldiers disapproved of the actions of their fellow troops. Indeed, a group of Vietnam veterans formed the organization Vietnam Veterans Against the War (VVAW). Small at first, it grew to perhaps as many as twenty thousand members. In April 1971, John Kerry, a former lieutenant in the U.S. Navy and a member of VVAW, testified before the U.S. Senate Committee on Foreign Relations about conditions in Vietnam based on his personal observations:

> I would like to talk on behalf of all those veterans and say that several months ago in Detroit we had an investigation at which over 150 honorably discharged, and many very highly decorated, veterans testified to war crimes committed in Southeast Asia. These were not isolated incidents but crimes committed on a day-to-day basis with the full awareness of officers at all levels of command. . . . They relived the absolute horror of what this country, in a sense, made them do.

> They told stories that at times they had personally raped, cut off ears, cut off heads . . . randomly shot at civilians, razed villages . . . and generally ravaged the countryside of South Vietnam in addition to the normal ravage of war and the normal and very particular ravaging which is done by the applied bombing power of this country. . . .

> We could come back to this country, we could be quiet, we could hold our silence, we could not tell what went on in Vietnam, but we feel because of what threatens this country, not the reds [Communists], but the crimes which we are committing that threaten it, that we have to speak out.
> —John Kerry, April 23, 1971

In what way did the actions of U.S. soldiers in Vietnam threaten the United States?

On March 16, 1968, men from the U.S. Army's Twenty-Third Infantry Division committed one of the most notorious atrocities of the war. About one hundred soldiers commanded by Captain Ernest Medina were sent to destroy the village of My Lai, which was suspected of hiding Viet Cong fighters. Although there was later disagreement regarding the captain's exact words, the platoon leaders believed the order to destroy the enemy included killing women and children. Having suffered twenty-eight casualties in the past three months, the men of Charlie Company were under severe stress and extremely apprehensive as they approached the village. Two platoons entered it, shooting randomly. A group of seventy to eighty unarmed people, including children and infants, were forced into an irrigation ditch by members of the First Platoon under the command of Lt. William L. Calley, Jr. Despite their proclamations of innocence, the villagers were shot (**Figure 9.13**). Houses were set on fire, and as the inhabitants tried to flee, they were killed with rifles, machine guns, and grenades. The U.S. troops were never fired upon, and one soldier later testified that he did not see any man who looked like a Viet Cong fighter.

Figure 9.13 Vietnamese civilians in My Lai await their fate. They were shot a few minutes after this 1968 photograph was taken.

The precise number of civilians killed that day is unclear: The numbers range from 347 to 504. None were armed. Although not all the soldiers in My Lai took part in the killings, no one attempted to stop the massacre before the arrival by helicopter of Warrant Officer Hugh Thompson, who, along with his crew, attempted to evacuate women and children. Upon returning to his base, Thompson immediately reported the events taking place at My Lai. Shortly thereafter, Medina ordered Charlie Company to cease fire. Although Thompson's crewmembers confirmed his account, none of the men from Charlie Company gave a report, and a cover-up began almost immediately. The army first claimed that 150 people, the majority of them Viet Cong, had been killed during a firefight with Charlie Company.

Hearing details from friends in Charlie Company, a helicopter gunner by the name of Ron Ridenhour began to conduct his own investigation and, in April 1969, wrote to thirty members of Congress, demanding an investigation. By September 1969, the army charged Lt. Calley with premeditated murder. Many Americans were horrified at the graphic footage of the massacre; the incident confirmed their belief that the war was unjust and not being fought on behalf of the Vietnamese people. However, nearly half of the respondents to a Minnesota poll did not believe that the incident at My Lai had actually happened. U.S. soldiers could not possibly do such horrible things, they felt; they were certain that American goals in Vietnam were honorable and speculated that the antiwar movement had concocted the story to generate sympathy for the enemy.

Calley was found guilty in March 1971, and sentenced to life in prison. Nationwide, hundreds of thousands of Americans joined a "Free Calley" campaign. Two days later, President Nixon released him from custody and placed him under him house arrest at Fort Benning, Georgia. In August of that same year, Calley's sentence was reduced to twenty years, and in September 1974, he was paroled. The only soldier convicted in the massacre, he spent a total of three-and-a-half years under house arrest for his crimes.

BATTLES AT HOME

As the conflict wore on and reports of brutalities increased, the antiwar movement grew in strength. To take the political pressure off himself and his administration, and find a way to exit Vietnam "with honor," Nixon began the process of **Vietnamization**, turning more responsibility for the war over to South Vietnamese forces by training them and providing American weaponry, while withdrawing U.S. troops from the field. At the same time, however, Nixon authorized the bombing of neighboring Cambodia, which had declared its neutrality, in an effort to destroy North Vietnamese and Viet Cong bases within that country and cut off supply routes between North and South Vietnam. The bombing was kept secret from both Congress and the American public. In April 1970, Nixon decided to follow up with an invasion of Cambodia.

The invasion could not be kept secret, and when Nixon announced it on television on April 30, 1970, protests sprang up across the country. The most tragic and politically damaging occurred on May 1, 1970, at Kent State University in Ohio. Violence erupted in the town of Kent after an initial student demonstration on campus, and the next day, the mayor asked Ohio's governor to send in the National Guard. Troops were sent to the university's campus, where students had set fire to the ROTC building and were fighting off firemen and policemen trying to extinguish it. The National Guard used teargas to break up the demonstration, and several students were arrested (**Figure 9.14**).

(a)   (b)

Figure 9.14 On April 30, 1970, Richard Nixon announces plans for the Cambodia Campaign (a), provoking protests on college campuses across the country. Within days, the governor of Ohio had called in the National Guard in response to student demonstrations at Kent State University. Bill Whitbeck, who was a student majoring in photo illustration at Kent State University in May 1970, captured this image (b) on campus on May 3, one day before the shootings that would result in four student deaths. (credit b: modification of work by Bill Whitbeck)

Tensions came to a head on May 4. Although campus officials had called off a planned demonstration, some fifteen hundred to two thousand students assembled, throwing rocks at a security officer who ordered them to leave. Seventy-seven members of the National Guard, with bayonets attached to their rifles, approached the students. After forcing most of them to retreat, the troops seemed to depart. Then, for reasons that are still unknown, they halted and turned; many began to fire at the students. Nine students were wounded; four were killed. Two of the dead had simply been crossing campus on their way to class. Peace was finally restored when a faculty member pleaded with the remaining students to leave.

Click and Explore

Read the *New York Times* account of the shootings at Kent State University (http://openstaxcollege.org/l/15KentState) and view (under the headline) one of the most iconic photographs in American history.

News of the Kent State shootings shocked students around the country. Millions refused to attend class, as strikes were held at hundreds of colleges and high schools across the United States. On May 8, an antiwar protest took place in New York City, and the next day, 100,000 protesters assembled in Washington,

DC. Not everyone sympathized with the slain students, however. Nixon had earlier referred to student demonstrators as "bums," and construction workers attacked the New York City protestors. A Gallup poll revealed that most Americans blamed the students for the tragic events at Kent State.

On May 15, a similar tragedy took place at Jackson State College, an African American college in Jackson, Mississippi. Once again, students gathered on campus to protest the invasion of Cambodia, setting fires and throwing rocks. The police arrived to disperse the protesters, who had gathered outside a women's dormitory. Shortly after midnight, the police opened fire with shotguns. The dormitory windows shattered, showering people with broken glass. Twelve were wounded, and two young men, one a student at the college and the other a local high school student, were killed.

PULLING OUT OF THE QUAGMIRE

Ongoing protests, campus violence, and the expansion of the war into Cambodia deeply disillusioned Americans about their role in Vietnam. Understanding the nation's mood, Nixon dropped his opposition to a repeal of the Gulf of Tonkin Resolution of 1964. In January 1971, he signed Congress's revocation of the notorious blanket military authorization. Gallup polls taken in May of that year revealed that only 28 percent of the respondents supported the war; many felt it was not only a mistake but also immoral.

Just as influential as antiwar protests and campus violence in turning people against the war was the publication of documents the media dubbed the **Pentagon Papers** in June 1971. These were excerpts from a study prepared during the Johnson administration that revealed the true nature of the conflict in Vietnam. The public learned for the first time that the United States had been planning to oust Ngo Dinh Diem from the South Vietnamese government, that Johnson meant to expand the U.S. role in Vietnam and bomb North Vietnam even as he stated publicly that he had no intentions of doing so, and that his administration had sought to deliberately provoke North Vietnamese attacks in order to justify escalating American involvement. Copies of the study had been given to the *New York Times* and other newspapers by Daniel Ellsberg, one of the military analysts who had contributed to it. To avoid setting a precedent by allowing the press to publish confidential documents, Nixon's attorney general, John Mitchell, sought an injunction against the *New York Times* to prevent its publication of future articles based on the Pentagon Papers. The newspaper appealed. On June 30, 1971, the U.S. Supreme Court held that the government could not prevent the publication of the articles.

Realizing that he must end the war but reluctant to make it look as though the United States was admitting its failure to subdue a small Asian nation, Nixon began maneuvering to secure favorable peace terms from the North Vietnamese. Thanks to his diplomatic efforts in China and the Soviet Union, those two nations cautioned North Vietnam to use restraint. The loss of strong support by their patrons, together with intensive bombing of Hanoi and the mining of crucial North Vietnamese harbors by U.S. forces, made the North Vietnamese more willing to negotiate.

Nixon's actions had also won him popular support at home. By the 1972 election, voters again favored his Vietnam policy by a ratio of two to one. On January 27, 1973, Secretary of State Henry Kissinger signed an accord with Le Duc Tho, the chief negotiator for the North Vietnamese, ending American participation in the war. The United States was given sixty days to withdraw its troops, and North Vietnam was allowed to keep its forces in places it currently occupied. This meant that over 100,000 northern soldiers would remain in the South—ideally situated to continue the war with South Vietnam. The United States left behind a small number of military advisors as well as equipment, and Congress continued to approve funds for South Vietnam, but considerably less than in earlier years. So the war continued, but it was clear the South could not hope to defeat the North.

As the end was nearing, the United States conducted several operations to evacuate children from the South. On the morning of April 29, 1975, as North Vietnamese and Viet Cong forces moved through the outskirts of Saigon, orders were given to evacuate Americans and South Vietnamese who had supported the United States. Unable to use the airport, helicopters ferried Americans and Vietnamese refugees who had fled to the American embassy to ships off the coast. North Vietnamese forces entered Saigon the next day, and the South surrendered.

The war had cost the lives of more than 1.5 million Vietnamese combatants and civilians, as well as over 58,000 U.S. troops. But the war had caused another, more intangible casualty: the loss of consensus, confidence, and a sense of moral high ground in the American political culture.

9.4 Watergate: Nixon's Domestic Nightmare

By the end of this section, you will be able to:
- Describe the actions that Nixon and his confederates took to ensure his reelection in 1972
- Explain the significance of the Watergate crisis
- Describe Gerald Ford's domestic policies and achievements in foreign affairs

Feeling the pressure of domestic antiwar sentiment and desiring a decisive victory, Nixon went into the 1972 reelection season having attempted to fashion a "new majority" of moderate southerners and northern, working-class whites. The Democrats, responding to the chaos and failings of the Chicago convention, had instituted new rules on how delegates were chosen, which they hoped would broaden participation and the appeal of the party. Nixon proved unbeatable, however. Even evidence that his administration had broken the law failed to keep him from winning the White House.

THE ELECTION OF 1972

Following the 1968 nominating convention in Chicago, the process of selecting delegates for the Democratic National Convention was redesigned. The new rules, set by a commission led by George McGovern, awarded delegates based on candidates' performance in state primaries (**Figure 9.15**). As a result, a candidate who won no primaries could not receive the party's nomination, as Hubert Humphrey had done in Chicago. This system gave a greater voice to people who voted in the primaries and reduced the influence of party leaders and power brokers.

(a)   (b)

Figure 9.15 In November 1968, Shirley Chisholm (a) became the first African American woman to be elected to the House of Representatives. In January 1972, she announced her intention to run for the Democratic presidential nomination. The nomination eventually went to George McGovern (b), an outspoken opponent of the war in Vietnam.

It also led to a more inclusive political environment in which Shirley Chisholm received 156 votes for the Democratic nomination on the first ballot (**Figure 9.15**). Eventually, the nomination went to George McGovern, a strong opponent of the Vietnam War. Many Democrats refused to support his campaign, however. Working- and middle-class voters turned against him too after allegations that he supported women's right to an abortion and the decriminalization of drug use. McGovern's initial support of vice presidential candidate Thomas Eagleton in the face of revelations that Eagleton had undergone electroshock treatment for depression, followed by his withdrawal of that support and acceptance of Eagleton's resignation, also made McGovern look indecisive and unorganized.

Nixon and the Republicans led from the start. To increase their advantage, they attempted to paint McGovern as a radical leftist who favored amnesty for draft dodgers. In the Electoral College, McGovern carried only Massachusetts and Washington, DC. Nixon won a decisive victory of 520 electoral votes to McGovern's 17. One Democrat described his role in McGovern's campaign as "recreation director on the Titanic."

HIGH CRIMES AND MISDEMEANORS

Nixon's victory over a Democratic party in disarray was the most remarkable landslide since Franklin D. Roosevelt's reelection in 1936. But Nixon's victory was short-lived, however, for it was soon discovered that he and members of his administration had routinely engaged in unethical and illegal behavior during his first term. Following the publication of the Pentagon Papers, for instance, the "**plumbers**," a group of men used by the White House to spy on the president's opponents and stop leaks to the press, broke into the office of Daniel Ellsberg's psychiatrist to steal Ellsberg's file and learn information that might damage his reputation.

During the presidential campaign, the Committee to Re-Elect the President (CREEP) decided to play "dirty tricks" on Nixon's opponents. Before the New Hampshire Democratic primary, a forged letter supposedly written by Democratic-hopeful Edmund Muskie in which he insulted French Canadians, one of the state's largest ethnic groups, was leaked to the press. Men were assigned to spy on both McGovern and Senator Edward Kennedy. One of them managed to masquerade as a reporter on board McGovern's press plane. Men pretending to work for the campaigns of Nixon's Democratic opponents contacted vendors in various states to rent or purchase materials for rallies; the rallies were never held, of course, and Democratic politicians were accused of failing to pay the bills they owed.

CREEP's most notorious operation, however, was its break-in at the offices of the Democratic National Committee (DNC) in the Watergate office complex in Washington, DC, as well as its subsequent cover-up. On the evening of June 17, 1972, the police arrested five men inside DNC headquarters (**Figure 9.16**). According to a plan originally proposed by CREEP's general counsel and White House plumber G. Gordon Liddy, the men were to wiretap DNC telephones. The FBI quickly discovered that two of the men had E. Howard Hunt's name in their address books. Hunt was a former CIA officer and also one of the plumbers. In the following weeks, yet more connections were found between the burglars and CREEP, and in October 1972, the FBI revealed evidence of illegal intelligence gathering by CREEP for the purpose of sabotaging the Democratic Party. Nixon won his reelection handily in November. Had the president and his reelection team not pursued a strategy of dirty tricks, Richard Nixon would have governed his second term with one of the largest political leads in the twentieth century.

Figure 9.16 The Watergate hotel and office complex, located on the Potomac River next to the John F. Kennedy Center for the Performing Arts, was the scene of the 1972 burglary and attempted wiretapping that eventually brought down the presidency of Richard Nixon.

In the weeks following the Watergate break-in, Bob Woodward and Carl Bernstein, reporters for *The Washington Post*, received information from several anonymous sources, including one known to them only as "**Deep Throat**," that led them to realize the White House was deeply implicated in the break-in. As the press focused on other events, Woodward and Bernstein continued to dig and publish their findings, keeping the public's attention on the unfolding scandal. Years later, Deep Throat was revealed to be Mark Felt, then the FBI's associate director.

THE WATERGATE CRISIS

Initially, Nixon was able to hide his connection to the break-in and the other wrongdoings alleged against members of CREEP. However, by early 1973, the situation quickly began to unravel. In January, the Watergate burglars were convicted, along with Hunt and Liddy. Trial judge John Sirica was not convinced that all the guilty had been discovered. In February, confronted with evidence that people close to the president were connected to the burglary, the Senate appointed the Watergate Committee to investigate. Ten days later, in his testimony before the Senate Judiciary Committee, L. Patrick Gray, acting director of the FBI, admitted destroying evidence taken from Hunt's safe by John Dean, the White House counsel, after the burglars were caught.

On March 23, 1973, Judge Sirica publicly read a letter from one of the Watergate burglars, alleging that perjury had been committed during the trial. Less than two weeks later, Jeb Magruder, a deputy director of CREEP, admitted lying under oath and indicated that Dean and John Mitchell, who had resigned as attorney general to become the director of CREEP, were also involved in the break-in and its cover-up. Dean confessed, and on April 30, Nixon fired him and requested the resignation of his aides John Ehrlichman and H. R. Haldeman, also implicated. To defuse criticism and avoid suspicion that he was participating in a cover-up, Nixon also announced the resignation of the current attorney general, Richard Kleindienst, a close friend, and appointed Elliot Richardson to the position. In May 1973, Richardson named Archibald Cox special prosecutor to investigate the Watergate affair.

Throughout the spring and the long, hot summer of 1973, Americans sat glued to their television screens, as the major networks took turns broadcasting the Senate hearings. One by one, disgraced former members of the administration confessed, or denied, their role in the Watergate scandal. Dean testified that Nixon was involved in the conspiracy, allegations the president denied. In March 1974, Haldeman, Ehrlichman, and Mitchell were indicted and charged with conspiracy.

Without evidence clearly implicating the president, the investigation might have ended if not for the testimony of Alexander Butterfield, a low-ranking member of the administration, that a voice-activated recording system had been installed in the Oval Office. The President's most intimate conversations had been caught on tape. Cox and the Senate subpoenaed them.

Click and Explore

Listen to excerpts (http://openstaxcollege.org/l/15NixonTapes) from Nixon's White House tapes. Some of the recordings are a bit difficult to hear because of static. Transcripts are also available at this site.

Nixon, however, refused to hand the tapes over and cited **executive privilege**, the right of the president to refuse certain subpoenas. When he offered to supply summaries of the conversations, Cox refused. On October 20, 1973, in an event that became known as the Saturday Night Massacre, Nixon ordered Attorney General Richardson to fire Cox. Richardson refused and resigned, as did Deputy Attorney General William Ruckelshaus when confronted with the same order. Control of the Justice Department then fell to Solicitor General Robert Bork, who complied with Nixon's order. In December, the House Judiciary Committee began its own investigation to determine whether there was enough evidence of wrongdoing to impeach the president.

The public was enraged by Nixon's actions. It seemed as though the president had placed himself above the law. Telegrams flooded the White House. The House of Representatives began to discuss impeachment. In April 1974, when Nixon agreed to release transcripts of the tapes, it was too little, too late (**Figure 9.17**). Yet, while revealing nothing about Nixon's knowledge of Watergate, the transcripts showed him to be coarse, dishonest, and cruel.

Figure 9.17 In April 1974, President Richard Nixon prepares to address the nation to clarify his position on releasing the White House tapes.

At the end of its hearings, in July 1974, the House Judiciary Committee voted to impeach. However, before the full House could vote, the U.S. Supreme Court ordered Nixon to release the actual tapes of his conversations, not just transcripts or summaries. One of the tapes revealed that he had in fact been told about White House involvement in the Watergate break-in shortly after it occurred. In a speech on August 5, 1974, Nixon, pleading a poor memory, accepted blame for the Watergate scandal. Warned by other Republicans that he would be found guilty by the Senate and removed from office, he resigned the presidency on August 8.

Nixon's resignation, which took effect the next day, did not make the Watergate scandal vanish. Instead, it fed a growing suspicion of government felt by many. The events of Vietnam had already showed that the government could not be trusted to protect the interests of the people or tell them the truth. For many, Watergate confirmed these beliefs, and the suffix "-gate" attached to a word has since come to mean a political scandal.

FORD NOT A LINCOLN

When Gerald R. Ford took the oath of office on August 9, 1974, he understood that his most pressing task was to help the country move beyond the Watergate scandal. His declaration that "Our long national nightmare is over. . . . [O]ur great Republic is a government of laws and not of men" was met with almost universal applause.

It was indeed an unprecedented time. Ford was the first vice president chosen under the terms of the Twenty-Fifth Amendment, which provides for the appointment of a vice president in the event the incumbent dies or resigns; Nixon had appointed Ford, a longtime House representative from Michigan known for his honesty, following the resignation of embattled vice president Spiro T. Agnew over a charge of failing to report income—a lenient charge since this income stemmed from bribes he had received as the governor of Maryland. Ford was also the first vice president to take office after a sitting president's resignation, and the only chief executive never elected either president or vice president. One of his first actions as president was to grant Richard Nixon a full pardon (**Figure 9.18**). Ford thus prevented Nixon's indictment for any crimes he may have committed in office and ended criminal investigations into his actions. The public reacted with suspicion and outrage. Many were convinced that the extent of Nixon's wrongdoings would now never been known and he would never be called to account for them. When Ford chose to run for the presidency in 1976, the pardon returned to haunt him.

Figure 9.18 In one of his first actions as president, Gerald R. Ford announced a full pardon for Richard Nixon on September 8, 1974. Nixon had appointed Ford vice president after the resignation of Spiro Agnew.

As president, Ford confronted monumental issues, such as inflation, a depressed economy, and chronic energy shortages. He established his policies during his first year in office, despite opposition from a heavily Democratic Congress. In October 1974, he labeled inflation the country's most dangerous public enemy and sought a grassroots campaign to curtail it by encouraging people to be disciplined in their consuming habits and increase their savings. The campaign was titled "Whip Inflation Now" and was advertised on brightly colored "Win" buttons volunteers were to wear. When recession became the nation's most serious domestic problem, Ford shifted to measures aimed at stimulating the economy. Still fearing inflation, however, he vetoed a number of nonmilitary appropriations bills that would have increased the already-large budget deficit.

Ford's economic policies ultimately proved unsuccessful. Because of opposition from a Democratic Congress, his foreign policy accomplishments were also limited. When he requested money to assist the South Vietnamese government in its effort to repel North Vietnamese forces, Congress refused. Ford was more successful in other parts of the world. He continued Nixon's policy of détente with the Soviet Union, and he and Secretary of State Kissinger achieved further progress in the second round of SALT talks. In August 1975, Ford went to Finland and signed the Helsinki Accords with Soviet premier Leonid Brezhnev. This agreement essentially accepted the territorial boundaries that had been established at the end of World War II in 1945. It also exacted a pledge from the signatory nations that they would protect human rights within their countries. Many immigrants to the United States protested Ford's actions, because it seemed as though he had accepted the status quo and left their homelands under Soviet domination. Others considered it a belated American acceptance of the world as it really was.

9.5 Jimmy Carter in the Aftermath of the Storm

By the end of this section, you will be able to:
- Explain why Gerald Ford lost the election of 1976
- Describe Jimmy Carter's domestic and foreign policy achievements
- Discuss how the Iranian hostage crisis affected the Carter presidency

At his inauguration in January 1977, President Jimmy Carter began his speech by thanking outgoing president Gerald Ford for all he had done to "heal" the scars left by Watergate. American gratitude had not been great enough to return Ford to the Oval Office, but enthusiasm for the new president was not much greater in the new atmosphere of disillusionment with political leaders. Indeed, Carter won his party's nomination and the presidency largely because the Democratic leadership had been decimated by assassination and the taint of Vietnam, and he had carefully positioned himself as an outsider who could not be blamed for current policies. Ultimately, Carter's presidency proved a lackluster one that was marked by economic stagnation at home and humiliation overseas.

THE ELECTION OF 1976

President Ford won the Republican nomination for the presidency in 1976, narrowly defeating former California governor Ronald Reagan, but he lost the election to his Democratic opponent Jimmy Carter. Carter ran on an "anti-Washington" ticket, making a virtue of his lack of experience in what was increasingly seen as the corrupt politics of the nation's capital. Accepting his party's nomination, the former governor of Georgia pledged to combat racism and sexism as well as overhaul the tax structure. He openly proclaimed his faith as a born-again Christian and promised to change the welfare system and provide comprehensive healthcare coverage for neglected citizens who deserved compassion. Most importantly, Jimmy Carter promised that he would "never lie."

Ford's pardon of Richard Nixon had alienated many Republicans. That, combined with the stagnant economy, cost him votes, and Jimmy Carter, an engineer and former naval officer who portrayed himself as a humble peanut farmer, prevailed, carrying all the southern states, except Virginia and Oklahoma (**Figure 9.19**). Ford did well in the West, but Carter received 50 percent of the popular vote to Ford's 48 percent, and 297 electoral votes to Ford's 240.

Figure 9.19 President Gerald Ford (right) and Democratic challenger Jimmy Carter dueled in Philadelphia in 1976, during the first televised presidential debate since that between Richard Nixon and John F. Kennedy in 1960.

Click and Explore

openstax

In the mid-1970s, the United States celebrated the two-hundredth anniversary of its independence from Great Britain. Peruse the collection of patriotic bicentennial memorabilia (http://openstaxcollege.org/l/15Bicent) at the Gerald R. Ford Presidential Library.

ON THE INSIDE

Making a virtue of his lack of political experience, especially in Washington, Jimmy Carter took office with less practical experience in executive leadership and the workings of the national government than any president since Calvin Coolidge. His first executive act was to fulfill a campaign pledge to grant unconditional amnesty to young men who had evaded the draft during the Vietnam War. Despite the early promise of his rhetoric, within a couple of years of his taking office, liberal Democrats claimed Carter was the most conservative Democratic president since Grover Cleveland.

In trying to manage the relatively high unemployment rate of 7.5 percent and inflation that had risen into the double digits by 1978, Carter was only marginally effective. His tax reform measure of 1977 was weak and failed to close the grossest of loopholes. His deregulation of major industries, such as aviation and trucking, was intended to force large companies to become more competitive. Consumers benefited in some ways: For example, airlines offered cheaper fares to beat their competitors. However, some companies, like Pan American World Airways, instead went out of business. Carter also expanded various social programs, improved housing for the elderly, and took steps to improve workplace safety.

Because the high cost of fuel continued to hinder economic expansion, the creation of an energy program became a central focus of his administration. Carter stressed energy conservation, encouraging people to insulate their houses and rewarding them with tax credits if they did so, and pushing for the use of coal, nuclear power, and alternative energy sources such as solar power to replace oil and natural gas. To this end, Carter created the Department of Energy.

CARTER AND A NEW DIRECTION IN FOREIGN AFFAIRS

Carter believed that U.S. foreign policy should be founded upon deeply held moral principles and national values. The mission in Vietnam had failed, he argued, because American actions there were contrary to moral values. His dedication to peace and human rights significantly changed the way that the United States conducted its foreign affairs. He improved relations with China, ended military support to Nicaraguan dictator Anastasio Somoza, and helped arrange for the Panama Canal to be returned to Panamanian control in 1999. He agreed to a new round of talks with the Soviet Union (SALT II) and brought Israeli prime minister Menachem Begin and Egyptian president Anwar Sadat to the United States to discuss peace between their countries. Their meetings at Camp David, the presidential retreat in Maryland, led to the signing of the Camp David Accords in September 1978 (**Figure 9.20**). This in turn resulted in the drafting of a historic peace treaty between Egypt and Israel in 1979.

Figure 9.20 President Jimmy Carter meets with Egypt's Anwar Sadat (left) and Israel's Menachem Begin (right) at Camp David in 1978. Sadat was assassinated in 1981, partly because of his willingness to make peace with Israel.

Despite achieving many successes in the area of foreign policy, Carter made a more controversial decision in response to the Soviet Union's 1979 invasion of Afghanistan. In January 1980, he declared that if the USSR did not withdraw its forces, the United States would boycott the 1980 Summer Olympic Games in Moscow. The Soviets did not retreat, and the United States did not send a team to Moscow. Only about half of the American public supported this decision, and despite Carter's call for other countries to join the boycott, very few did so.

HOSTAGES TO HISTORY

Carter's biggest foreign policy problem was the Iranian hostage crisis, whose roots lay in the 1950s. In 1953, the United States had assisted Great Britain in the overthrow of Prime Minister Mohammad Mossadegh, a rival of Mohammad Reza Pahlavi, the shah of Iran. Mossadegh had sought greater Iranian control over the nation's oil wealth, which was claimed by British companies. Following the coup, the shah assumed complete control of Iran's government. He then disposed of political enemies and eliminated dissent through the use of SAVAK, a secret police force trained by the United States. The United States also supplied the shah's government with billions of dollars in aid. As Iran's oil revenue grew, especially after the 1973 oil embargo against the United States, the pace of its economic development and the size of its educated middle class also increased, and the country became less dependent on U.S. aid. Its population increasingly blamed the United States for the death of Iranian democracy and faulted it for its consistent support of Israel.

Despite the shah's unpopularity among his own people, the result of both his brutal policies and his desire to Westernize Iran, the United States supported his regime. In February 1979, the shah was overthrown when revolution broke out, and a few months later, he departed for the United States for medical treatment. The long history of U.S. support for him and its offer of refuge greatly angered Iranian revolutionaries. On November 4, 1979, a group of Iranian students and activists, including Islamic fundamentalists who wished to end the Westernization and secularization of Iran, invaded the   American embassy in Tehran and seized sixty-six embassy employees. The women and African Americans were soon released, leaving fifty-three men as hostages. Negotiations failed to free them, and in April 1980, a rescue attempt fell through when the aircraft sent to transport them crashed. Another hostage was released when he developed serious medical problems. President Carter's inability to free the other captives hurt his performance in the 1980 elections. The fifty-two men still held in Iran were finally freed on January 20, 1981, the day Ronald Reagan took office as president (**Figure 9.21**).

Figure 9.21 The fifty-two American hostages return from Iran in January 1981. They had been held for 444 days.

Carter's handling of the crisis appeared even less effective in the way the media portrayed it publicly. This contributed to a growing sense of malaise, a feeling that the United States' best days were behind it and the country had entered a period of decline. This belief was compounded by continuing economic problems, and the oil shortage and subsequent rise in prices that followed the Iranian Revolution. The president's decision to import less oil to the United States and remove price controls on oil and gasoline did not help matters. In 1979, Carter sought to reassure the nation and the rest of the world, especially the Soviet Union, that the United States was still able to defend its interests. To dissuade the Soviets from making additional inroads in southwest Asia, he proposed the **Carter Doctrine**, which stated that the United States would regard any attempt to interfere with its interests in the Middle East as an act of aggression to be met with force ifnecessary.

Carter had failed to solve the nation's problems. Some blamed these problems on dishonest politicians; others blamed the problems on the Cold War obsession with fighting Communism, even in small nations like Vietnam that had little influence on American national interests. Still others faulted American materialism. In 1980, a small but growing group called the Moral Majority faulted Carter for betraying his southern roots and began to seek a return to traditional values.

CHAPTER 10

From Cold War to Culture Wars, 1980-2000

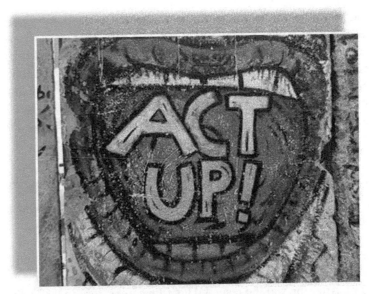

Figure 10.1 This striking piece of graffiti from the Berlin Wall, now housed in the Newseum in Washington, DC, contains the name of the AIDS Coalition to Unleash Power (ACT UP), a group formed in 1987 in New York City to combat the spread of AIDS and the perception that AIDS was the product of immoral behavior.

Chapter Outline

10.1 The Reagan Revolution
10.2 Political and Cultural Fusions
10.3 A New World Order
10.4 Bill Clinton and the New Economy

Introduction

"Act up!" might be called the unofficial slogan of the 1980s. Numerous groups were concerned by what they considered disturbing social, cultural, and political trends in the United States and lobbied for their vision of what the nation should be. Conservative politicians cut taxes for the wealthy and shrank programs for the poor, while conservative Christians blamed the legalization of abortion and the increased visibility of gays and lesbians for weakening the American family. When the U.S. Centers for Disease Control first recognized the Acquired Immune Deficiency Syndrome (AIDS) in 1981, the Religious Right regarded it as a plague sent by God to punish homosexual men for their "unnatural" behavior. Politicians, many of whom relied on religious conservatives for their votes, largely ignored the AIDS epidemic. In response, gay men and women formed organizations such as ACT UP to draw attention to their cause **(Figure 10.1)**.

Toward the end of the decade in 1989, protesters from both East and West Berlin began "acting up" and tearing down large chunks of the Berlin Wall, essentially dismantling the Iron Curtain. This symbolic act was the culmination of earlier demonstrations that had swept across Eastern Europe, resulting in the collapse of Communist governments in both Central and Eastern Europe, and marking the beginning of the end of the Cold War.

10.1 The Reagan Revolution

By the end of this section, you will be able to:
- Explain Ronald Reagan's attitude towards government
- Discuss the Reagan administration's economic policies and their effects on the nation

Ronald Reagan entered the White House in 1981 with strongly conservative values but experience in moderate politics. He appealed to moderates and conservatives anxious about social change and the seeming loss of American power and influence on the world stage. Leading the so-called Reagan Revolution, he appealed to voters with the promise that the principles of conservatism could halt and revert the social and economic changes of the last generation. Reagan won the White House by citing big government and attempts at social reform as the problem, not the solution. He was able to capture the political capital of an unsettled national mood and, in the process, helped set an agenda and policies that would affect his successors and the political landscape of the nation.

REAGAN'S EARLY CAREER

Although many of his movie roles and the persona he created for himself seemed to represent traditional values, Reagan's rise to the presidency was an unusual transition from pop cultural significance to political success. Born and raised in the Midwest, he moved to California in 1937 to become a Hollywood actor. He also became a reserve officer in the U.S. Army that same year, but when the country entered World War II, he was excluded from active duty overseas because of poor eyesight and spent the war in the army's First Motion Picture Unit. After the war, he resumed his film career; rose to leadership in the Screen Actors Guild, a Hollywood union; and became a spokesman for General Electric and the host of a television series that the company sponsored. As a young man, he identified politically as a liberal Democrat, but his distaste for communism, along with the influence of the social conservative values of his second wife, actress Nancy Davis, edged him closer to conservative Republicanism (**Figure 10.3**). By 1962, he had

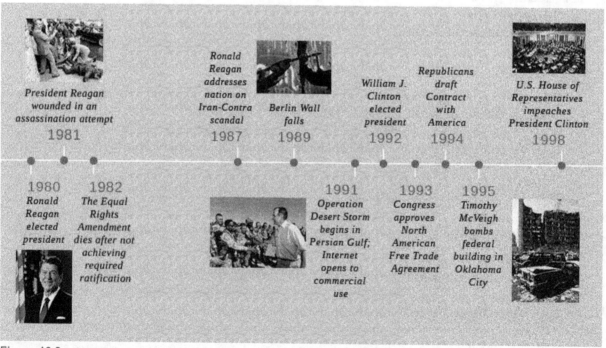

Figure 10.2

formally switched political parties, and in 1964, he actively campaigned for the Republican presidential nominee Barry Goldwater.

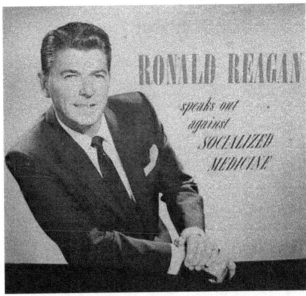

Figure 10.3 In 1961, when Congress began to explore nationwide health insurance for the elderly under Social Security, Reagan made a recording for the American Medical Association in which he denounced the idea—which was later adopted as Medicare—as "socialized medicine." Such a program, Reagan warned his listeners, was the first step to the nation's demise as a free society.

Reagan launched his own political career in 1966 when he successfully ran for governor of California. His opponent was the incumbent Pat Brown, a liberal Democrat who had already served two terms. Reagan, quite undeservedly, blamed Brown for race riots in California and student protests at the University of California at Berkeley. He criticized the Democratic incumbent's increases in taxes and state government, and denounced "big government" and the inequities of taxation in favor of free enterprise. As governor, however, he quickly learned that federal and state laws prohibited the elimination of certain programs and that many programs benefited his constituents. He ended up approving the largest budget in the state's history and approved tax increases on a number of occasions. The contrast between Reagan's rhetoric and practice made up his political skill: capturing the public mood and catering to it, but compromising when necessary.

REPUBLICANS BACK IN THE WHITE HOUSE

After two unsuccessful Republican primary bids in 1968 and 1976, Reagan won the presidency in 1980. His victory was the result of a combination of dissatisfaction with the presidential leadership of Gerald Ford and Jimmy Carter in the 1970s and the growth of the **New Right**. This group of conservative Americans included many very wealthy financial supporters and emerged in the wake of the social reforms and cultural changes of the 1960s and 1970s. Many were evangelical Christians, like those who joined Jerry Falwell's Moral Majority, and opposed the legalization of abortion, the feminist movement, and sex education in public schools. Reagan also attracted people, often dubbed neoconservatives, who would not previously have voted for the same candidate as conservative Protestants did. Many were middle- and working-class people who resented the growth of federal and state governments, especially benefit programs, and the subsequent increase in taxes during the late 1960s and 1970s. They favored the tax revolts that swept the nation in the late 1970s under the leadership of predominantly older, white, middle-class Americans, which had succeeded in imposing radical reductions in local property and state income taxes.

Voter turnout reflected this new conservative swing, which not only swept Reagan into the White House but created a Republican majority in the Senate. Only 52 percent of eligible voters went to the polls in 1980, the lowest turnout for a presidential election since 1948. Those who did cast a ballot were older, whiter, and wealthier than those who did not vote (**Figure 10.4**). Strong support among white voters, those over forty-five years of age, and those with incomes over $50,000 proved crucial for Reagan's victory.

Figure 10.4 Ronald Reagan campaigns for the presidency with his wife Nancy in South Carolina in 1980. Reagan won in all the Deep South states except Georgia, although he did not come from the South and his opponent Jimmy Carter did.

REAGANOMICS

Reagan's primary goal upon taking office was to stimulate the sagging economy while simultaneously cutting both government programs and taxes. His economic policies, called **Reaganomics** by the press, were based on a theory called supply-side economics, about which many economists were skeptical. Influenced by economist Arthur Laffer of the University of Southern California, Reagan cut income taxes for those at the top of the economic ladder, which was supposed to motivate the rich to invest in businesses, factories, and the stock market in anticipation of high returns. According to Laffer's argument, this would eventually translate into more jobs further down the socioeconomic ladder. Economic growth would also increase the total tax revenue—even at a lower tax rate. In other words, proponents of "trickle-down economics" promised to cut taxes and balance the budget at the same time. Reaganomics also included the deregulation of industry and higher interest rates to control inflation, but these initiatives preceded Reagan and were conceived in the Carter administration.

Many politicians, including Republicans, were wary of Reagan's economic program; even his eventual vice president, George H. W. Bush, had referred to it as "voodoo economics" when competing with him for the Republican presidential nomination. When Reagan proposed a 30 percent cut in taxes to be phased in over his first term in office, Congress balked. Opponents argued that the tax cuts would benefit the rich and not the poor, who needed help the most. In response, Reagan presented his plan directly to the people (**Figure 10.5**).

Figure 10.5 Ronald Reagan outlines his plan for tax reduction legislation in July 1981. Data suggest that the supply-side policies of the 1980s actually produced less investment, slightly slower growth, and a greater decline in wages than the non–supply side policies of the 1990s.

Reagan was an articulate spokesman for his political perspectives and was able to garner support for his policies. Often called "The Great Communicator," he was noted for his ability, honed through years as an actor and spokesperson, to convey a mixture of folksy wisdom, empathy, and concern while taking humorous digs at his opponents. Indeed, listening to Reagan speak often felt like hearing a favorite uncle recall stories about the "good old days" before big government, expensive social programs, and greedy politicians destroyed the country (**Figure 10.6**). Americans found this rhetorical style extremely compelling. Public support for the plan, combined with a surge in the president's popularity after he survived an assassination attempt in March 1981, swayed Congress, including many Democrats. On July 29, 1981, Congress passed the Economic Recovery Tax Act, which phased in a 25 percent overall reduction in taxes over a period of three years.

Figure 10.6 President Ronald Reagan signs economic reform legislation at his ranch in California. Note the blue jeans, denim jacket, and cowboy boots he wears.

MY STORY

⊘ *Richard V. Allen on the Assassination Attempt on Ronald Reagan*

On March 30, 1981, just months into the Reagan presidency, John Hinckley, Jr. attempted to assassinate the president as he left a speaking engagement at the Washington Hilton Hotel. Hinckley wounded Reagan and three others in the attempt. Here, National Security Adviser Richard V. Allen recalls what happened the day President Reagan was shot:

> By 2:52 PM I arrived at the White House and went to [Chief of Staff James] Baker's office . . . and we placed a call to Vice President George H. W. Bush. . . .
>
> [W]e sent a message with the few facts we knew: the bullets had been fired and press secretary Jim Brady had been hit, as had a Secret Service agent and a DC policeman. At first, the President was thought to be unscathed.
>
> Jerry Parr, the Secret Service Detail Chief, shoved the President into the limousine, codenamed "Stagecoach," and slammed the doors shut. The driver sped off. Headed back to the safety of the White House, Parr noticed that the red blood at the President's mouth was frothy, indicating an internal injury, and suddenly switched the route to the hospital. . . . Parr saved the President's life. He had lost a serious quantity of blood internally and reached [the emergency room] just in time. . . .
>
> Though the President never lost his sense of humor throughout, and had actually walked into the hospital under his own power before his knees buckled, his condition became grave.

Why do you think Allen mentions the president's sense of humor and his ability to walk into the hospital on his own? Why might the assassination attempt have helped Reagan achieve some of his political goals, such as getting his tax cuts through Congress?

Click and Explore

The largest of the presidential libraries, the Ronald Reagan Presidential Library (http://openstaxcollege.org/l/15ReaganLib) contains Reagan's most important speeches and pictures of Ronald and Nancy Reagan.

Reagan was successful at cutting taxes, but he failed to reduce government spending. Although he had long warned about the dangers of big government, he created a new cabinet-level agency, the Department of Veterans Affairs, and the number of federal employees increased during his time in office. He allocated a smaller share of the federal budget to antipoverty programs like Aid to Families with Dependent Children (AFDC), food stamps, rent subsidies, job training programs, and Medicaid, but Social Security and Medicare entitlements, from which his supporters benefited, were left largely untouched except for an increase in payroll taxes to pay for them. Indeed, in 1983, Reagan agreed to a compromise with the Democrats in Congress on a $165 billion injection of funds to save Social Security, which included this payroll tax increase.

But Reagan seemed less flexible when it came to deregulating industry and weakening the power of labor unions. Banks and savings and loan associations were deregulated. Pollution control was enforced less strictly by the Environmental Protection Agency, and restrictions on logging and drilling for oil on public lands were relaxed. Believing the free market was self-regulating, the Reagan administration had little use for labor unions, and in 1981, the president fired twelve thousand federal air traffic controllers who had gone on strike to secure better working conditions (which would also have improved the public's safety). His action effectively destroyed the Professional Air Traffic Controllers Organization (PATCO) and ushered in a new era of labor relations in which, following his example, employers simply replaced striking workers. The weakening of unions contributed to the leveling off of real wages for the average American family during the1980s.

Reagan's economic policymakers succeeded in breaking the cycle of stagflation that had been plaguing the nation, but at significant cost. In its effort to curb high inflation with dramatically increased interest rates, the Federal Reserve also triggered a deep recession. Inflation did drop, but borrowing became expensive and consumers spent less. In Reagan's first years in office, bankruptcies increased and unemployment reached about 10 percent, its highest level since the Great Depression. Homelessness became a significant problem in cities, a fact the president made light of by suggesting that the press exaggerated the problem and that many homeless people chose to live on the streets. Economic growth resumed in 1983 and gross domestic product grew at an average of 4.5 percent during the rest of his presidency. By the end of Reagan's second term in office, unemployment had dropped to about 5.3 percent, but the nation was nearly $3 trillion in debt. An increase in defense spending coupled with $3.6 billion in tax relief for the 162,000 American families with incomes of $200,000 or more made a balanced budget, one of the president's campaign promises in 1980, impossible to achieve.

The Reagan years were a complicated era of social, economic, and political change, with many trends operating simultaneously and sometimes at cross-purposes. While many suffered, others prospered. The 1970s had been the era of the hippie, and *Newsweek* magazine declared 1984 to be the "year of the Yuppie." Yuppies, whose name derived from "(y)oung, (u)rban (p)rofessionals," were akin to hippies in being young people whose interests, values, and lifestyle influenced American culture, economy, and politics, just as the hippies' credo had done in the late 1960s and 1970s. Unlike hippies, however, yuppies were materialistic and obsessed with image, comfort, and economic prosperity. Although liberal on some social issues, economically they were conservative. Ironically, some yuppies were former hippies or yippies, like Jerry Rubin, who gave up his crusade against "the establishment" to become a businessman.

Click and Explore

Read more about yuppie culture (http://openstaxcollege.org/l/15YuppieCult) and then use the table of contents to access other information about the culture of the 1980s.

10.2 Political and Cultural Fusions

By the end of this section, you will be able to:
- Discuss the culture wars and political conflicts of the Reagan era
- Describe the Religious Right's response to the issues of the Reagan era

Ronald Reagan's victory in 1980 suggested to conservatives that the days of liberalism were over and the liberal establishment might be dismantled. Many looked forward to the discontinuation of policies like affirmative action. Conservative Christians sought to outlaw abortion and stop the movement for gay and lesbian rights. Republicans, and some moderate Democrats, demanded a return to "traditional" family values, a rhetorical ploy to suggest that male authority over women and children constituted a natural order that women's rights and the New Left had subverted since the 1960s. As the conservative message regarding the evils of government permeated society, distrust of the federal government grew, inspiring some to form organizations and communities that sought complete freedom from government control.

CREATING CONSERVATIVE POLICY

Ronald Reagan's popularity and effectiveness as a leader drew from his reputation as a man who fought for what he believed in. He was a very articulate spokesperson for a variety of political ideas based on conservative principles and perspectives. Much of the intellectual meat of the Reagan Revolution came from conservative think tanks (policy or advocacy groups) that specifically sought to shape American political and social dialogues. The **Heritage Foundation**, one such group, soon became the intellectual arm of the conservative movement.

Launched in 1973 with a $250,000 contribution from Joseph Coors (of Coors Brewing Company) and support from a variety of corporations and conservative foundations, the Heritage Foundation sought to counteract what conservatives believed to be Richard Nixon's acceptance of a liberal consensus on too many issues. In producing its policy position papers and political recommendations to conservative candidates and politicians, it helped contribute to a sanitization of U.S. history and a nostalgic glorification of what it deemed to be traditional values, seemingly threatened by the expansion of political and personal freedoms. The foundation had lent considerable support and encouragement to the conservative dialogues that helped carry Ronald Reagan into office in 1980. Just a year later, it produced a document entitled *Mandate for Leadership* that catalogued some two thousand specific recommendations on how to shrink the size and reach of the federal government and implement a more consistent conservative agenda. The newly elected Reagan administration looked favorably on the recommendations and recruited several of the paper's authors to serve in the White House.

CONSERVATIVE CHRISTIANS AND FAMILY VALUES

Among the strongest supporters of Ronald Reagan's campaign for president were members of the Religious Right, including Christian groups like the Moral Majority, 61 percent of whom voted for him. By 1980, evangelical Christians had become an important political and social force in the United States (**Figure 10.7**). Some thirteen hundred radio stations in the country were owned and operated by evangelicals. Christian television programs, such as Pat Robertson's *The 700 Club* and Jim Bakker's *The PTL* (Praise the Lord) *Club*, proved enormously popular and raised millions of dollars from viewer contributions. For some, evangelism was a business, but most conservative Christians were true believers who were convinced that premarital and extramarital sex, abortion, drug use, homosexuality, and "irreligious" forms of popular and high culture were responsible for a perceived decline in traditional family values that threatened American society.

YES, ANITA!

I want to help you bring America back to God and morality. Please send me all issues of your Protect America's Children Newsletter.

Name
Address
City   State   Zip

Protect America's Children   P.O. Box 40-2608   Miami Beach, Florida 33140

Figure 10.7 This fundraising card was used by Anita Bryant, singer and beauty pageant winner, to gather support for Save Our Children Inc., a political coalition she formed in the late 1970s to overturn a Florida ordinance banning discrimination based on sexual orientation. Many of the group's strategies were soon embraced by the Moral Majority.

Despite the support he received from Christian conservative and family values voters, Reagan was hardly an ideologue when it came to policy. Indeed, he was often quite careful in using hot button, family-value issues to his greatest political advantage. For example, as governor of California, one of the states that ratified the Equal Rights Amendment (ERA) in its first year, he positioned himself as a supporter of the amendment. When he launched his bid for the Republican nomination in 1976, however, he withdrew his support to gain the backing of more conservative members of his party. This move demonstrated both political savvy and foresight. At the time he withdrew his support, the Republican National Convention was still officially backing the amendment. However, in 1980, the party began to qualify its stance, which dovetailed with Reagan's candidacy for the White House.

Reagan believed the Fourteenth Amendment to the Constitution was sufficient protection for women against discrimination. Once in office, he took a mostly neutral position, neither supporting nor working against the ERA. Nor did this middle position appear to hurt him at the polls; he attracted a significant number of votes from women in 1980, and in 1984, he polled 56 percent of the women's vote compared to 44 percent for the Democratic ticket of Walter Mondale and Geraldine Ferraro, the first female candidate for vice president from a major party.

DEFINING "AMERICAN"

⊙ *Phyllis Schlafly and the STOP ERA Movement*

In 1972, after a large number of states jumped to ratify the Equal Rights Amendment, most observers believed its ultimate ratification by all the necessary states was all but certain. But, a decade later, the amendment died without ever getting the necessary votes. There are many reasons it went down in defeat, but a major one was Phyllis Schlafly.

On the surface, Schlafly's life might suggest that she would naturally support the ERA. After all, she was a well-educated, professional woman who sought advancement in her field and even aspired to high political office. Yet she is a fascinating historical character, precisely because her life and goals don't conform to expected norms.

Schlafly's attack on the ERA was ingenious in its method and effectiveness. Rather than attacking the amendment directly as a gateway to unrestrained and immoral behavior as some had, she couched her opposition in language that was sensitive to both privilege and class. Her instrument was the STOP ERA movement, with the acronym STOP, standing for "Stop Taking our Privileges." Schlafly argued that women enjoyed special privileges such as gender-specific restrooms and exemption from the military draft. These, she claimed, would be lost should the ERA be ratified. But she also claimed to stand up for the dignity of being a homemaker and lambasted the feminist movement as elitist. In this, she was keenly aware of the power of class interests. Her organization suggested that privileged women could afford to support the ERA. Working women and poor housewives, however, would ultimately bear the brunt of the loss of protection it would bring. In the end, her tactics were successful in achieving exactly what the movement's name suggested; she stopped the ERA.

Reagan's political calculations notwithstanding, his belief that traditional values were threatened by a modern wave of immoral popular culture was genuine. He recognized that nostalgia was a powerful force in politics, and he drew a picture for his audiences of the traditional good old days under attack by immorality and decline. "Those of us who are over thirty-five or so years of age grew up in a different America," he explained in his farewell address. "We were taught, very directly, what it means to be an American. And we absorbed, almost in the air, a love of country and an appreciation of its institutions. . . . The movies celebrated democratic values and implicitly reinforced the idea that America was special." But this America, he insisted, was being washed away. "I'm warning of an eradication of the American memory that could result, ultimately, in an erosion of the American spirit."

Concern over a decline in the country's moral values welled up on both sides of the political aisle. In 1985, anxiety over the messages of the music industry led to the founding of the Parents Music Resource Center (PMRC), a bipartisan group formed by the wives of prominent Washington politicians including Susan Baker, the wife of Reagan's treasury secretary, James Baker, and Tipper Gore, the wife of then-senator Al Gore, who later became vice president under Bill Clinton. The goal of the PMRC was to limit the ability of children to listen to music with sexual or violent content. Its strategy was to get the recording industry to adopt a voluntary rating system for music and recordings, similar to the Motion Picture Association of America's system for movies.

The organization also produced a list of particularly offensive recordings known as the "filthy fifteen." By August 1985, nearly twenty record companies had agreed to put labels on their recordings indicating "explicit lyrics," but the Senate began hearings on the issue in September (**Figure 10.8**). While many parents and a number of witnesses advocated the labels, many in the music industry rejected them as censorship. *Twisted Sister*'s Dee Snider and folk musician John Denver both advised Congress against the restrictions. In the end, the recording industry suggested a voluntary generic label. Its effect on children's exposure to raw language is uncertain, but musicians roundly mocked the effort.

Figure 10.8 Tipper Gore, wife of then-senator (and later vice president) Al Gore, at the 1985 Senate hearings into rating labels proposed by the PMRC, of which she was a cofounder.

Click and Explore

Listen to the testimony of Dee Snider (http://openstaxcollege.org/l/15DeeSnider) and John Denver (http://openstaxcollege.org/l/15JohnDenver) to learn more about the contours of this debate.

THE AIDS CRISIS

In the early 1980s, doctors noticed a disturbing trend: Young gay men in large cities, especially San Francisco and New York, were being diagnosed with, and eventually dying from, a rare cancer called Kaposi's sarcoma. Because the disease was seen almost exclusively in male homosexuals, it was quickly dubbed "gay cancer." Doctors soon realized it often coincided with other symptoms, including a rare form of pneumonia, and they renamed it "Gay Related Immune Deficiency" (GRID), although people other than gay men, primarily intravenous drug users, were dying from the disease as well. The connection between gay men and GRID—later renamed human immunodeficiency virus/autoimmune deficiency syndrome, or **HIV/AIDS**—led heterosexuals largely to ignore the growing health crisis in the gay community, wrongly assuming they were safe from its effects. The federal government also overlooked the disease, and calls for more money to research and find the cure were ignored.

Even after it became apparent that heterosexuals could contract the disease through blood transfusions and heterosexual intercourse, HIV/AIDS continued to be associated primarily with the gay community, especially by political and religious conservatives. Indeed, the Religious Right regarded it as a form of divine retribution meant to punish gay men for their "immoral" lifestyle. President Reagan, always politically careful, was reluctant to speak openly about the developing crisis even as thousands faced certain death from the disease.

With little help coming from the government, the gay community quickly began to organize its own response. In 1982, New York City men formed the Gay Men's Health Crisis (GMHC), a volunteer organization that operated an information hotline, provided counseling and legal assistance, and raised money for people with HIV/AIDS. Larry Kramer, one of the original members, left in 1983 and formed his own organization, the AIDS Coalition to Unleash Power (ACT UP), in 1987. ACT UP took a more militant approach, holding demonstrations on Wall Street, outside the U.S. Food and Drug Administration (FDA), and inside the New York Stock Exchange to call attention and shame the government into action. One of the images adopted by the group, a pink triangle paired with the phrase "Silence = Death," captured media attention and quickly became the symbol of the AIDS crisis (**Figure 10.9**).

Figure 10.9 The pink triangle was originally used in Nazi concentration camps to identify those there for acts of homosexuality. Reclaimed by gay activists in New York as a symbol of resistance and solidarity during the 1970s, it was further transformed as a symbol of governmental inaction in the face of the AIDS epidemic during the 1980s.

THE WAR ON DRUGS AND THE ROAD TO MASS INCARCERATION

As Ronald Reagan took office in 1981, violent crime in the United States was reaching an all-time high. While there were different reasons for the spike, the most important one was demographics: The primary category of offenders, males between the ages of sixteen and thirty-six, reached an all-time peak as the baby-boomer generation came of age. But the phenomenon that most politicians honed in on as a cause for violent crime was the abuse of a new, cheap drug dealt illegally on city streets. Crack cocaine, a smokable type of cocaine popular with poorer addicts, was hitting the streets in the 1980s, frightening middle-class Americans. Reagan and other conservatives led a campaign to "get tough on crime" and promised the nation a "**war on drugs**." Initiatives like the "Just Say No" campaign led by First Lady Nancy Reagan implied that drug addiction and drug-related crime reflected personal morality.

Nixon had first used the term in 1971, but in the 1980s the "war on drugs" took on an ominous dimension, as politicians scrambled over each other to enact harsher sentences for drug offenses so they could market themselves as tough on crime. State after state switched from variable to mandatory minimum sentences that were exceedingly long and particularly harsh for street drug crimes. The federal government supported the trend with federal sentencing guidelines and additional funds for local law enforcement agencies. This law-and-order movement peaked in the 1990s, when California introduced a "three strikes" law that mandated life imprisonment without parole for any third felony conviction—even nonviolent ones. As a result, prisons became crowded, and states went deep into debt to build more. By the end of the century, the war began to die down as the public lost interest in the problem, the costs of the punishment binge became politically burdensome, and scholars and politicians began to advocate the decriminalization of drug use. By this time, however, hundreds of thousands of people had been incarcerated for drug offenses and the total number of prisoners in the nation had grown four-fold in the last quarter of the century. Particularly glaring were the racial inequities of the new age of mass incarceration, with African Americans being seven times more likely to be in prison (**Figure 10.10**).

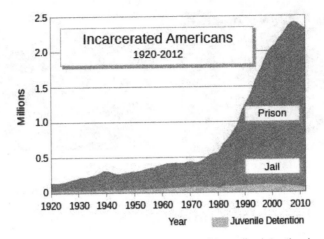

Figure 10.10 This graph of the number of people in jail, prison, and juvenile detention by decade in the United States shows the huge increase in incarceration during the war on drugs that began in the 1980s, during the Reagan administration. (Prisons are long-term state or federal facilities; jails are local, short-term facilities.)

10.3 A New World Order

By the end of this section, you will be able to:
- Describe the successes and failures of Ronald Reagan's foreign policy
- Compare the policies of Ronald Reagan with those of George H. W. Bush
- Explain the causes and results of the Persian Gulf War
- Discuss the events that constituted the end of the Cold War

In addition to reviving the economy and reducing the size of the federal government, Ronald Reagan also wished to restore American stature in the world. He entered the White House a "cold warrior" and referred to the Soviet Union in a 1983 speech as an "evil empire." Dedicated to upholding even authoritarian governments in foreign countries to keep them safe from Soviet influence, he was also desperate to put to rest **Vietnam Syndrome**, the reluctance to use military force in foreign countries for fear of embarrassing defeat, which had influenced U.S. foreign policy since the mid-1970s.

THE MIDDLE EAST AND CENTRAL AMERICA

Reagan's desire to demonstrate U.S. readiness to use military force abroad sometimes had tragic consequences. In 1983, he sent soldiers to Lebanon as part of a multinational force trying to restore order following an Israeli invasion the year before. On October 23, more than two hundred troops were killed in a barracks bombing in Beirut carried out by Iranian-trained militants known as Hezbollah (**Figure 10.11**). In February 1984, Reagan announced that, given intensified fighting, U.S. troops were being withdrawn.

(a)   (b)

Figure 10.11 The suicide bombing of the U.S. Embassy in Beirut (a) on April 18, 1983, marked the first of a number of attacks on U.S. targets in the region. Less than six months later, a truck bomb leveled the U.S. Marine barracks at the Beirut airport (b), part of a coordinated attack that killed 299 U.S and French members of the multinational peacekeeping force in Lebanon.

Two days after the bombing in Beirut, Reagan and Secretary of State George P. Shultz authorized the invasion of Grenada, a small Caribbean island nation, in an attempt to oust a Communist military junta that had overthrown a moderate regime. Communist Cuba already had troops and technical aid workers stationed on the island and were willing to defend the new regime, but the United States swiftly took command of the situation, and the Cuban soldiers surrendered after two days.

Reagan's intervention in Grenada was intended to send a message to Marxists in Central America. Meanwhile, however, decades of political repression and economic corruption by certain Latin American governments, sometimes generously supported by U.S. foreign aid, had sown deep seeds of revolutionary discontent. In El Salvador, a 1979 civil-military coup had put a military junta in power that was engaged in a civil war against left-leaning guerillas when Reagan took office. His administration supported the right-wing government, which used death squads to silence dissent.

Neighboring Nicaragua was also governed by a largely Marxist-inspired group, the Sandinistas. This organization, led by Daniel Ortega, had overthrown the brutal, right-wing dictatorship of Anastasio Somoza in 1979. Reagan, however, overlooked the legitimate complaints of the Sandinistas and believed that their rule opened the region to Cuban and Soviet influence. A year into his presidency, convinced it was folly to allow the expansion of Soviet and Communist influence in Latin America, he authorized the Central Intelligence Agency (CIA) to equip and train a group of anti-Sandinista Nicaraguans known as the Contras (*contrarevolucionários* or "counter-revolutionaries") to oust Ortega.

Reagan's desire to aid the Contras even after Congress ended its support led him, surprisingly, to Iran. In September 1980, Iraq had invaded neighboring Iran and, by 1982, had begun to gain the upper hand. The Iraqis needed weapons, and the Reagan administration, wishing to assist the enemy of its enemy, had agreed to provide Iraqi president Saddam Hussein with money, arms, and military intelligence. In 1983, however, the capture of Americans by Hezbollah forces in Lebanon changed the president's plans. In 1985, he authorized the sale of anti-tank and anti-aircraft missiles to Iran in exchange for help retrieving three of the American hostages.

A year later, Reagan's National Security Council aide, Lieutenant Colonel Oliver North, found a way to sell weapons to Iran and secretly use the proceeds to support the Nicaraguan Contras—in direct violation of a congressional ban on military aid to the anti-Communist guerillas in that Central American nation. Eventually the Senate became aware, and North and others were indicted on various charges, which were all dismissed, overturned on appeal, or granted presidential pardon. Reagan, known for delegating much authority to subordinates and unable to "remember" crucial facts and meetings, escaped the scandal with nothing more than criticism for his lax oversight. The nation was divided over the extent to which the president could go to "protect national interests," and the limits of Congress's constitutional authority to oversee the activities of the executive branch have yet to be resolved.

Click and Explore

Visit the Brown University site (http://openstaxcollege.org/l/15IranContra) to learn more about the Iran-Contra congressional hearings. Read transcripts of the testimony and watch the video of President Reagan's address to the nation regarding the operation.

THE COLD WAR WAXES AND WANES

While trying to shrink the federal budget and the size of government sphere at home, Reagan led an unprecedented military buildup in which money flowed to the Pentagon to pay for expensive new forms of weaponry. The press drew attention to the inefficiency of the nation's military industrial complex, offering as examples expense bills that included $640 toilet seats and $7,400 coffee machines. One of the most controversial aspects of Reagan's plan was the Strategic Defense Initiative (SDI), which he proposed in 1983. SDI, or "Star Wars," called for the development of a defensive shield to protect the United States from a Soviet missile strike. Scientists argued that much of the needed technology had not yet been developed and might never be. Others contended that the plan would violate existing treaties with the Soviet Union and worried about the Soviet response. The system was never built, and the plan, estimated to have cost some $7.5 billion, was finally abandoned.

Anticipating his reelection campaign in 1984, Reagan began to moderate his position toward the Soviet Union, largely at the initiative of his new counterpart, Mikhail Gorbachev. The new and comparatively young Soviet premier did not want to commit additional funds for another arms race, especially since the war in Afghanistan against mujahedeen—Islamic guerilla fighters—had depleted the Soviet Union's resources severely since its invasion of the central Asian nation in 1979. Gorbachev recognized that economic despair at home could easily result in larger political upheavals like those in neighboring Poland, where the Solidarity movement had taken hold. He withdrew troops from Afghanistan, introduced political reforms and new civil liberties at home—known as *perestroika* and *glasnost*—and proposed arms reduction talks with the United States. In 1985, Gorbachev and Reagan met in Geneva to reduce armaments and shrink their respective military budgets. The following year, meeting in Reykjavík, Iceland, they surprised the world by announcing that they would try to eliminate nuclear weapons by 1996. In 1987, they agreed to eliminate a whole category of nuclear weapons when they signed the Intermediate-Range Nuclear Forces (INF) Treaty at the White House (**Figure 10.12**). This laid the foundation for future agreements limiting nuclear weapons.

Figure 10.12 In the East Room of the White House, President Reagan and Soviet general secretary Mikhail Gorbachev sign the 1987 INF Treaty, eliminating one category of nuclear weapons.

Click and Explore

You can view President Reagan delivering one of his most memorable addresses (http://openstaxcollege.org/l/15BerlinWall) in 1987. Standing in front of the Brandenburg Gate in West Berlin, he called on General Secretary Gorbachev to "tear down this wall."

"NO NEW TAXES"

Confident they could win back the White House, Democrats mounted a campaign focused on more effective and competent government under the leadership of Massachusetts governor Michael Dukakis. When George H. W. Bush, Reagan's vice president and Republican nominee, found himself down in the polls, political advisor Lee Atwater launched an aggressively negative media campaign, accusing Dukakis of being soft on crime and connecting his liberal policies to a brutal murder in Massachusetts. More importantly, Bush adopted a largely Reaganesque style on matters of economic policy, promising to shrink government and keep taxes low. These tactics were successful, and the Republican Party retained the White House.

Although he promised to carry on Reagan's economic legacy, the problems Bush inherited made it difficult to do so. Reagan's policies of cutting taxes and increasing defense spending had exploded the federal budget deficit, making it three times larger in 1989 than when Reagan took office in 1980. Bush was further constrained by the emphatic pledge he had made at the 1988 Republican Convention—"read my lips: no new taxes"—and found himself in the difficult position of trying to balance the budget and reduce the deficit without breaking his promise. However, he also faced a Congress controlled by the Democrats, who wanted to raise taxes on the rich, while Republicans thought the government should drastically cut domestic spending. In October, after a brief government shutdown when Bush vetoed the budget Congress delivered, he and Congress reached a compromise with the Omnibus Budget Reconciliation Act of 1990. The budget included measures to reduce the deficit by both cutting government expenditures and raising taxes, effectively reneging on the "no new taxes" pledge. These economic constraints are one reason why Bush supported a limited domestic agenda of education reform and antidrug efforts, relying on private volunteers and community organizations, which he referred to as "a thousand points of light," to address most social problems.

When it came to foreign affairs, Bush's attitude towards the Soviet Union differed little from Reagan's. Bush sought to ease tensions with America's rival superpower and stressed the need for peace and cooperation. The desire to avoid angering the Soviets led him to adopt a hands-off approach when, at the beginning of his term, a series of pro-democracy demonstrations broke out across the Communist Eastern Bloc.

In November 1989, the world—including foreign policy experts and espionage agencies from both sides of the Iron Curtain—watched in surprise as peaceful protesters in East Germany marched through checkpoints at the Berlin Wall. Within hours, people from both East and West Berlin flooded the checkpoints and began tearing down large chunks of the wall. Months of earlier demonstrations in East Germany had called on the government to allow citizens to leave the country. These demonstrations were one manifestation of a larger movement sweeping across East Germany, Poland, Hungary, Czechoslovakia, Bulgaria, and Romania, which swiftly led to revolutions, most of them peaceful, resulting in the collapse of Communist governments in Central and Eastern Europe.

In Budapest in 1956 and in Prague in 1968, the Soviet Union had restored order through a large show of force. That this didn't happen in 1989 was an indication to all that the Soviet Union was itself collapsing. Bush's refusal to gloat or declare victory helped him maintain the relationship with Gorbachev that Reagan had established. In July 1991, Gorbachev and Bush signed the Strategic Arms Reduction Treaty, or **START**, which committed their countries to reducing their nuclear arsenals by 25 percent. A month later, attempting to stop the changes begun by Gorbachev's reforms, Communist Party hardliners tried to remove him from power. Protests arose throughout the Soviet Union, and by December 1991, the nation had collapsed. In January 1992, twelve former Soviet republics formed the Commonwealth of Independent States to coordinate trade and security measures. The Cold War was over.

AMERICAN GLOBAL POWER IN THE WAKE OF THE COLD WAR

The dust had barely settled on the crumbling Berlin Wall when the Bush administration announced a bold military intervention in Panama in December 1989. Claiming to act on behalf of human rights, U.S. troops deposed the unpopular dictator and drug smuggler Manuel Noriega swiftly, but former CIA connections between President Bush and Noriega, as well as U.S. interests in maintaining control of the Canal Zone, prompted the United Nations and world public opinion to denounce the invasion as a power grab.

As the Soviet Union was ceasing to be a threat, the Middle East became a source of increased concern. In the wake of its eight-year war with Iran from 1980 to 1988, Iraq had accumulated a significant amount of foreign debt. At the same time, other Arab states had increased their oil production, forcing oil prices down and further hurting Iraq's economy. Iraq's leader, Saddam Hussein, approached these oil-producing states for assistance, particularly Saudi Arabia and neighboring Kuwait, which Iraq felt directly benefited from its war with Iran. When talks with these countries broke down, and Iraq found itself politically and economically isolated, Hussein ordered the invasion of oil-rich Kuwait in August 1990. Bush faced his first full-scale international crisis.

In response to the invasion, Bush and his foreign policy team forged an unprecedented international coalition of thirty-four countries, including many members of NATO (North Atlantic Treaty Organization) and the Middle Eastern countries of Saudi Arabia, Syria, and Egypt, to oppose Iraqi aggression. Bush hoped that this coalition would herald the beginning of a "new world order" in which the nations of the world would work together to deter belligerence. A deadline was set for Iraq to withdraw from Kuwait by January 15, or face serious consequences. Wary of not having sufficient domestic support for combat, Bush first deployed troops to the area to build up forces in the region and defend Saudi Arabia via Operation Desert Shield (**Figure 10.13**). On January 14, Bush succeeded in getting resolutions from Congress authorizing the use of military force against Iraq, and the U.S. then orchestrated an effective air campaign, followed by **Operation Desert Storm**, a one-hundred-hour land war involving over 500,000

U.S. troops and another 200,000 from twenty-seven other countries, which expelled Iraqi forces from Kuwait by the end of February.

Figure 10.13 George H. W. Bush greets U.S. troops stationed in Saudi Arabia on Thanksgiving Day in 1990. The first troops were deployed there in August 1990, as part of Operation Desert Shield, which was intended to build U.S. military strength in the area in preparation for an eventual military operation.

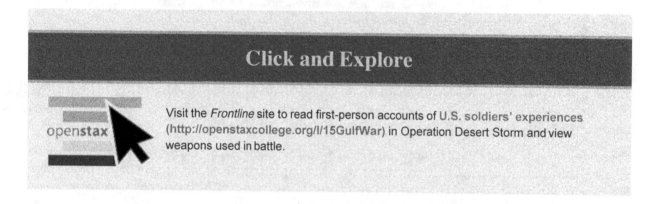

Click and Explore

Visit the *Frontline* site to read first-person accounts of U.S. soldiers' experiences (http://openstaxcollege.org/l/15GulfWar) in Operation Desert Storm and view weapons used in battle.

Some controversy arose among Bush's advisors regarding whether to end the war without removing Saddam Hussein from power, but General Colin Powell, the head of the Joint Chiefs of Staff, argued that to continue to attack a defeated army would be "un-American." Bush agreed and troops began moving out of the area in March 1991. Although Hussein was not removed from power, the war nevertheless suggested that the United States no longer suffered from "Vietnam Syndrome" and would deploy massive military resources if and when it thought necessary. In April 1991, United Nations (UN) Resolution 687 set the terms of the peace, with long-term implications. Its concluding paragraph authorizing the UN to take such steps as necessary to maintain the peace was later taken as the legal justification for the further use of force, as in 1996 and 1998, when Iraq was again bombed. It was also referenced in the lead-up to the second invasion of Iraq in 2003, when it appeared that Iraq was refusing to comply with other UN resolutions.

A CHANGING DOMESTIC LANDSCAPE

By nearly every measure, Operation Desert Storm was a resounding success. Through deft diplomatic efforts on the international stage, Bush had ensured that many around the world saw the action as legitimate. By making the goals of the military action both clear and limited, he also reassured an American public still skeptical of foreign entanglements. With the Soviet Union vanishing from the world stage, and the United States demonstrating the extent of its diplomatic influence and military potency with President Bush at the helm, his reelection seemed all but inevitable. Indeed, in March 1991, the president had an approval rating of 89 percent.

Despite Bush's successes internationally, the domestic situation at home was far more complicated. Unlike Reagan, Bush was not a natural culture warrior. Rather, he was a moderate, Connecticut-born Episcopalian, a pragmatic politician, and a life-long civil servant. He was not adept at catering to post-Reagan conservatives as his predecessor had been. By the same token, he appeared incapable of capitalizing on his history of moderation and pragmatism regarding women's rights and access to abortion. Together with a Democratic Senate, Bush broke new ground in civil rights with his support of the Americans with Disabilities Act, a far-reaching law that prohibited discrimination based on disability in public accommodations and by employers.

President Bush's weaknesses as a culture warrior were on full display during the controversy that erupted following his nomination of a new Supreme Court judge. In 1991, Justice Thurgood Marshall, the first African American ever to sit on the Supreme Court, opted to retire, thus opening a position on the court. Thinking he was doing the prudent thing by appealing to multiple interests, Bush nominated Clarence Thomas, another African American but also a strong social conservative. The decision to nominate Thomas, however, proved to be anything but prudent. During Thomas' confirmation hearings before the Senate Judiciary Committee, Anita Hill, a lawyer who had worked for Thomas when he was chairman of the Equal Employment Opportunity Commission (EEOC), came forward with allegations that he had sexually harassed her when he was her supervisor. Thomas denied the accusations and referred to the televised hearings as a "high tech lynching." He survived the controversy and was appointed to the Supreme Court by a narrow Senate vote of fifty-two to forty-eight. Hill, also African American, noted later in frustration: "I had a gender, he had a race." In the aftermath, however, sexual harassment of women in the workplace gained public attention, and harassment complaints made to the EEOC increased 50 percent by the fall of 1992. The controversy also reflected poorly on President Bush and may have hurt him with female voters in 1992.

10.4 Bill Clinton and the New Economy

By the end of this section, you will be able to:
- Explain political partisanship, antigovernment movements, and economic developments during the Clinton administration
- Discuss President Clinton's foreign policy
- Explain how George W. Bush won the election of 2000

By 1992, many had come to doubt that President George H. W. Bush could solve America's problems. He had alienated conservative Republicans by breaking his pledge not to raise taxes, and some faulted him for failing to remove Saddam Hussein from power during Operation Desert Storm. Furthermore, despite living much of his adult life in Texas, he could not overcome the stereotypes associated with his privileged New England and Ivy League background, which hurt him among working-class Reagan Democrats.

THE ROAD TO THE WHITE HOUSE

The contrast between George H. W. Bush and William Jefferson Clinton could not have been greater. Bill Clinton was a baby boomer born in 1946 in Hope, Arkansas. His biological father died in a car wreck three months before he was born. When he was a boy, his mother married Roger Clinton, an alcoholic who abused his family. However, despite a troubled home life, Clinton was an excellent student. He took an interest in politics from an early age. On a high school trip to Washington, DC, he met his political idol, President John F. Kennedy. As a student at Georgetown University, he supported both the civil rights and antiwar movements and ran for student council president (**Figure 10.14**).

Figure 10.14 During his 1967 campaign for student council president at Georgetown University, Bill Clinton told those who voted for him that he would invite them to the White House when he became president of the United States. He kept his promise.

In 1968, Clinton received a prestigious Rhodes scholarship to Oxford University. From Oxford he moved on to Yale, where he earned his law degree in 1973. He returned to Arkansas and became a professor at the University of Arkansas's law school. The following year, he tried his hand at state politics, running for Congress, and was narrowly defeated. In 1977, he became attorney general of Arkansas and was elected governor in 1978. Losing the office to his Republican opponent in 1980, he retook the governor's mansion in 1982 and remained governor of Arkansas until 1992, when he announced his candidacy for president.

During his campaign, Bill Clinton described himself as a New Democrat, a member of a faction of the Democratic Party that, like the Republicans, favored free trade and deregulation. He tried to appeal to the middle class by promising higher taxes on the rich and reform of the welfare system. Although Clinton garnered only 43 percent of the popular vote, he easily won in the Electoral College with 370 votes to President Bush's 188. Texas billionaire H. Ross Perot won 19 percent of the popular vote, the best showing by any third-party candidate since 1912. The Democrats took control of both houses of Congress.

"IT'S THE ECONOMY, STUPID"

Clinton took office towards the end of a recession. His administration's plans for fixing the economy included limiting spending and cutting the budget to reduce the nation's $60 billion deficit, keeping interest rates low to encourage private investment, and eliminating protectionist tariffs. Clinton also hoped to improve employment opportunities by allocating more money for education. In his first term, he expanded the Earned Income Tax Credit, which lowered the tax obligations of working families who were just above the poverty line. Addressing the budget deficit, the Democrats in Congress passed the Omnibus Budget Reconciliation Act of 1993 without a single Republican vote. The act raised taxes for the top 1.2 percent of the American people, lowered them for fifteen million low-income families, and offered tax breaks to 90 percent of small businesses.

Clinton also strongly supported ratification of the North American Free Trade Agreement (NAFTA), a treaty that eliminated tariffs and trade restrictions among the United States, Canada, and Mexico. The treaty had been negotiated by the Bush administration, and the leaders of all three nations had signed it in December 1992. However, because of strong opposition from American labor unions and some in Congress who feared the loss of jobs to Mexico, the treaty had not been ratified by the time Clinton took office. To allay the concerns of unions, he added an agreement to protect workers and also one to protect the environment. Congress ratified NAFTA late in 1993. The result was the creation of the world's largest common market in terms of population, including some 425 million people.

During Clinton's administration, the nation began to experience the longest period of economic expansion in its history, almost ten consecutive years. Year after year, job growth increased and the deficit shrank. Increased tax revenue and budget cuts turned the annual national budget deficit from close to $290 billion in 1992 to a record budget surplus of over $230 billion in 2000. Reduced government borrowing freed up capital for private-sector use, and lower interest rates in turn fueled more growth. During the Clinton years, more people owned homes than ever before in the country's history (67.7 percent). Inflation dipped to 2.3 percent and the unemployment rate declined, reaching a thirty-year low of 3.9 percent in 2000.

Much of the prosperity of the 1990s was related to technological change and the advent of new information systems. In 1994, the Clinton administration became the first to launch an official White House website and join the revolution of the electronically mediated world. By the 1990s, a new world of instantaneous global exposure was at the fingertips of billions worldwide.

AMERICANA

☼ *Hope and Anxiety in the Information Age*

While the roots of innovations like personal computers and the Internet go back to the 1960s and massive Department of Defense spending, it was in the 1980s and 90s that these technologies became part of everyday life. Like most technology-driven periods of transformation, the information age was greeted with a mixture of hope and anxiety upon its arrival.

In the late 1970s and early 1980s, computer manufacturers like Apple, Commodore, and Tandy began offering fully assembled personal computers. (Previously, personal computing had been accessible only to those adventurous enough to buy expensive kits that had to be assembled and programmed.) In short order, computers became a fairly common sight in businesses and upper-middle-class homes (Figure 10.15). Soon, computer owners, even young kids, were launching their own electronic bulletin board systems, small-scale networks that used modems and phone lines, and sharing information in ways not dreamed of just decades before. Computers, it seemed, held out the promise of a bright, new future for those who knew how to use them.

Figure 10.15 This ad for the Apple II appeared in *Byte* magazine in 1977.

Casting shadows over the bright dreams of a better tomorrow were fears that the development of computer technology would create a dystopian future in which technology became the instrument of society's undoing. Film audiences watched a teenaged Matthew Broderick hacking into a government computer and starting a nuclear war in *War Games*, Angelina Jolie being chased by a computer genius bent on world domination in *Hackers*, and Sandra Bullock watching helplessly as her life is turned inside out by conspirators who manipulate her virtual identity in *The Net*. Clearly, the idea of digital network connections as the root of our demise resonated in this period of rapid technological change.

DOMESTIC ISSUES

In addition to shifting the Democratic Party to the moderate center on economic issues, Clinton tried to break new ground on a number of domestic issues and make good on traditional Democratic commitments to the disadvantaged, minority groups, and women. At the same time, he faced the challenge of domestic terrorism when a federal building in Oklahoma City was bombed, killing 168 people and injuring hundreds more.

Healthcare Reform

An important and popular part of Clinton's domestic agenda was healthcare reform that would make universal healthcare a reality. When the plan was announced in September of the president's first year in office, pollsters and commentators both assumed it would sail through. Many were unhappy with the way the system worked in the United States, where the cost of health insurance seemed increasingly unaffordable for the middle class. Clinton appointed his wife, Hillary Clinton, a Yale Law School graduate and accomplished attorney, to head his Task Force on National Health Care Reform in 1993. The 1,342-page Health Security Act presented to Congress that year sought to offer universal coverage (**Figure 10.16**). All Americans were to be covered by a healthcare plan that could not reject them based on pre-existing medical conditions. Employers would be required to provide healthcare for their employees. Limits would be placed on the amount that people would have to pay for services; the poor would not have to pay at all.

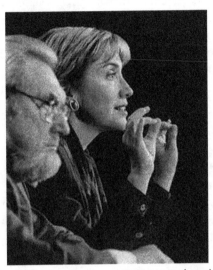

Figure 10.16　C. Everett Koop, who had served as surgeon general under Ronald Reagan and was a strong advocate of healthcare reform, helped First Lady Hillary Clinton promote the Health Security Act in the fall of 1993.

The outlook for the plan looked good in 1993; it had the support of a number of institutions like the American Medical Association and the Health Insurance Association of America. But in relatively short order, the political winds changed. As budget battles distracted the administration and the midterm elections of 1994 approached, Republicans began to recognize the strategic benefits of opposing reform. Soon they were mounting fierce opposition to the bill. Moderate conservatives dubbed the reform proposals "Hillarycare" and argued that the bill was an unwarranted expansion of the powers of the federal government that would interfere with people's ability to choose the healthcare provider they wanted. Those further to the right argued that healthcare reform was part of a larger and nefarious plot to control the public.

To rally Republican opposition to Clinton and the Democrats, Newt Gingrich and Richard "Dick" Armey, two of the leaders of the Republican minority in the House of Representatives, prepared a document entitled **Contract with America**, signed by all but two of the Republican representatives. It listed eight specific legislative reforms or initiatives the Republicans would enact if they gained a majority in Congress in the 1994 midterm elections.

Lacking support on both sides, the healthcare bill was never passed and died in Congress. The reform effort finally ended in September 1994. Dislike of the proposed healthcare plan on the part of conservatives and the bold strategy laid out in the Contract with America enabled the Republican Party to win seven Senate seats and fifty-two House seats in the November elections. The Republicans then used their power to push for conservative reforms. One such piece of legislation was the Personal Responsibility and Work Opportunity Reconciliation Act, signed into law in August 1996. The act set time limits on welfare benefits and required most recipients to begin working within two years of receiving assistance.

Don't Ask, Don't Tell

Although Clinton had campaigned as an economically conservative New Democrat, he was thought to be socially liberal and, just days after his victory in the 1992 election, he promised to end the fifty-year ban on gays and lesbians serving in the military. However, in January 1993, after taking the oath of office, Clinton amended his promise in order to appease conservatives. Instead of lifting the longstanding ban, the armed forces would adopt a policy of "don't ask, don't tell." Those on active duty would not be asked their sexual orientation and, if they were gay, they were not to discuss their sexuality openly or they would be dismissed from military service. This compromise satisfied neither conservatives seeking the exclusion of gays nor the gay community, which argued that homosexuals, like heterosexuals, should be able to live without fear of retribution because of their sexuality.

Clinton again proved himself willing to appease political conservatives when he signed into law the Defense of Marriage Act (DOMA) in September 1996, after both houses of Congress had passed it with such wide margins that a presidential veto could easily be overridden. DOMA defined marriage as a heterosexual union and denied federal benefits to same-sex couples. It also allowed states to refuse to recognize same-sex marriages granted by other states. When Clinton signed the bill, he was personally opposed to same-sex marriage. Nevertheless, he disliked DOMA and later called for its repeal. He also later changed his position on same-sex marriage. On other social issues, however, Clinton was more liberal. He appointed openly gay and lesbian men and women to important positions in government and denounced discrimination against people with AIDS. He supported the idea of the ERA and believed that women should receive pay equal to that of men doing the same work. He opposed the use of racial quotas in employment, but he declared affirmative action programs to be necessary.

As a result of his economic successes and his moderate social policies, Clinton defeated Senator Robert Dole in the 1996 presidential election. With 49 percent of the popular vote and 379 electoral votes, he became the first Democrat to win reelection to the presidency since Franklin Roosevelt. Clinton's victory was partly due to a significant **gender gap** between the parties, with women tending to favor Democratic candidates. In 1992, Clinton won 45 percent of women's votes compared to Bush's 38 percent, and in 1996, he received 54 percent of women's votes while Dole won 38 percent.

Domestic Terrorism

The fears of those who saw government as little more than a necessary evil appeared to be confirmed in the spring of 1993, when federal and state law enforcement authorities laid siege to the compound of a religious sect called the Branch Davidians near Waco, Texas. The group, which believed the end of world was approaching, was suspected of weapons violations and resisted search-and-arrest warrants with deadly force. A standoff developed that lasted nearly two months and was captured on television each day. A final assault on the compound was made on April 19, and seventy-six men, women, and children died in a fire probably set by members of the sect. Many others committed suicide or were killed by fellow sect members.

During the siege, many antigovernment and militia types came to satisfy their curiosity or show support for those inside. One was Timothy McVeigh, a former U.S. Army infantry soldier. McVeigh had served in Operation Desert Storm in Iraq, earning a bronze star, but he became disillusioned with the military and the government when he was deemed psychologically unfit for the Army Special Forces. He was convinced that the Branch Davidians were victims of government terrorism, and he and his coconspirator, Terry Nichols, determined to avenge them.

Two years later, on the anniversary of the day that the Waco compound burned to the ground, McVeigh parked a rented truck full of explosives in front of the Alfred P. Murrah Federal Building in Oklahoma City and blew it up (**Figure 10.17**). More than 600 people were injured in the attack and 168 died, including nineteen children at the daycare center inside. McVeigh hoped that his actions would spark a revolution against government control. He and Nichols were both arrested and tried, and McVeigh was executed on June 11, 2001, for the worst act of terrorism committed on American soil. Just a few months later, the terrorist attacks of September 11, 2001 broke that dark record.

(a)   (b)

Figure 10.17 The remains of automobiles stand in front of the bombed federal building in Oklahoma City in 1995 (a). More than three hundred nearby buildings were damaged by the blast, an attack perpetrated at least partly to avenge the Waco siege (b) exactly two years earlier.

CLINTON AND AMERICAN HEGEMONY

For decades, the contours of the Cold War had largely determined U.S. action abroad. Strategists saw each coup, revolution, and civil war as part of the larger struggle between the United States and the Soviet Union. But with the Soviet Union vanquished, the United States was suddenly free of this paradigm, and President Clinton could see international crises in the Middle East, the Balkans, and Africa on their own terms and deal with them accordingly. He envisioned a post-Cold War role in which the United States used its overwhelming military superiority and influence as global policing tools to preserve the peace. This foreign policy strategy had both success and failure.

One notable success was a level of peace in the Middle East. In September 1993, at the White House, Yitzhak Rabin, prime minister of Israel, and Yasser Arafat, chairman of the Palestine Liberation Organization, signed the Oslo Accords, granting some self-rule to Palestinians living in the Israeli-occupied territories of the Gaza Strip and the West Bank (**Figure 10.18**). A year later, the Clinton administration helped facilitate the second settlement and normalization of relations between Israel and Jordan.

Figure 10.18 Yitzhak Rabin (left) and Yasser Arafat (right), shown with Bill Clinton, signed the Oslo Accords at the White House on September 13, 1993. Rabin was killed two years later by an Israeli who opposed the treaty.

As a small measure of stability was brought to the Middle East, violence erupted in the Balkans. The Communist country of Yugoslavia consisted of six provinces: Serbia, Croatia, Bosnia and Herzegovina, Slovenia, Montenegro, and Macedonia. Each was occupied by a number of ethnic groups, some of which shared a history of hostile relations. In May 1980, the leader of Yugoslavia, Josip Broz Tito, died. Without him to hold the country together, ethnic tensions increased, and this, along with the breakdown of Communism elsewhere in Europe, led to the breakup of Yugoslavia. In 1991, Croatia, Slovenia, and Macedonia declared their independence. In 1992, Bosnia and Herzegovina did as well. Only Serbia and Montenegro remained united as the Serbian-dominated Federal Republic of Yugoslavia.

Almost immediately, ethnic tensions within Bosnia and Herzegovina escalated into war when Yugoslavian Serbs aided Bosnian Serbs who did not wish to live in an independent Bosnia and Herzegovina. These Bosnian Serbs proclaimed the existence of autonomous Serbian regions within the country and attacked Bosnian Muslims and Croats. During the conflict, the Serbs engaged in genocide, described by some as "ethnic cleansing." The brutal conflict also gave rise to the systematic rape of "enemy" women—generally Muslim women exploited by Serbian military or paramilitary forces. The International Criminal Tribunal of Yugoslavia estimated that between twelve thousand and fifty thousand women were raped during the war.

NATO eventually intervened in 1995, and Clinton agreed to U.S. participation in airstrikes against Bosnian Serbs. That year, the Dayton Accords peace settlement was signed in Dayton, Ohio. Four years later, the United States, acting with other NATO members, launched an air campaign against Serbian-dominated Yugoslavia to stop it from attacking ethnic Albanians in Kosovo. Although these attacks were not sanctioned by the UN and were criticized by Russia and China, Yugoslavia withdrew its forces from Kosovo in June 1999.

The use of force did not always bring positive results. For example, back in December 1992, George H. W. Bush had sent a contingent of U.S. soldiers to Somalia, initially to protect and distribute relief supplies to civilians as part of a UN mission. Without an effective Somali government, however, the warlords who controlled different regions often stole food, and their forces endangered the lives of UN workers. In 1993, the Clinton administration sent soldiers to capture one of the warlords, Mohammed Farah Aidid, in the city of Mogadishu. The resulting battle proved disastrous. A Black Hawk helicopter was shot down, and

U.S. Army Rangers and members of Delta Force spent hours battling their way through the streets; eighty-four soldiers were wounded and nineteen died. The United States withdrew, leaving Somalia to struggle with its own anarchy.

The sting of the Somalia failure probably contributed to Clinton's reluctance to send U.S. forces to end the 1994 genocide in Rwanda. In the days of brutal colonial rule, Belgian administrators had given control to Tutsi tribal chiefs, although Hutus constituted a majority of the population. Resentment over ethnic privileges, and the discrimination that began then and continued after independence in 1962, erupted into civil war in 1980. The Hutu majority began to slaughter the Tutsi minority and their Hutu supporters. In 1998, while visiting Rwanda, Clinton apologized for having done nothing to save the lives of the 800,000 massacred in one hundred days of genocidal slaughter.

IMPEACHMENT

Public attention was diverted from Clinton's foreign policing actions by a series of scandals that marked the last few years of his presidency. From the moment he entered national politics, his opponents had attempted to tie Clinton and his First Lady to a number of loosely defined improprieties, even accusing him of murdering his childhood friend and Deputy White House Counsel Vince Foster. One accusation the Clintons could not shake was of possible improper involvement in a failed real estate venture associated with the Whitewater Development Corporation in Arkansas in the 1970s and 1980s. Kenneth Starr, a former federal appeals court judge, was appointed to investigate the matter in August 1994.

While Starr was never able to prove any wrongdoing, he soon turned up other allegations and his investigative authority was expanded. In May 1994, Paula Jones, a former Arkansas state employee, filed a sexual harassment lawsuit against Bill Clinton. Starr's office began to investigate this case as well. When a federal court dismissed Jones's suit in 1998, her lawyers promptly appealed the decision and submitted a list of other alleged victims of Clinton's harassment. That list included the name of Monica Lewinsky, a young White House intern. Both Lewinsky and Clinton denied under oath that they had had a sexual relationship. The evidence, however, indicated otherwise, and Starr began to investigate the possibility that Clinton had committed perjury. Again, Clinton denied any relationship and even went on national television to assure the American people that he had never had sexual relations with Lewinsky.

However, after receiving a promise of immunity, Lewinsky turned over to Starr evidence of her affair with Clinton, and the president admitted he had indeed had inappropriate relations with her. He nevertheless denied that he had lied under oath. In September, Starr reported to the House of Representatives that he believed Clinton had committed perjury. Voting along partisan lines, the Republican-dominated House of Representatives sent articles of impeachment to the Senate, charging Clinton with lying under oath and obstructing justice. In February 1998, the Senate voted forty-five to fifty-five on the perjury charge and fifty-fifty on obstruction of justice (**Figure 10.19**). Although acquitted, Clinton did become the first president to be found in contempt of court. Nevertheless, although he lost his law license, he remained a popular president and left office at the end of his second term with an approval rating of 66 percent, the highest of any U.S. president.

Figure 10.19 Floor proceedings in the U.S. Senate during the 1998 impeachment trial of Bill Clinton, who was narrowly acquitted of both charges.

THE ELECTION OF 2000

Despite Clinton's high approval rating, his vice president and the 2000 Democratic nominee for president, Al Gore, was eager to distance himself from scandal. Unfortunately, he also alienated Clinton loyalists and lost some of the benefit of Clinton's genuine popularity. Gore's desire to emphasize his concern for morality led him to select Connecticut senator Joseph I. Lieberman as his running mate. Lieberman had been quick to denounce Clinton's relationship with Monica Lewinsky. Consumer advocate Ralph Nader ran as the candidate of the **Green Party**, a party devoted to environmental issues and grassroots activism, and Democrats feared that he would attract votes that Gore might otherwise win.

On the Republican side, where strategists promised to "restore honor and dignity" to the White House, voters were divided between George W. Bush, governor of Texas and eldest son of former president Bush, and John McCain, an Arizona senator and Vietnam War veteran. Bush had the robust support of both the Christian Right and the Republican leadership. His campaign amassed large donations that it used to defeat McCain, himself an outspoken critic of the influence of money in politics. The nomination secured, Bush selected Dick Cheney, part of the Nixon and Ford administrations and secretary of defense under George H. W. Bush, as his running mate.

One hundred million votes were cast in the 2000 election, and Gore topped Bush in the popular vote by 540,000 ballots, or 0.5 percent. The race was so close that news reports declared each candidate the winner at various times during the evening. It all came down to Florida, where early returns called the election in Bush's favor by a mere 527 of 5,825,000 votes. Whoever won Florida would get the state's twenty-five electoral votes and secure the presidency (**Figure 10.20**).

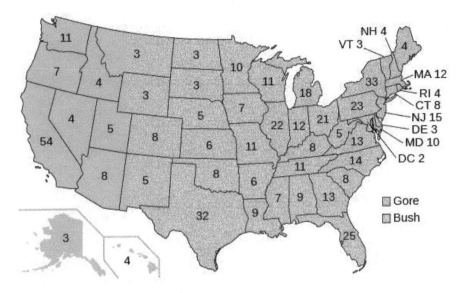

Figure 10.20 The map shows the results of the 2000 U.S. presidential election. While Bush won in the majority of states, Gore dominated in the more populous ones, winning the popular vote overall.

Because there seemed to be irregularities in four counties traditionally dominated by Democrats, especially in largely African American precincts, Gore called for a recount of the ballots by hand. Florida's secretary of state, Katherine Harris, set a deadline for the new vote tallies to be submitted, a deadline the counties could not meet. When the Democrats requested an extension, the Florida Supreme Court granted it, but Harris refused to accept the new tallies unless the counties could explain why they had not met the original deadline. When the explanations were submitted, they were rejected. Gore then asked the Florida Supreme Court for an injunction that would prevent Harris from declaring a winner until the recount was finished. On November 26, Harris declared Bush the winner in Florida. Gore protested that not all votes had been recounted by hand. When the Florida Supreme Court ordered the recount to continue, the Republicans appealed to the U.S. Supreme Court, which decided 5–4 to stop the recount. Bush received Florida's electoral votes and, with a total of 271 votes in the Electoral College to Gore's 266, became the forty-third president of the United States.

CHAPTER 11

The Challenges of the Twenty-First Century

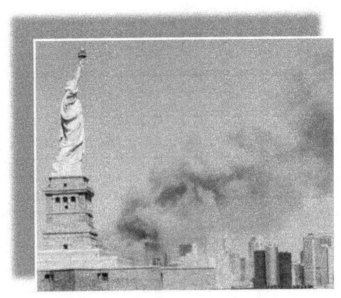

Figure 11.1 In 2001, almost three thousand people died as a result of the September 11 attacks, when members of the terrorist group al-Qaeda hijacked four planes as part of a coordinated attack on sites in New York City and Washington, DC.

Chapter Outline

Introduction

On the morning of September 11, 2001, hopes that the new century would leave behind the conflicts of the previous one were dashed when two hijacked airliners crashed into the twin towers of New York's World Trade Center. When the first plane struck the north tower, many assumed that the crash was a horrific accident. But then a second plane hit the south tower less than thirty minutes later. People on the street watched in horror, as some of those trapped in the burning buildings jumped to their deaths and the enormous towers collapsed into dust. In the photo above, the Statue of Liberty appears to look on helplessly, as thick plumes of smoke obscure the Lower Manhattan skyline (**Figure 11.1**). The events set in motion by the September 11 attacks would raise fundamental questions about the United States' role in the world, the extent to which privacy should be protected at the cost of security, the definition of exactly who is an American, and the cost of liberty.

11.1 The War on Terror

By the end of this section, you will be able to:
- Discuss how the United States responded to the terrorist attacks of September 11, 2001
- Explain why the United States went to war against Afghanistan and Iraq
- Describe the treatment of suspected terrorists by U.S. law enforcement agencies and the U.S. military

As a result of the narrow decision of the U.S. Supreme Court in *Bush v. Gore*, Republican George W. Bush was the declared the winner of the 2000 presidential election with a majority in the Electoral College of 271 votes to 266, although he received approximately 540,000 fewer popular votes nationally than his Democratic opponent, Bill Clinton's vice president, Al Gore. Bush had campaigned with a promise of "compassionate conservatism" at home and nonintervention abroad. These platform planks were designed to appeal to those who felt that the Clinton administration's initiatives in the Balkans and Africa had unnecessarily entangled the United States in the conflicts of foreign nations. Bush's 2001 education reform act, dubbed No Child Left Behind, had strong bipartisan support and reflected his domestic interests. But before the president could sign the bill into law, the world changed when terrorists hijacked four American airliners to use them in the deadliest attack on the United States since the Japanese bombing of Pearl Harbor in December 1941. Bush's domestic agenda quickly took a backseat, as the president swiftly changed course from nonintervention in foreign affairs to a "war on terror."

9/11

Shortly after takeoff on the morning of September 11, 2001, teams of hijackers from the Islamist terrorist group **al-Qaeda** seized control of four American airliners. Two of the airplanes were flown into the twin towers of the World Trade Center in Lower Manhattan. Morning news programs that were filming the moments after the first impact, then assumed to be an accident, captured and aired live footage of the

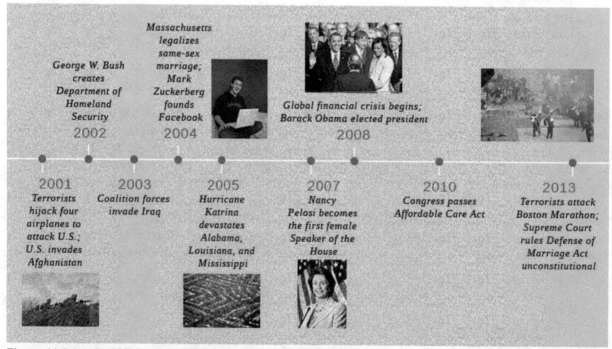

Figure 11.2 (credit "2004": modification of work by Elaine and Priscilla Chan; credit "2013": modification of work by Aaron Tang; credit "2001": modification of work by "DVIDSHUB"/Flickr)

second plane, as it barreled into the other tower in a flash of fire and smoke. Less than two hours later, the heat from the crash and the explosion of jet fuel caused the upper floors of both buildings to collapse onto the lower floors, reducing both towers to smoldering rubble. The passengers and crew on both planes, as well as 2,606 people in the two buildings, all died, including 343 New York City firefighters who rushed in to save victims shortly before the towers collapsed.

The third hijacked plane was flown into the Pentagon building in northern Virginia, just outside Washington, DC, killing everyone on board and 125 people on the ground. The fourth plane, also heading towards Washington, crashed in a field near Shanksville, Pennsylvania, when passengers, aware of the other attacks, attempted to storm the cockpit and disarm the hijackers. Everyone on board was killed (**Figure 11.3**).

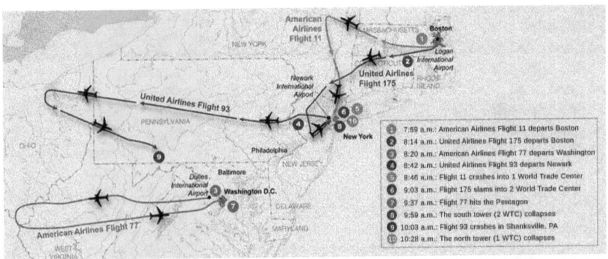

Figure 11.3 Three of the four airliners hijacked on September 11, 2001, reached their targets. United 93, presumably on its way to destroy either the Capitol or the White House, was brought down in a field after a struggle between the passengers and the hijackers.

That evening, President Bush promised the nation that those responsible for the attacks would be brought to justice. Three days later, Congress issued a joint resolution authorizing the president to use all means necessary against the individuals, organizations, or nations involved in the attacks. On September 20, in an address to a joint session of Congress, Bush declared war on terrorism, blamed al-Qaeda leader Osama bin Laden for the attacks, and demanded that the radical Islamic fundamentalists who ruled Afghanistan, the **Taliban**, turn bin Laden over or face attack by the United States. This speech encapsulated what became known as the **Bush Doctrine**, the belief that the United States has the right to protect itself from terrorist acts by engaging in pre-emptive wars or ousting hostile governments in favor of friendly, preferably democratic, regimes.

World leaders and millions of their citizens expressed support for the United States and condemned the deadly attacks. Russian president Vladimir Putin characterized them as a bold challenge to humanity itself. German chancellor Gerhard Schroder said the events of that day were "not only attacks on the people in the United States, our friends in America, but also against the entire civilized world, against our own freedom, against our own values, values which we share with the American people." Yasser Arafat, chairman of the Palestinian Liberation Organization and a veteran of several bloody struggles against Israel, was dumbfounded by the news and announced to reporters in Gaza, "We completely condemn this very dangerous attack, and I convey my condolences to the American people, to the American president and to the American administration."

In May 2014, a Museum dedicated to the memory of the victims was completed. Watch this video (http://openstaxcollege.org/l/15CBSstory) and learn more about the victims and how the country seeks to remember them.

GOING TO WAR IN AFGHANISTAN

When it became clear that the mastermind behind the attack was Osama bin Laden, a wealthy Saudi Arabian national who ran his terror network from Afghanistan, the full attention of the United States turned towards Central Asia and the Taliban. Bin Laden had deep roots in Afghanistan. Like many others from around the Islamic world, he had come to the country to oust the Soviet army, which invaded Afghanistan in 1979. Ironically, both bin Laden and the Taliban received material support from the United States at that time. By the late 1980s, the Soviets and the Americans had both left, although bin Laden, by that time the leader of his own terrorist organization, al-Qaeda, remained.

The Taliban refused to turn bin Laden over, and the United States began a bombing campaign in October, allying with the Afghan Northern Alliance, a coalition of tribal leaders opposed to the Taliban. U.S. air support was soon augmented by ground troops (**Figure 11.4**). By November 2001, the Taliban had been ousted from power in Afghanistan's capital of Kabul, but bin Laden and his followers had already escaped across the Afghan border to mountain sanctuaries in northern Pakistan.

Figure 11.4 Marines fight against Taliban forces in Helmand Province, Afghanistan. Helmand was a center of Taliban strength. (credit: "DVIDSHUB"/Flickr)

IRAQ

At the same time that the U.S. military was taking control of Afghanistan, the Bush administration was looking to a new and larger war with the country of Iraq. Relations between the United States and Iraq had been strained ever since the Gulf War a decade earlier. Economic sanctions imposed on Iraq by the United Nations, and American attempts to foster internal revolts against President Saddam Hussein's government, had further tainted the relationship. A faction within the Bush administration, sometimes labeled neoconservatives, believed Iraq's recalcitrance in the face of overwhelming U.S. military superiority represented a dangerous symbol to terrorist groups around the world, recently emboldened by the dramatic success of the al-Qaeda attacks in the United States. Powerful members of this faction, including Vice President Dick Cheney and Secretary of Defense Donald Rumsfeld, believed the time to strike Iraq and solve this festering problem was right then, in the wake of 9/11. Others, like Secretary of State Colin Powell, a highly respected veteran of the Vietnam War and former chair of the Joint Chiefs of Staff, were more cautious about initiating combat.

The more militant side won, and the argument for war was gradually laid out for the American people. The immediate impetus to the invasion, it argued, was the fear that Hussein was stockpiling weapons of mass destruction (**WMDs**): nuclear, chemical, or biological weapons capable of wreaking great havoc. Hussein had in fact used WMDs against Iranian forces during his war with Iran in the 1980s, and against the Kurds in northern Iraq in 1988—a time when the United States actively supported the Iraqi dictator. Following the Gulf War, inspectors from the United Nations Special Commission and International Atomic Energy Agency had in fact located and destroyed stockpiles of Iraqi weapons. Those arguing for a new Iraqi invasion insisted, however, that weapons still existed. President Bush himself told the nation in October 2002 that the United States was "facing clear evidence of peril, we cannot wait for the final proof—the smoking gun—that could come in the form of a mushroom cloud." The head of the United Nations Monitoring, Verification and Inspection Commission, Hanx Blix, dismissed these claims. Blix argued that while Saddam Hussein was not being entirely forthright, he did not appear to be in possession of WMDs. Despite Blix's findings and his own earlier misgivings, Powell argued in 2003 before the United Nations General Assembly that Hussein had violated UN resolutions. Much of his evidence relied on secret information provided by an informant that was later proven to be false. On March 17, 2003, the United States cut off all relations with Iraq. Two days later, in a coalition with Great Britain, Australia, and Poland, the United States began "Operation Iraqi Freedom" with an invasion of Iraq.

Other arguments supporting the invasion noted the ease with which the operation could be accomplished. In February 2002, some in the Department of Defense were suggesting the war would be "a cakewalk." In November, referencing the short and successful Gulf War of 1990–1991, Secretary of Defense Rumsfeld told the American people it was absurd, as some were claiming, that the conflict would degenerate into a long, drawn-out quagmire. "Five days or five weeks or five months, but it certainly isn't going to last any longer than that," he insisted. "It won't be a World War III." And, just days before the start of combat operations in 2003, Vice President Cheney announced that U.S. forces would likely "be greeted as liberators," and the war would be over in "weeks rather than months."

Early in the conflict, these predictions seemed to be coming true. The march into Bagdad went fairly smoothly. Soon Americans back home were watching on television as U.S. soldiers and the Iraqi people worked together to topple statues of the deposed leader Hussein around the capital. The reality, however, was far more complex. While American deaths had been few, thousands of Iraqis had died, and the seeds of internal strife and resentment against the United States had been sown. The United States was not prepared for a long period of occupation; it was also not prepared for the inevitable problems of law and order, or for the violent sectarian conflicts that emerged. Thus, even though Bush proclaimed a U.S. victory in May 2003, on the deck of the USS *Abraham Lincoln* with the banner "Mission Accomplished" prominently displayed behind him, the celebration proved premature by more than seven years (**Figure 11.5**).

Figure 11.5 President Bush gives the victory symbol on the aircraft carrier USS *Abraham Lincoln* in May 2003, after American troops had completed the capture of Iraq's capitol Baghdad. Yet, by the time the United States finally withdrew its forces from Iraq in 2011, nearly five thousand U.S. soldiers had died.

MY STORY

⊛ *Lt. General James Conway on the Invasion of Baghdad*

Lt. General James Conway, who commanded the First Marine Expeditionary Force in Iraq, answers a reporter's questions about civilian casualties during the 2003 invasion of Baghdad.

"As a civilian in those early days, one definitely had the sense that the high command had expected something to happen which didn't. Was that a correct perception?"

—We were told by our intelligence folks that the enemy is carrying civilian clothes in their packs because, as soon as the shooting starts, they're going put on their civilian clothes and they're going go home. Well, they put on their civilian clothes, but not to go home. They put on civilian clothes to blend with the civilians and shoot back at us. . . .

"There's been some criticism of the behavior of the Marines at the Diyala bridge [across the Tigris River into Baghdad] in terms of civilian casualties."

—Well, after the Third Battalion, Fourth Marines crossed, the resistance was not all gone. . . . They had just fought to take a bridge. They were being counterattacked by enemy forces. Some of the civilian vehicles that wound up with the bullet holes in them contained enemy fighters in uniform with weapons, some of them did not. Again, we're terribly sorry about the loss of any civilian life where civilians are killed in a battlefield setting. I will guarantee you, it was not the intent of those Marines to kill civilians. [The civilian casualties happened because the Marines] felt threatened, [and] they were having a tough time distinguishing from an enemy that [is violating] the laws of land warfare by going to civilian clothes, putting his own people at risk. All of those things, I think, [had an] impact [on the behavior of the Marines], and in the end it's very unfortunate that civilians died.

Who in your opinion bears primary responsibility for the deaths of Iraqi civilians?

DOMESTIC SECURITY

The attacks of September 11 awakened many to the reality that the end of the Cold War did not mean an end to foreign violent threats. Some Americans grew wary of alleged possible enemies in their midst and hate crimes against Muslim Americans—and those thought to be Muslims—surged in the aftermath.

Fearing that terrorists might strike within the nation's borders again, and aware of the chronic lack of cooperation among different federal law enforcement agencies, Bush created the Office of Homeland Security in October 2001. The next year, Congress passed the Homeland Security Act, creating the Department of Homeland Security, which centralized control over a number of different government functions in order to better control threats at home (**Figure 11.6**). The Bush administration also pushed the USA Patriot Act through Congress, which enabled law enforcement agencies to monitor citizens' e-mails and phone conversations without a warrant.

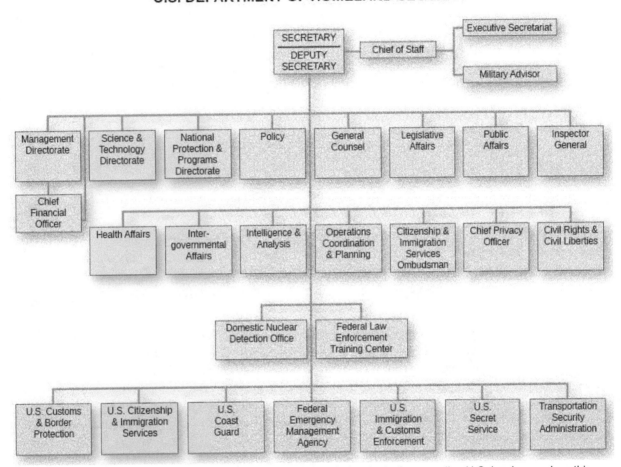

U.S. DEPARTMENT OF HOMELAND SECURITY

Figure 11.6 The Department of Homeland Security has many duties, including guarding U.S. borders and, as this organizational chart shows, wielding control over the Coast Guard, the Secret Service, U.S. Customs, and a multitude of other law enforcement agencies.

The Bush administration was fiercely committed to rooting out threats to the United States wherever they originated, and in the weeks after September 11, the Central Intelligence Agency (CIA) scoured the globe, sweeping up thousands of young Muslim men. Because U.S. law prohibits the use of torture, the CIA transferred some of these prisoners to other nations—a practice known as rendition or extraordinary rendition—where the local authorities can use methods of interrogation not allowed in the United States.

While the CIA operates overseas, the Federal Bureau of Investigation (FBI) is the chief federal law enforcement agency within U.S. national borders. Its activities are limited by, among other things, the Fourth Amendment, which protects citizens against unreasonable searches and seizures. Beginning in 2002, however, the Bush administration implemented a wide-ranging program of warrantless domestic wiretapping, known as the Terrorist Surveillance Program, by the National Security Agency (NSA). The shaky constitutional basis for this program was ultimately revealed in August 2006, when a federal judge in Detroit ordered the program ended immediately.

The use of unconstitutional wire taps to prosecute the war on terrorism was only one way the new threat challenged authorities in the United States. Another problem was deciding what to do with foreign terrorists captured on the battlefields in Afghanistan and Iraq. In traditional conflicts, where both sides are uniformed combatants, the rules of engagement and the treatment of prisoners of war are clear. But in the new war on terror, extracting intelligence about upcoming attacks became a top priority that superseded human rights and constitutional concerns. For that purpose, the United States began transporting men suspected of being members of al-Qaeda to the U.S. naval base at Guantanamo Bay, Cuba, for questioning. The Bush administration labeled the detainees "unlawful combatants," in an effort to avoid affording them the rights guaranteed to prisoners of war, such as protection from torture, by international treaties such as the Geneva Conventions. Furthermore, the Justice Department argued that the prisoners were unable to sue for their rights in U.S. courts on the grounds that the constitution did not apply to U.S. territories. It was only in 2006 that the Supreme Court ruled in *Hamdan v. Rumsfeld* that the military tribunals that tried Guantanamo prisoners violated both U.S. federal law and the Geneva Conventions.

11.2 The Domestic Mission

By the end of this section, you will be able to:
- Discuss the Bush administration's economic theories and tax policies, and their effects on the American economy
- Explain how the federal government attempted to improve the American public education system
- Describe the federal government's response to Hurricane Katrina
- Identify the causes of the Great Recession of 2008 and its effect on the average citizen

By the time George W. Bush became president, the concept of supply-side economics had become an article of faith within the Republican Party. The oft-repeated argument was that tax cuts for the wealthy would allow them to invest more and create jobs for everyone else. This belief in the self-regulatory powers of competition also served as the foundation of Bush's education reform. But by the end of 2008, however, Americans' faith in the dynamics of the free market had been badly shaken. The failure of the homeland security apparatus during Hurricane Katrina and the ongoing challenge of the Iraq War compounded the effects of the bleak economic situation.

OPENING AND CLOSING THE GAP

The Republican Party platform for the 2000 election offered the American people an opportunity to once again test the rosy expectations of supply-side economics. In 2001, Bush and the Republicans pushed through a $1.35 trillion tax cut by lowering tax rates across the board but reserving the largest cuts for those in the highest tax brackets. This was in the face of calls by Republicans for a balanced budget, which Bush insisted would happen when the so-called job creators expanded the economy by using their increased income to invest in business.

The cuts were controversial; the rich were getting richer while the middle and lower classes bore a proportionally larger share of the nation's tax burden. Between 1966 and 2001, one-half of the nation's income gained from increased productivity went to the top 0.01 percent of earners. By 2005, dramatic examples of income inequity were increasing; the chief executive of Wal-Mart earned $15 million that year, roughly 950 times what the company's average associate made. The head of the construction company K. B. Homes made $150 million, or four thousand times what the average construction worker earned that same year. Even as productivity climbed, workers' incomes stagnated; with a larger share of the   wealth, the very rich further solidified their influence on public policy. Left with a smaller share of the economic pie, average workers had fewer resources to improve their lives or contribute to the nation's prosperity by, for example, educating themselves and their children.

Another gap that had been widening for years was the education gap. Some education researchers had argued that American students were being left behind. In 1983, a commission established by Ronald Reagan had published a sobering assessment of the American educational system entitled *A Nation at Risk*. The report argued that American students were more poorly educated than their peers in other countries, especially in areas such as math and science, and were thus unprepared to compete in the global marketplace. Furthermore, test scores revealed serious educational achievement gaps between white students and students of color. Touting himself as the "education president," Bush sought to introduce reforms that would close these gaps.

His administration offered two potential solutions to these problems. First, it sought to hold schools accountable for raising standards and enabling students to meet them. The No Child Left Behind Act, signed into law in January 2002, erected a system of testing to measure and ultimately improve student performance in reading and math at all schools that received federal funds (**Figure 11.7**). Schools whose students performed poorly on the tests would be labeled "in need of improvement." If poor performance continued, schools could face changes in curricula and teachers, or even the prospect of closure.

Figure 11.7 President Bush signed the No Child Left Behind Act into law in January 2002. The act requires school systems to set high standards for students, place "highly qualified" teachers in the classroom, and give military recruiters contact information for students.

The second proposed solution was to give students the opportunity to attend schools with better performance records. Some of these might be **charter schools**, institutions funded by local tax monies in much the same way as public schools, but able to accept private donations and exempt from some of the rules public schools must follow. During the administration of George H. W. Bush, the development of charter schools had gathered momentum, and the American Federation of Teachers welcomed them as places to employ innovative teaching methods or offer specialized instruction in particular subjects. President George W. Bush now encouraged states to grant educational funding vouchers to parents, who could use them to pay for a private education for their children if they chose. These vouchers were funded by tax revenue that would otherwise have gone to public schools.

THE 2004 ELECTION AND BUSH'S SECOND TERM

In the wake of the 9/11 attacks, Americans had rallied around their president in a gesture of patriotic loyalty, giving Bush approval ratings of 90 percent. Even following the first few months of the Iraq war, his approval rating remained historically high at approximately 70 percent. But as the 2004 election approached, opposition to the war in Iraq began to grow. While Bush could boast of a number of achievements at home and abroad during his first term, the narrow victory he achieved in 2000 augured poorly for his chances for reelection in 2004 and a successful second term.

Reelection

As the 2004 campaign ramped up, the president was persistently dogged by rising criticism of the violence of the Iraq war and the fact that his administration's claims of WMDs had been greatly overstated. In the end, no such weapons were ever found. These criticisms were amplified by growing international concern over the treatment of prisoners at the Guantanamo Bay detention camp and widespread disgust over the torture conducted by U.S. troops at the prison in Abu Ghraib, Iraq, which surfaced only months before the election (Figure 11.8).

(a) (b)

Figure 11.8 The first twenty captives were processed at the Guantanamo Bay detention camp on January 11, 2002 (a). From late 2003 to early 2004, prisoners held in Abu Ghraib, Iraq, were tortured and humiliated in a variety of ways (b). U.S. soldiers jumped on and beat them, led them on leashes, made them pose naked, and urinated on them. The release of photographs of the abuse raised an outcry around the world and greatly diminished the already flagging support for American intervention in Iraq.

In March 2004, an ambush by Iraqi insurgents of a convoy of private military contractors from Blackwater USA in the town of Fallujah west of Baghdad, and the subsequent torture and mutilation of the four captured mercenaries, shocked the American public. But the event also highlighted the growing insurgency against U.S. occupation, the escalating sectarian conflict between the newly empowered Shia Muslims and the minority of the formerly ruling Sunni, and the escalating costs of a war involving a large number of private contractors that, by conservative estimates, approached $1.7 trillion by 2013. Just as importantly, the American campaign in Iraq had diverted resources from the war against al-Qaeda in Afghanistan, where U.S troops were no closer to capturing Osama bin Laden, the mastermind behind the 9/11 attacks.

With two hot wars overseas, one of which appeared to be spiraling out of control, the Democrats nominated a decorated Vietnam War veteran, Massachusetts senator John Kerry (Figure 11.9), to challenge Bush for the presidency. As someone with combat experience, three Purple Hearts, and a foreign policy background, Kerry seemed like the right challenger in a time of war. But his record of support for the invasion of Iraq made his criticism of the incumbent less compelling and earned him the byname "Waffler" from Republicans. The Bush campaign also sought to characterize Kerry as an elitist out of touch with regular Americans—Kerry had studied overseas, spoke fluent French, and married a wealthy foreign-born heiress. Republican supporters also unleashed an attack on Kerry's Vietnam War record, falsely claiming he had lied about his experience and fraudulently received his medals. Kerry's reluctance to embrace his past leadership of Vietnam Veterans Against the War weakened the enthusiasm of antiwar Americans while opening him up to criticisms from veterans groups. This combination compromised the impact of his challenge to the incumbent in a time of war.

Figure 11.9 John Kerry served in the U.S. Navy during the Vietnam War and represented Massachusetts in the U.S. Senate from 1985 to 2013. Here he greets sailors from the USS *Sampson*. Kerry was sworn in as President Obama's Secretary of State in 2013.

Urged by the Republican Party to "stay the course" with Bush, voters listened. Bush won another narrow victory, and the Republican Party did well overall, picking up four seats in the Senate and increasing its majority there to fifty-five. In the House, the Republican Party gained three seats, adding to its majority there as well. Across the nation, most governorships also went to Republicans, and Republicans dominated many state legislatures.

Despite a narrow win, the president made a bold declaration in his first news conference following the election. "I earned capital in this campaign, political capital, and now I intend to spend it." The policies on which he chose to spend this political capital included the partial privatization of Social Security and new limits on court-awarded damages in medical malpractice lawsuits. In foreign affairs, Bush promised that the United States would work towards "ending tyranny in the world." But at home and abroad, the president achieved few of his second-term goals. Instead, his second term in office became associated with the persistent challenge of pacifying Iraq, the failure of the homeland security apparatus during Hurricane Katrina, and the most severe economic crisis since the Great Depression.

A Failed Domestic Agenda

The Bush administration had planned a series of free-market reforms, but corruption, scandals, and Democrats in Congress made these goals hard to accomplish. Plans to convert Social Security into a private-market mechanism relied on the claim that demographic trends would eventually make the system unaffordable for the shrinking number of young workers, but critics countered that this was easily fixed. Privatization, on the other hand, threatened to derail the mission of the New Deal welfare agency and turn it into a fee generator for stock brokers and Wall Street financiers. Similarly unpopular was the attempt to abolish the estate tax. Labeled the "death tax" by its critics, its abolishment would have benefitted only the wealthiest 1 percent. As a result of the 2003 tax cuts, the growing federal deficit did not help make the case for Republicans.

The nation faced another policy crisis when the Republican-dominated House of Representatives approved a bill making the undocumented status of millions of immigrants a felony and criminalizing the act of employing or knowingly aiding illegal immigrants. In response, millions of illegal and legal immigrants, along with other critics of the bill, took to the streets in protest. What they saw as the civil rights challenge of their generation, conservatives read as a dangerous challenge to law and national security. Congress eventually agreed on a massive build-up of the U.S. Border Patrol and the construction of a seven-hundred-mile-long fence along the border with Mexico, but the deep divisions over immigration and the status of up to twelve million undocumented immigrants remained   unresolved.

Hurricane Katrina

One event highlighted the nation's economic inequality and racial divisions, as well as th e Bush administration's difficulty in addressing them effectively. On August 29, 2005, Hurricane Katrina came ashore and devastated coastal stretches of Alabama, Mississippi, and Louisiana. The city of New Orleans, no stranger to hurricanes and floods, suffered heavy damage when the levees, embankments designed to protect against flooding, failed during the storm surge, as the Army Corps of Engineers had warned they might. The flooding killed some fifteen hundred people and so overwhelmed parts of the city that tens of thousands more were trapped and unable to evacuate (**Figure 11.10**). Thousands who were elderly, ill, or too poor to own a car followed the mayor's directions and sought refuge at the Superdome, which lacked adequate food, water, and sanitation. Public services collapsed under the weight of the crisis.

Figure 11.10 Large portions of the city of New Orleans were flooded during Hurricane Katrina. Although most of the city's population managed to evacuate in time, its poorest residents were left behind.

Click and Explore

See pictures of the aftermath of Hurricane Katrina (http://openstaxcollege.org/l/15Katrina) and read and view accounts of survivors of the disaster.

Although the U.S. Coast Guard managed to rescue more than thirty-five thousand people from the stricken city, the response by other federal bodies was less effective. The Federal Emergency Management Agency (FEMA), an agency charged with assisting state and local governments in times of natural disaster, proved inept at coordinating different agencies and utilizing the rescue infrastructure at its disposal. Critics argued that FEMA was to blame and that its director, Michael D. Brown, a Bush friend and appointee with no background in emergency management, was an example of cronyism at its worst. The failures of FEMA were particularly harmful for an administration that had made "homeland security" its top priority. Supporters of the president, however, argued that the scale of the disaster was such that no amount of preparedness or competence could have allowed federal agencies to cope.

While there was plenty of blame to go around—at the city, state, and national levels—FEMA and the Bush administration got the lion's share. Even when the president attempted to demonstrate his concern with a personal appearance, the tactic largely backfired. Photographs of him looking down on a flooded New

Orleans from the comfort of Air Force One only reinforced the impression of a president detached from the problems of everyday people. Despite his attempts to give an uplifting speech from Jackson Square, he was unable to shake this characterization, and it underscored the disappointments of his second term. On the eve of the 2006 midterm elections, President Bush's popularity had reached a new low, as a result of the war in Iraq and Hurricane Katrina, and a growing number of Americans feared that his party's economic policy benefitted the wealthy first and foremost. Young voters, non-white Americans, and women favored the Democratic ticket by large margins. The elections handed Democrats control of the Senate and House for the first time since 1994, and, in January 2007, California representative Nancy Pelosi became the first female Speaker of the House in the nation's history.

THE GREAT RECESSION

For most Americans, the millennium had started with economic woes. In March 2001, the U.S. stock market had taken a sharp drop, and the ensuing recession triggered the loss of millions of jobs over the next two years. In response, the Federal Reserve Board cut interest rates to historic lows to encourage consumer spending. By 2002, the economy seemed to be stabilizing somewhat, but few of the manufacturing jobs lost were restored to the national economy. Instead, the "outsourcing" of jobs to China and India became an increasing concern, along with a surge in corporate scandals. After years of reaping tremendous profits in the deregulated energy markets, Houston-based Enron imploded in 2003 over allegations of massive accounting fraud. Its top executives, Ken Lay and Jeff Skilling, received long prison sentences, but their activities were illustrative of a larger trend in the nation's corporate culture that embroiled reputable companies like JP Morgan Chase and the accounting firm Arthur Anderson. In 2003, Bernard Ebbers, the CEO of communications giant WorldCom, was discovered to have inflated his company's assets by as much as $11 billion, making it the largest accounting scandal in the nation's history. Only five years later, however, Bernard Madoff's Ponzi scheme would reveal even deeper cracks in the nation's financial economy.

Banks Gone Wild

Notwithstanding economic growth in the 1990s and steadily increasing productivity, wages had remained largely flat relative to inflation since the end of the 1970s; despite the mild recovery, they remained so. To compensate, many consumers were buying on credit, and with interest rates low, financial institutions were eager to oblige them. By 2008, credit card debt had risen to over $1 trillion. More importantly, banks were making high-risk, high-interest mortgage loans called **subprime mortgages** to consumers who often misunderstood their complex terms and lacked the ability to make the required payments.

These subprime loans had a devastating impact on the larger economy. In the past, a prospective home buyer went to a local bank for a mortgage loan. Because the bank expected to make a profit in the form of interest charged on the loan, it carefully vetted buyers for their ability to repay. Changes in finance and banking laws in the 1990s and early 2000s, however, allowed lending institutions to securitize their mortgage loans and sell them as bonds, thus separating the financial interests of the lender from the ability of the borrower to repay, and making highly risky loans more attractive to lenders. In other words, banks could afford to make bad loans, because they could sell them and not suffer the financial consequences when borrowers failed to repay.

Once they had purchased the loans, larger investment banks bundled them into huge packages known as collateralized debt obligations (CDOs) and sold them to investors around the world. Even though CDOs consisted of subprime mortgages, credit card debt, and other risky investments, credit ratings agencies had a financial incentive to rate them as very safe. Making matters worse, financial institutions created instruments called **credit default swaps**, which were essentially a form of insurance on investments. If the investment lost money, the investors would be compensated. This system, sometimes referred to as the securitization food chain, greatly swelled the housing loan market, especially the market for subprime mortgages, because these loans carried higher interest rates. The result was a housing bubble, in which the value of homes rose year after year based on the ease with which people now could buy them.

Banks Gone Broke

When the real estate market stalled after reaching a peak in 2007, the house of cards built by the country's largest financial institutions came tumbling down. People began to default on their loans, and more than one hundred mortgage lenders went out of business. American International Group (AIG), a multinational insurance company that had insured many of the investments, faced collapse. Other large financial institutions, which had once been prevented by federal regulations from engaging in risky investment practices, found themselves in danger, as they either were besieged by demands for payment or found their demands on their own insurers unmet. The prestigious investment firm Lehman Brothers was completely wiped out in September 2008. Some endangered companies, like Wall Street giant Merrill Lynch, sold themselves to other financial institutions to survive. A financial panic ensued that revealed other fraudulent schemes built on CDOs. The biggest among them was a pyramid scheme organized by the New York financier Bernard Madoff, who had defrauded his investors by at least $18 billion.

Realizing that the failure of major financial institutions could result in the collapse of the entire U.S. economy, the chairman of the Federal Reserve, Ben Bernanke, authorized a bailout of the Wall Street firm Bear Stearns, although months later, the financial services firm Lehman Brothers was allowed to file for the largest bankruptcy in the nation's history. Members of Congress met with Bernanke and Secretary of the Treasury Henry Paulson in September 2008, to find a way to head off the crisis. They agreed to use $700 billion in federal funds to bail out the troubled institutions, and Congress subsequently passed the Emergency Economic Stabilization Act, creating the Troubled Asset Relief Program (TARP). One important element of this program was aid to the auto industry: The Bush administration responded to their appeal with an emergency loan of $17.4 billion—to be executed by his successor after the November election—to stave off the industry's collapse.

The actions of the Federal Reserve, Congress, and the president prevented the complete disintegration of the nation's financial sector and warded off a scenario like that of the Great Depression. However, the bailouts could not prevent a severe recession in the U.S. and world economy. As people lost faith in the economy, stock prices fell by 45 percent. Unable to receive credit from now-wary banks, smaller businesses found that they could not pay suppliers or employees. With houses at record prices and growing economic uncertainty, people stopped buying new homes. As the value of homes decreased, owners were unable to borrow against them to pay off other obligations, such as credit card debt or car loans. More importantly, millions of homeowners who had expected to sell their houses at a profit and pay off their adjustable-rate mortgages were now stuck in houses with values shrinking below their purchasing price and forced to make mortgage payments they could no longer afford.

Without access to credit, consumer spending declined. Some European nations had suffered similar speculation bubbles in housing, but all had bought into the mortgage securities market and suffered the losses of assets, jobs, and demand as a result. International trade slowed, hurting many American businesses. As the **Great Recession** of 2008 deepened, the situation of ordinary citizens became worse. During the last four months of 2008, one million American workers lost their jobs, and during 2009, another three million found themselves out of work. Under such circumstances, many resented the expensive federal bailout of banks and investment firms. It seemed as if the wealthiest were being rescued by the taxpayer from the consequences of their imprudent and even corrupt practices.

11.3 New Century, Old Disputes

By the end of this section, you will be able to:
- Describe the efforts to reduce the influence of immigrants on American culture
- Describe the evolution of twenty-first-century American attitudes towards same-sex marriage
- Explain the clash over climate change

As the United States entered the twenty-first century, old disputes continued to rear their heads. Some revolved around what it meant to be American and the rights to full citizenship. Others arose from religious conservatism and the influence of the Religious Right on American culture and society. Debates over gay and lesbian rights continued, and arguments over abortion became more complex and contentious, as science and technology advanced. The clash between faith and science also influenced attitudes about how the government should respond to climate change, with religious conservatives finding allies among political conservatives who favored business over potentially expensive measures to reduce harmful emissions.

WHO IS AN AMERICAN?

There is nothing new about anxiety over immigration in the United States. For its entire history, citizens have worried about who is entering the country and the changes that might result. Such concerns began to flare once again beginning in the 1980s, as Americans of European ancestry started to recognize the significant demographic changes on the horizon. The number of Americans of color and multiethnic Americans was growing, as was the percentage of people with other than European ancestry. It was clear the white majority would soon be a demographic minority (**Figure 11.11**).

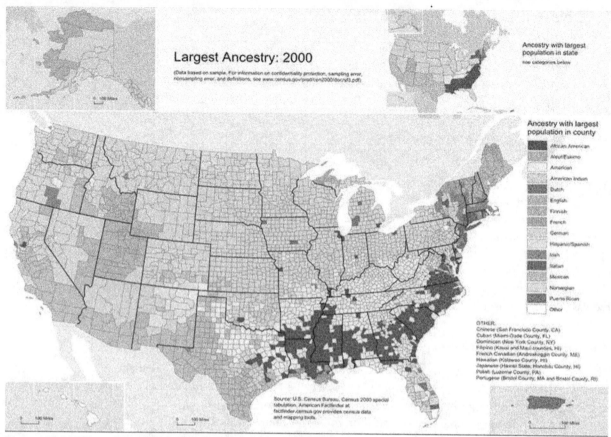

Figure 11.11 This map, based on the 2000 census, indicates the dominant ethnicity in different parts of the country. Note the heavy concentration of African Americans (dark purple) in the South, and the large numbers of those of Mexican ancestry (pink) in California and the Southwest. Why do you think so many in the Upper South are designated as simply American (light yellow)?

The nation's increasing diversity prompted some social conservatives to identify American culture as one of European heritage, including the drive to legally designate English the official language of the United States. This movement was particularly strong in areas of the country with large Spanish-speaking populations such as Arizona, where, in 2006, three-quarters of voters approved a proposition to make English the official language in the state. Proponents in Arizona and elsewhere argued that these laws were necessary, because recent immigrants, especially Hispanic newcomers, were not being sufficiently acculturated to white, middle-class culture. Opponents countered that English was already the *de facto* official language, and codifying it into law would only amount to unnecessary discrimination.

DEFINING "AMERICAN"

☉ *Arizona Bans Mexican American Studies*

In 2010, Arizona passed a law barring the teaching of any class that promoted "resentment" of students of other races or encouraged "ethnic solidarity." The ban, to take effect on December 31 of that year, included a popular Mexican American studies program taught at elementary, middle, and high schools in the city of Tucson. The program, which focused on teaching students about Mexican American history and literature, was begun in 1998, to convert high absentee rates and low academic performance among Latino students, and proved highly successful. Public school superintendent Tom Horne objected to the course, however, claiming it encouraged resentment of whites and of the U.S. government, and improperly encouraged students to think of themselves as members of a race instead of as individuals.

Tucson was ordered to end its Mexican American studies program or lose 10 percent of the school system's funding, approximately $3 million each month. In 2012, the Tucson school board voted to end the program. A former student and his mother filed a suit in federal court, claiming that the law, which did not prohibit programs teaching Indian students about their culture, was discriminatory and violated the First Amendment rights of Tucson's students. In March 2013, the court found in favor of the state, ruling that the law was not discriminatory, because it targeted classes, and not students or teachers, and that preventing the teaching of Mexican studies classes did not intrude on students' constitutional rights. The court did, however, declare the part of the law prohibiting classes designed for members of particular ethnic groups to be unconstitutional.

What advantages or disadvantages can you see in an ethnic studies program? How could an ethnic studies course add to our understanding of U.S. history? Explain.

The fear that English-speaking Americans were being outnumbered by a Hispanic population that was not forced to assimilate was sharpened by the concern that far too many were illegally emigrating from Latin America to the United States. The Comprehensive Immigration Reform Act proposed by Congress in 2006 sought to simultaneously strengthen security along the U.S.-Mexico border (a task for the Department of Homeland Security), increase the number of temporary "guest workers" allowed in the United States, and provide a pathway for long-term U.S. residents who had entered the country illegally to gain legal status. It also sought to establish English as a "common and unifying language" for the nation. The bill and a similar amended version both failed to become law.

With unemployment rates soaring during the Great Recession, anxiety over illegal immigration rose, even while the incoming flow slowed. State legislatures in Alabama and Arizona passed strict new laws that required police and other officials to verify the immigration status of those they thought had entered the country illegally. In Alabama, the new law made it a crime to rent housing to undocumented immigrants, thus making it difficult for these immigrants to live within the state. Both laws have been challenged in court, and portions have been deemed unconstitutional or otherwise blocked.

Beginning in October 2013, states along the U.S.-Mexico border faced an increase in the immigration of children from a handful of Central American countries. Approximately fifty-two thousand children, some unaccompanied, were taken into custody as they reached the United States. A study by the United Nations High Commissioner for Refugees estimated that 58 percent of those migrants, largely from El Salvador and Honduras, were propelled towards the United States by poverty, violence, and the potential for exploitation in their home countries. Because of a 2008 law originally intended to protect victims of human trafficking, these Central American children are guaranteed a court hearing. Predictably, the crisis has served to underline the need for comprehensive immigration reform. But, as of late 2014, a 2013 Senate immigration reform bill that combines border security with a guest worker program and a path to citizenship has yet to be enacted as law.

WHAT IS A MARRIAGE?

In the 1990s, the idea of legal, same-sex marriage seemed particularly unlikely; neither of the two main political parties expressed support for it. Things began to change, however, following Vermont's decision to allow same-sex couples to form state-recognized **civil unions** in which they could enjoy all the legal rights and privileges of marriage. Although it was the intention of the state to create a type of legal relationship equivalent to marriage, it did not use the word "marriage" to describe it.

Following Vermont's lead, several other states legalized same-sex marriages or civil unions among gay and lesbian couples. In 2004, the Massachusetts Supreme Judicial Court ruled that barring gays and lesbians from marrying violated the state constitution. The court held that offering same-sex couples the right to form civil unions but not marriage was an act of discrimination, and Massachusetts became the first state to allow same-sex couples to marry. Not all states followed suit, however, and there was a backlash in several states. Between 1998 and 2012, thirty states banned same-sex marriage either by statute or by amending their constitutions. Other states attempted, unsuccessfully, to do the same. In 2007, the Massachusetts State Legislature rejected a proposed amendment to the state's constitution that would have prohibited such marriages.

Click and Explore

Watch this **detailed documentary** (http://openstaxcollege.org/l/15HolyWar) on the attitudes that prevailed in Colorado in 1992, when the voters of that state approved Amendment 2 to the state's constitution and consequently denied gay and lesbian Coloradans the right to claim relief from local levels of discrimination in public accommodations, housing, or jobs.

While those in support of broadening civil rights to include same-sex marriage were optimistic, those opposed employed new tactics. In 2008, opponents of same-sex marriage in California tried a ballot initiative to define marriage strictly as a union between a man and a woman. Despite strong support for broadening marriage rights, the proposition was successful. This change was just one of dozens that states had been putting in place since the late 1990s to make same-sex marriage unconstitutional at the state level. Like the California proposition, however, many new state constitutional amendments have faced challenges in court (**Figure 11.12**). As of 2014, leaders in both political parties are more receptive than ever before to the idea of same-sex marriage.

(a)   (b)

Figure 11.12 Supporters and protesters of same-sex marriage gather in front of San Francisco's City Hall (a) as the California Supreme Court decides the fate of Proposition 8, a 2008 ballet measure stating that "only marriage between a man and a woman" would be valid in California. Following the Iowa Supreme Court's decision to legalize same-sex marriage, supporters rally in Iowa City on April 3, 2009 (b). The banner displays the Iowa state motto: "Our liberties we prize and our rights we will maintain." (credit a: modification of work by Jamison Wieser; credit b: modification of work by Alan Light)

Click and Explore

Visit the **Pew Research site** (http://openstaxcollege.org/l/15GayMarriage) to read more about the current status of same-sex marriage in the United States and the rest of the world.

WHY FIGHT CLIMATE CHANGE?

Even as mainstream members of both political parties moved closer together on same-sex marriage, political divisions on scientific debates continued. One increasingly polarizing debate that baffles much of the rest of the world is about global climate change. Despite near unanimity in the scientific community that climate change is real and will have devastating consequences, large segments of the American population, predominantly on the right, continue to insist that it is little more than a complex hoax and a leftist conspiracy. Much of the Republican Party's base denies that global warming is the result of human activity; some deny that the earth is getting hotter at all. This popular denial has had huge global consequences. In 1998, the United States, which produces roughly 36 percent of the **greenhouse gases** like carbon dioxide that prevent the earth's heat from escaping into space, signed the **Kyoto Protocol**, an agreement among the world's nations to reduce their emissions of these gases. President Bush objected to the requirement that major industrialized nations limit their emissions to a greater extent than other parts of the world and argued that doing so might hurt the American economy. He announced that the United States would not be bound by the agreement, and it was never ratified by Congress.

Instead, the Bush administration appeared to suppress scientific reporting on climate change. In 2006, the progressive-leaning Union of Concerned Scientists surveyed sixteen hundred climate scientists, asking them about the state of federal climate research. Of those who responded, nearly three-fourths believed that their research had been subjected to new administrative requirements, third-party editing to change their conclusions, or pressure not to use terms such as "global warming." Republican politicians, citing the altered reports, argued that there was no unified opinion among members of the scientific community that humans were damaging the climate.

Countering this rejection of science were the activities of many environmentalists, including Al Gore, Clinton's vice president and Bush's opponent in the disputed 2000 election. As a new member of Congress in 1976, Gore had developed what proved a steady commitment to environmental issues. In 2004, he established Generation Investment Management, which sought to promote an environmentally responsible system of equity analysis and investment. In 2006, a documentary film, *An Inconvenient Truth*, represented his attempts to educate people about the realities and dangers of global warming, and won the 2007 Academy Award for Best Documentary. Though some of what Gore said was in error, the film's main thrust is in keeping with the weight of scientific evidence. In 2007, as a result of these efforts to "disseminate greater knowledge about man-made climate change," Gore shared the Nobel Peace Prize with the Intergovernmental Panel on Climate Change.

11.4 Hope and Change

By the end of this section, you will be able to:
- Describe how Barack Obama's domestic policies differed from those of George W. Bush
- Discuss the important events of the war on terror during Obama's two administrations
- Discuss some of the specific challenges facing the United States as Obama's second term draws to a close

In 2008, American voters, tired of war and dispirited by the economic downturn, elected a relative newcomer to the political scene who inspired them and made them believe that the United States could rise above political partisanship. Barack Obama's story resembled that of many Americans: a multicultural background; a largely absent father; a single working mother; and care provided by maternal grandparents. As president, Obama would face significant challenges, including managing the economic recovery in the wake of the Great Recession, fighting the war on terror inherited from the previous administration, and implementing the healthcare reform upon which he had campaigned.

OBAMA TAKES OFFICE

Born in Hawaii in 1961 to a Kenyan father and an American woman from Kansas, Obama excelled at school, going on to attend Occidental College in Los Angeles, Columbia University, and finally Harvard Law School, where he became the first African American president of the *Harvard Law Review*. As part of his education, he also spent time in Chicago working as a community organizer to help those displaced by the decline of heavy industry in the early 1980s. Obama first came to national attention when he delivered the keynote address at the 2004 Democratic National Convention while running for his first term in the U.S. Senate. Just a couple of years later, he was running for president himself, the first African American nominee for the office from either major political party.

Obama's opponent in 2008 was John McCain, a Vietnam veteran and Republican senator with the reputation of a "maverick" who had occasionally broken ranks with his party to support bipartisan initiatives. The senator from Arizona faced a number of challenges. As the Republican nominee, he remained closely associated with the two disastrous foreign wars initiated under the Bush administration. His late recognition of the economic catastrophe on the eve of the election did not help matters and further damaged the Republican brand at the polls. At seventy-one, he also had to fight accusations that he was too old for the job, an impression made even more striking by his energetic young challenger. To minimize this weakness, McCain chose a young but inexperienced running mate, Governor Sarah Palin of Alaska. This tactic backfired, however, when a number of poor performances in television interviews convinced many voters that Palin was not prepared for higher office (**Figure 11.13**).

Figure 11.13 John McCain (on the far right) campaigns with his wife Cindy (in green), Sarah Palin (in black), and Palin's husband Todd. Palin was a controversial choice for running mate. The campaign never succeeded in erasing the charges that she was ignorant of foreign policy—an impression she enforced in her own ad-lib statements. (credit: Rachael Dickson)

Senator Obama, too, was criticized for his lack of experience with foreign policy, a deficit he remedied by choosing experienced politician Joseph Biden as his running mate. Unlike his Republican opponent, however, Obama offered promises of "hope and change." By sending out voter reminders on Twitter and connecting with supporters on Facebook, he was able to harness social media and take advantage of grassroots enthusiasm for his candidacy. His youthful vigor drew independents and first-time voters, and he won 95 percent of the African American vote and 44 percent of the white vote (**Figure 11.14**).

Figure 11.14 Barack Obama takes the oath of office as the forty-fourth president of the United States. Standing next to him is First Lady Michelle Obama. Like her husband, she graduated from Harvard Law School.

DEFINING "AMERICAN"

⊙ *Politicking in a New Century*

Barack Obama's campaign seemed to come out of nowhere to overcome the widely supported frontrunner Hillary Clinton in the Democratic primaries. Having won the nomination, Obama shot to the top with an exuberant base of youthful supporters who were encouraged and inspired by his appeal to hope and change. Behind the scenes, the Obama campaign was employing technological innovations and advances in social media to both inform and organize its base.

The Obama campaign realized early that the key to political success in the twenty-first century was to energize young voters by reaching them where they were: online. The organizing potential of platforms like Facebook, YouTube, and Twitter had never before been tapped—and they were free. The results were groundbreaking. Using these social media platforms, the Obama campaign became an organizing and fundraising machine of epic proportions. During his almost two-year-long campaign, Obama accepted 6.5 million donations, totaling $500 million. The vast majority of online donations were less than $100. This accomplishment stunned the political establishment, and they have been quick to adapt. Since 2008, nearly every political campaign has followed in Obama's footsteps, effecting a revolution in campaigning in the United States.

ECONOMIC AND HEALTHCARE REFORMS

Barack Obama had been elected on a platform of healthcare reform and a wave of frustration over the sinking economy. As he entered office in 2009, he set out to deal with both. Taking charge of the TARP program instituted under George W. Bush to stabilize the country's financial institutions, Obama oversaw the distribution of some $7.77 trillion designed to help shore up the nation's banking system. Recognizing that the economic downturn also threatened major auto manufacturers in the United States, he sought and received congressional authorization for $80 billion to help Chrysler and General Motors. The action was controversial, and some characterized it as a government takeover of industry. The money did, however, help the automakers earn a profit by 2011, reversing the trend of consistent losses that had hurt the industry since 2004. It also helped prevent layoffs and wage cuts. By 2013, the automakers had repaid over $50 billion of bailout funds. Finally, through the 2009 American Recovery and Reinvestment Act (ARRA), the Obama administration pumped almost $800 billion into the economy to stimulate economic growth and job creation.

More important for Obama supporters than his attempts to restore the economy was that he fulfill his promise to enact comprehensive healthcare reform. Many assumed such reforms would move quickly through Congress, since Democrats had comfortable majorities in both houses, and both Obama and McCain had campaigned on healthcare reform. However, as had occurred years before during President Clinton's first term, opposition groups saw attempts at reform as an opportunity to put the political brakes on the Obama presidency. After months of political wrangling and condemnations of the healthcare reform plan as socialism, the Patient Protection and Affordable Care Act (**Figure 11.15**) was passed and signed into law.

The act, which created the program known as **Obamacare**, represented the first significant overhaul of the American healthcare system since the passage of Medicaid in 1965. Its goals were to provide all Americans with access to affordable health insurance, to require that everyone in the United States acquire some form of health insurance, and to lower the costs of healthcare. The plan, which made use of government funding, created private insurance company exchanges to market various insurance packages to enrollees.

Figure 11.15 President Obama signs the Patient Protection and Affordable Care Act into law on March 23, 2010, as Vice President Biden, Speaker of the House Nancy Pelosi, Senate Majority Leader Harry Reid, and others look on. (credit: Pete Souza)

Although the plan implemented the market-based reforms that they had supported for years, Republicans refused to vote for it. Following its passage, they called numerous times for its repeal, and more than twenty-four states sued the federal government to stop its implementation. Discontent over the Affordable Care Act helped the Republicans capture the majority in the House of Representatives in the 2010 midterm elections. It also helped spawn the **Tea Party**, a conservative movement focused primarily on limiting government spending and the size of the federal government.

THE ELECTION OF 2012

By the 2012 presidential election, the Republicans, convinced Obama was vulnerable because of opposition to his healthcare program and a weak economy, nominated Mitt Romney, a well-known business executive-turned politician who had earlier signed healthcare reform into state law as governor of Massachusetts (**Figure 11.16**). Romney had unsuccessfully challenged McCain for the Republican nomination in 2008, but by 2012, he had remade himself politically by moving towards the party's right wing and its newly created Tea Party faction, which was pulling the traditional conservative base further to the right with its strong opposition to abortion, gun control, and immigration.

Figure 11.16 Former governor of Massachusetts Mitt Romney became the first member of the Mormon Church to run for president. He claimed his experience as a member of the Mormon lay clergy had made him sympathetic to the needs of the poor, but some of his campaign decisions contradicted this stance. (credit: Mark Taylor)

Romney appealed to a new attitude within the Republican Party. While the percentage of Democrats who agreed that the government should help people unable to provide for themselves had remained relatively stable from 1987 to 2012, at roughly 75 to 79 percent, the percentage of Republicans who felt the same way had decreased from 62 to 40 percent over the same period, with the greatest decline coming after 2007. Indeed, Romney himself revealed his disdain for people on the lower rungs of the socioeconomic ladder when, at a fundraising event attended by affluent Republicans, he remarked that he did not care to reach the 47 percent of Americans who would always vote for Obama because of their dependence on government assistance. In his eyes, this low-income portion of the population preferred to rely on government social programs instead of trying to improve their own lives.

Click and Explore

Read the transcript (http://openstaxcollege.org/l/1547percent2) of "On the 47 percent," the secretly recorded speech (http://openstaxcollege.org/l/1547percent) given by Mitt Romney at a Republican fundraiser.

Starting out behind Obama in the polls, Romney significantly closed the gap in the first of three presidential debates, when he moved towards more centrist positions on many issues. Obama regained momentum in the remaining two debates and used his bailout of the auto industry to appeal to voters in the key states of Michigan and Ohio. Romney's remarks about the 47 percent hurt his position among both poor Americans and those who sympathized with them. A long-time critic of FEMA who claimed that it should be eliminated, Romney also likely lost votes in the Northeast when, a week before the election, Hurricane Sandy devastated the New England, New York, and New Jersey coasts. Obama and the federal government had largely rebuilt FEMA since its disastrous showing in New Orleans in 2005, and the agency quickly swung into action to assist the 8.5 million people affected by the disaster.

Obama won the election, but the Republicans retained their hold on the House of Representatives and the Democratic majority in the Senate grew razor-thin. Political bickering and intractable Republican resistance, including a 70 percent increase in filibusters over the 1980s, a refusal to allow a vote on some legislation, such as the 2012 "jobs bill," and the glacial pace at which the Senate confirmed the President's judicial nominations, created political gridlock in Washington, interfering with Obama's ability to secure any important legislative victories.

ONGOING CHALLENGES

As Obama entered his second term in office, the economy remained stagnant in many areas. On average, American students continued to fall behind their peers in the rest of the world, and the cost of a college education became increasingly unaffordable for many. Problems continued overseas in Iraq and Afghanistan, and another act of terrorism took place on American soil when bombs exploded at the 2013 Boston Marathon. At the same time, the cause of same-sex marriage made significant advances, and Obama was able to secure greater protection for the environment. He raised fuel-efficiency standards for automobiles to reduce the emissions of greenhouse gases and required coal-burning power plants to capture their carbon emissions.

Learning and Earning

The quality of American education remains a challenge. The global economy is dominated by those nations with the greatest number of "knowledge workers:" people with specialized knowledge and skills like engineers, scientists, doctors, teachers, financial analysts, and computer programmers. Furthermore, American students' reading, math, and critical thinking skills are less developed than those of their peers in other industrialized nations, including small countries like Estonia.

The Obama administration sought to make higher education more accessible by increasing the amount that students could receive under the federally funded Pell Grant Program, which, by the 2012–13 academic year, helped 9.5 million students pay for their college education. Obama also worked out a compromise with Congress in 2013, which lowered the interest rates charged on student loans. However, college tuition is still growing at a rate of 2 to 3 percent per year, and the debt burden has surpassed the $1 trillion mark and is likely to increase. With debt upon graduation averaging about $29,000, students may find their economic options limited. Instead of buying cars or paying for housing, they may have to join the **boomerang generation** and return to their parents' homes in order to make their loan payments. Clearly, high levels of debt will affect their career choices and life decisions for the foreseeable future.

Many other Americans continue to be challenged by the state of the economy. Most economists calculate that the Great Recession reached its lowest point in 2009, and the economy has gradually improved since then. The stock market ended 2013 at historic highs, having experienced its biggest percentage gain since 1997. However, despite these gains, the nation struggled to maintain a modest annual growth rate of 2.5 percent after the Great Recession, and the percentage of the population living in poverty continues to hover around 15 percent. Income has decreased (**Figure 11.17**), and, as late as 2011, the unemployment rate was still high in some areas. Eight million full-time workers have been forced into part-time work, whereas 26 million seem to have given up and left the job market.

Median Household Income in February 2013 Dollars

Figure 11.17 Median household income trends reveal a steady downward spiral. The Great Recession may have ended, but many remain worse off than they were in 2008.

LGBT Rights

During Barack Obama's second term in office, courts began to counter efforts by conservatives to outlaw same-sex marriage. A series of decisions declared nine states' prohibitions against same-sex marriage to be unconstitutional, and the Supreme Court rejected an attempt to overturn a federal court ruling to that effect in California in June 2013. Shortly thereafter, the Supreme Court also ruled that the Defense of Marriage Act of 1996 was unconstitutional, because it violated the Equal Protection Clause of the Fourteenth Amendment. These decisions seem to allow legal challenges in all the states that persist in trying to block same-sex unions.

The struggle against discrimination based on gender identity has also won some significant victories. In 2014, the U.S. Department of Education ruled that schools receiving federal funds may not discriminate against transgender students, and a board within the Department of Health and Human Services decided that Medicare should cover sexual reassignment surgery. Although very few people eligible for Medicare are transgender, the decision is still important, because private insurance companies often base their coverage on what Medicare considers appropriate and necessary forms of treatment for various conditions. Undoubtedly, the fight for greater rights for LGBT (lesbian, gay, bisexual, transsexual) individuals will continue.

Violence

Another running debate questions the easy accessibility of firearms. Between the spring of 1999, when two teens killed twelve of their classmates, a teacher, and themselves at their high school in Columbine, Colorado, and the early summer of 2014, fifty-two additional shootings or attempted shootings had occurred at schools (**Figure 11.18**). Nearly always, the violence was perpetrated by young people with severe mental health problems, as at Sandy Hook elementary school in Newtown, Connecticut, in 2012. After killing his mother at home, twenty-year-old Adam Lanza went to the school and fatally shot twenty six- and seven-year-old students, along with six adult staff members, before killing himself. Advocates of stricter gun control noted a clear relationship between access to guns and mass shootings. Gun rights advocates, however, disagreed. They argued that access to guns is merely incidental.

Figure 11.18 A candlelight vigil at Virginia Polytechnic Institute and State University in Blacksburg, Virginia, in the wake of the 2007 murder of thirty-two people by a student. The incident remains the deadliest school shooting to date. (credit: "alka3en"/Flickr)

Another shocking act of violence was the attack on the Boston Marathon. On April 15, 2013, shortly before 3:00 p.m., two bombs made from pressure cookers exploded near the finish line (**Figure 11.19**). Three people were killed, and more than 250 were injured. Three days later, two suspects were identified, and a manhunt began. Later that night, the two young men, brothers who had immigrated to the United States from Chechnya, killed a campus security officer at the Massachusetts Institute of Technology, stole a car, and fled. The older, Tamerlan Tsarnaev, was killed in a fight with the police, and Dzhokhar Tsarnaev was captured the next day. In his statements to the police, Dzhokhar Tsarnaev reported that he and his brother, who he claimed had planned the attacks, had been influenced by the actions of fellow radical Islamists in Afghanistan and Iraq, but he denied they had been affiliated with any larger terrorist group.

Figure 11.19 Bystanders at the finish line of the Boston Marathon help carry the injured to safety after the April 2013 attack. Two bombs exploded only a few seconds and a few hundred yards apart, killing three people. (credit: Aaron Tang)

America and the World

In May 2014, President Obama announced that, for the most part, U.S. combat operations in Afghanistan were over. Although a residual force of ninety-eight hundred soldiers will remain to continue training the Afghan army, by 2016, all U.S. troops will have left the country, except for a small number to defend U.S. diplomatic posts.

The years of warfare have brought the United States few rewards. In Iraq, 4,475 American soldiers died and 32,220 were wounded. In Afghanistan, the toll through February 2013 was 2,165 dead and 18,230 wounded. By some estimates, the total monetary cost of the wars in Iraq and Afghanistan could easily reach $4 trillion, and the Congressional Budget Office believes that the cost of providing medical care for the veterans might climb to $8 billion by 2020.

In Iraq, the coalition led by then-Prime Minister Nouri al-Maliki was able to win 92 of the 328 seats in parliament in May 2014, and he seemed poised to begin another term as the country's ruler. The elections, however, did not stem the tide of violence in the country. In June 2014, the Islamic State of Iraq and Syria (ISIS), a radical Islamist militant group consisting of mostly Sunni Muslims and once affiliated with al-Qaeda, seized control of Sunni-dominated areas of Iraq and Syria. On June 29, 2014, it proclaimed the formation of the Islamic State with Abu Bakr al-Baghdadi as caliph, the state's political and religious leader.

APPENDIX A
Presidents of the United States of America

Table A1 Presidents of the United States of America

Order	Election Year	President
1	1788–1789	George Washington
2	1792	George Washington
3	1796	John Adams
4	1800	Thomas Jefferson
5	1804	Thomas Jefferson
6	1808	James Madison
7	1812	James Madison
8	1816	James Monroe
9	1820	James Monroe
10	1824	John Quincy Adams
11	1828	Andrew Jackson
12	1832	Andrew Jackson
13	1836	Martin Van Buren
14	1840	William Henry Harrison
15	1844	James K. Polk
16	1848	Zachary Taylor
17	1852	Franklin Pierce
18	1856	James Buchanan
19	1860	Abraham Lincoln
20	1864	Abraham Lincoln
21	1868	Ulysses S. Grant
22	1872	Ulysses S. Grant
23	1876	Rutherford B. Hayes
24	1880	James A. Garfield

Table A1 Presidents of the United States of America

Order	Election Year	President
25	1884	Grover Cleveland
26	1888	Benjamin Harrison
27	1892	Grover Cleveland
28	1896	William McKinley
29	1900	William McKinley
30	1904	Theodore Roosevelt
31	1908	William Howard Taft
32	1912	Woodrow Wilson
33	1916	Woodrow Wilson
34	1920	Warren G. Harding
35	1924	Calvin Coolidge
36	1928	Herbert Hoover
37	1932	Franklin D. Roosevelt
38	1936	Franklin D. Roosevelt
39	1940	Franklin D. Roosevelt
40	1944	Franklin D. Roosevelt
41	1948	Harry S. Truman
42	1952	Dwight D. Eisenhower
43	1956	Dwight D. Eisenhower
44	1960	John F. Kennedy
45	1964	Lyndon B. Johnson
46	1968	Richard Nixon
47	1972	Richard Nixon
48	1976	Jimmy Carter
49	1980	Ronald Reagan
50	1984	Ronald Reagan
51	1988	George H. W. Bush

Table A1 Presidents of the United States of America

Order	Election Year	President
52	1992	Bill Clinton
53	1996	Bill Clinton
54	2000	George W. Bush
55	2004	George W. Bush
56	2008	Barack Obama
57	2012	Barack Obama

APPENDIX B

U.S. Political Map

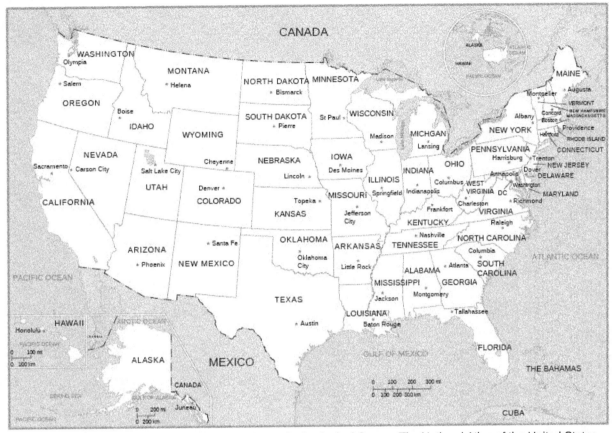

Figure B1 (credit: U.S. Department of the Interior, U.S. Geological Survey, The National Atlas of the United States of America/nationalatlas.gov)

APPENDIX C

U.S. Topographical Map

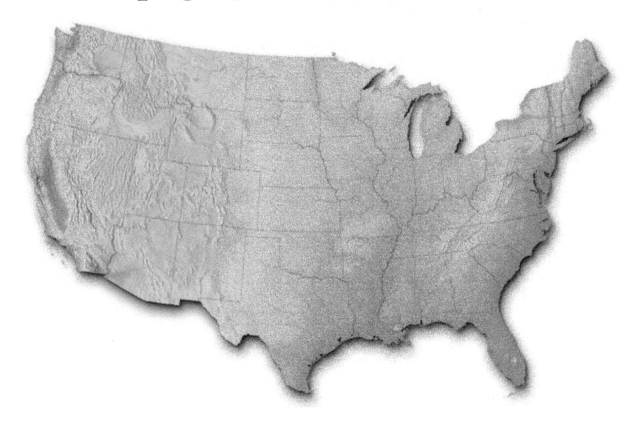

APPENDIX D

United States Population Chart

Table D1 United States Population Chart[1]

Census Year	Population	Census Year	Population
1610	350	1820	9,638,453
1620	2,302	1830	12,866,020
1630	4,646	1840	17,069,453
1640	26,634	1850	23,191,876
1650	50,368	1860	31,443,321
1660	75,058	1870	38,558,371
1670	111,935	1880	50,189,209
1680	151,507	1890	62,979,766
1690	210,372	1900	76,212,168
1700	250,888	1910	92,228,496
1710	331,711	1920	106,021,537
1720	466,185	1930	123,202,624
1730	629,445	1940	132,164,569
1740	905,563	1950	151,325,798
1750	1,170,760	1960	179,323,175
1760	1,593,625	1970	203,211,926
1770	2,148,076	1980	226,656,805
1780	2,780,369	1990	248,709,873
1790	3,929,214	2000	281,421,906
1800	5,308,483	2010	308,745,538
1810	7,239,881		

1. Population figures for the decades before the first U.S. census in 1790 are estimates.

CPSIA information can be obtained
at www.ICGtesting.com
Printed in the USA
FFHW02n2059210818
47808349-51500FF